Windows 95 for Network Administrators

Nicolas Behrmann
Craig Chambers
Scott Fuller
Forrest Houlette
Kevin Pagan

New Riders Publishing, Indianapolis, IN

Windows 95 for Network Administrators

By Nicolas Behrmann, Craig Chambers, Scott Fuller,
Forrest Houlette, and Kevin Pagan

Published by:
New Riders Publishing
201 West 103rd Street
Indianapolis, IN 46290 USA

Printed in the United States of America 1 2 3 4 5 6 7 8 9 0

CIP data available upon request

Warning and Disclaimer

This book is designed to provide information about the NetWare computer program. Every effort has been made to make this book as complete and as accurate as possible, but no warranty or fitness is implied.

The information is provided on an "as is" basis. The author and New Riders Publishing shall have neither liability nor responsibility to any person or entity with respect to any loss or damages arising from the information contained in this book or from the use of the disks or programs that may accompany it.

Publisher *Don Fowley*
Publishing Manager *Emmett Dulaney*
Marketing Manager *Ray Robinson*
Acquisitions Manager *Jim LeValley*
Managing Editor *Tad Ringo*

Acquisitions Editor
Alicia Buckley

Development Editor
Ian Sheeler

Production Editor
John Sleeva

Copy Editors
Amy Bezek, Sarah Kearns, Pete Kuhns, Stacia Mellinger Cliff Shubs, Suzanne Snyder Phil Worthington

Technical Editor
Kim Green

Assistant Marketing Manager
Tamara Apple

Acquisitions Coordinator
Tracy Turgeson

Publisher's Assistant
Karen Opal

Cover Designer
Sandra Schroeder

Cover Photographer
© Robert Bullivant/Tony Stone Images

Book Designer
Sandra Schroeder

Manufacturing Coordinator
Paul Gilchrist

Production Manager
Kelly Dobbs

Production Team Supervisor
Laurie Casey

Graphic Image Specialists
Jason Hand, Clint Lahnen, Laura Robbins, Craig Small, Todd Wente

Production Analysts
Angela D. Bannan, Bobbi Satterfield, Mary Beth Wakefield

Production Team
Angela Calvert, Kim Cofer, Aleata Howard, Shawn MacDonald, Gina Rexrode Christine Tyner, Karen Walsh

Indexers
Christopher Cleveland, Brad Herriman

About the Authors

Nicolas L. Behrmann is the President of Information Management Consulting, a business productivity and network management company in Palm Springs, California. In partnership with DataTech Institute, a national training company, Mr. Behrmann has lead networking seminars for thousands of network managers. He has developed and taught seminars dealing with NetWare 3.*x* and 4.*x*, Windows and NetWare integration, and network management. He has over ten years of practical experience in the planning, installation, and implementation of networks and business productivity applications. With over thirty years of organizational development and training experience, Mr. Behrmann is currently working on team development and groupware support projects. He is a Certified NetWare Engineer, an Enterprise Certified NetWare Engineer, and Microsoft Certified Professional, certified in more than eight of the Microsoft network and desktop products.

Craig Chambers is presently working as an OS/2 consultant. He has authored and co-authored several magazine articles and five books about OS/2, including *OS/2 Warp Professional Reference* and *LAN Server Certification Handbook,* published by New Riders Publishing.

Scott M. Fuller is President of IDEAS, a computer consulting group specializing in law firms. Mr. Fuller has an extensive background in system design, operations management, and technical training for a wide variety of clients. He has contributed to several books, including *Learn Windows 95 in a Day, Upgrade to Windows 95 Quick & Easy, Learn Timeslips in a Day, Learn CompuServe in a Day,* and *Learn Prodigy in a Day.*

Forrest Houlette is a computer writer and consultant who lives in Muncie, Indiana. Forrest holds a Ph.D. in Linguistics and Rhetoric from the University of Louisville. He began working with computers when he took a course in FORTRAN in 1979. Since then, he has programmed in BASIC, the Digital Authoring Language, C, C++, WordBasic, and Visual Basic. During his career as a university professor, he taught linguistics and focused on using artificial intelligence techniques to improve software for writing. He has written computer-based education programs for the teaching of writing, one of which won the Zenith Masters of Innovation competition. Forrest now focuses on writing about computers and creating custom software. He teaches courses on Windows 95, Windows NT, and Visual Basic for Learning Tree International.

Kevin D. Pagan is an attorney specializing in civil trial law. Mr. Pagan has a bachelor's degree in accounting and is currently a member of both the Texas Bar Association and the American Bar Association. He is the co-author of *Learn Timeslips in a Day* and *Learn CompuServe in a Day.*

Trademark Acknowledgments

Contents at a Glance

Table of Contents

Windows 95 and NetWare: A Management Approach

Just about when the network administrator has wrestled in to control the network and its workstations and software, here comes Windows 95. Even with the reality testing by the beta users and the approximately 500,000 Windows 95 previews, there is still a prevailing sense of excitement and positive press that stresses the ease of networking, and especially network integration. The purpose of this book as outlined in this introductory chapter is to lay out the criteria of network management as a background against which to see Windows 95 and the realties of network management.

Windows 95 for Network Administrators has been written to address the questions and concerns that network administrators have about the impact of Windows 95 on their structured and well-behaved network. As with any new product that has benefits and features of interest, there are installation, implementation, and training issues that must be addressed.

As with other innovations, there are a vast number of innovations with Windows 95 that will need fixing when field experience shows them not to be up to the goals of the designers and marketers. Even as

Windows 95 is being installed on desktops, there are supplements being planned for the new desktop. What is presented in the pages of this book is not as much technical reference as guidelines and strategy for implementing the Windows 95 client-based network.

Windows 95 for Network Administrators is also written for the network manager who is reluctant to change the status quo of the existing network on the theory that "if it ain't broke, don't fix it." Just because Windows 95 is out there doesn't mean it should be implemented immediately in your organization. The power and depth of Windows 95 requires not only the appropriate hardware platform, but also the proper amount of network manager knowledge and thought, to say nothing of the time to properly accomplish the installation and implementation. The same guidelines developed in these pages for the network manager who is ready to begin the process can be used by the reluctant manager to develop, over time, the proper foundation for later implementation.

As you will learn in Chapter 5, "Location Issues: Server or Workstation," the network manager who is concerned about where to put the files and computer memory-disk access and traffic load needs to make sure that either the server or the workstations can sustain the load before a final decision can be made. Indeed, part of the decision process might be the costs of either or both implementations as a deciding factor.

One of the major themes set by Microsoft in conjunction with Windows 95 is the network management features such as remote Registry management, remote system monitoring, user versus system configuration, and moveable user profiles. Although Windows 95 addresses many network management issues, it does not address all of them.

Unfortunately, because of the new technologies involved with Windows 95 (especially the protected mode operation), in the short run network administrators will experience the lack of those network management tools that have become critical to managing the network. The lag is also a factor of the changes that have been made up to the freeze point for Windows 95 code. Third-party developers need to know their starting point for application development.

Regardless of the benefits of a Windows 95 implementation on the network client desktop, there will be time, energy, and financial costs involved in the placement of Windows 95 on the desktops. Both the ready and the reluctant network manager must plan out the implementation blueprints. A significant difference between the results of these two positions will be timing. The network administrator whose setting is ripe for Windows 95 will want to follow a set of policy setting and implementation procedures based on solid network management principles. The reluctant organization or network manager will need to create a similar set of documentation along with explanations as to the reasons why such implementation will need to be done over a longer period of time.

The network administrator considering Windows 95 and the network will be faced with the following choices:

- Where to install Windows 95—on the workstation or on the server?
- Which network client to use when setting up the Windows 95 computer as a NetWare client?
- Whether to enable or disable sharing, and what kind of sharing—resource or user—is to provide security?
- What restrictions to place on the workstation?
- What restrictions to place on the user?
- Should there be user profiles used on the workstation?
- Should the server be configured to support long file names?

These and other matters will make the difference between a successful Windows 95-based network and one for which there are a steady stream of support calls. A successful network is one for which there are relatively few support calls.

Does Windows 95 Address Windows 3.*x* Management Issues?

Whereas Windows 3.*x* and NetWare provide the administrator with almost no tools for managing either the Windows workstation or the Windows user across the network, Windows 95 presents the network administrator with a whole set of tools for this purpose. These tools, while giving the network manager more control over the network, require significant planning and decision making in their implementation. The network administrator is well-advised to think out the implications of each set of tools to determine whether indeed these features should be implemented.

The Windows 3.*x*-based NetWare network administrator became aware that Windows 3.1 is not a network application because there are no centralized means of administrating it. The SYSCON (NetWare 3.*x*) and NWADMIN (NetWare 4.*x*) utilities are examples of centralized administrative applications that enable the administrator to access the users NetWare environment from any workstation and impact the rights that users have on the network. Microsoft published a site license program, called WinLogin, that was supposed to provide a centralized means of coordinating the user and the workstation configuration needs. Unfortunately the program did not live up to its promises.

Among the issues facing the administrator, for example, is the "roving user" who needs to use multiple workstations each with its own video card or network driver. Although the user might be expecting his or her favorite colors, the network administrator is more concerned with making sure that the user has access to his or her required applications.

Workstation Versus User Configuration Issues

The administrator of the Windows 3.*x*-based network found that schemes had to be evolved to solve the problem of providing users with their user-based configurations as they move from one workstation to another, while also providing users with the workstation-based configuration specific to the computer they were currently using.

With Windows 3.*x*, the Win.com and System.ini files are workstation specific, whereas the Win.ini and Control.ini files are user-related files. Many administrators worked out batch files to either copy user files from the network to the local machines or system files from the local machines to the users' server directories so that at run time all five files were together.

The Windows 95 Registry, which replaces the Ini text files for Windows 3.*x*, is constructed to easily split out the user and the system configuration information. At run time, the System.dat file of the workstation and the User.dat file of the user are brought together to properly configure the user and the hardware aspects of the system session.

When working with network users and appropriately configured, the Windows 95 system can find the user's User.dat file either on the workstation or the network, and when it is found in both locations, choose the latest copy of it as the operational version. When the user session is completed, Windows 95 updates both copies so that they are synchronized.

Managing Menus and Access to Applications

Another set of Windows 3.*x* and network issues involves how to control the user's access to program icons without having to go to each desktop. The term *effective rights* is used to cover the total rights that a user has on the network because of being a member of multiple groups. The term "effective icons" could be used to cover the icons that a user should have on his or her Windows desktop because of membership in various network groups. One of the tools that has been missing with the Windows 3.*x* system is the ability to change the user's desktop icons by changing the user's underlying network group membership. The ability to add or delete icons by modifying the user's membership in network groups would provide "effective icons."

Although some administrators use the NetWare login script variable "if member of group" as the basis for copying the Progman.ini file to the user, other NetWare administrators have turned to third-party software to solve the problem of personalizing a user's icons. Among third-party vendors providing effective icon support for Windows 3.*x* are Saber, McAfee, Symantec, Lanovation, and Digital Communications Associates.

Windows 95 has a structure beyond the User.dat and the System.dat files that is called user profiles. These user profiles, when established as permissible on the workstation, are a combination of the user's User.dat and the object linking and embedding shortcut icons used in the Windows 95 menu structure. The use of an open-ended menu structure in Windows 95 rather than the binary closed program groups of Windows 3.*x* gives the administrator more control. It is relatively easy to distribute files to users through some login batch file or by placing these files in the network location of the user profile copies. These profiles are placed in the user's home directory on the Windows NT server and the user's mail directory on the NetWare server.

Remote Configuration Matters

One of the biggest support issues facing the network administrator with the Windows 3.*x*-based client is the need to support the seven or eight configuration text files: Config.sys, Autoexec.bat, Net.cfg, System.ini, Win.ini, Progman.ini, and Control.ini. Changing the number of files open in the Config.sys file or a setting in System.ini, for example, can be anywhere from 15 minutes to an hour if the technician has to go to the desktop to make the changes.

Because these files are often specific to a workstation or a user, they cannot just be copied over through such utilities as NetWare's WSUPDATE. Vendors such as Saber, McAfee, Lanovation, On Demand, and Symantec devised applications that administrators can use to remotely reconfigure these text files.

Windows 95 is designed to maintain both the workstation and the user configurations through the run time combination of the User.dat and the System.dat files. Through the remote Registry service on the workstation and the server-based System Policy Editor, the administrator of the Windows 95-based network can provide for the central maintenance of the workstation. Third-party vendors will make this process even easier as time goes on through applications that can apply changes based on other Registry settings as can now be done with many Windows 3.*x* programs that can modify configurations for either users or specific hardware and software configurations.

Planning Issues for Windows 95 User and Workstation Management

Windows 95 gives you the ability to manage workstations and users by implementing system policies for each. The ability to implement these policies is technical; the decision to establish them is and should be organizational.

You should design user policy packages as suggested in the *Microsoft Resource Kit for Windows 95* and present these sets for review by management.

After reviewing the policy options, you might want to consult the *Microsoft Resource Kit for Windows 95* for instructions on how to create customized policies for other matters. More discussion about the structure for establishing these policies is covered in Chapter 4, "Managing the Workstation and User."

User Restrictions

You should make up a checklist of all the features that can be controlled for users and fill it out for each classification of users or groups. The following is an outline of these categories.

- **Control Panel access**

  Disable display control
  Disable network control
  Disable printer control
  Disable system control
  Disable passwords Control

- **Shell restrictions**

  Remove Run command
  Remove Find command
  Hide drives in My Computer
  Hide Network Neighborhood
  Do not show entire network
  Do not show workgroups in Network Neighborhood
  Do not save settings on exit
  Remove Taskbar
  Hide all items on desktop
  Remove Settings item on menu

- **Others**

  Disable file sharing controls
  Disable print sharing controls
  Disable Registry editing tools
  Only run allowed Windows applications
  Disable MS-DOS prompt
  Disable single-mode MS-DOS applications
  Disable dial-up networking

You can establish combinations of these for each user, or create one or any number of mandatory User.man profiles that cannot be changed by the users who are given these profiles in their NetWare \mail\user-id.

Another option is to create profiles determined by user group membership (for example, clerical staff, programmers, MIS staff, managers, and similar groups).

Workstation Configurations and Restrictions

Among the matters that should be decided is the nature of the network client mode that is to be used on the workstations. As discussed in Chapter 3, "Integrating Windows 95 and NetWare," the options are as follows:

- **Option one.** Running the real mode Ipx.com or IPXODI protocol along with the real mode NETX or VLMS client shell

- **Option two.** Running the real mode Ipx.com or IPXODI with the Microsoft Client for NetWare

- **Option three.** Running the Microsoft IPX/SPX-compatible protocol, the 32-bit implementation of the IPX protocol, along with the 32-bit Microsoft Client for NetWare

- **Option four.** Running the Novell Netware Client 32, which is a protected mode 32-bit implementation of both the IPX/SPX protocol and the former NETX/VLM client shell

It would make for stronger planning and decision making to make up a checklist of all the features that can be controlled on the workstation and fill it out for each named workstation or classification of workstation.

- Enable user-level security

- Require validation by network server

- Microsoft Client for NetWare settings

  Indicate preferred server
  Support long file names
  Choose a search mode
  Disable automatic NetWare logon

- Microsoft Client for Microsoft network setting

  Log on to Windows NT
  Display domain logon validation
  Disable caching of domain passwords
  Participate in specific workgroup
  Alternative Workgroup

- Password settings

  Hide passwords with asterisks
  Disable password caching
  Require alphanumeric Windows password
  Require minimum length for Windows password

- Sharing Settings

  Disable file sharing
  Disable print sharing

- Others

  Enable user profiles versus default user profile
  Run applications and utilities at logon startup
  Run services at system startup
  Enable Remote Registry and system monitoring

Other installation options for each workstation on the checklist include whether or not the workstation has single Windows 95 boot or dual boot allowing for a previous DOS version.

On this checklist of workstations might also be a field for workstation functions. You might want to make up categories of functional types of workstations that are on the network.

You need to have a systematic means of naming the workstations. What should each workstation be named to identify function and/or department location?

You should review the organizational structure of purposes, users, and workstation locations and functions before the Windows 95 roll out begins. This process should enable the network design and implementation to better fit the organization that exists now.

Network Management Context of Windows 95

Because the typical Windows 95 business workstation will be on the network, you will benefit from reviewing the network environment of the Windows 95 client. Some of the features of Windows 95 fit into network management categories, and some of the network categories must be considered within the configuration of the network location for Windows 95 and the applications. Other categories should be considered for matters such as security and software distribution; other matters such as network mapping help to provide a better managed network context for the Windows 95 workstations.

The importance of viewing Windows 95 within the network management context is that unless the underlying network is managed properly, the user will experience difficulties at the Windows 95 workstation when working with the network. The well-managed network means fewer network and workstation problems.

ISO Network Management Areas

The International Organization for Standards (ISO) has established the following five categories of network management. The ISO has also provided the seven network layers, known as the Open System Interconnection (OSI). For a more detailed discussion of these layers, please see Chapter 5, "Location Issues: Server or Workstation."

- **Fault management.** This area tells you that something is wrong and helps you figure out how to get out of trouble.
- **Configuration management.** This area tells you what workstations, hubs, routers, gateways, and servers exist and how these items should be set up to avoid problems.
- **Security management.** In this area, you learn to identify the users and the groups they are part of and what rights are assigned to either users or groups for server login, application access, and print queue use. This area also deals with passwords and acceptable login times.

- **Performance management.** In this area, you learn about packet rates, CPU utilization, and other measurable statistics.
- **Accounting management.** The definition for this area varies, ranging from accountability for performance and faults to charging departments for services rendered. Also covered are financial matters such as assets and depreciation.

LAN Management Areas

Working with LAN managers and administrators, and through research into the management tools available in the marketplace, has led me to expand these standards into some broader concerns and specific areas. This section explores these areas with some indication as to the implications for viewing the impact of Windows 95 on the NetWare network.

Network Documentation Management

Having documentation on all aspects of the network is a mark of the well-designed network. Such documentation makes troubleshooting and upgrading significantly more manageable than it would be otherwise. If this is true for normal events and software upgrades, it is even more so in the case of implementing what will be in many situations an upgrade of existing Windows clients.

Before presenting the outlines of the network management category in general and a description of what you should have after the implementation of Windows 95, it would prove helpful to list the categories of information that will be necessary to have available in making management decisions about the Windows 95 implementation.

Windows 95 is designed to align with the existing NetWare servers and users and make the following elements part of a new workstation environment. You should document each of these items as part of the known elements in the Windows 95-based NetWare network.

- **Servers.** What is the primary purpose of each server? How much disk space is available on each volume? Are there volumes that can be used for long file names through the addition of the OS/2 name space? Are there servers that host all users and can be used as validating name servers for the Windows 95 workstation?
- **Users.** Who are the users and what use might they have with access to peer-to-peer workstations? What restrictions might be placed on these users in terms of Windows 95 features?
- **Groups.** What groups exist on the servers and how can they be used to manage the Windows 95 desktop through group-oriented restrictions on access to the Windows 95 environment? These groups must be carefully examined on the

servers, because they can be used to validate access to workstation-based resources if the file and printer sharing for NetWare networks is used on a workstation. How will the user who wants to apply these groups to their workstation know who is in the groups? Should there be a listing of public groups and their members, if only within a department that is contained in that group?

- **Print queues.** Who has access to each of the queues as either themselves or as a member of a user group? Keep in mind that within Windows 95, users will see the print queues to which they have access.
- **Space usage by user.** Many network administrators utilize the NetWare user space restrictions. These restrictions might have to be revised upward as the user-owned files and space will increase.
- **Network applications.** When planning a user's access to network applications, it is important to gather the user's requirements for these applications. For the administrator who will be installing Windows 95 over existing Windows 3.1 and Windows for Workgroups 3.11 installations, the conversions will be made by the Windows 95 setup process. For the new installs or the machines coming equipped with preinstalled Windows 95, the installations must be done "manually" through a Control Panel icon.

Icons versus shortcut keys? As programs are installed or you try to manually make connections to programs, keep in mind that when an icon is erased from a file directory, the underlying file is erased as well. When a shortcut key is erased, only the object linking and embedding connection is deleted.

- **Workstations.** You should perform a careful analysis of each workstation on the network, not only for its physical capability to receive and run the Windows 95 system, but also in terms of who will be using the workstation. You can customize the setup process for a single workstation or a number of workstations with the Msbatch.inf file with or other structured setup files. Also through the centralized server-based Config.pol or similar policy file, you can manage each named workstation in terms of what users can do on that workstation. One example might be the ability to use file and printer sharing for NetWare networks on that workstation. Needing explicit action is the naming of each workstation on the network with a unique and identifiable name.
- **Login scripts.** All system login scripts and individual user login scripts, and the NetWare 4.*x* profile login scripts for groups need to be examined before any real mode programs run. If the 32-bit Microsoft Client for NetWare is used in place of the real mode IPXODI/NETX or VLM combination, then the logon process takes place through the Windows 95 protected mode logon processor for NetWare. For the Windows 95 workstation and user, these login scripts must be adjusted so they do not call up these real mode programs.

In the startup phase of Windows 95, you might add a SET command to the Autoexec.bat file, establishing a workstation variable such as "set wks = "W95"" and then use this variable in the NetWare login script to identify the Windows 95 stations. Such a NetWare login script might read like this: " If <wks> = W95 then " and have the "then" portion skip past the real mode programs evoked in the login script process. The "then" portion might be a real mode workstation inventory program or a real mode virus protection executable program.

Through both online and printed documentation, you should have a centralized and easy to understand set of documentation that places all necessary information in one place. A handbook about your network provides information about users, workstation data, maps of your network, applications being used and by whom, and so forth. For security purposes, you should keep this manual under limited access.

Workstation Inventory Management

As covered in Chapter 5, you need to know about the potential Windows 95 workstation. The organization will have to evolve a standard configuration that it will support for the Windows 95 system. Among the matters of concern are RAM memory, disk size and free space, video cards, and network adapters. After you decide on a standard for the new operating system and user interface hardware platform, you need to inventory the existing network nodes to see which stations can be recycled, and which can be upgraded.

As you familiarize yourself with the Windows 95 features you want to implement, you can, through this inventory process, identify nodes that can serve some special purposes. You also need to identify those workstations that need to be cleared of old or unnecessary programs and files to make room for the 30–40 MB of Windows 95 programs.

You need to create a list of all workstations, printers, hubs, routers, and so forth that exist on the network, including financial information such as warranty dates and which have a maintenance contract. This list enables you to know who needs what and who can run what software. Although you can create a checklist of items that should be gathered, there are applications that can be run at user login to gather that information into a network database, saving the administrator a great deal of work.

Remote software distribution, configuration text files, or Registry change distribution over the network cable with some specially written applications can use the workstation inventory as part of the criteria involved in deciding who gets what changes or applications. It makes no sense for a workstation with no disk space to be set up to receive a 10 MB set of application files. Indeed, workstation inventory management applications enable you to know which users on the network are running out of disk space and head off any potential problems.

Among the inventory management software vendors in the LAN workplace are Symantec, McAfee, Frye, Tally Systems, and Lan Support Group. A specific example of the use of the Norton Administrator for Networks Inventory Module is described in Chapter 5.

Although there are quite a few inventory or asset management packages available, their mode of operation presents a challenge to the network administrator. These packages usually are run during the login script and take their snapshots of the workstation as part of the process of updating the workstation's record in the corporate database. The challenge for the developer of such applications is not only to create a protected mode client for their "fact finding," but also to adjust the facts they find for the new Windows 95 operating system and disk management. The network administrator needs to wait until his current vendor makes this adjustment or needs to find a vendor whose package can function in this new environment.

The new technology of Plug and Play will, over the long haul, enable the network manager not to have to worry as much about both the physical hardware and the workstation configuration. New machines such as those from HP and Compaq are now shipping with built-in agents and network management modules to monitor these stations across the cable. These Plug and Play items will better identify themselves to the inventory management packages.

Workstation Configuration Management

The first questions from any technical support staff usually deal with the workstations' configuration files. With Windows 3.*x* installed on the workstation, you need to know what the settings are in the various Ini files. With Windows 95 there is the Registry and some settings in the System.ini and Win.ini files. At the most basic level, workstation configuration management is an extension of the workstation inventory process (with the collection of the configuration files being included in the network database).

Such a gathering of the configuration files into a central database helps with a typical support problem: a vendor often needs to return a support call, and the network manager needs to move on to other tasks while waiting. Online access to a copy of the configuration file enables you to be away from the workstation in question and have the ability to review its configuration files.

In addition to understanding the role of the configuration files and having online access to a copy of the files, there is the question of managing these files remotely. Remote management of these files can be done through remote control of the workstation or an e-mail like distribution program. When changes need to be made, must you physically run to that workstation or can you make the changes from any workstation? This question has financial implications. If you don't have to go to that station, you save time for yourself and the user. And time is worth money to the company. Remote control is better than having to physically go to the other workstation.

In addition to the question of the support person's time is that of the user's time. Adjustments to the user's configuration files often means moving the user away from his or her machine or rescheduling a visit for another time. Remote changes make better use of support time, but may not fit into the user's time frame. Rather than having to worry about such scheduling issues, you might want to think about distributing changes as a form of e-mail. Under an e-mail scheme of things, you can make the changes on your time, and the user would receive them or accept them on his or her time.

Microsoft Windows 3.1 and Windows for Workgroups 3.11 present the network manager with significant challenges dealing with configuration file changes. If the network has Windows installed on each workstation then the support staff needs to visit each station to adjust these files. If the users' Windows files are maintained on the file server, then the support staff can make adjustments from their own workstations. But even with this convenience, it might just be more economical to use some configuration file management software that would distribute the adjustments without the support person needing to open each user's files and using a text edit to make and save the changes. This advantageous use of a third-party software application to distribute the changes might make even more financial sense when the distribution needs to be made on some criteria and the administrator does not have to do the list making manually.

Windows 95 in the long run replaces the Ini files with its central Registry file, which is more structured and is divisible into user and workstation configurations. The phrase "in the long run" is used here to mean when the users are switched over to the 32-bit applications and devices that are maintained in the Registry. The remote Registry service enables you to connect to one workstation at a time to make adjustments in that station's Registry. This remote management tool, along with the System Policy Editor and the resulting Config.pol file, makes it possible for changes to be distributed at logon time and on a station-by-station basis. There is even a group management feature that enables you to manage users by their group membership as long as there is no specific user configuration existing.

Rather than replacing the need for third-party software, Windows 95 in a network environment requires additional management tools than are already provided through Windows 95. Microsoft is positioning its System Management Server system as a provider of such support. What provides the need for third-party vendors is that there is neither any way of upgrading or modifying a group of workstation registries by any criteria devised by the administrator, nor a way of making changes to either specific users or groups of users without creating a NetWare or Windows NT server group for that purpose. Nor is there a way of utilizing that group function for such changes.

The central Registry system is a source of concern for network managers. It should not be accessible to the user, so you should take two steps to keep users from this file. You should remove the Registry Editor program from the workstation, and keep the user from accessing it.

Application Management

Application management is an amplification of configuration management focused on running software applications successfully. Application management is at the top level of the seven OSI layers and concerns us with a system of recognizing and dealing with what the user experiences when working with applications. Put simply, application management is dealing with the problems of using applications.

Of all the areas of LAN management discussed here, application management is the least developed in terms of the marketplace, but will become important as vendors write programs to monitor all aspects of the application's relationship to the local Windows 95 software operating system, the local workstation, and the network.

Users are all too familiar with error messages that do not necessarily mean anything other than that Windows software is not sure of what to make of a situation. Application management software intercepts the system messages and makes them available to those who support the network and the application.

Typically, problems are caused by not having enough open files set in the configuration files, slow network problems that cause the application to time out, or issues specific to Windows such as the lack of enough system resources. These problems often cause the application to fail or crash, but don't tell the user why.

Application management involves running a workstation agent, a TSR program, or Windows virtual device driver on the workstation that sends real-time messages to a central monitoring station on the network or to an e-mail system or pager. The items monitored include such things as system resources or disk space available, or some network traffic measurement.

As the network support staff becomes more experienced with a particular application, they develop a body of knowledge of the common problems and their solutions. This knowledge is useful in reducing response time. As an extension of this experience, it is even more beneficial and cost saving, if there were a system that allowed a software application to receive the alerts and carry out predefined procedures based on those alerts. These procedures would be messages to the problem workstation indicating actions for that workstation to do or actual remote control of the workstation by the central monitoring station to accomplish these procedures.

The costs of any such application management software would need to be justified based on the time savings for both the user and the support staff. Another such matter that would need to be worked out is the issue of live monitoring of workstations. Is the workstation and its activity the province of the user or the employer? If it is the users, should there be a choice of being monitored or not? There are issues raised in the legal sense about what is on e-mail systems and workstation/network files as to ownership and rights of the individual for privacy—do these principles apply here?

Although Windows 95 gives you the ability to monitor a workstation's performance in areas like CPU and swap file usage, there are not yet any programs such as Intel's Alertview for monitoring applications and their relationship to the operating system and the network. Intel's Alertview is a Windows 3.*x* program that sits between the application, the workstation operating system, and the network and picks up specific application failure messages.

With the complexity of the Windows 95 Registry and the increased sophistication of applications running in the Windows 95 environment, such application management programs will be created by third-party vendors interested in filling this market need.

The Desktop Management Task Force (DTMF) is an organization that is creating standards for agents embedded in hardware and software to report back to central monitoring stations about the health and performance of the workstations and applications. Windows 95 will at some time support a special Windows 95 DTMF agent.

Software License Management

Computer monitors are licensed for singular use, but what about software that could be installed on multiple computers or accessed by multiple users? The use of software is governed by federal and state laws of intellectual properties. You need to make sure you are not using pirated software. How do you survey for licensed versus unlicensed copies, and what can you do when you discover unauthorized software? Is the network manager at risk if there is no policy?

After your organization adopts a policy, what are the best means of monitoring corporate use of software to maintain the licensing? Some companies install software that shuts down the individual workstation if unauthorized software is discovered. From a political point of view is there a way of insuring that the Vice President of the company always has access to an application? Or from a practical point of view is there a way of politely asking a user of an application to relinquish his copy if it has not been used for a long period of time? These are some of the many issues that need to be discussed about the legal aspects of software management.

The section "Security Management" later in this chapter covers the user's rights to application directories and files. Software management, on the other hand, governs access to applications in keeping with license agreements.

Windows 95 presents some special concerns for maintaining the legal contracts you have with software vendors. Because of the protected mode operation of Windows 95, even before the GUI is initiated and before the 32-bit network client is started, the TSR scheme that monitors the applications run on the workstation does not work. Until vendors catch up with the Windows 95 developers and provide a means of monitoring the applications run on the Windows 95 workstation, there will be a lapse in software metering.

Another aspect of software management is the access through menu systems (or what has been described earlier as "effective icons"). Initially, the administrator has little control over the application desktop of the user. Third-party tools, such as SABER LAN workstation, Net Tools, Norton Desktop for Windows, Habitat, Netwizard, and LAN Escort, enable the network manager to maintain the effective icons, the user's icons, and application desktops. These tools, however, are written for earlier versions of Windows and either replace the Program Manager, or run TSR or real mode batch files to solve the remote management problem of the user's icons and GUI access to applications. These vendors will be issuing Windows 95-specific applications to provide a Windows 95 virtual device driver means of controlling the user's desktop.

Network Traffic Management

The area of traffic management deals with the process of getting messages from your desk to other locations on the network, and includes monitoring cables and packet rates, and visually mapping the network. The seven OSI layers of computer communication take us from the application running on the workstation down to the physical network card connected by cable to the file server or host. As the message travels down to the physical layer it accumulates an envelope-like covering that deals with how the traffic is controlled on the cable and what language the computers on the cable are speaking.

Traffic management applications help you track down problems dealing with getting message packets to and from the file server. When there is too much traffic, the network seems to be very slow. Sometimes the traffic is simply a single faulty network card that sends out too much traffic or faulty packets that impede passage on the cable highway. You might need to look at packets traveling on the network cable to determine their type and content. These tasks are in the realm of network traffic or protocol analyzers.

Traffic management also enables you to alert the network manager to either potential or real problems, ideally before they occur. The threshold of network cable traffic might be set, for example, so that the manager is alerted by e-mail or pager when the network bandwidth reaches fifty percent or the number of detected errors on the network reaches 10 percent of network traffic.

Besides this problem solving process, network management enables the network manager to better understand network traffic and the structure of the protocols and requests made over the network. This understanding is helpful in the overall design and care of the network.

One of the criteria for the location of Windows 95 and applications is the impact on the network. Server-based shared installations of Windows 95 and/or applications means the creation of traffic as packets travel from the workstation to the server and back. Another traffic concern is the potential peer-to-peer aspect of Windows 95 and then the traffic consideration inherent in using the NetWare Service Advertising Protocol to support the user security level of peer-to-peer functionality inherent in the Microsoft Client for NetWare. You also need to examine the remote Registry and remote system monitor facilities in terms of their impact on network traffic.

One of the contributions Microsoft is making to the network traffic management area is the inclusion of the Simple Network Management Protocol (SNMP) agent. The SNMP agent adds to your ability to manage the Windows 95 workstation within the broader context of network traffic management. Through the SNMP agent the workstation can be monitored by network traffic monitoring applications that use this protocol as a means of establishing communication across the network.

Network Design Management

As an off-shoot of network traffic management, there are an increasing number of design tools that enable you to create visual maps of your networks and to validate the design issues involved. These design maps can be used to create lists of parts for the networks and then as the actual maps of the network.

There are network management applications that discover nodes on the network. This discovery process is common to applications that monitor devices on the networks. Generally, this discovery process is facilitated by the network card node address. After it is discovered, the application can use this node information. This discovery is different from the registration of machine information at user login time. The application might then utilize inventory information collected at login or take advantage of information embedded on the hardware circuits. Simple Network Management Protocols, or standards established by the Desktop Management Task Force, dictate system or software information that is polled by a central monitor or reported by the nodes-devices directly to that console.

Although some products enable you to move the icons of the discovered node from a logical to a physical map representation of the network, there are a number of products that enable you to create visual maps of the network. Some of the products take data from the discovery process and others need to be created without benefit of discovery. Most have stencils or images that you can drag from a palette to the drawing area where a map of the network can be created. Some of the products create an underlying database record when the image is placed on the map and even enable you to import and export workstation data. These visual maps are useful for network analysis and troubleshooting.

Visual mapping of the network gives the administrator a better means of managing the network by clearly representing the what and where of network nodes, printers, bridges, routers, and gateways. It would be fitting to have such a visual map of the network so that there is a better handle on the known network before the Windows 95 systems are placed on the network.

A significant aspect of network design is the anticipation of growth of the existing network. You can use design management tools to simulate network traffic and test for potential growth. Through the use of accumulated data, you can project the trends of the network into the future. The accumulated data can then be compared so that you can see the relationship between users and traffic, and then project out traffic load implications of adding 50 additional users.

You can perform the stress testing or load analysis of the network first with a pilot network running the established Windows 3.1 or Windows for Workgroups 3.11 for benchmarking, and then with the same number of Windows 95 workstations in their various configurations, including Microsoft Client for NetWare and file and printer sharing for NetWare networks.

Server Management

The impact on the server is a major factor in the integration of Windows 95 and the file server-based network. The impact on performance of either or both Windows 95 and applications being located on the server is a major concern of the network administrator. Another concern is the space requirement of the shared program and installation files required for installing Windows 95 from the network server.

The file server, the center of the networked universe, needs to be closely monitored for disk space and memory usage and fine-tuned for performance. The CPU and its activity is of concern to us to register how hard the unit is working. An overworked CPU means slower performance, which increases how long the user must wait for data. The disk channel is also a potential problem. You might, therefore, want to note the use of the channel and its queue for reads and writes. The use of server memory is a vital concern, as are the measurements of how the server is using memory. A server with too little memory is slow in delivering data to users.

You also should be concerned with traffic coming to and going out from the server. The network card needs to be able to handle all the traffic addressed to the server, and the server needs to be able to receive the packets for processing. If not, the workstations will resend the packets until they are either received or the workstation times out. The resending of these packets means more network traffic added to a busy network.

Server management also means accumulating these performance statistics over a period of time for patterns and trends. As with network traffic, you are then in position to be able to make judgments and recommendations about resolving current problems or averting problems and anticipate growth needs. You should also stress test the server with application software that simulates activity and resulting loads on the server.

Servers also have fine-tuning capabilities that you can utilize. Software is available that helps you understand these settings and when to adjust them for particular tasks.

Such tasks include network backups during which you might want to disable logins so that users don't open files that would then not be backed up. You can use such software to schedule the changes in server settings to make adjustments and then schedule a time that the settings revert back to their original values.

A key aspect of server management is the increased desire by network managers to be alerted to potential problems before they affect the server. There are growing capabilities being developed to send alerts to the network manager when the server is being threatened by changes that could bring the file server down.

Server management also entails being able to support servers remotely, whether using the network operating systems' built-in capabilities or an application that tracks and supports servers on the network.

Support Management

Software upgrades and software distribution are handled by support personnel. Network management includes keeping track of all support calls so that you know what is happening on the network. With proper record keeping, you can isolate one time events from patterns that require your attention.

Despite their best intentions, Microsoft and other vendors will have their hands full during the first months (if not years) of Windows 95. Publications such as this book, online resources such as the Internet, CompuServe, and the Microsoft network, user groups, and other resources will be an invaluable source for help.

As a network administrator, you need to develop record keeping skills to note as much as possible about problems that develop with the installation and running of applications and devices. Users should be briefed on making such notes so that they can be part of the corporate learning machine. No matter how much beta testing there has been, the reality of your environment with your machines and programs will yield problems that need to be documented.

You need to examine the types of issues users raise and how quickly your support staff responds to them. The larger the network, the more important it is to both build up your in-house expertise through building our own "knowledgebase" of the applications you support, but also to avail yourself to vendor bulletin boards and such online services as their CD-ROM support databases.

As mentioned previously, there is a growing set of applications that enable you to distribute configuration files and applications over the network in order to save having to physically go to each of your workstations to install new software or upgrade existing installations. Some of the Electronic Software Distribution applications enable you to base the distributions on the existing hardware and software configurations and status. Applications include software that allows for distribution over both local and wide area networks.

The Software Distribution vendors, such as Symantec, Frye, McAfee, On Demand, and Lanovations, are all busy at work re-creating their applications for the Windows 95 platform, so the tools for this network management function will not be immediately available.

Security Management

Network security is a broad area encompassing anything that might disturb the well-being of the network and the organization that it serves. Although there are some performance issues that might be considered technical, there are also important policy decisions that must be established and supported by management. Virus attacks are breaches in security, and you need to prevent them through checks on both local workstations and the network, along with policies about what software can be run on workstations and the best way of creating gates to keep viruses from entering the network.

The emphasis today is on the C2 security rating that ups the security requirements from simply having passwords and access control lists (ACLs) for files and directories, to preventing passwords from being read by traffic analyzers and providing auditing of what users do on the network. Although C2 security is more involved, these are the major implications. Building in these security levels means overhead on the network and the server. Decisions need to be made about these practices.

A number of issues arise when auditing what users do on the network, including the pervasive question about monitoring users, and whether users should be informed that they are using corporate equipment and software, and thus subject to monitoring. What should be the auditing policy when the operating systems themselves provide this ability? Should such monitoring software be acquired when the network operating system does not provide it? What or who should be audited?

Network managers often face difficult situations when they have to establish and support sensitive areas such as the President's office or accounting/payroll/human resources. As supervisors, the network manager has access to all resources needed to do their jobs, but also access to all files on the network. In these areas the network manager and the appropriate manager might set up an auditing system that tracks the network manager in relationship to sensitive data areas.

A key area of security management is tracking "effective rights," which are the totality of rights that a user has as a member of various network groups. The typical network operating system does not provide printouts of the effective rights of users. Third-party security management packages enable you to analyze the effective rights of users or of a specific user, and their rights to the server file directories or a specific directory.

Looking at users, the area of access and passwords involves issues such as what might be called "dangerous users," which are the users for whom the security system is not tight enough. A report listing these "dangerous users" enables you to examine these users and exercise critical judgment in tightening up the security system. You can, for example, assign passwords or increase the length of the passwords in use, or set up policies that disallow any passwords that can be found in the dictionary or are variations of the user's name or birthday.

Windows 95 enables you to piggyback or borrow the bindery from a NetWare server or the user security list from a Windows NT server in a number of situations without delving deeply in the security system. As with Windows 3.1 and Windows for Workgroups 3.11, users can see the servers and directories/files for which they have file scanning access rights. Users are able to see any print queues for which they have access. These facts have caused some NetWare administrators to change queue access rights from the default group everyone. Others have attempted to remove the file scan rights from the application directory.

Most specifically, you can establish a NetWare or Windows NT Server as a validating source for a user wanting to use a workstation. This function means that you can require a Windows 95 user to be a recognized and valid user on a specified server in order to be able to log on to the Windows 95 workstation.

If you establish a workstation to use file and print sharing for NetWare or Microsoft networks, you can have a server provide the list of users and groups that you can then use to create the user-based security for shared resources on that Windows 95 workstation. In either situation, one particular server must be the reference point, even if users do not specifically log on to that server, or have any rights on that server.

Beyond these aspects is the use of the NetWare user's mail directory for the replication of their profile, which consists of their User.dat segment of the Windows 95 Registry and the link files that provide object linking and embedding links to actual programs (whether on the local disk or server). From a security point of view this means additional matters to be concerned with in an area of the NetWare server that has been of only minor concern. The increased use of this area means that the administrator has to be able to access information about the bindery or NetWare Directory Services (NDS) identity as the system tracks the user's mail directory with his or her eight-digit security identity. For the administrator to modify Mary's profile on the network, the administrator will have to know her security ID to find her mail\user directory. Even to use the User.man file (a user profile that the user cannot change), the administrator has to place this User.man in the mail\user directory.

Network File Storage Management

Chapter 2, "Key Issues Networking with Windows 95," discusses the challenge of long file names. Beyond that is the storage space used by the user profile Lnk files, which are small files that use up 4 KB storage blocks in NetWare 3.*x*.

For backup and other file management matters, administrators should keep in mind that users using shared Windows 95 program files from the server will have their virtual memory or swap files kept on the server. These files need to be accounted for in terms of space used, and should not be backed up, because they are empty files. It is not clear what algorithm or method the Windows 95 system uses to create and size these permanent, but expanding and contracting, files. Indeed, when considering the location of the Windows 95 programs for users, these swap files need to be part of the process. Unlike Windows 3.*x*, which created the server located swap files with each session and deleted the files after, Windows 95 creates but does not delete the swap file after a session.

With the increase in network activity and the increase in file size for databases and document imaging, the management of server storage space occupies more of your attention. Network management involves determining the usefulness of stored files and finding methods of file compression and hierarchical storage management for offloading files to less expensive storage media, such as optical disks, as well as establishing procedures for backing up data files and protecting the file server from loss of power and other electrical power problems. System fault tolerance, such as mirroring, duplexing, RAID, duplicate servers, and online backup systems, is also an issue of network file storage management.

In addition to encouraging users to clean up older files, network managers might want to utilize applications that "age" files by last use and enable managers to archive files or move them offline. Disk or file compression is also an option worth considering. Management of the disk file system is something that operating systems usually manage. When the file server crashes, you need to perform external repair of the file systems. You also need to consider software applications that help keep the server file system working and efficient.

File storage space is usually at a premium on the server. There are means of assessing the use of disk space and even to limit the space users might fill. You need to examine creative approaches that eliminate the need to keep multiple copies of files in instances such as group projects. Many document or word-processing packages enable you to include non-printing comments, and spreadsheet packages allow for multiple scenarios that eliminate the need for multiple copies. There are also applications that create "virtual file cabinets," which are sets of files that can be made available to other users for their access and changes. These virtual file cabinet approaches bring the aliases and linking of file names to specific and real files that operating systems provide to users.

You need to examine file backup policies and practices to make sure that critical data is not lost. Many companies back up user workstation files. You should periodically test the tape backup unit and software to ensure proper and accurate backup of data files.

LAN Team Management

Beyond technology, the network is run by people. The effective network manager must work with both the end user and the network support staff. This means often stepping beyond one's technical competence into the people management area. Tracking the performance of team members is important and needs to be documented and dealt with in a constructive, business-like manner. Members of your team, end users, and staff members alike should be cultivated and recognized for contributions.

Many network managers have found that having a network users' group is an invaluable source of suggestions and support when working with upper management. The network manager and staff need to be "internal sales" staff for the services of the network to make sure that the users are buying and using the network's resources. In some cases, this group helps to develop stringent policies to support the network administrator in terms of the software management and virus protection concerns.

As part of LAN team management, it is important to emphasize that the technology of the LAN must support the business and productivity goals of the organization. An example of this point is the user group for a large law firm that suggested and helped develop a set of word processing macros that enabled the construction of complicated legal documents in a matter of minutes rather than the hours of typing that used to be needed.

The involvement of the end user in the implementation process of Windows 95 would be a very important management technique. With Windows 95, every insight offers important data for you as you move into uncharted territory. The end user can be alerted to the need to track problems with as much detail as possible and even make suggestions as to what training or support might be needed.

Remote Task Management

Network management applications enable you to manage the network from the desktop. What if, however, you could schedule a database application report to run on Mary's new Pentium processor while she is on vacation next week; or what if you could remotely try out that new application on John's workstation while he is at the annual sales meeting?

More and more tools are available that enable you to distribute tasks to inactive or remote workstations, thus giving you far more distributed processing power. These tools now depend on running memory resident programs or TSRs on workstations, which with Windows 95 will give way to Windows Dynamic Link Libraries (DLLs) and virtual device drivers running within the large amounts of memory on these workstations for running Windows 95.

As this 32-bit virtual device driver technology expands, you need to think about what to do with these powerful and expensive machines the other 128 hours a week that they are now not being used during the current 40 hours a week that we consider the work week.

Key Issues Networking with Windows 95

For the NetWare administrator, Windows 95 presents some key issues from the outset that need analysis, decision and policy making, and then action. Among these matters are the following:

- The protected mode operation of the Windows 95 workstation
- The replacement of the Ini files with the Windows 95 Registry
- The introduction of long file names
- The matter of Windows 95 workstation security
- The question of administration across the network

Each of these matters marks a departure from the Windows 3.*x* and NetWare experiences of the past three years. Windows 95 has the workstation booting into what some might call protected mode DOS and logging to the network in protected mode, rather than starting DOS in 640 KB real mode and attaching to the network in real mode and then starting Windows. Even though you can still—and might have to—continue using the current NetWare clients to log on to NetWare and then start Windows 95, many of the advanced networking and network administration features are only available if the protected mode network process is used.

The replacement of the System.ini, Win.ini, Control.ini, and Progman.ini files with a single Windows 95 Registry leads to better control over the computer and user, but it also introduces a whole new set of tools, terms, and operations. With more control, you need to make decisions about the levels of control you want to establish and the consequences of such control.

Long file names that break out of the DOS 8.3-character naming system will be both a popular feature for users and a source of significant concern for the administrator. It will be a matter of time before application vendors catch up with this long file name feature with support in their applications for this new file name attribute. Administrators should educate users about some of the traps of long file names. The NetWare file server requires setup for long file names, maintenance of settings such as directory caching, and additional server memory to service the long file names through the NetWare server Name Space service.

Windows 95 contains peer-to-peer connectivity in addition to the previously mentioned features. Peer-to-peer networks have always raised concerns for network administrators, who are trained to be concerned about network performance and security. Until personal NetWare, Windows for Workgroups 3.11, and Windows 95, peer-to-peer networking in the NetWare environment meant multiple protocols. Windows 95 provides IPX/SPX support for accessing both the NetWare server and the Windows 95 workstation. Windows 95 also enables the establishment of user-level security for peer-to-peer access, rather than the less secure share-level security. The bindery of the Windows 95 workstation's preferred NetWare server could provide user-level security to the workstation. This security approach is not without administration preparation and traffic concerns.

User-level security can be based on the NetWare 3.*x* bindery or the Windows NT Server's security system. This user-level security in effect borrows the list from the server, making sure that the user is on that list, but sets the specific security access on the Windows 95 station itself.

Windows 95 has the significant capability to manage both user and computer configurations across the network and at logon time. You need to become quite familiar with the range and how-to's of these management features. Careful planning is required to establish policies that govern individuals and groups. A well thought out set of policies and restrictions will help prevent an endless cycle of granting and restricting after the fact of the initial Windows 95 installation.

Windows 95 and Protected Mode

Windows 3.*x* has worked in the memory area above 1 MB or extended memory area protected memory mode sitting on top of DOS, which operates in the real memory mode. Your workstation network components, the network card driver, the network protocol, and the client shell have been 16-bit real mode memory-resident software. In addition to taking up either base memory or upper memory space, these real mode items require supporting virtual mode drivers to manage connections between protected mode and real mode software. Problems arise when the virtual or protected mode drivers Netware.drv and Vnetware.386 being used in Windows do not match the real mode Netx or VLM client version.

By noting the developments from DOS to Windows 3.1 through Windows for Workgroups, and then to Windows 95 by way of Windows NT, you can see a transition from real mode to protected mode operation. Windows 95, although briefly running real mode at boot time, quickly switches into protected mode.

Protected Versus Real Mode Memory

Workstation memory is divided into three location types: base memory, adapter segment or upper memory, and above 1 MB memory, which is extended memory or can be made to look like the older expanded memory. Another memory designation refers to the mode of operation, either real mode memory or protected mode memory.

Although the definitions are not as clear as they could be, you might say that anything below 1 MB in real mode designates memory usage possible with the 286 processor. Memory above 1 MB, designated as extended memory, enables you to take special advantage of the 386 and higher processor to run processes such as virtual machines in Windows (see fig. 2.1). Simply said, protected mode is protected from all the rules that apply in real mode. Among these rules are the amount of memory that can be added. You cannot add memory chips and increase the size of the 640 KB base memory or the 384 KB adapter segment memory area. You can, however, add memory to the above 1 MB extended memory area.

Real mode covers both the 640 KB base application memory and the 384 KB upper memory of adapter segment area range. Thus, whether you load a memory resident program in base memory or upper memory, it is being loaded in real mode. Network protocols and shells that can be loaded in either base memory or upper memory are nonetheless loaded in real mode. Being able to load these memory resident network software items into upper memory has helped the applications have enough memory within DOS and within the DOS virtual machines in Windows.

Figure 2.1

Real versus protected computer memory locations.

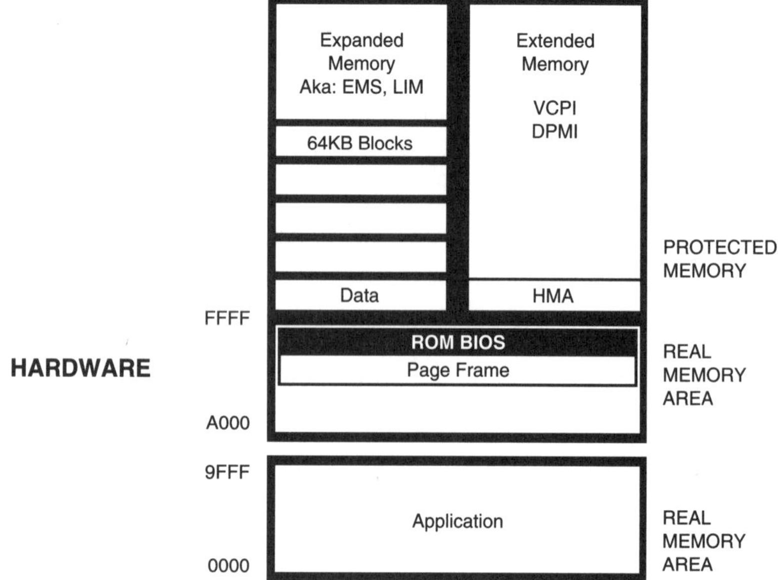

The design of Windows 95, especially in relationship to the network adapter, protocol, and client shell, is to have 32-bit protected mode network components that do not take up any base memory. What Windows 95 has in common with Windows 3.*x* is that as it moves into extended memory or protected mode operation, it takes a snapshot of the existing base memory. This snapshot is used to create the DOS virtual machine in which the DOS application runs. This snapshot includes any resident programs and this means that the DOS application has that much less memory to use for its purposes in that virtual machine. Windows applications also look at the base memory area for usable memory and some may fail to work properly if there is not enough base memory available. The goal of memory management is to remove the DOS memory resident programs from base memory.

The problem with real mode software is that it takes up base memory or upper memory, both of which are limited and, hence, at a premium on our workstations. For practical considerations, protected mode software is preferred.

The Need for Virtual Device Drivers

Virtual is a term that has become associated with protected mode operation. Put most succinctly, virtual means "not real," (see fig. 2.2). Virtual machines (VMs) exist in protected mode which is not real mode. There are virtual device drivers (VxDs) that operate in protected mode, not real mode. Another use of the word virtual refers to virtual memory or the swap file. The swap file is not real chip memory, but a holding place for the former contents of real chip memory, and hence it is not real or virtual memory.

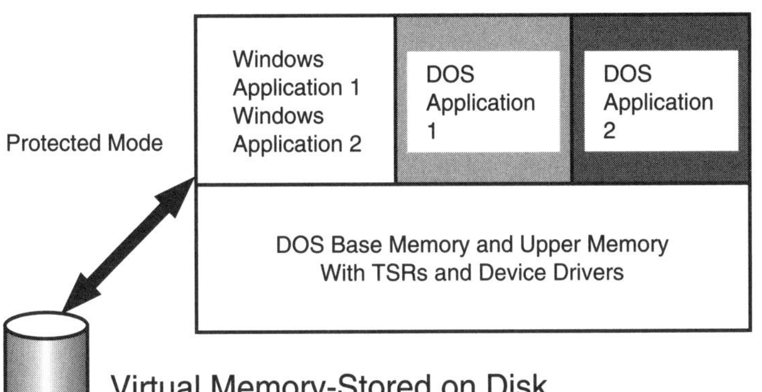

Figure 2.2

Virtual means "not real," as in virtual machines and virtual memory.

Because Windows 3.*x* and Windows 95 GUIs are run in protected mode and there are many aspects of the workstation's operation that are in real mode, there is a whole classification of software known as virtual device drivers (VxDs) (see fig. 2.3). These VxDs are designated by the 386 file extensions in Windows 3.*x* and the Vxd extension in Windows 95. There are two types of virtual device driver: the support layer type, which provides a virtual mode counterpart to a real mode software (as with the NetWare Vnetware.386, which provides protected mode connection to the real mode client shell); and the protected mode Vxd such as Vshare.386 explained below.

With the publication of Windows-based suites of applications comes the need to share specific files. This has brought about the need for real mode Share.exe, which enables this sharing without the DOS error announcing a sharing violation. The difficulty with Share.exe is that it is real mode and, therefore, a memory user. Without much notice, Microsoft made a protected mode version available for Windows 3.1. This protected mode version of Share.exe, which allows the taking of the share function out of real mode operation is Vshare.386. The V and the 386 stand for virtual device driver. You can now take Share.exe. out of real mode use and add a "DEVICE=Vshare.386" line into the 386 Enhanced section of System.ini. In the System.ini of Windows 95, which is provided for backward compatibility, a statement in the [386Enh] section reads "device=*vshare." This translates, "device= the internal virtual device drive vshare.vxd, which is now built into the operating system."

Figure 2.3

Virtual mode requires virtual device drivers to get to real mode.

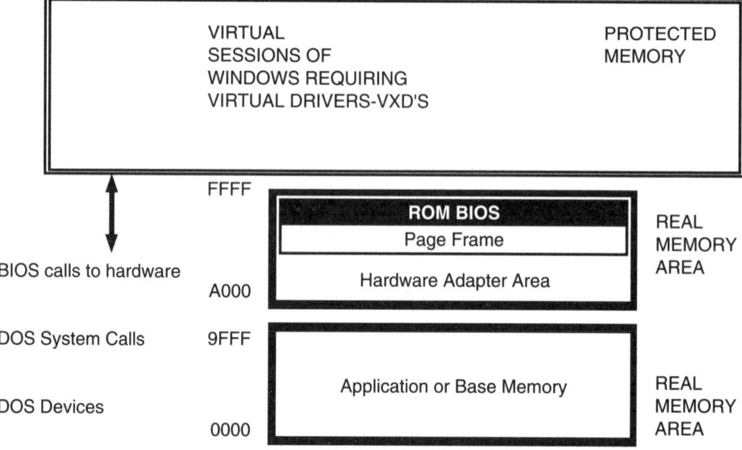

The adventurous administrator who wants to become familiar with the Registry and the Registry Editor and/or who wants to see if a particular VxD has translated from Windows 3.*x* to Windows 95, can find the Vshare.vxd in the Registry by accessing the Registry Editor and selecting **F**ind from the **E**dit menu, and then searching for the file in "My Computer/HKEY/LOCAL_MACHINE/System/Current Control Set/control/VMM32Files/Vshare.vxd."

32-bit is another term used to describe device drivers that function in the protected mode arena. Windows 3.*x* brought 32-bit disk access (see fig. 2.4). Windows 3.11 brought you 32-bit file access. Neither of these 32-bit processes actually changed hardware from 16-bit to 32-bit devices, rather they moved the focus of their efforts from real mode to protected mode.

32-bit disk access is an option for Windows 3.1 that provides faster and more efficient access to the local workstation disk. Without it, a protected mode Windows application needing a file on the local disk must push that request into real mode where the request seeks the physical disk location of the file and forwards that request to the BIOS-based disk controller to fetch the file, which then must be pushed back up into protected mode.

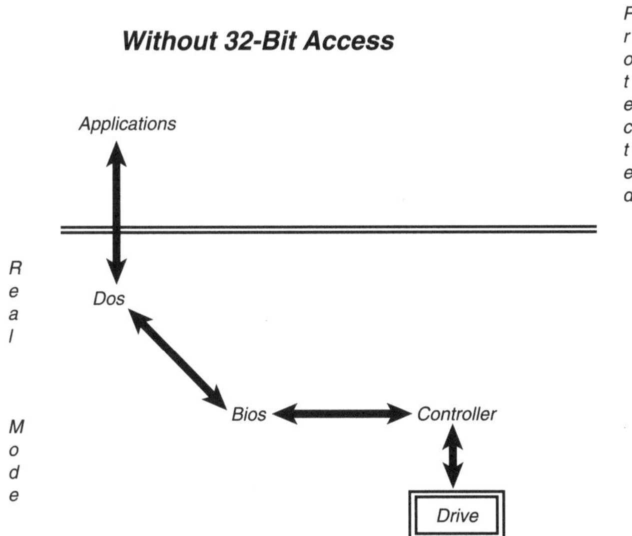

Figure 2.4

The real mode disk controller device without 32-bit virtualizing.

The translation between modes is inefficient, using up more CPU cycles. It also means that Windows must be careful about not running DOS applications unless all its code is in memory. This issue of DOS applications comes about to prevent the situation in which part of the application resides in memory and other pieces are still in virtual memory or in the disk swap file. It is feared that the memory part of the application might make the disk request, but the receiving or processing part of the program might still be on disk. In this situation the program could not access the data until the rest of the program is brought back, but that cannot happen until the data request is completed. This impasse would be impossible to solve because 16-bit or real mode processing is one dimensional. Windows must take steps to avoid this impasse, and the safeguards contribute to the inefficient processing of disk requests.

32-bit disk access works by virtualizing the hard disk controller. This means it acts as if the disk existed in protected mode bypassing the real mode system BIOS. 32-bit protected mode code can act more freely and make the fetching of disk files much more efficient and thus faster for the user. Unfortunately, this feature is only supported by Western Digital 1003-compatible disk controllers or disks with special supporting software. The other major limitation is that it is incompatible with the APM or power management features of notebooks that power down the disk drive during inactive periods.

32-bit disk access is the default setting of Windows 95. The Windows 95 operating system software now provides for ESDI controllers and SCSI controllers, which were not supported with this feature in Windows 3.*x*. Windows 95 also now supports IDE drives with logical block addressing (LBA), which allows IDE drives greater than 28 MB.

32-bit disk access is supported by using virtual device driver support for the real mode disk controller. Such a Windows 95 feature speeds up local disk access. 32-bit file access (see fig. 2.5) on the other hand deals with caching files into memory and finding them quickly on disk. 32-bit file access also illustrates the move from real mode operation to 32-bit protected mode operation, first with Windows for Workgroups 3.11 and then with Windows 95.

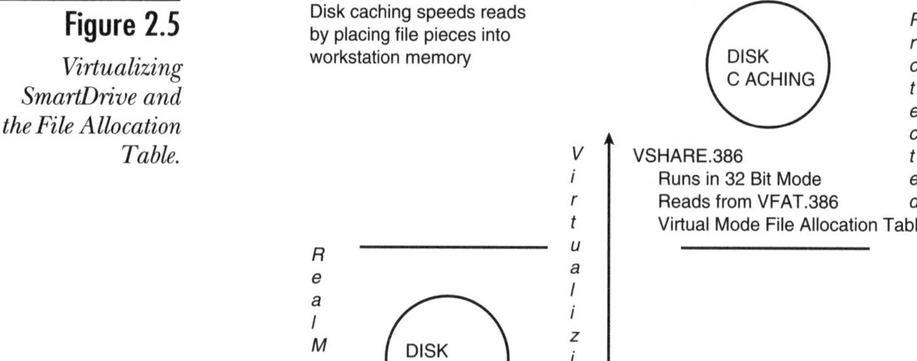

Figure 2.5

Virtualizing SmartDrive and the File Allocation Table.

With Windows for Workgroups 3.11, Microsoft introduces 32-bit file access, which improves the speed of access to files by caching files into memory. Files accessed from memory are obtained faster than through disk reads. This feature was originally introduced in the memory resident SmartDrive. Aside from problems caused by users turning off machines before SmartDrive had completed its writes to disk, SmartDrive took up valuable real mode memory and turned out not to be "smart." Users of older DOS-based Lotus applications were told by technical support personnel to disable the SmartDrive executable because it interfered with the Lotus products' use of memory, and other users discovered that SmartDrive robbed them of valuable memory.

Beyond memory use, the method by which SmartDrive chooses what files to cache into memory is not too intelligent. It reads the location of files being accessed from disk and caches a certain amount of disk storage space units contiguous to the location. Only if the disk had just been defragmented is there a chance that cached memory file pieces are at all related to the files being used. 32-bit file access provides two marked improvements: the movement of the caching program from real mode to the Vcache.386 protected mode virtual device driver, and making the feature more rational by having it access the File Access Table for the real physical locations of the rest of the file. Because Vcache.386 works in protected mode it needs to access the

FAT table which is now made accessible through the protected mode Vfat.386 device driver.

This process of 'virtualizing' the real mode devices into protected mode virtual device drivers accomplishes two purposes:

- The moving of the devices out of base memory, leaving more available and useable memory in the snapshot of memory used by Windows to create the DOS virtual machine.
- The protected mode or virtual device driver can take advantage of the protected mode to be more efficient in the processing of its tasks.

Users that still had the NETX redirector client on their machines discovered that this 32-bit file access feature did not speed up the processing of files. Instead the NETX and 32-bit file access combination actually slowed the machines. By switching to the newer VLM clients, users were able to take advantage of the 32-bit file access. This switching to the VLM DOS requester client was beneficial because the VLM client was designed to work with DOS rather than in opposition to it, which was how the NETX redirector worked. The NETX redirector had to review every call to DOS and the system to determine whether it was for DOS or the NetWare Server software. The 32-bit file access is built into Windows 95 and is fully supported by the 32-bit Microsoft Client for NetWare.

VLMs also were attractive to the Windows for Workgroups 3.11 workstation because of drive mappings. The NETX client started drive mappings after the last drive as configured in the Config.sys file. The traditional F for the user's home directory was chosen because F is the next drive after the default last DOS drive of E. Because both Windows for Workgroups and the VLM client remap DOS drives, both programs work best when they have all the DOS drives to remap—a result of the Config.sys setting "last drive z."

Note The drive mapping issue in Windows 95 is resolved in the default configuration for the workstation as the last drive being the Z drive and the Microsoft Client for NetWare having a setting for the first network drive.

From Support Drivers to 32-Bit Network Clients

When you deal with Windows 3.*x* and NetWare, you run into the problem of how to get there from here. Windows operates in protected mode, and the NetWare protocol and client shell are loaded in real mode, regardless of whether they are in base memory or upper memory. The solution to this problem is provided by the development of three virtual device drivers, Vipx.386, Vnetware.386 and Netware.drv (see fig. 2.6). These VxDs provide virtual mode support for the real mode networking elements.

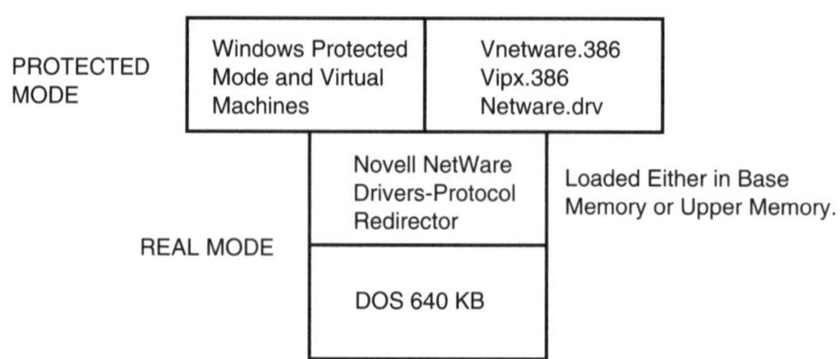

Figure 2.6

*NetWare and the required VxDs to support Windows 3.*x.

Specific functions of the virtual mode drivers are made clearer in figure 2.7, which depicts the relationship of the virtual components to their corresponding real mode software. For example, Vipx.386 provides protected mode support for the real mode IPX protocol, allowing DOS applications within a DOS virtual machine access to the network. Netware.drv supports the network icon in the Windows 3.*x* Control Panel.

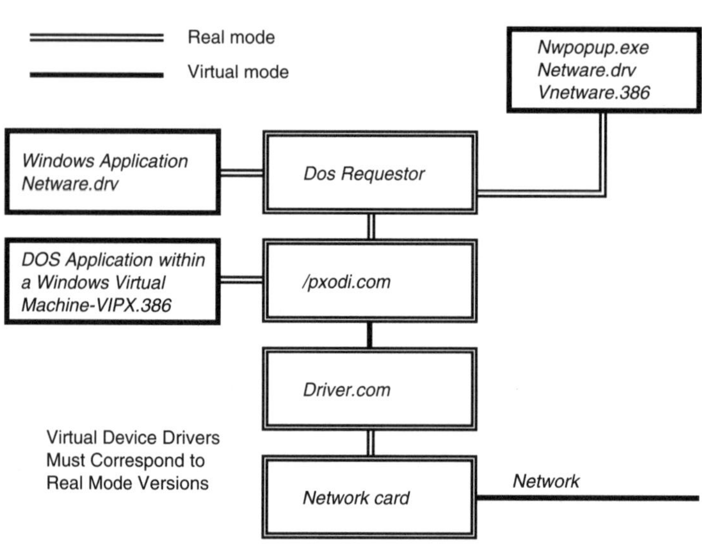

Figure 2.7

*NetWare and the required VxDs to support Windows 3.*x *highlighting version issues.*

A significant problem facing NetWare administrators supporting Windows on NetWare networks is version control and matching between the real mode networking pieces and their protected mode support counterparts. Every switch in shell version requires a new set of virtual device drivers, and whenever Novell has issued a new VLM version (which was fairly often), it meant also replacing the Windows support drivers for NetWare. Behavior problems of all sorts are caused by a mismatch between the IPX and client shell and their protected mode support layer device drivers. To complicate this matter, well-intentioned vendors often gave the user a newer version of the virtual device driver, making it out of sequence with the real mode component.

Windows for Workgroups 3.11 introduces the 32-bit client model for networks. To make the peer-to-peer networking process work within the Windows framework, Microsoft created the 32-bit Windows for Workgroups 3.11 server function on the workstation to share directories and printers. Built in to the client part of the workstation is the ability to map drive letters to directories on other Windows for Workgroups 3.11 stations and to access printing devices on these other computers. These client and server operations are conducted in protected mode and require only a few kilobytes of the 640 KB base memory. Because of the need to run Server.386 and Vredir.386 in enhanced mode, Windows for Workgroups 3.11 only can run in enhanced mode. This elmination of the earlier standard mode is also brought forward into Windows 95.

Windows for Workgroups 3.11 uses the Microsoft NetBEUI protocol, which is a fine-tuned version of the NetBIOS peer protocol. NetBEUI works fine on a single segment or token ring, but it cannot be routed between rings or segments. In order to gain more corporate acceptance for Windows for Workgroups 3.11, Microsoft needed to make this protocol more interactive with routeable protocols such as Novell's IPX protocol. Microsoft's solution to running multiple protocols with NetBEUI is Network Device Interface Specification (NDIS), as shown in figure 2.8. Novell's solution to running multiple protocols on the same network card is Open Datalink Interface (ODI).

The problem with both NDIS and ODI is that they are mutually incompatible. NetWare administrators faced this issue when trying to interface NetWare with other platforms such as the IBM AS/400, which used NDIS-based LAN support software. A number of years ago, a solution to this problem was available from Novell—but only through a somewhat secretive method. People had to call Novell technical support and be given that day's password to a guarded section on CompuServe. Once in that section, they could download a set of files that contained the Odinsup.com file. This Odinsup.com program was a patch that enabled the ODI Drivers to coexist with the NDIS drivers. Although discouraged by Microsoft, the Odinsup program allowed for better functionality using the IPXODI drivers with Windows for Workgroups 3.1 than the Microsoft supplied version of IPX. Figure 2.9 illustrates the changes that take place with Windows for Workgroups 3.11 and the NetWare coexistence.

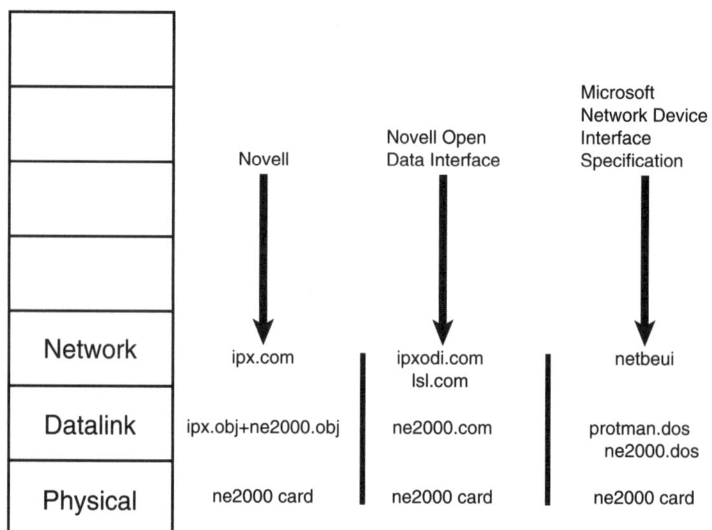

Figure 2.8
Ipx.com, IPXODI, and NetBEUI-NDIS.

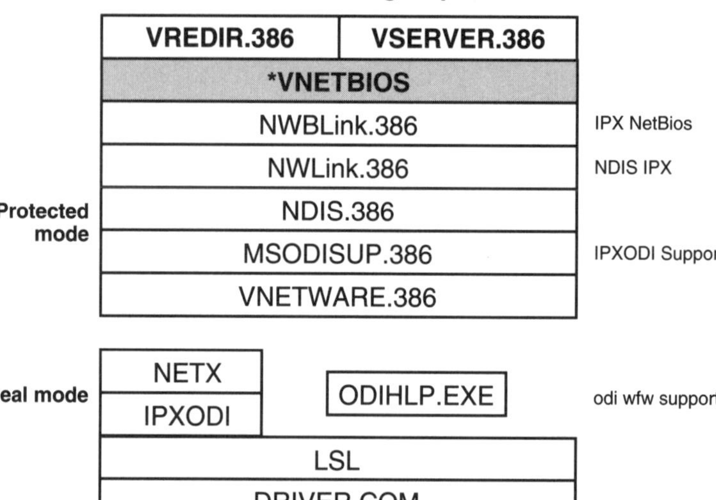

Figure 2.9
Windows for Workgroups 3.11 and its NetWare VxDs.

Windows for Workgroups 3.11 has built-in support for coexistence with NetWare. An Odinsup-like ODI-NDIS interface functionality shows up in the Msodisup.386 device driver, allowing a relationship between the Microsoft NDIS.386 and its NetBEUI protocol. Nwblink.386 and Nwlink.386 provide IPX NetBIOS protocol support and NDIS IPX protocol support, respectively. Windows for Workgroups 3.11 provides these VxDs to work with the protected-mode support drivers for the NetWare real-mode networking protocol and client shell.

This discussion of the virtual device drivers need for the NetWare workstation and for Windows for Workgroups 3.11 was for the purpose of showing the differences between the two situations.

- The need for support layers in protected mode with NetWare and Windows 3.*x*.
- The protected mode operation of Windows for Workgroups 3.11 in which there are no real mode components other than the network card.

As shown in figure 2.10, there is a transition that continues into Windows 95 in which even the network card can be loaded into protected mode as a virtual device driver.

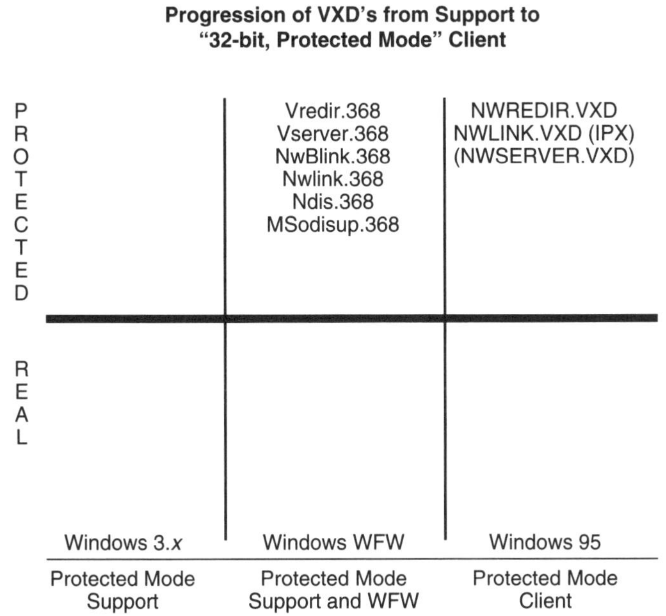

Figure 2.10

The progression of VxDs from support layers to true '32' functionality.

Because Windows 95 quickly moves you from a brief real-mode bootup session into the protected mode session, NetWare networking issues need to be addressed. Although you might have to continue using the real mode IPX and NetWare client, there is a 32-bit client for NetWare. The Microsoft Client for NetWare, the Nwredir.vxd, and the companion 32-bit IPX-SPX compatible protocol, Nwlink.vxd, exist as protected mode entities that do not need real mode components. (Note that, in Windows 95, VxDs are those files with the Vxd file extensions.) Also reflected in figure 2.10 is Nwserver.vxd, which is the protected-mode device driver that supports the use of NetWare server-based bindery security for local Windows 95 workstation directories, files, and printers.

Although, at this writing, NetWare's 32-bit protocol and client are not available outside of Novell testing labs, both Novell and Microsoft agree that a 32-bit protected mode client would be advantageous for workstation Windows 95 operation with the network. Although it comes with its own set of operational planning issues for the NetWare administrator, a 32-bit client is still a means of freeing up real mode memory for applications and other uses of upper memory. The Microsoft 32-bit client for NetWare is required for supporting long file names on the server for the Windows 95 workstation, but this Microsoft client for NetWare does not initially support NetWare 4.*x* NetWare Directory Services.

The Problem of TSRs and Windows 95

An immediate challenge to the use of the protected mode protocol and client are TSRs run as part of the logon process and before you start Windows. These TSRs include the NetWare IP connectivity and real mode 3270 emulation support software, as well as DOS memory resident Bquestor support for Btrieve-based applications. Network management software is another example of TSRs that cannot be used with the 32-bit protected mode client support for NetWare from Microsoft.

These TSRs can be run in the batch files that start DOS applications in DOS virtual machines. When run as a specific DOS virtual machine these programs are only available to applications running in that virtual machine. Some DOS TSRs do well in that virtual machine setting; some do not.

Tremendous strides have been made by third-party vendors such as Saber, Symantec, McAfee, Intel, LAN Support Group, and others whose programs require TSRs to run. These memory-resident programs provide any number of management features, including the following:

- Remote control over other network nodes for end user support, file transfer, and text file changes.

- Software metering and license protection. Also allows for tracking actual use of packages to determine whether users are actually using installed software.
- Virus checking on workstations.
- Workstation inventory readings at logon time.
- Text file change distribution such as "files=" in Config.sys, or Autoexec.bat changes, or Windows' System.ini. (These files will be with us in some format for a while.)
- E-mail-like software distribution, such as Norton Administrator for Networks, McAfee Bright Works, and Frye's Software Update and Distribution System. These applications use a real mode program to check for distribution jobs either for the user or that are intended for workstations that meet certain configuration criteria.
- Network utilities such as Norton's Disk Doctor, which checks disks at logon time and leaves messages for administrators about workstation disks needing attention.
- Real time applications that run a memory resident program on the workstation, which reports the status of Windows systems resources to a central monitoring station. This is to alert an administrator of potential problems involved with the workstation running out of system resources.
- Real time application management programs such as Intel's AlertView, which runs a TSR on the workstation. This TSR picks up error messages from applications and reports them to a central monitor station.
- Remote printing by server to local workstation.

Over a period of time network management program vendors will be publishing versions that will work with Windows 95 protected mode following the example set by Microsoft. Microsoft sets such an example of the moving of a TSR into protected mode operation with its Mspserve.exe. Mspserve.exe functions like NetWare's RPRINTER utility, providing a local workstation's printer port for the file server's use. Both enable the workstation to receive print jobs sent to a particular print queue on the server. NetWare's RPRINTER, however, is a real mode memory resident program, whereas Mspserve.exe is loaded as a virtual mode.

Until software vendors begin to provide 32-bit virtual device drivers or executables of their own to support their functionality, and until NetWare provides us with their 32-bit protocol and client, and until Microsoft provides us with NetWare Directory Services support for NetWare 4.*x*, there will be some hard choices for the NetWare administrator with regard to NetWare connectivity with Windows 95. These choices will be covered more fully in Chapter 3, "Integrating Windows 95 and NetWare."

- **Option one:** Run the real mode Ipx.com or IPXODI protocol with the real mode NETX or VLMS client shell.
- **Option two:** Run the real mode Ipx.com or IPXODI with the Microsoft Client for NetWare.
- **Option three:** Run the Microsoft IPX/SPX-compatible protocol—their 32-bit implementation of the IPX protocol—along with the 32-bit Microsoft Client for NetWare.
- **Option four:** Run the Novell NetWare Client 32, which is a protected mode 32-bit implementation of both the IPX/SPX protocol and the former NETX/ VLM client shell.

Until the vendors do indeed supply the virtual or protected mode versions of their software, the network administrator who desires the network management functions listed above might want to hold off the use of the 32-bit client. The balance would be between the use of these network management applications and the tools that Microsoft has provided by way of user and workstation management. The use of these tools, as Microsoft has intended them to be used, is dependent upon the presence on the workstation of the Microsoft Client for NetWare.

The Registry Replaces the Ini Text Files

A significant change in the structure of Windows 95 is the introduction of the Registry. The Registry is a central file that controls the user and the workstation. In providing one central file for these matters, Microsoft has greatly simplified management of the workstation and the user.

The Role of the Windows 95 Registry

Windows 95 replaces the flat text file configuration approach in Windows 3.*x* with the hierarchical directory type of structure Microsoft has had so much success with in Windows NT. System.ini, Win.ini, and Control.ini of Windows 3.*x* are replaced with the Registry, which cannot be edited through an ASCII text editor but requires the use of the Registry Editor (see fig. 2.11) or the administrative Policy Editor. As in Windows 3.*x*, some items dealing with configuration can be changed through the Control Panel.

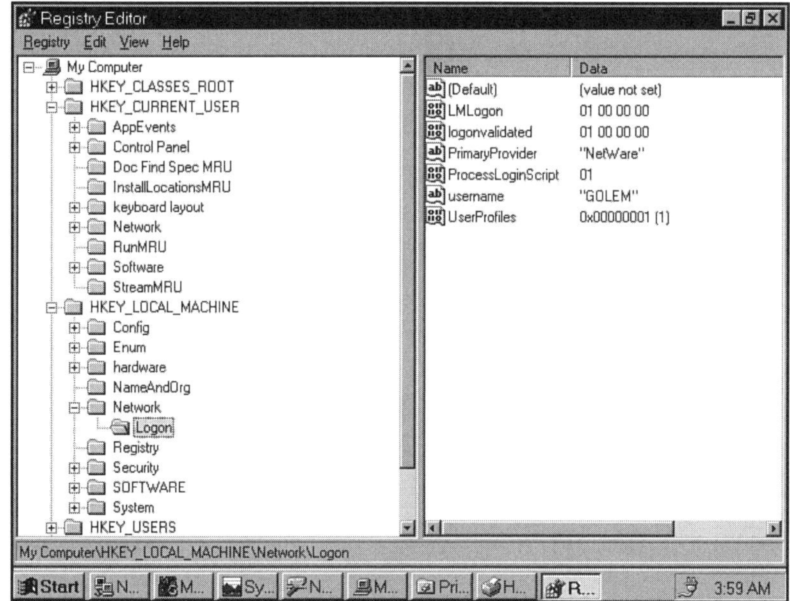

Figure 2.11

The Registry as seen through the Registry Editor.

Besides having to understand a whole new structure of Windows 95 configuration choices and details, the administrator needs to understand that there are various ways to make changes in both workstation and user configuration. One of these ways is a remote registry feature that enables us to make registry changes over cable to another's machine.

What is significant is that the Windows 95 Registry structure gives the administrator much more control over the user and the workstation than was available in the Windows 3.*x* environment. In the setup process, you can establish default settings for users and workstations that preset restrictions and the environment. You can either restrict choices, eliminate activities, or allow users free choice in a large number of items—from the relatively insignificant choice of wallpaper screen backgrounds to restricting access to specific Control Panel items. Among the items that can be restricted are the network and systems icon. You can also disable the **Run** command from the Start menu (see fig. 2.12), which replaces the Windows 3.1 Program Manager interface.

Such restrictions, which impact what a user can do, are somewhat limited within the Windows 3.*x* setting. Administrators can establish restrictions for the user within the Program.ini text file. These restrictions include preventing the use of the **Run** command as well as restrictions against saving session settings that involve the appearance of Program Manager, icons, or groups. One of the limitations of this approach is that Program.ini is a text file that cannot be write protected. Users get an error message upon starting Windows that the program is being started in read-only mode.

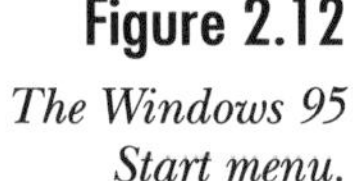

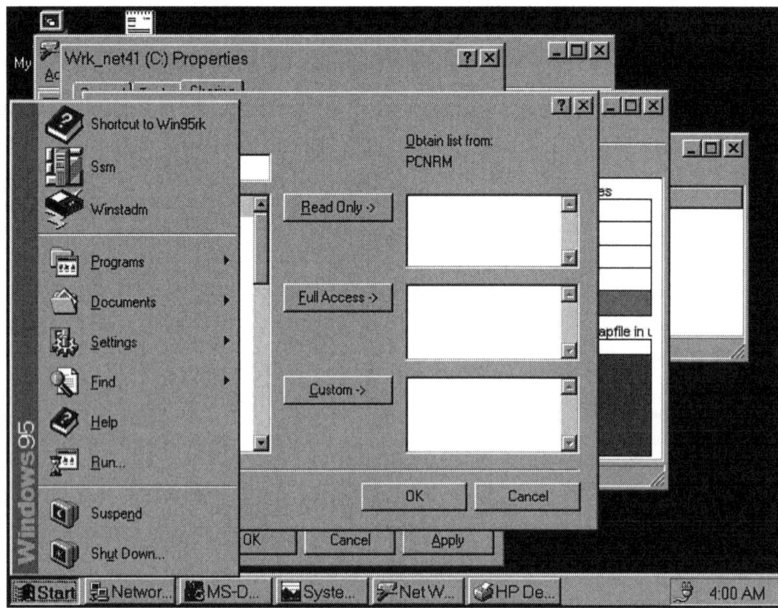

Figure 2.12
The Windows 95 Start menu.

Many administrators discovered the capability to add a section in Control.ini—the [don't load] section. In this section, the label under the Control Panel icon, such as `Network` or `386 enhanced`, could be added as an entry with the syntax being "Network=yes." The logic then was "yes, don't load" this icon when Control Panel is started. This meant the user would not see the icon and thus be unable to make Control Panel changes.

In reality, though, the administrator could make changes through the Ini text files directly, rather than going through the time consuming process of loading Windows and starting the Control Panel. In fact, many administrators turned to third-party packages that could distribute text file changes, including changing the values in entry lines. One such example would be changing the spooler=yes statement in the [Windows] section of Win.ini from yes to no in some cases to avoid lengthy double spooling at both Windows and the NetWare server.

As you will see in Chapter 4, "Managing the Workstation and User," you can set restrictions in the Registry for individual users, groups of users, and workstations. These restrictions cover almost all areas of Windows 95 operation, including networking in general and NetWare networking specifically.

Many, but not all, items have been moved to the Registry. Some functions remain in the System.ini, which is still used for backward compatibility. To provide for the current 16-bit Windows applications, the network administrator will still benefit from network management applications that can remotely modify the text configuration files, such as System.ini.

An example of items that appear in the Windows 95 System.ini follows:

```
[boot]
shell=Explorer.exe
Networks32=NWNP32 MSNP32
 [386Enh]
Paging File=C:/WINDOWS/WIN386.SWP
```

The shell in Windows 95 is the Explorer, which replaces the Program Manager of Windows 3.*x*. Explorer displays local disk and network drive structures in the folder and icon graphic manner, which is more user friendly than the directory and file structure.

`Networks32` indicates 32-bit network drivers; `NWNP32` indicates the Microsoft Client for NetWare Networks; and `MSNP32` indicates the Microsoft Client for Microsoft Networks that might use the Windows NT Server.

The paging file bolded in the System.ini file is the swap file created by Windows 95 at each boot time. It is much like the temporary swap file of Windows 3.*x*, including having the same name and default location.

User Versus Hardware Configuration Issues

A major headache for many NetWare administrators is the user who moves around from one Windows workstation to another. One set of issues involves the problem of users wanting their color choices to follow them around from computer to computer. Another set of issues involves our wanting to make sure users have access to the icons they need to do their jobs. Yet another set of issues that come up are the problems of impacting such workstation configurations as the permanent swap file on the workstation by using the wrong swap file location pointer file, the spart.par file. Of course, complicating this issue of the roving user is whether Windows is installed locally on the workstation or on the server.

With Windows 3.*x*, solutions for the matching of the user configuration to the user and the hardware configuration to the workstation are provided by dividing the configuration files as follows: System.ini and Win.com are specific to the workstation hardware and configuration; Win.ini, Control.ini, and Progman.ini are specific to the user. It does not matter where these files are stored, as long as they are brought together at startup. Batch file copying schemes could be designed to copy, at run time, the local workstation's System.ini, Win.com, and perhaps even the Spart.par file to the server user's home or Windows directory, bringing them together with the user's Win.ini, Control.ini, and Progman.ini. Another approach would be to copy the user files to the local hard drive for that Windows session, then copy them back to the network afterward in case the user made changes.

Fortunately, the Registry has been written to allow two binary files that split out the workstation and user matters. User.dat is the Registry file that supports the user, and System.dat is the file that supports the workstation's configuration. Windows 95 is written to support multiple users with their own personal preferences. With local workstation installations of Windows 95, multiple copies of User.dat are maintained on the workstation, and a copy of a user's User.dat can be stored in the NetWare user's mail directory so as to be available at logon time. When a user moves to another workstation, the latest version of User.dat is brought down to the workstation from the server. In fact, Windows 95 can be set up to compare the workstation's copy against the /mail/user's copy, and automatically use the latest copy and update the older version. On diskless workstations, the Windows 95 system pulls the User.dat from the user's mail directory of the server, and the System.dat from the home directory setup for that diskless workstation.

This clear and clean split between user and system, in addition to Windows 95's capability to manage the user's configuration, benefits the administrator. A significant issue, however, is that this highly structured automation is dependent upon using the Microsoft client for NetWare. Novell, on the other hand, is working on a NetWare Application Launcher for their 32-bit client. This NetWare feature will pull user data and application data for the user from the NetWare Services and thus create a user-specific environment within Windows 95. Once again, there are choices and consequences that will not become clear or known to us until Novell releases their client 32.

Managing Configurations across the Network

The Remote Registry service loaded as a virtual mode program on the workstation enables real time remote access to the workstation's Registry. System Management maintenance of system, group, and specific user policies for users of the network will make the required changes during the user's logon process. These two sets of management tools contribute to the ability to manage workstation and user configurations over the network. Microsoft's own System Management Server and other third-party packages will be written to support remote workstation and user configurations in exciting, creative, and important ways.

Long File Names

Among the end-user features that have been built in to Windows 95 is the capability to use file names that are up to 255 characters in length. This feature will make it easier for users to work more meaningfully with files than they have been able to with the 8.3 character structure. On the other hand, these long file names will present some administrative problems both in tracking these files and accomodating them on the NetWare file server.

Changes in File System to Allow New Naming Structure

One of the new features of Windows 95 is the capability to move beyond the 8.3 file name rule of 8 characters as the main file name and a 3 character file extension. This 8.3 structure has caused us to have to both be inventive in giving file names and have the mind of the detective to recall the name of a file or remember what is in the file. Under the 8.3 structure a file might be called "Strclnf.doc," while the new file name in the long file name format might be "the structure of the long file name.doc." The Macintosh, Unix, and OS/2 worlds all have had this long file-name capability that only now has come to the Windows desktop.

Please be aware that long file names mean much more than the length of file names or directories. In Windows 95, the feature also provides for extended file information such as when the file was last accessed, and folder names (Windows 95 term for directories) that are included in a user profile.

The user profile enables users to move between machines and have not only their color preferences follow them but the Windows 95 shortcut icons as well. These icons provide click access to applications, and network administrators will find it handy to modify profiles on the network and have Windows 95 automatically modify the user's workstation profiles as well.

Long file-name features can be turned off through an adjustment to the Registry or through a setting reached through the Control Panel. Choose the System object from the Control Panel, then the Performance tab to display the Performance property page. Choose File System, then the Troubleshooting tab to display the Troubleshooting page. Place a check in the check box labeled disable long name preservation for old programs.

The feature also can be turned off by reverting back to Windows 3.1 file system. You can change the setting with the Registry Editor. The user can click on the directory-like structure items starting with the HkeyLocal Machine, then on System, then on Current Control Set, then on Control, then on File System. The bottom of the Registry editor will display Hkey_Local_Machine/System/Current Control Set/Control/File System. At that setting the value would be set to 1.

For the network client on a file server that does not have Name Space support for long file names, add an additional section to the System.ini file [NWRedir], and the line "support LFN=0," which means off.

Advantages to the Users

Instead of having to conform to the 8.3 file structure of DOS, users can now use file names with up to 255 characters. A directory name can be up to 260 characters. In practical terms, however, file names beyond 50 to 70 characters long can get quite unwieldy and difficult to deal with. There is an absolute limit of 270 characters in a full path name. There is also a visual problem in having to see a file that has too long of a file name.

The 270 character limit to the path means the full file name that includes the disk drive letter and the directory name and the file name, as in C:\accounting\spreadsheets\data\firstquarter1995. On a network that can also include the Universal Naming Convention designation: \\marketing\product\accounting\spreadsheets\data\firstquarter1995.

To make these files compatible with the traditional DOS file structure, *aliases* are created, using the first six characters of the file name, a tilde "~", and a number assigned to the file. This number will be incremented when a short file name of the same name having a "~" and a number already exists. Users also can right mouse click on a file or folder to view both the DOS 8.3 name and the long file name in the Properties view of the file. As an example, with a long file name structure you can have a directory called "The Microsoft Network," which has an MS-DOS name of THEMIC~1. Users of the Microsoft client for NetWare and, according to Novell, the users of its announced Client 32 see the long file names, whereas the DOS user sees the shorted version name.

Challenges to Network and Application Administration

The real mode NetWare client doesn't support long file names. Rather, you must have the Microsoft Client for NetWare or the announced NetWare Client 32—which is one reason administrators might want or be compelled to use the Microsoft-supplied client for NetWare.

Another challenge to network and application administration is disk maintenance.

Disk Maintenance and Long File Names

Disk utilities such as the Norton Utilities and others do not support long file names and can actually damage this new structure. Virus scanning programs are likely to see these long file names as being symptoms of a virus. When in doubt about the use of such programs, you should use the Lfnbk.exe utility supplied with Windows 95. Lfnbk.exe lets you turn off and then restore long file names without destroying their structure or names.

You can find the Lfnbk.exe utility on the Windows 95 CD-ROM, accompanied by a text file that provides information about the operation of the utility.

The Lfnbk.exe utility is intended to be used for the backing up of the long file names that exist on the workstation hard drive. When you run Lfnbk.exe with the /B argument, the program creates a backup of the long file names for the files existing on the disk. After the disk utilities are run, you can then use the restore setting Lfnbk.exe /R.

Lfnbk.exe creates a file named Lfnbk.dat in the root of the drive you process. You need this file to restore your long file names, so don't delete it. Lfnbk.exe deletes it during the restore, providing it encounters no problems.

The restore process restores the long file name for each file in Lfnbk.dat, but Windows 95 assigns the old style 8.3 (short) name, so the process occasionally might change it.

Running the Lfnbk utility backs up long file names into the Lfnbk.dat file. Among the long file names backed up is the Start menu, which is itself a long file name. Upon restarting, Windows 95 reverts back to the default Start menu. Running the restore process restores the Start menu as well.

Long File Name Convention Policy

You should establish and publish naming conventions for long file names. Your organization might, for example, want users to include a short file name as part of the long file name so that the short file name and the long file name for the file are somewhat similar. A variation might be to use deferential terms, such as "Oct Status Report" rather than "Status Report October." The former would shorten to OCTSTA~1 rather than STATUS~1.

You need to set up the file server to support long file names if you are committed to full user profile support, so users can move freely about among multiple machines. The ability to fully support users moving around the network depends not only on the split of Registry data between System.dat and User.dat, but also on the capability to track and copy folders, such as Start menu and Network Neighborhood, which are themselves long file names.

A certain period of time can be expected to expire during which applications do not support long file names, until the vendors retrofit their applications to cover this new structure or publish their own 32-bit application that runs in the Windows 95 environment and supports the long file-name structure.

NetWare Name Space Administration on Server

Before you can support the Windows 95 long file names, you must configure the NetWare server to provide for long file-name attributes. You can adjust NetWare volumes to store the longer file names by installing the Name Space feature. Windows 95 long file names are structured to conform to the OS/2 Name Space.

Because the Windows 95 user profiles are based on long file names, and they are replicated to the user's mail directory on volume SYS, Name Space for OS/2 must be installed for that volume.

To install the OS/2 Name Space feature, type the following at the file server console:

```
LOAD OS/2
ADD NAME SPACE OS/2 TO VOLUMR SYS
```

Because this impacts the configuration of the file server volume, you need to add the following to the configuration file Startup.ncf:

```
LOAD OS/2
```

You then need to down the server and bring it back up to make this OS/2 Name Space feature functional at the server.

Adding Name Space without adding server memory can present problems. Adding the OS/2 Name Space to the server volume involves memory and support issues. The added information that must be maintained causes the file server to need more RAM memory so that it can handle the Name Space feature.The remedy to this is to place more RAM on the server. You also need to consider the Name Space feature when you have to do maintenance on the volumes, specifically when you run VREPAIR. There is no server-based program that backs up and then restores the long file names stored in the extra Name Space provided in the Name Space feature.

Server Memory Requirements for Name Space Requirements

You need more server memory before you can load and support Name Space. The following chart indicates the difference between memory calculations for normal NetWare volumes and those that support Name Space. Another thing: Name Space volumes require 39 percent more memory than normal volumes. Listed on the following page are two calculations for server memory requirements, the first without and the second with Name Space figured in the calculations.

- **DOS Volume without Name Space**

  Formula: M=.023 × Volume size in MB / Block Size

  Calculation: DOS volume of 1000 MB =.023 × 1000 MB /4 MB = 5.75 MB

- **Volume with Added Name Space**

  Formula: M= .032 × Volume size in MB / Block Size

  Calculation: Name Space volume of 1000 MB = .032 × 1000 MB /4 MB =8 MB

Supporting drives and volumes requires the preceding memory as calculated, and then adding the server program memory requirements and the NLM requirements to ascertain total memory. Continuing this mode of calculation would lead you to conclude that you need an additional 39 percent of memory to support the NetWare volume.

Under the older calculation for Name Space, 39 percent more memory would be needed on the server to support the volumes that would house Windows 95 long file names.

New Server Memory Calculation

The new server memory calculations from Novell add other factors, such as number of users volume size, disk storage size, cache memory requirements, and now bases the calculation of Name Space on Directory Entry Table (DET) entries. That is, after you apply the new calculations to the server you can make your Name Space adjustments in the DET calculations. The DET includes not only the file name but the long file name as well. The DET for a Name Space volume is then only able to contain half as many file entries as it does on a standard NetWare volume.

Calculating memory also applies to resolving the Windows 95 program and application location question, because it relates to Windows 95 programs and all Windows applications. You should consider the following:

- Placing all Windows 95 programs and applications on the local workstation places no memory load on the NetWare file server.
- Placing only data files makes some demands on the server for storage purposes.
- Keeping server stored files in long file format increases memory requirements because of the need for an extra entry in the Directory Entry Table.
- Placing all Windows applications on the server for administrative reasons adds to disk storage needs and the file caching memory needs because of the additions to the open files.

- Running Windows 95 from the shared Windows 95 program directories also adds greatly to both the storage and file cache memory requirements.

Having files open on the server also greatly impacts network traffic and makes moving memory from the file cache memory sector to the communication packet receive buffer section necessary. This potential loss of some file cache memory (between 100 KB and 8 MB), forces you to plan for adequate file cache memory right from the beginning.

The Name Space feature to support long file names requires that two entries be made in the DET, one for the DOS name and the second for the long file name (specifically, the OS/2 Name Space) entry. Thus only half as many files can fit into allocated DET memory.

Memory Requirement Calculations

Novell has established a different means of calculating server memory requirements that covers NetWare 3.*x* and 4.*x*. They have broken up the new calculation process into three separate processes:

1. Establish seven variables, including volume storage block size, and number of users.
2. Calculate memory requirements based on operating system, FAT requirements, and caching needs.
3. Round off the total to the next MB for better results.

    - Total number of MB on disks attached to the server
    - Total number of MB on disks attached to the server usable for storage

Keep in mind as you calculate that for duplexed disks you should count only half of the available MB as usable for storage, because you are using the second drive for keeping a duplicate of the first drive.

- Storage block size

NetWare 4.*x* automatically assigns the size based on volume size, whereas the default size in NetWare 3.*x* is 4 KB.

- Number of disk blocks per megabyte (divide 1,024 by the storage block size)

- Total usable storage (number of disk blocks per megabyte × number of megabytes usable for storage)
- Maximum number of users attached to server at any one time
- Maximum number of files that can be stored on the file server (if using NetWare 4.*x* with its ability to place multiple small (512 byte size) files in the same storage block to save storage blocks wasted in the previous versions)

4. Calculate memory requirements based on operating system, FAT requirements, caching needs:

   - 2,048 KB system memory for Netware 3.*x*; 5,120 KB system memory for NetWare 4.*x*
   - Media Manager memory (10 percent of system memory: system memory (2,048 KB or 5,120 KB) × .10)
   - Add 250 KB (if you use NetWare 4.*x* with file compression on)
   - Suballocation feature memory requirement (if you use suballocation or multiple files in the same storage block): approximate total number of files on server × .005
   - Memory required to keep the FAT table in cache memory: total number of disk blocks × .008
   - Memory required for file cache memory (use the following table, which assumes that the file cache requirements per user decreases as the number of actual users increases, because multiple users then access the cached files):

Number of Users	Formula To Determine File Cache Memory
1–100	Number of users × 400 KB
101–250	40,000 + ((Number of users – 100) × 200)
251–500	70,000 + ((Number of users – 250) × 100)
501–1000	95,000 + ((Number of users – 500) × 50)

   - Kilobytes of memory required for the NetWare Loadable Modules: 2,000 KB recommended, which would be used to load the most common NLMs, such as Pserver (200 KB), Install (600 KB), Clib (500 KB), and Btrieve (700 KB); if other NLMs are required adjust upward the memory required

- Memory required for other services, such as NetWare for the Macintosh, for SAA Host connectivity NetWare Management System (2 MB is not unrealistic)

5. Round off the total to the next MB Total for better results:

   - Total KB: add all figures in step 4
   - Total MB: divide total KB by 1,024 and then round up to nearest MB

Under this new set of memory calculations there are quite a few more steps to establishing the server memory requirements. These new steps and their calculations take into consideration all the new features of NetWare. In general, the memory of the server is vital to the well being of the server and the network serving the Windows 95 workstations depending upon the network. Chapter 5, dealing with Windows 95 locations, has a more detailed discussion of the server health as registered in the NetWare Server Monitor screen. Briefly, the amount of free memory needs to be more than half of the original server memory after it is started up. But the Name Space calculation still needs to be made.

New Name Space Calculation—Directory Caching

The preceding newer memory calculation is only half of the calculation process to account for the Name Space feature you need to support Windows 95's long file-name structure.

The newer Novell Server memory requirement calculation requires you to calculate Name Space requirements on totally different terms than did the old method. It focuses on the directory cache that maintains the most recently used Directory Entry Table blocks in memory in anticipation of them soon being used again. In NetWare 2.*x*, the entire Directory Entry Table was cached, which required a great deal of memory (Novell quotes 65 MB for 500,000 files), but NetWare 3.*x* and 4.*x* use the most recently used (MRU) cache, which uses the least recently used (LRU) algorithm to displace older entries and thereby makes room for new DET caching.

You need to remember certain terms because they crop up so often: MRU and LRU. NetWare uses MRU here for DET caching, whereas Windows 95 uses MRU in the Registry (most recently used drive mappings). Windows 95 uses LRU for swapping out real chip memory locations to virtual memory (also known as the swap file) and NetWare uses LRU when it reuses file cache memory, that is, when it needs to flush out cache items to make room for new files—but NetWare doesn't have virtual memory.

Name Space volumes have extended Directory Entry Table entries. A directory cache buffer normally stores 32 file names. When you divide the 32 file number by the number of Name Spaces, you find that you diminish the normal capability to cache 32 files per DET block into memory. The 32 file number divided by one Name Space, namely, the DOS Name Space, gives you 32 files. Add just the OS/2 Name Space to support long file names (which gives you two Name Spaces) and you cache only 16 files per DET block, your end result being that each Name Space you add diminishes the efficiency of the directory caching.

The default server settings for directory cache buffers are:

```
MINIMUM DIRECTORY CACHE BUFFERS=20
```

and

```
MAXIMUM DIRECTORY CACHE BUFFERS=500.
```

These are 4 KB cache buffers dedicated to bringing the Directory Entry Table entries into cache for fast access. The default of a 4 KB buffer × 512 buffers brings the default memory allocation to 2 MB.

The maximum number of the directory cache buffers is 4,000, which would require 16 MB of server memory. The following settings:

```
MINIMUM DIRECTORY CACHE BUFFERS=
```

and

```
MAXIMUM DIRECTORY CACHE BUFFERS=
```

are set in the server's Autoexec.ncf configuration file. You should set a heavily used server to at least 2,000 buffers (which would mean 8 MB of server memory), and probably more.

These calculations are significant to the Windows 95 workstation and the Novell NetWare server. When long file names are supported on the NetWare server, you must manage the file server to take into account the long file names; this means adding Name Space to the volumes and watching the memory for the server in general and the way that NetWare operating system on the server is managing the directory entry caching process.

Basically, here's the rule of thumb: For every .4 MB of file cache RAM, you can allocate the server 100 directory cache buffers, allowing for some 3,200 directory entries with only DOS Name Space, or 1,600 directory entries with just OS/2 Name Space added. You need to watch the Directory Cache Buffer Statistics line that appears on the NetWare Server Monitor screen.

Applying the rule of thumb, Novell suggests that you just let the server function for awhile (a set period of time) and set a watermark that you can view in the Monitor.nlm. You should then take the figure of allocated Directory Entry Table cache buffers × the number of Name Spaces (remember: DOS Name Space counts as 1). By doing so, you create the minimum cache buffers that must be allocated during server startup. You can set the maximum cache buffers above that amount with an estimate ceiling. Set the number at first at one hundred more than the minimum to see if that is enough, and then gradually add to the number as experience warrants for performance.

Directory cache buffers for supporting the Directory Entry Table come from the server's file cache memory, so keep in mind, therefore, that it might need to be refreshed or added to by setting the number of directory cache buffers higher through the "Set Maximum directory cache buffer =" console command.

Vrepair reestablishes the coordination between the File Allocation Tables and the Directory Entry Tables. NetWare keeps two copies of each on disk and loads a copy of each into memory every time the server boots. During the NetWare session, both sets of FAT files and both sets of the DETs are updated continuously, with approximately 28 second gaps between updates. During standard shutdown, you, as administrator, type **down** at the server prompt and the NetWare operating system synchronizes these four files with each other. If an abnormal shutdown occurs, the FAT and DET files can fall out of synchronization. You run VREPAIR to reestablish this synchronization.

Be careful when you read the documentation and the instructions for running VREPAIR so that when VREPAIR is run you don't accidentally eliminate Name Space support on the server. NetWare has no provisions for saving long file names without Name Space. You can run VREPAIR with Name Space functional, even though one option you do have is REMOVE NAME SPACE SUPPORT FROM VOLUME QUIT IF A VREPAIR NAME SPACE SUPPORT NLM IS NOT LOADED. Name Space does not have to be removed to run VREPAIR.

Actually, running VREPAIR is the only way you can eliminate Name Space from the volumes, and you might need to do so if the volume or its support for long file names becomes corrupted. Novell's documentation suggests that if you run out of memory, you might need to remove Name Space, but doing so is final and you can lose these long file names for your users. A better solution to the space problem is to keep the server under better maintenance by periodically eliminating unnecessary files.

Professionally, whenever I discuss VREPAIR, I always recommend On-Track's Data Recovery for NetWare as a disaster recovery tool for NetWare. You can run the application even if you can't bring up the server using the Server.exe program, and it enables you to guide the resynchronization of the FAT and the DET entries. You can choose which copy of the FAT to use with which copy of the DET to conduct this realignment, after you determine which combination poses the fewest errors.

OnTrack's Data Recovery for NetWare usually also can access the NetWare partition so it can copy files from the volumes to floppies or a tape backup system attached to the server. This feature is not only invaluable for times when you don't have a good backup, but especially for midday crashes when a backup has not been run since the night before and a proposal or report is due on a timely basis, and probably before the server can be brought back online.

Windows 95 as Peer Client

A Windows 95 workstation can run the NetWare IPX as the native protocol for access to both the NetWare server and other Windows 95 workstations in a peer-to-peer function. You even can configure the Windows 95 workstation to appear as a NetWare peer-to-peer server that offers NetWare-based bindery security for accessing directories, files, and print queues on the workstation (see fig. 2.13). This appearance as a "server" would be transparent to other Windows 95 clients, Windows For Workgroups 3.11 users, and even DOS-based workstations. Beyond this, the workstation also could run Mspserv, a Microsoft-written 32-bit replacement for the problematic DOS-based and real mode Rprinter that allows a NetWare-server–based print queue to service the workstation printer.

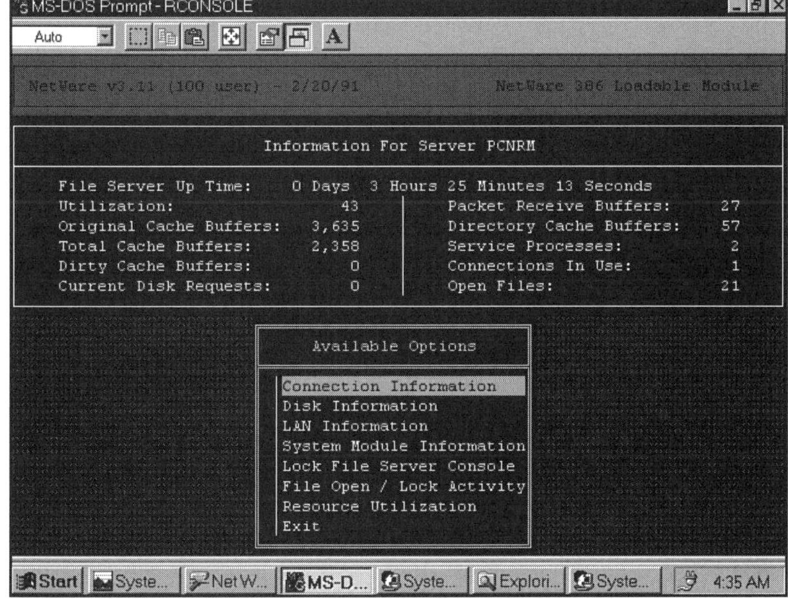

Figure 2.13

A Windows 95 station appearing as a server on a network.

The Windows 95 or non-Windows 95 workstation can attach to the server like a Windows 95 workstation and then map drives to that station (see fig. 2.14). In the example, the station shares its entire hard disk to the network, but could share just specific directories one at a time (see fig. 2.15). There are levels of sharing based on the NetWare user that can give different users or groups different access rights.

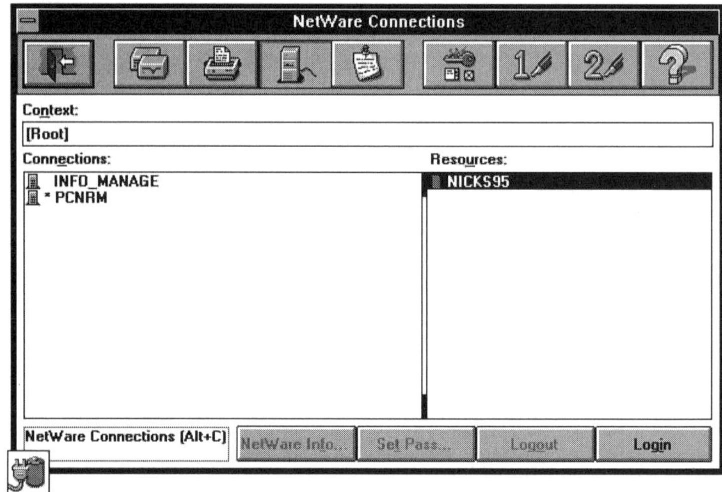

Figure 2.14
Windows 3.x client logon or attaching to a Windows 95 station appearing as a server.

Once attached to a Windows 95 workstation running file and printer sharing for NetWare networks, the user can see the directories that have been offered for sharing.

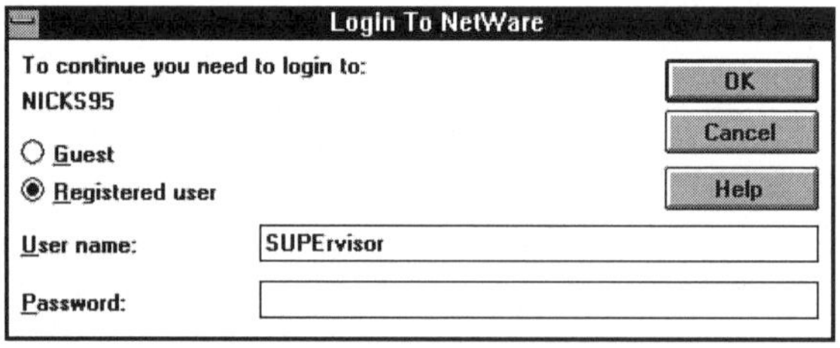

Figure 2.15
The Windows 3.x user can map the drive to particular directories to which he or she has access or to the one shared directory.

The file and printer sharing for NetWare networks configured client can offer its files to specific users who have access to and map their drives to a shared directory. The Windows 95 directories here look like those on a real NetWare server. After you map the drive, the user can click on the drive information button (see fig. 2.16) and see his or her rights just as if on a real NetWare server directory.

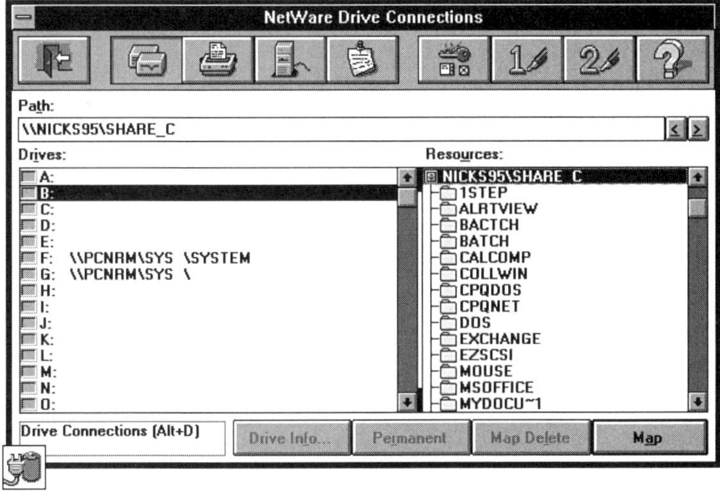

Figure 2.16

*A Windows 95 station appearing as a server on a network even to the DOS or Windows 3.*x *user.*

The significance of this discussion is that the Windows 95 workstation can be made to appear as a NetWare file server to provide user-level security for peer-to-peer networking and to give the end user ease of use as this function enables the NetWare utilities to work here. The user does not need new training to use the peer-to-peer functionaliy.

Enabling or Disabling File and Printer Sharing

You can allow or disallow Microsoft peer-to-peer resource sharing. You can configure the workstation to look like a NetWare user security based resource by using the NetWare Service Advertising Protocol as a way of being seen on the network and providing NetWare Core Protocol type services to other NetWare clients.

NetWare Service Advertising Protocol and NetWare Core Protocol are two communication structures used by the Novell server and client to communicate. SAP is used by the workstation to find a server and by the server to make its presence known to servers and workstations. NCP is the structure of requests made by the workstation to the server and the structure of the replies from the server to the workstation.

When you consider this peer-to-peer functionality, you need to think about the workstation as a resource in ways not possible before because you now can use 32-bit virtual device drivers for these functions rather than real mode and somewhat limited TSR applications.

Security Issues of File and Printer Sharing

You can set up the Windows 95 station to receive its authorized used list from a designated server. This user list then can be used to choose which users or groups can access the workstation's directories, either one by one or the hard disk as a whole unit. After users are Chosen, they can be assigned one of three levels of access, as shown in figure 2.17. The Custom screen option opens a screen that closely resembles the Bindery screen. Among the bindery-like set of access rights that can be set in the custom screen are those that control the following file operations:

- Reading from a file
- Finding a file
- Writing to a file
- Making a new file or directory
- Deleting a file
- Changing a directory or file attribute

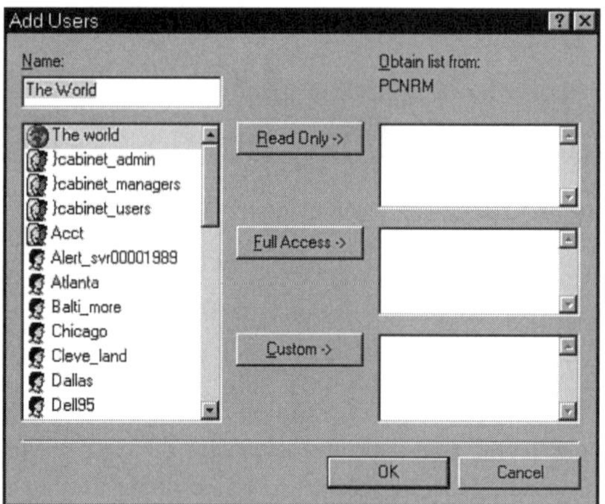

Figure 2.17

NetWare bindery-like security can be applied to the Windows 95 station.

If you think of the workstation as more than just a user workstation, you might begin to realize the potential of using a Windows 95 workstation as a file server. Peer-to-peer networking servers in any setting work best at providing access to files that are then copied back to the client workstation. These servers do not have file and directory caching that enable NetWare servers to provide speedy access to open files and programs. Keeping this factor in mind, you could place CD-ROMs on a Windows 95 workstation and use bindery security to control access. You actually could use a Windows 95 workstation as a file server to provide secure access to a storehouse of relatively seldom used data files. The following are among the types of such files that could be kept there:

- Large graphic files
- Engineering and CAD drawings
- Legal documents that need to be maintained but are not used on a daily basis
- Document images

You could use a machine with a large disk drive for secure access to relatively seldom used data files.

Network Management of the Windows 95 Workstation and User

Although you must pick and choose features, Windows 95 does enable you to manage the Windows 95 workstation and user across the network rather than physically attending to each workstation to make configuration changes. You need to consider which features you can support and determine the side effects or consequences of your choices in terms of the way the Windows 95 workstation and user relates to the NetWare network and servers.

Windows 95's developers have paid attention to the complaints and observations of network administrators, and in many ways have created a respectable product for the network client workstation. This book examines the role that Windows 95 can have on the NetWare network, and the powerful tools that enable you to design, control, and maintain specific workstations and specific users on the network. These management tools will be discussed in Chapter 4, "Managing the Workstation and User."

What network administrators have learned from Windows 3.*x* and NetWare and find equally true with Windows 95 and NetWare is that the NetWare network must be under even tighter administrative control with the Windows GUI than it was under the DOS menu environment (see fig. 2.18). Among the matters of concern are drive mappings, print queue assignments, and group membership.

At the DOS-based menu, the user had choices in terms of applications, and these choices contained underlying DOS batch files that perhaps reassigned drive

Figure 2.18

DOS-based login authentication, user environment creation, and menu control.

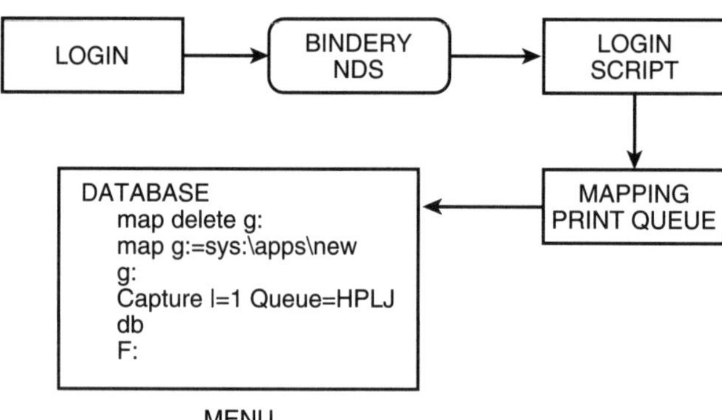

mappings and print queues for the chosen application. Users might have been offered printer choices at the application or network level, but these choices were highly controlled by the writer of the menu system. The administrator would have this DOS-based menu for several important reasons:

- To make the network easier for users who had explicit choices to make that would eliminate confusion
- To keep users from the DOS prompt and from making print queue choices that would mean laser jet printers receiving dot matrix print jobs
- To keep users from seeing menu choices for programs that they did not have security clearance to be able to use
- To keep the users from seeing the underlying NetWare server directories and files that they might have bindery or NetWare Directory Services access to, but should not be seeing or have direct access to for a variety of reasons

With Windows 3.*x*, the control the network administrator had worked so hard to achieve with DOS all but disappeared with the placement of Windows as the client from which the user accessed the network after login. This lack of upfront control is also true with Windows 95.

- The user can access File Manager or the Windows 95 Network Neighborhood and remap network drive letters.
- The user of either Windows or Windows 95 can reassign print queue assignments.

- The user can designate these mapping and print queue changes as permanent, which means that Windows attempts to re-create these connections every time Windows starts.

Novell uses the term "permanent" to designate the changes in drive mappings and print queue assignments that should be reconnected during the Windows startup. Microsoft uses the term "persistent" to refer to these types of connections.

Although the NetWare security established in the NetWare 3.*x* bindery or the NetWare 4.*x* NetWare Directory Services is not impacted by the Windows environment, that environment, whether Windows 3.1, Windows for Workgroups 3.11, or Windows 95 does make the NetWare security environment for the user highly visible. Consider for example the NetWare print queue assignments. Within the DOS menu structure the user only sees what the menu writer chooses for the user to see.

In the Windows 3.*x* or Windows 95 environment, the user sees whatever print queues the Bindery or NDS provides them access to use. Unless you change it in the NetWare PCONSOLE utility , the default print queue assignment in terms of queue users is group "EVERYONE"—which means that regardless of whether it appears as a choice for the user in the DOS-based menu, the user can access that print queue as a default member of group EVERYONE.

Within Windows 3.*x* and Windows 95, the user can see all print queues assigned to groups that he or she is a member of, including group EVERYONE. The means that the NetWare administrator needs to review the print queue users and groups for each print queue, so that a typical user will only see those print queues that the administrator wanted them to be able to choose.

The visibility of print queues also calls for the administrator to be more systematic in the choice of NetWare print queue names which can be up to 20 alpha-numeric characters and should have a systematic structure to their format such as that adopted by many networks, namely, location department printer type. Uniformity of such queue names makes moving to the NetWare Directory Services multiserver structure easier as well, so that printers from various servers could appear in a meaningful sort list.

In terms of the server file and directory structure, you might want to reexamine the assumptions about file and directory access rights (see fig. 2.19). With Windows 3.1 and Windows for Workgroups 3.11 File Manager, users had visual access to all the files and directories for which they had NetWare file scan rights. Within Windows 95 this translates into the ability to see file folders and files that they have the NetWare file scan rights to see. You should review your network applications and their directories to determine if indeed users need this file scan right. Some applications might need these files to be visible to the user, while others might allow for making the files invisible to the user.

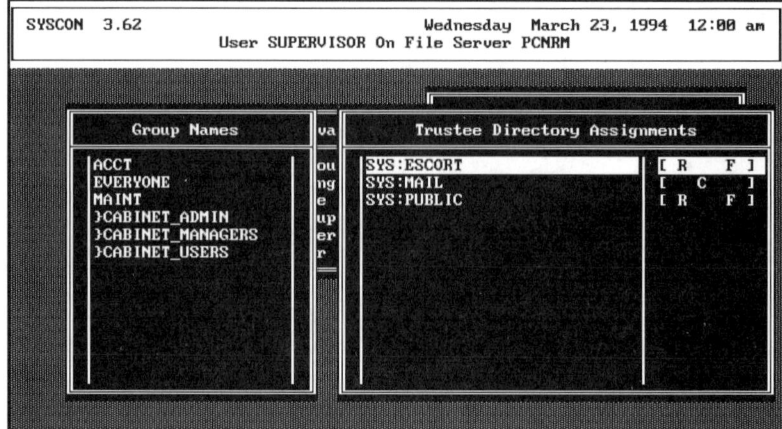

Figure 2.19 *Rights assignment through NetWare 3.11's SYSCON.*

Although you can limit what the Windows 95 user sees through the Neighborhood Network and Explorer programs, users might still be able to access programs, files, and directories using the DOS prompt or the network mapping prompt if they know the Universal Naming Convention of "\\server\path."

Although these matters have not changed from Windows 3.*x* to Windows 95, there are a number of changes that Microsoft has made to make the role of the administrator significantly more structured and meaningful in placing the Windows 95 client on the NetWare network.

There are some strings attached, to many of the management features that the developers make available to the NetWare administrator, these conditions relate to the adoption of the Microsoft Client for NetWare as a facilitator. The Registry, which replaces the Ini files except for backward compatibility, gives the administrator a central control file. You can manage almost all aspects of Windows 95 and handle the management in the setup for the user. With downloads of the policies controlling the user and the workstation, these items can be managed across the network at logon. Many of these features require the Microsoft Client for NetWare. Administrators, however, may elect not to use this client option because of the need for real mode memory resident programs or to provide VLM access to NetWare 4.*x*. With the real mode clients many of the network management features of Windows 95 will not be available.

For the administrator who recognizes that peer-to-peer networking has a role on the network but is concerned with security, there is the ability to use NetWare bindery-based user access to the specially configured workstation. There is also the ability to establish protected mode remote printer capability on specified workstations to support network server print queues. There are specific printing features for having users download print drivers as necessary for printing to network printers and other labor saving printing issues for the administrator.

Microsoft developers have also created Windows 95 workstation-based services to support remote monitoring of network and workstation functions and an industry standard Simple Network Management Protocol agent that will enable the NetWare administrator to monitor the station through such Network management tools as NetWare's NMS, NetWare Management System. Microsoft is revising their own System Management Server and have provided other vendors such as Symantec and McAfee with the necessary knowledge to revise their network management tools to provide remote management of the workstation beyond the Remote Registry.

The NetWare administrator who is used to the centralized user management of NetWare's SYSCON for NetWare 3.*x* and NWADMIN for NetWare 4.*x* will be pleased to note that the administrator will be able to set system policies for the users and maintain them on the NetWare login server for the users. These policies determine what users can change on their own and what they cannot, where they can make changes, and what the limits are to their choices.

One of the realities of Windows 95 and NetWare is that the bindery and the NetWare Directory Services will be of even greater significance. With Windows 95 these security structures can be used for Windows logon validation, and the listings used as the basis for user-level security on the Windows 95 workstation. You need to become quite clear as to the structure and specific entries in that system security process. You should review the user lists and group memberships because these can be used on the Windows 95 workstation when establishing access control.

In tuning up the NetWare server in this administrative security area, the administrator might be well advised to turn to a third-party vendor such as Preferred Systems and their AuditWare, LAN Support Group, and their Bindview or other vendors and their programs that provide reporting facilities not supplied by NetWare.

One specific matter is the Windows 95 use of the \Mail\User_ id directories for the storage of the users configuration file and the user profiles. Because the NetWare User_id is the eight digit bindery or NDS ID and not the user name, having a reference list of users and their user ID might be beneficial at times. You might want to figure out shortcuts to getting that information.

One such report might be a listing of users by the bindery IDs or a list of users and their bindery IDs to make access to the user's Windows 95 profiles easier. No doubt that someone will provide a program that does this lookup for you, but in the meantime you might want to access a user's profile to modify it so that the user gets an updated profile during his or her next logon.

Because Windows 95 with its NetWare connectivity and integration features becomes so heavily dependent upon the NetWare Server, the NetWare administrator must see to it that the server is properly structured and maintained.

Integrating Windows 95 and NetWare

Windows 95 has been designed to integrate into the network environment and provide the network administrator with the tools to support this integration. The focus in this chapter is specifically on the Windows 95 workstation and its relationship to the NetWare network setting. The attention is on the choices that the NetWare administrator must make in moving from the basic hardware and software components that provide connectivity to the server (see fig. 3.1), to the Windows 95-based workstation as a NetWare client of the NetWare server(s).

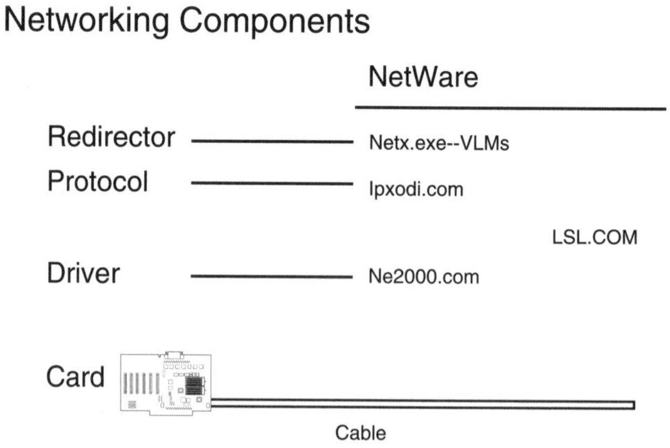

Figure 3.1
The hardware and software levels required for NetWare connectivity.

The process of integrating the Windows 95 workstation into the NetWare network requires reviewing the hardware and software components of networking, and outlining the steps that must be taken to install these items into the Windows 95 system. With this background established, you need to make decisions as to which version of these network components will be used on the Windows 95 workstation to provide the user with NetWare server access.

Hardware and Software Requirements for Windows 95 Networks

The networking elements required to provide the connectivity to the NetWare server are the network interface card, software drivers to support that card, protocols or a language of communciation, and a network shell or client that makes requests to the server and receives responses from the server. This chapter examines each of these for its implications in the Windows 95 network client setting. You also need to pay attention to the class of programs that many network administrators use to help manage their networks—the memory resident program that is loaded on the workstation after the server connection has been established.

The Network Interface Card

The network interface card (NIC) provides the hardware physical connection to the networking cable. This brief discussion is generic and covers the basics. The good news in the industry is that Windows 95 provides support for what is called Plug and Play, which is a structure that allows manufacturers to build peripherals to a certain standard that allows the operating system to automatically detect the peripheral and adjust the operating system to the new card's configuration.

The interrupt settings in a network card identify the card to the CPU. Actual communication is through the memory or I/O (input/output) address. An Ethernet card might have an interrupt number of 5 and an I/O address of 300.

Some network interface cards also use memory for buffering incoming and outgoing message packets. The memory used for buffering is in the adapter segment area, the 384 KB area above the 640 KB base memory. Memory managers might also claim the use of this segment of memory when the computer boots, restricting this area from the NIC. If this occurs, you have to prevent the memory manager from accessing this memory range. Some of these memory issues go away with Windows 95, especially when 32-bit adapter settings are used.

NIC Drivers

The software component necessary to network a Windows 95 workstation is either a network interface card driver or what the Windows 95 system calls the network card adapter. A common example of such a driver might be the Ne2000.com, which in the Windows 95 setting could be an adapter chosen from a list of vendor-supplied software. The software wakes up the card and notifies the CPU of its presence. The driver and the software serve as the foundation for interfacing with the protocol.

An NIC driver has default settings for the interrupt and memory addresses of the network interface card. Changes in the default setting had to be compiled into the older Ipx.com, and with the newer Ipxodi.com, these changes are text edited into the Net.cfg configuration file. Common drivers are distributed by Novell with the NetWare software client updates. Drivers are also available over CompuServe or through the Internet from ftp.novell.com.

One of the issues that needs to be resolved is the nature of the network card driver. Will the network card driver be loaded in real 16-bit mode that takes up memory, or will it be a 32-bit adapter driver that does not?

Network Protocols

The protocol level, which with NetWare is the IPX/SPX protocol, established the common ground for communication between computers on the network cabling. Referred to as a language or standard of communication, this protocol makes dialogue possible by setting up the ground rules. The IPX/SPX protocol is the default protocol for the Novell NetWare network. TCP/IP is the protocol used for Unix and Internet connectivity.

Both of these protocols have a simple level—IPX or IP—and a more complicated higher overhead but more assured connectivity mode, the SPX or TCP protocols. (The NetBEUI protocol is used by Windows for Workgroups.)

Protocols were originally "monolithic" or singular non-sharing protocols. As multiple platform connectivity became more critical, the protocols needed to be able to co-exist with other protocols. Novell's IPX became IPXODI or open Data Interlink with support for its own and other protocols on the same network interface card. Microsoft's NetBEUI uses a Network Device Interface Specification (NDIS) layer to coexist with other protocols.

One of the issues that needs to be resolved is the nature of the network protocol. Will the network protocol be loaded in real 16-bit mode that takes up memory, or will it be a 32-bit protocol that does not?

Client Shell

The client shell first provides a connection to a file server and then conducts the communication between the node and the server(s).

In the NetWare world, the client shell was, until fairly recently, the Netx redirector. Now the client shell is the Virtual Loadable Module (VLM) with its Netx.vlm component. The Netx.com or Netx.exe as a memory resident program reviewed every transaction of the networked workstation to determine whether a response was needed by DOS or NetWare. The VLM architecture allows DOS to make specific requests to NetWare if necessary. VLMs also are modular so that specific components can be used or not, and administrators can provide more control over features on the workstation.

One of the issues that needs to be resolved is the nature of the network client. Will the network client be loaded in real 16-bit mode that takes up memory, or will it be a 32-bit client that does not?

Memory Resident Network Management Programs

Network administrators have found great usefulness in programs that provide remote control, software metering, virus protection, connectivity, and other network management services. These network management memory resident programs usually are loaded after the network software, drivers, protocol, and shell load on the workstation. The networking elements listed earlier are evoked before the login process. Next, memory resident programs specified in the NetWare login script are initialized during the logon process. Some of these memory resident programs are called from a batch file after the login script is completed. The problem with these real mode network management programs under Windows 95 is that the logon process takes place in protected mode when using the 32-bit network client. Until there are 32-bit replacements for these programs, you might have to stay with the existing network client software.

In Windows 95, real mode memory resident programs become "services" that you can run on the workstation in protected mode. The services are installed with Windows 95 (see fig. 3.2). As time goes by more vendors will provide services or 32-bit protected mode virtual device driver-based programs for network management.

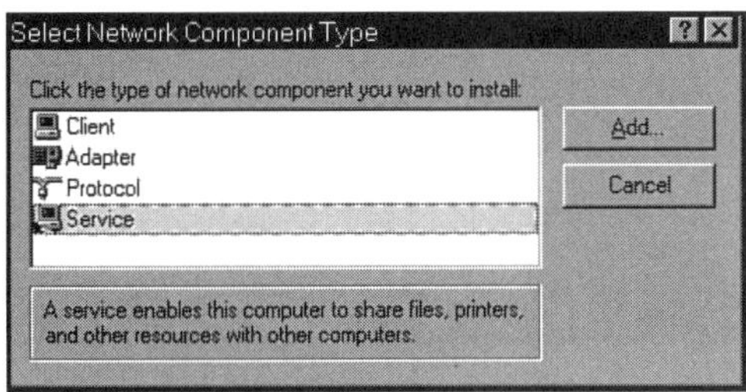

Figure 3.2
Windows 95 adds services on top of the adaptor, protocol, and client.

Windows 95 workstations can, regardless of protocol and client mode, access and use NetWare server-based services, including file access and printing services. Windows 95 workstations can also be configured to provide services to the network administrator or to network users. This book discusses the way in which Windows 95 accesses and uses these services. This chapter focuses on the ease of access, also known as the level of integration, of the NetWare protocol and NetWare client into the Windows 95 workstation.

With the new program Microsoft Client for NetWare, the Windows 95 workstation can appear as a NetWare server for file and print sharing or as remote printers for a NetWare server.

Installing Network Components

This section provides an overview of the steps necessary to set up Windows 95 on a network. Part of the Windows 95 setup process is the detection of existing network cards, protocols, and clients to ensure that the workstation is set up for the network. These items can also be established in the batch file setup, which enables the administrator to customize by computer name and user. This section shows you the steps necessary for installing the network components you read about earlier—the network interface card, NIC driver, protocols, and network shells.

To install network pieces you first double-click on the Control Panel Network icon, as shown in figure 3.3. Double-click on the Network icon. The network install screen (see fig. 3.4) lists the currently installed items. Your choices for these items are an Add button, a Remove button, and a Properties button.

Figure 3.3

The Control Panel highlighting the Network icon.

Figure 3.4

The Network Configuration add screen.

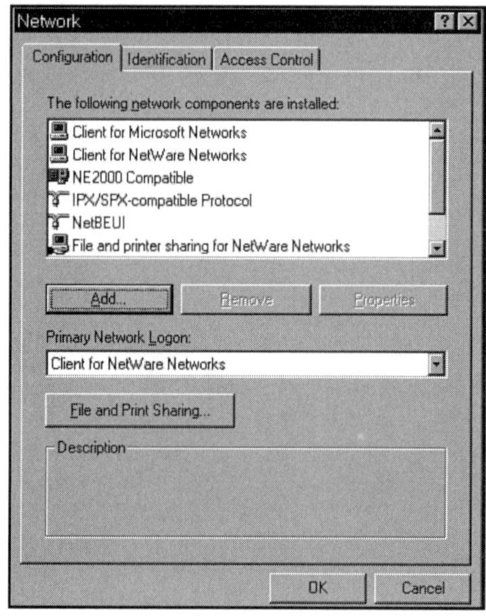

Click on the Add button to select a network component type. You will be provided with four categories: adapter or network card, protocol, client, and service.

Configuring the Network Adapter Card

When you select the adapter card, a list of vendors that have provided Microsoft with their card drivers appears (see fig. 3.5). You can also choose a disk of drivers in this list.

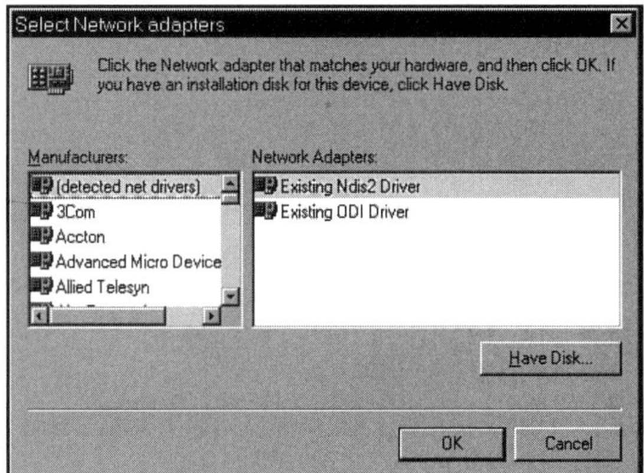

Figure 3.5
The Select Network Adapter screen.

Note: Be aware that the drivers should have the OEM's .Inf file, or the message `the specified location does not contain information about your hardware` will appear.

Selecting the NIC Driver

After you highlight the now installed adapter on the network screen, click on the Properties button (see fig. 3.6)and indicate the mode of the driver—16-bit NDIS or 16-bit ODI or the 32-bit Enhanced Mode adapter card driver.

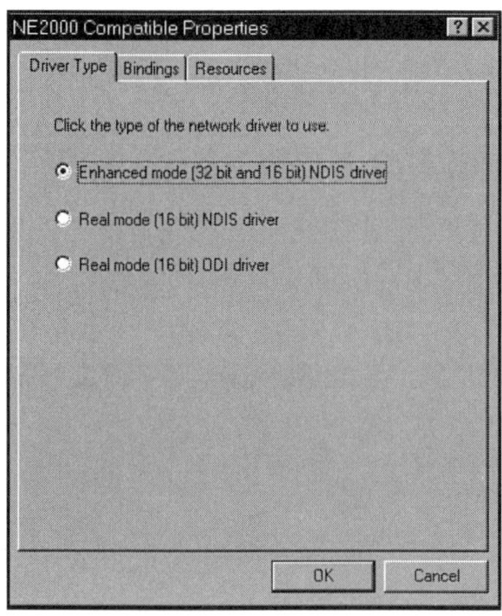

Figure 3.6
The Network Card Adapter properties screen.

Selecting the Correct Protocol

You then can configure the protocols that are bound to the network card. In figure 3.7 the 32 IPX/SPX-compatible protocol and NetBEUI and TCP/IP are installed on this workstation and are bound to this card. The hardware settings must be set within the Windows 95 environment (see fig. 3.8). Within the Network Card Adapter properties screen, you can set the interrupt and I/O address range of the card. This is especially helpful for non-default settings.

You then must establish the network protocol. This process means choosing the vendor and then the protocol (see fig. 3.9). If you are using the 16-bit real mode IPXODI protocol, you would then choose the Novell vendor and see that IPXODI protocol choice. If you are going to the Microsoft Client for NetWare, you would choose Microsoft as the vendor and the IPX/SPX-compatible protocol.

Setting Frame Type

After you choose the IPX/SPX-compatible protocol, click on the Network Configuration Properties button to access the Advanced Properties screen (see fig. 3.10). At this point, you can set the frame type. The *frame type* is the format the protocol uses to conduct its communication. The term *frame* actually refers to what the packet looks like. A packet appears as a fixed field length record; a number of digits refers to a field and the next number of digits to another and so forth. This allows for the easy reading of the packets. The frame type determines the structure of the record.

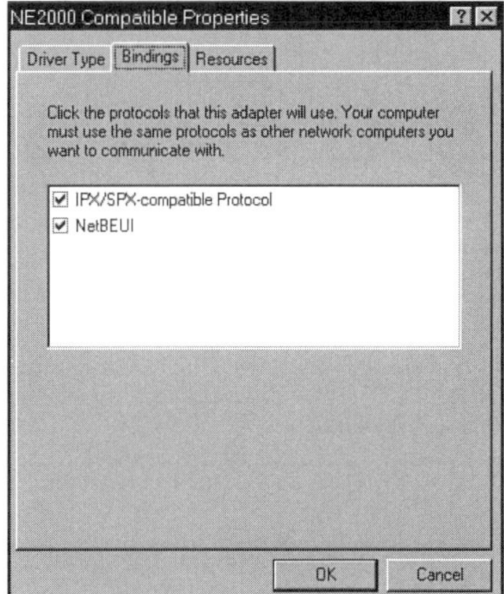

Figure 3.7

Protocol bound to the network card adapters.

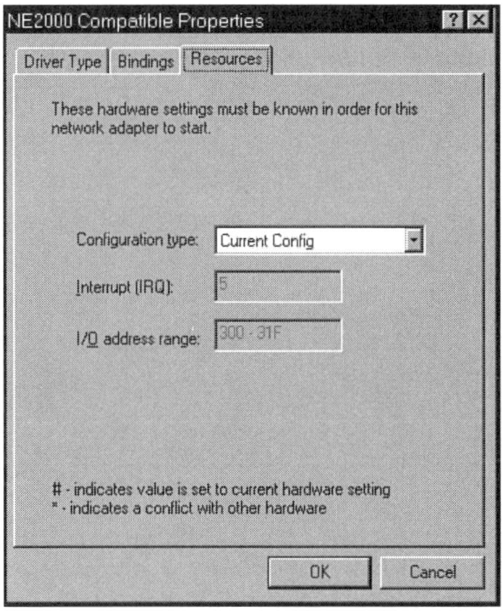

Figure 3.8

Network Card Adapter Properties.

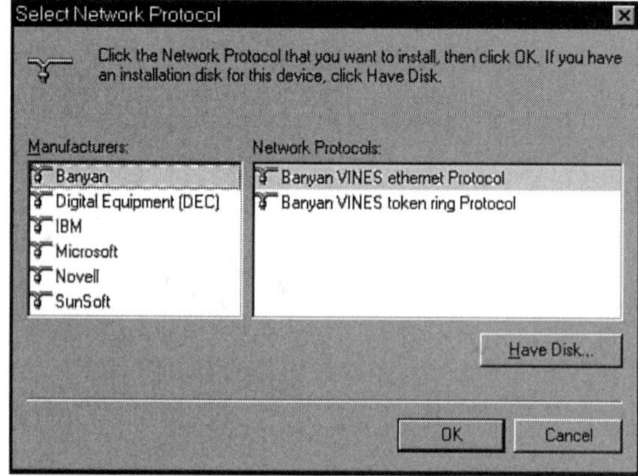

Figure 3.9
Selecting the network protocol by vendor.

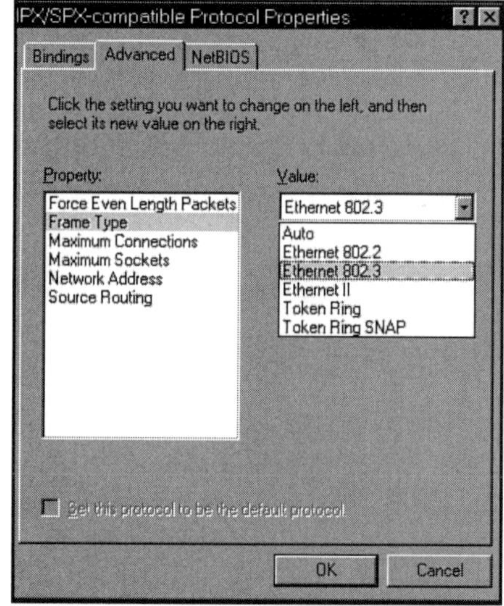

Figure 3.10
Configuring the IPX protocol.

When you set the frame type, keep in mind that Novell has switched its official Ethernet protocol to 802.2 with the VLMs. If you are the administrator, make sure the frame type is the appropriate one for the network and the NetWare server.

Installing the Network Client

After the adapter and protocol are established, you can install the client (see fig. 3.11). If the 16-bit real mode clients from Novell are to be used, choose the Novell Vendor and pick the appropriate client—workstation shell 3.*x* for NETX and 4.0 for the VLMs.

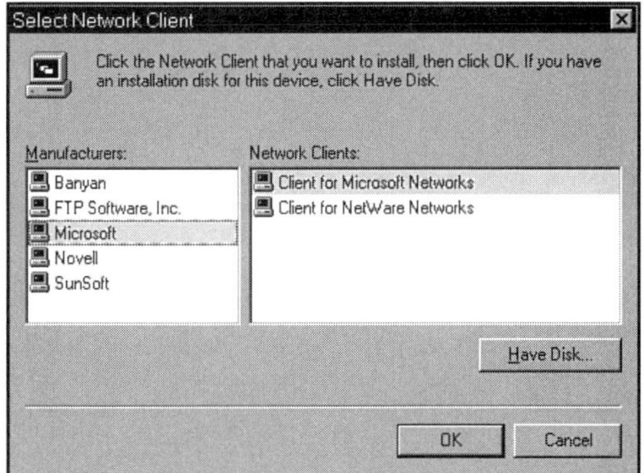

Figure 3.11

Choosing the network client.

If you are using Microsoft Client for NetWare, choose Microsoft as the vendor and then that client. If you choose the Microsoft Client for NetWare you need to configure its properties.

The properties configurable for the NetWare client are the preferred server, the first network drive, and then whether to enable login script processing (see fig. 3.12). You can modify the preferred server by using the universal naming convention of \\servername if the server does not appear in the lists. This will be the server listed in the opening logon box when Windows 95 starts up and recognizes a NetWare network.

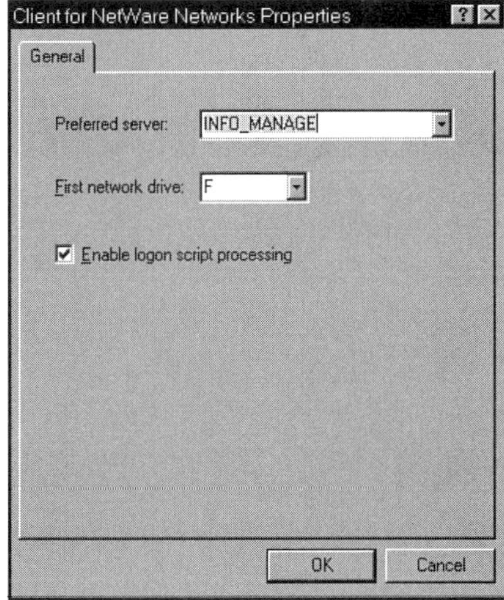

Figure 3.12

Configuring the Microsoft Client for NetWare properties.

Keep in mind the purpose for the preferred server. This setting is to account for another server than the logon server responding to the client's "any server out there?" or get nearest server broadcast. What actually happens is that the first available server that hears that broadcast responds, and then checks its internal router table for the actual preferred server, and then re-routes the packet.

One problem this re-routing creates is that the user remains "not logged on" according to the user slot in the re-routing server. User slots can be lost quickly on the faster low user license server. One way to get around this problem is to adjust the set commands to turn off the responses to "get nearest server" and have another higher licensed server be the re-router.

Client Configuration Settings

The other two settings for network configuration are on the Identification and the Access Control screens. On these screens you can establish a computer name for the workstation, a workgroup the client will belong to, and a computer description, such as the main user's name or department location. The computer name is used by the administrator to connect to the computer for a number of administrative matters, and is used by the computer to announce its presence on the network.

Access control settings determine whether the share level or resource level access control is used, or whether a particular NetWare server's bindery is to be used for authentication and validation.

Windows 95 Network Configuration Considerations

Whenever a new network is set up, ease of user access and workstation management are two goals of the NetWare administrator. The more control the administrator has over both the workstation and the user, the more efficient and the more cost efficient the network will be. The 32-bit Microsoft Client for NetWare has made great strides in these two areas. This version has set the pace for 32-bit client and network management components. Nevertheless, there are some for which the Microsoft implementation may not be the most appropriate.

This section discusses the considerations network administrators must think about when setting up Windows 95 with NetWare. To overcome any obstacles, the network administrator has several options for connecting Windows 95 to a NetWare network:

- **Option one:** Run the real mode Ipx.com or IPXODI protocol with the real mode NETX or VLMS client shell.
- **Option two:** Run the real mode Ipx.com or IPXODI with the Microsoft Client for NetWare.
- **Option three:** Run the Microsoft IPX/SPX-compatible protocol—their 32-bit implementation of the IPX protocol—along with the 32-bit Microsoft Client for NetWare.
- **Option four:** Run the Novell NetWare Client 32, which is a protected mode 32-bit implementation of both the IPX/SPX protocol and the former NETX/VLM client shell.

Each option has advantages and disadvantages on the Windows 95-based network. In the early stages of the Windows 95 transition, you might have to make some choices as to the best configuration per workstation.

Some examples of the types of concerns you must consider include the need to access a NetWare 4.*x* server through its native NetWare Directory Services, or the DOS virtual machine global drive mappings—an unchangeable default of the Microsoft client for NetWare. Another important consideration, is whether there is any need for the use of any 16-bit real mode memory resident programs.

Architecture Considerations with NetWare and Windows 95

In the design of Windows 95, the developers built support for a number of network options. As background for the choices presented above and prior to a more detailed discussion of each area, it would be helpful to have a sense of the structure of the network support within Windows 95, especially for NetWare connectivity.

Windows 95 Support Layers for NetWare

The basis for Windows 95 support of a variety of network configuration options is Mpr.dll (see fig. 3.13). Mpr.dll is the Microsoft-supplied multiple provider router. This dynamic link library file provides the ability to use one of several network sets of files and configurations with Windows 95. Mpr.dll provides access to the Windows 95 32-bit application program interface to the Windows 95 applications above and a service provider interface to network providers below.

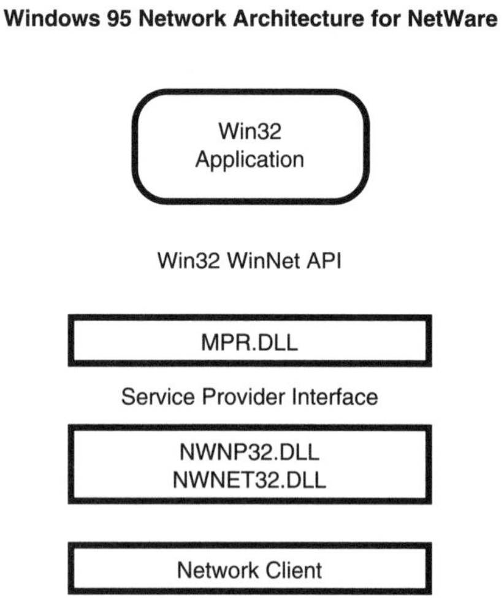

Figure 3.13
Windows 95 network architecture to support NetWare from the workstation.

Windows 95 Network Architecture for NetWare

Win32 Application
Win32 WinNet API
MPR.DLL
Service Provider Interface
NWNP32.DLL NWNET32.DLL
Network Client

Underneath Mpr.dll are the two dynamic link library files that support the NetWare connectivity: Nwnp32.dll and Nwnet32.dll. Nwnet32.dll provides NetWare networking features for Nwnp32.dll and Nwpp32.dll, which are network provider and printer support files respectively. Nwnp32.dll provides access to NetWare resources for the user through such Windows 95 features as the Windows Explorer and the Network Neighborhood.

Mpr.dll, Nwnp32.dll, and Nwnet32.dll are layers that provide support for whichever client shell will be used. At this point the client could be the Microsoft Client for NetWare or either of the real mode clients—NETX or the VLMS. As of the writing of this book, the structural details of the NetWare Client 32 have not been released.

Windows 95 Support Layers for the Microsoft Client for NetWare

In providing full 32-bit support for the Windows 95 NetWare client workstation, Microsoft has supplied virtual device drivers that replace the real mode 16-bit network card driver, protocol, and client shell (see fig. 3.14).

In the 32-bit mode client support, the Installable File Service Manager, Ifsmgr.vxd, and the Microsoft-supplied Nwredir.vxd or 32 client for NetWare are required. Other required components include the 32-bit IPX/SPX compatible protocol, Nwlink.vxd, and the supporting Microsoft Network Device Interface Specification layer (Ndis.vxd), and the network card/adapter driver.

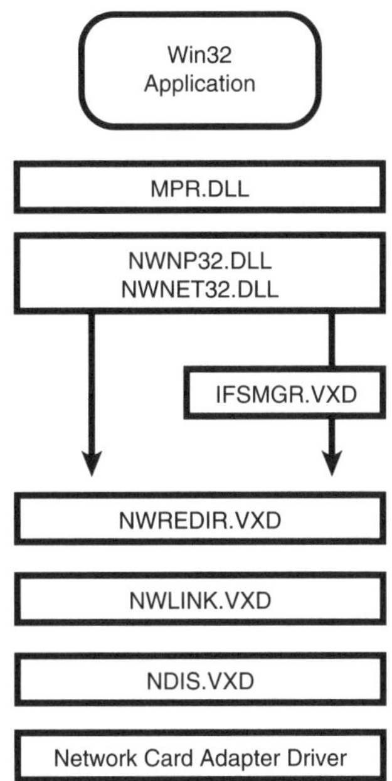

Figure 3.14
Windows 95 network architecture to support Microsoft Client for NetWare.

Windows 95 Support Layers for the Real Mode NetWare Client

For reasons discussed in the "Real Mode NetWare Advantages and Disadvantages" section on the following page, there may be reasons for staying with the existing NetWare server connectivity pieces, real mode network card adapter, Ipxodi.com, and either the Netx.exe or the Vlm.exe with its Netx.vlm module. As shown in figure 3.15, Windows 95 supports this set of options.

If a real mode client is used, the Novell Netware.drv and Vnetware.386 provide the protected mode support layer as they do with Windows 3.*x*. Note that for the older 16-bit applications Windows 95 must supply the Nw16.dll to translate the 16-bit code and transactions into 32-bit mode. Referred to by Microsoft as a "thunk" layer, Nw16.dll also passes 32-bit calls to the 16-bit NetWare application program.

There are two different Netware.drv files. There is the one provided by NetWare whose version must correspond to whichever real mode NetWare client is used. There is a Microsoft version supplied for Windows 95 for use with the Microsoft Client for NetWare. Problems arise when switching from one client to another.

Figure 3.15

Windows 95 network architecture to support the real mode NETX or VLMS client.

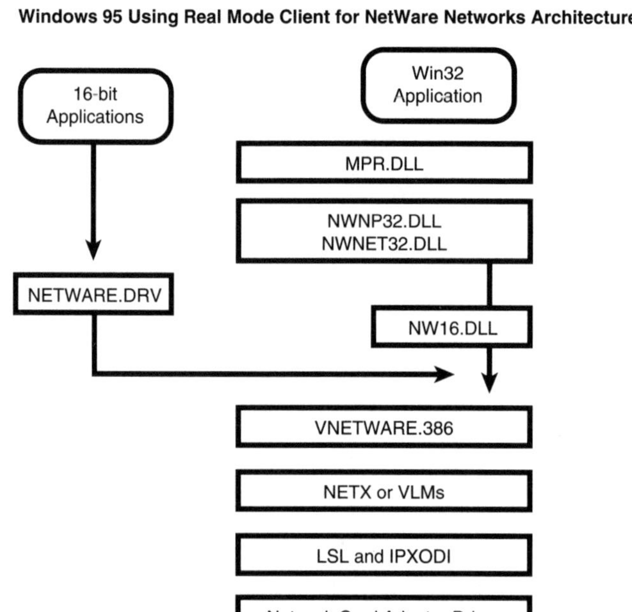

If real mode pieces are being used, the traditional NetWare Startnet.bat file should be called from the Autoexec.bat file so that it is executed before Windows 95 moves into protected mode. Another way to accomplish this would be to move the network connectivity files into Autoexec.bat.

This brief examination of architecture shows that Windows 95 can support choices for real mode versus protected mode by providing the 32-bit support for either choice, and one supposes for the NetWare Client 32 as well.

Real Mode NetWare Advantages and Disadvantages

The protected mode 32-bit client is far more integrated into the Windows 95 operating system than the 16-bit real mode networking protocol and clients. Nevertheless, several situations will, in the short run, prevent the use of the Microsoft Client for NetWare's 32-bit client, such as whenever:

- Memory resident programs are required for various connectivity applications.
- Memory resident programs might be required to be run between NetWare logon and the loading of Windows.
- The workstation is used for access to NetWare 4.*x* and utilizes the NetWare Directory Services features.
- You are running VLM features such as Personal NetWare that are not supported with Microsoft Client for NetWare.

16-bit real mode components would be most appropriate whenever:

- NetWare Core Protocol packet signature is required.
- NetWare IP (Nwip.exe) is required to support Unix-based Transmission Control Protocol/Internet Protocol Communications.
- Mainframe 3270 emulation is required and is DOS-based, or real mode memory resident 3270 connectivity support is required.
- VLM components such as Personal NetWare are required.
- NetWare's communication server components exist on the Windows 95 workstation.
- The workstation is a NetWare 4.*x* client and needs access to NetWare Directory Services features.
- The user needs to use the VLM implementation NWUSER. This is the tool set that provides access to drive mappings, logon servers, and print queues from a central interface.
- The user needs to use NetWare Directory Services names in Windows 95 dialog boxes.

What about RPRINTER, the real mode memory resident program that makes the workstation printer port available to the network to service a printer queue? RPRINTER and the Windows 95 replacement are discussed at the end of this chapter, but the question serves as an opportunity to discuss the implications of the Windows 95 32-bit protected mode logon process.

Problems with Real Mode TSRs

When a real mode TSR such as RPRINTER is evoked in the logon process, Windows 95 creates a DOS virtual machine to start the TSR. This setup seems fine because RPRINTER is system-based and not needed by other DOS programs. The problem with running RPRINTER this way is that Windows 95 then precedes to close the logon DOS virtual machine, effectively vaporizing the TSR.

When a real mode TSR is run on the NetWare workstation before the startup of Windows 3.*x*, it is usually run through a batch file that you've established to make the transition between the login script and the system menu or the start of Windows. The problem of running Windows 95 with its 32-bit network adapter, protocols, and client is that the logon process is place in protected mode, and when the login script is completed the workstation stays in protected mode.

RPRINTER is also an example of a memory-resident program that cannot be run effectively unless the network connection exists. The reason for this is that RPRINTER must make contact with a network component to work.

To work around these problems, the NetWare administrator who needs to support the workstation serving as remote printer port for the server functionality of the real mode RPRINTER program has the following two choices:

- Run the traditional 16-bit NetWare RPRINTER and real mode network driver, protocol, and shell.
- Use the implementation provided by Microsoft, which runs with the protected mode Microsoft Client for NetWare.

It is expected that network management software vendors whose applications need to run a real mode memory client program will be providing 32-bit protected more versions that could become part of the startup applications within Windows 95. These programs would then make their network component connections after the NetWare login script finishes.

Real Mode Considerations

If your situation calls for the use of real mode NetWare clients, several issues need to be considered. Probably the best way to handle real mode NetWare clients is to move them to the Autoexec.bat file.

NetWare 16-Bit DLLs and Windows 95

The NetWare dynamic link library files that support NetWare Application Program Interfaces in the Windows protected mode operation of both Windows 3.*x* and Windows 95 include the following:

- **Nwcalls.dll.** Controls NetWare core protocol communication back and forth between the server and the workstation.
- **Nwgdi.dll.** Supports NetWare graphic needs such as the NetWare logo that was added to the VLM 1.20 version. This DLL also causes a brief flash of a red NetWare logo after the Microsoft opening logo and before Program Manager appears.
- **Nwipxspx.dll.** Provides vendors with access to the NetWare protocol layer.
- **Nwlocale.dll.** Provides local support for applications.
- **Nwnet.dll.** A VLM-specific module that calls out to NDS features.
- **Nwpsrv.dll.** Provides access to print server features.

These NetWare files are available on CompuServe and the Internet as the Nwdll*x*.exe files. The *x* stands for the current version of the set. The version will also be the same for the Vlmup*x*.exe and the Windr*x*.exe downloadable files.

Winstart.bat and Real Mode TSRs

You should become familiar with the Winstart.bat feature, which was part of the Windows 3.*x* environment, and has been included in the Windows 95 system (see fig. 3.16). Winstart.bat addresses the problem of DOS real mode-based TSRs that must be loaded before Windows moves into protected mode operation.

These TSRs typically are only needed either by the system or by Windows applications. TSRs required by DOS applications running in virtual machines must either have had the TSRs loaded prior to Windows or have their TSRs loaded in a batch file that loads the application in its virtual machine.

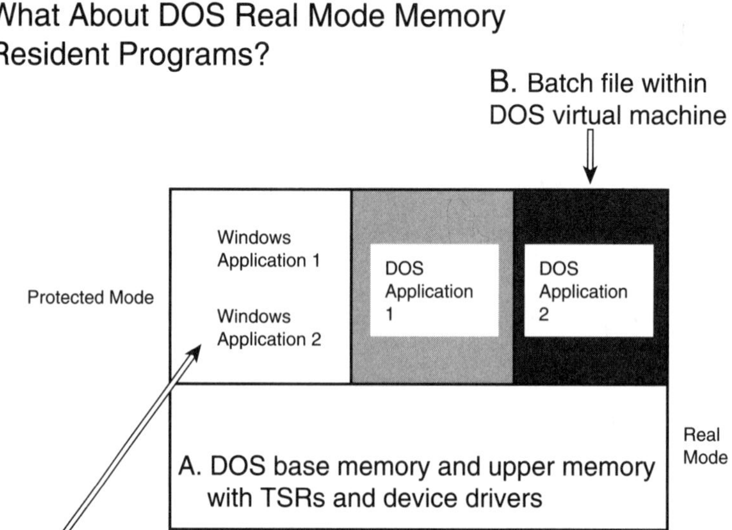

Figure 3.16
The Winstart.bat and its function to load memory resident programs into Windows global memory.

If Winstart.bat is in the user's search path, it will execute as Windows loads. The memory resident programs within it will be loaded into Windows global memory, and will only be accessible to Windows applications and the workstation.

Although this Winstart.bat function is quite useful for Windows 3.*x* because of its ability to load application-required DOS memory programs out of base memory, it is not as useful with Windows 95 protected mode clients and protected mode login script processing.

With Windows 95 in protected mode, the Winstart.bat memory resident programs are loaded before server connectivity has been established and before connections with server-based applications on NetWare are made. TSR applications that require connectivity with the server before the transition into Windows protected mode operation either need to be replaced by the vendor's virtual device drivers or will require the use of real mode 16-bit clients, NETX or VLMs, for the immediate future.

Winstart.bat and its functionality becomes a good tool for the network administrator who is running the real mode protocol and the real mode NetWare client and needs to load DOS memory resident programs to support existing 16-bit Windows applications. Loading these TSRs into Windows global memory with Winstart.bat saves base memory needed by the DOS virtual machines and their DOS applications.

Real Mode Components—Two Special Considerations

There are two more reasons to consider using the real mode network components. The first involves drive mappings in the DOS virtual machines, and the second involves NetWare version 4.*x*.

The first special condition involves how NetWare drive mappings are handled by the DOS virtual machine session; whether the drive mappings are global to all DOS virtual machines, and whether this change will be made in the other existing DOS virtual machines as well. This matter can be set with the real mode client and the System.ini, but not when using the Microsoft Client for NetWare. (We do not know yet about NetWare Client 32.)

The second special consideration is when Windows 95 is to work with a NetWare 4.*x* server. The NetWare 4.*x* administrator, and those NetWare 3.*x* supervisors contemplating a system upgrade, must face the problem that the Windows 95 Microsoft Client for NetWare does not yet support the Netware 4.*x* NetWare Directory Services, and the NetWare Client 32 described in this chapter has yet to be released. For the near future this leaves only the real mode virtual loadable modules as the only means of accessing the NetWare 4.*x* server.(For NetWare Directory Services features, bindery emulation, which is supported by Microsoft Client for NetWare, is not sufficient as it is a limited access set to the NetWare 4.*x* server treating it simply as another NetWare 3.*x* server.)

Drive Mappings in the DOS Virtual Machine

Drive mappings are a significant tool that enable the administrator or the user to assign a network drive letter to subdirectories on the NetWare network server volume. NetWare login script drive mappings established by the administrator are considered static drive mappings. Dynamic drive mappings are those that can be typed at the DOS prompt or from within a DOS-based menu system. This difference creates an administrative problem: users can adjust drive mappings within Windows and designate them as "persistent connections," which NetWare users know as "permanent drive mappings." These persistent or permanent drive mappings ensure that as Windows comes up on the workstation, these drive mappings are reestablished for that Windows session.

Beyond the administrator's concern about the user remapping drives is the concern with DOS virtual machine dynamic drive mappings. Whenever DOS drive mappings are localized and a batch file is used to start the application, the same drive letter can be used in each DOS virtual machine. Each drive letter designation points to the unique server location in the virtual machine. If, on the other hand, DOS drive mappings are global to all DOS virtual machines, and a batch file is run in a DOS virtual machine that assigns drive G, for example, to a particular server location, G gets reassigned in every DOS virtual machine.

To illustrate this problem, suppose you run a database application in DOS virtual machine1, map G to run WordPerfect DOS word-processing in DOS virtual machine2, and again map G to the WordPerfect document directory. This configuration will work until you decide to go back to the DOS virtual machine1 database application. If you press Alt+Tab to get back to the database application, G is now mapped to the WordPerfect files—not the database file location. The database application will not work properly because it cannot find its files in G. This is obviously a problem for the administrator and the old logic of reusing drive letters.

In the Windows 3.*x* environment the local or global state of a DOS virtual machine is controlled by the [NetWare] section and the setting NWSharehandles= in the System.ini file. The NWSharehandles setting is one of those that has a text setting line in the System.ini file and a check box in the Network section of Windows Control Panel (see fig. 3.17). Whatever the Control Panel icon has to offer, it is really controlled by the System.ini setting. If the setting NWSharehandles=false in the [NetWare] section of System.ini, then mapping is local to the DOS virtual machine; if NWSharehandles=true, then mapping is global for all DOS virtual machines.

Figure 3.17

*Global drive mappings as a Windows 3.*x *Control Panel choice.*

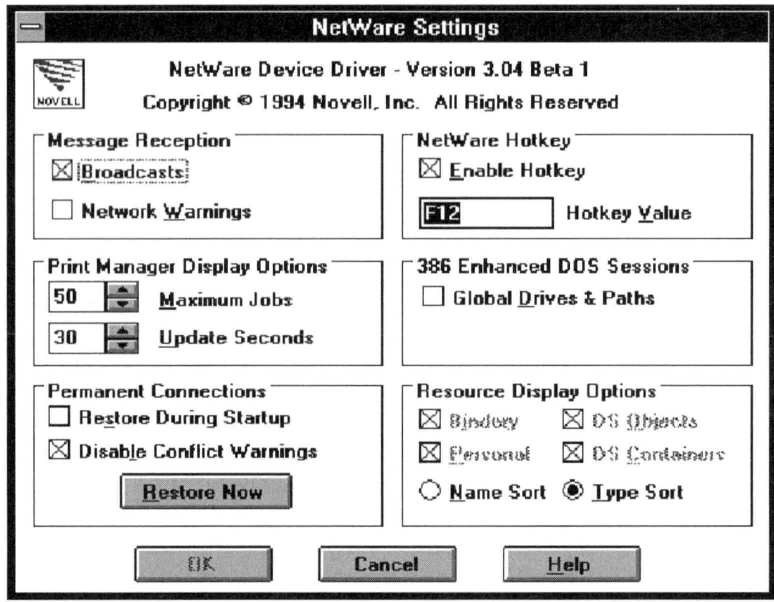

The impact for the NetWare administrator is that if DOS virtual machine mappings are global, the batch file or dynamic drive mapping used must be unique for each DOS application. This causes two problems for the administrator, aside from the extra effort necessary to maintain all these mappings. First, for each user's drive mapping 16 bytes of short term alloc memory are used in NetWare 3.*x*; this can add up in a large user server environment. Second, more workstation DOS environment space is used on each workstation.

What do all these mapping problems mean for the NetWare network administrator concerned about Windows 95? If the Microsoft Client for NetWare is used, the drive mappings for DOS VMs are global and no options are available for getting around these problems. This means that if a group of users are going to use the Microsoft Client for NetWare and run DOS legacy applications, dynamic drive mappings for these DOS virtual machines are global and require special attention from the NetWare administrator.

You should also note that while drive mappings in Window 3.1 are local or global, depending on the value of NWSharehandles=, print queues are global in Windows 95. This means that changing the print queue of a port for a specific DOS virtual machine application through a batch file changes the print queue assignments in all Windows virtual machines, including the Windows virtual machine where Windows applications are loaded.

NetWare 4.*x* NetWare Directory Services

Until Microsoft publishes its Microsoft Client for NetWare support for NetWare's NetWare Directory Services, and until Novell publishes its Client 32 that supports NetWare Directory Services, the Netware 4.*x* administrator wanting to implement Windows 95 on the workstation will have to use the real mode adapter, IPXODI protocol and the virtual loadable module client shell.

NetWare 4.*x* has significant network management features for the administrator to consider. Among these feature are the following:

- Clients attach to the network not just to an individual server.
- The NetWare Directory Services structure provides a network perspective as opposed to just a single server-based view.
- NetWare Directory Services offers the administrator an object-oriented structure that enables information and network items to be managed in an easier administrative format.
- NetWare 4.*x* offers more disk management and file management features such as sub block allocation for file storage, disk compresssion, as well as support for data migration of less used files.

Netware 4.x Is Network-Based Versus Server-Based

Each server on a NetWare 3.11 network has its own bindery system. Each user and each print queue has a unique binder ID that is assigned when the entity is created.

If a user wants to work with more than one server, he or she logs on to the preferred server and uses the ATTACH command to log on to another server (see fig. 3.18). The SLIST command, replaced in NetWare 4.*x* with NLIST SERVER, enables users to see the other servers available on the network. With NetWare 3.11, however, only eight servers are visible; NetWare 4.*x* enables users to see and attach to up to 50 file servers.

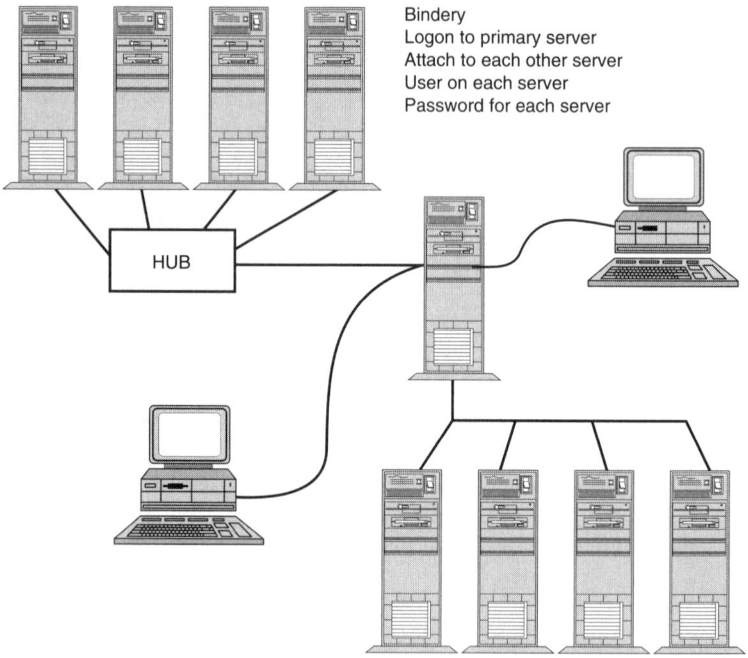

Figure 3.18
*NetWare 3.*x *requires specific attach statements to each server.*

If you have the same password on the other servers and the same name, the ATTACH *servername* command gets you to the other server(s) without any additional effort. If you have different passwords or different logon names for each server, you have to specify each logon name and a password for each server.

NetWare Directory Services has been created by Novell to allow LAN and WAN servers to be part of the same system. A user need only log on once to have a distinct identity on the network (see fig. 3.19). A significant part of these directory services is designed so that a user can have, given the user rights, easy access to files, printers, and other peripherals across the network.

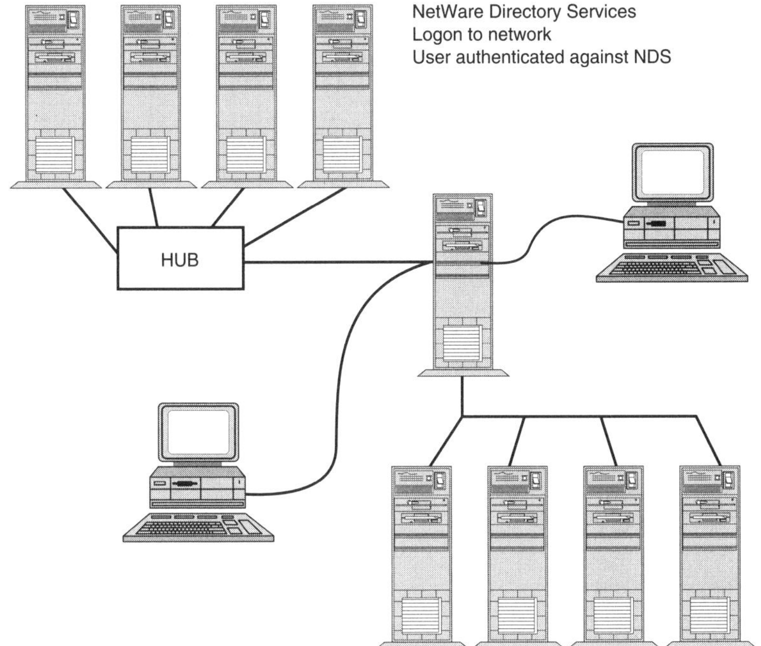

Figure 3.19

You can log on to the network through NetWare Directory Services.

Novell's solution to providing this one global network system is the NDS or NetWare Directory Services. Under NDS all related servers are seen as being on the same NDS tree, where they can be seen by each other. All servers, users, volumes, and printers are constructed as objects on the NDS and have special properties and unique values assigned to those properties. In Windows-based NWADMIN, the administrator can configure and adjust more of these settings than the older bindery-based SYSCON or system configuration provided.

The directory tree is the hierarchical organization of NDS. Figure 3.20 shows how you can transfer from a physical site map of an organization to an organizational chart, to a visual NDS tree.

With this tree structure, computer heritage requires the use of an upside down tree that starts at a root level and branches out. In this example of a large organization with two departments that each have a file server, the two file servers have a separate SYS volume that is recognized as being the name of the file server SYS. This makes mapping and object manipulation easier later on.

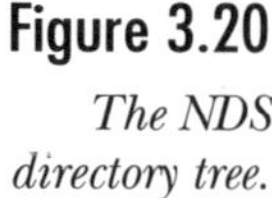

Figure 3.20

The NDS directory tree.

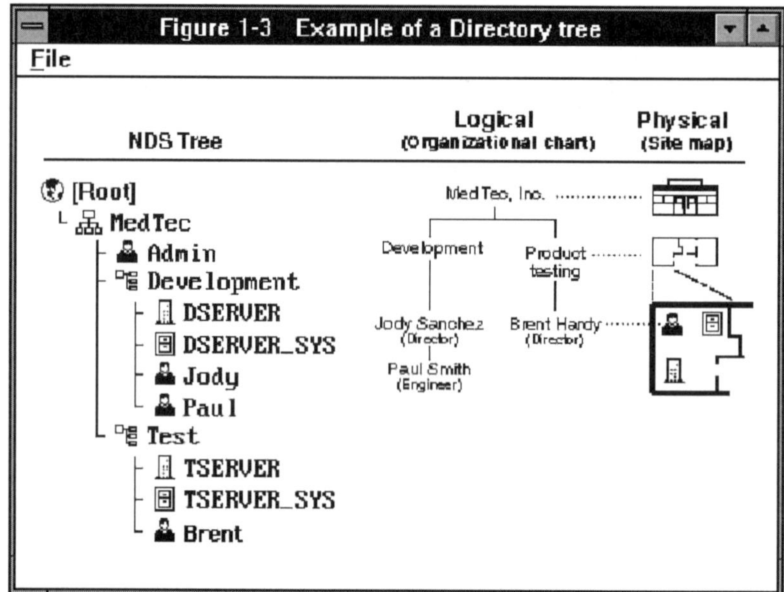

Note that if Bront logs on to the Test server and is in context a user on Test, he still can, assuming rights, change his context by typing a command similar to CD, namely CX, and get to DSERVER SYS should he need to do so.

Bindery Versus an NDS Structure

Figure 3.21 sums up the difference between the traditional Novell bindery and the new NetWare Directory Services. The bindery is a flat file of all the items on the server. In other words, the bindery is organized by logical organization, and is searchable by object type ("printers," for example).

NDS is global for all servers rather than specific to a single server, just as passwords are global rather than for a single server. Database information is distributed across the server, which provides fault tolerance of the directory structure or database and faster access over a wide area network. By using this method, you can look up a replica on your local server of database items on a distant server.

	Bindery	versus	NDS
Logical Structure	Flat		Hierarchical
Users / groups	Single server		Network wide
Volumes	Single server		Global objects
Logon	Password per server		System wide password
Location	Single server		Distributed

Figure 3.21

The bindery compared to the NDS structure.

Two NDS Examples

One type of NDS directory structure is illustrated in figure 3.22—flat file bindery. This illustration of a screen from a third-party shareware program illustrates the nature of the bindery. The item highlighted in the Objects section is a print queue named "12345678901234567890" that shows how many characters can be used in a queue name. This item also appears as a type 003, but whose real identity is 0600001. With print queues, the challenge for administrators is to set up the queue so that a user only sees a name. Hidden from the user is the queue's real name and path. The print queue is in reality a directory under SYSTEM subdirectory as the \system\queue-Identity or in this case \SYSTEM\0600001.

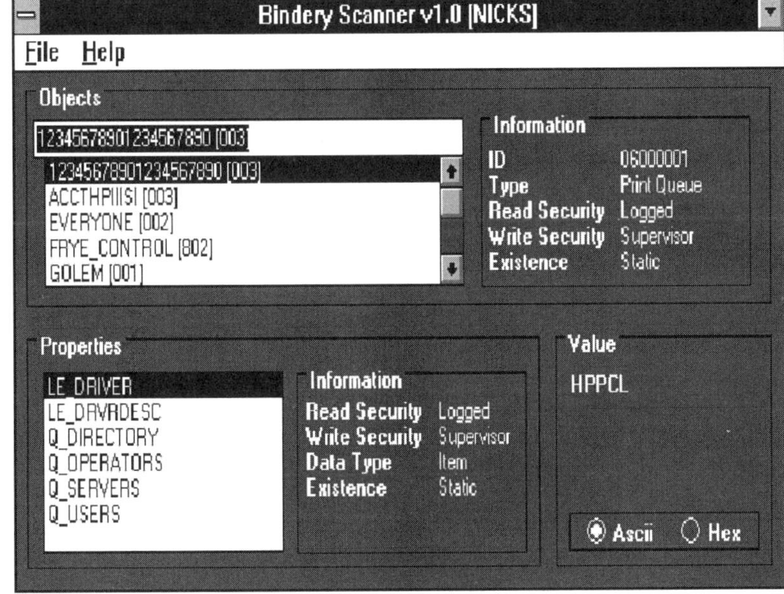

Figure 3.22

The third-party program BINDSCAN provides a view of the bindery for the administrator.

Another type of NDS directory structure uses the directory tree. This directory tree example is patterned after the hypothetical organization MEDTEC used in figure 3.20, which has two organizational units, Development and Test. Each unit has a server and at least two server volumes.

The challenge to the tree designers is how to organize the directory tree to reflect the organization. In this two server company, the tree is organized by departmental functions. Later examples in this chapter use a structure based at the highest level by country, then by department, then by location.

NDS Object Orientation

The illustrations so far in this chapter graphically depict the resources on the network under the NDS format. The icons are symbolic representations of the objects. Each object has its own properties or database fields of information.

For the object User, for example, you have properties such as first name, last name, title, location, telephone, and fax number. Each of these properties has values that you fill-in, such as Nicolas L. Behrmann, Vice President for Training, Palm Springs, 619-555-1234, 619-555-1235. Although another user might see my logon name as NBEHRMANN, unless they have appropriate rights, they will not have access to my data or values.

NDS provides you not only with more data fields for the user, but also with objects that can be used as time and effort savers. See figure 3.23 for the items that can be created.

With object orientation you might at times refer to the object and at other times the item that is represented by the object. In GUI programs you can simply click on the object and see the property screens and statistics for the object. The following are objects that you might create:

- **AFP Server.** AppleTalk file server.
- **Alias.** A simple means of referencing an object in another organizational unit, rather than having to use the full network tree, network container, and network name.
- **Computer.** Purely for database storage such as serial number and node address.
- **Directory Map.** Holds MAP commands so that an application can be referenced here rather than for each user.
- **Group.** List of users in a group, addressed to group with e-mail. Rights can be assigned to groups and they apply to all users within the group.

- **NetWare Server.** Shows a Novell NetWare server.
- **Organizational Role.** An object with specific trustee rights.
- **Organizational Unit.** A branch on the NDS tree.
- **Printer.** Printer attached to the file server, workstation, or print box.
- **Print Server.** File server or stand-alone resource serving the function of controlling printers.
- **Profile.** A login script that is loaded after the SYSTEM login script but before the USER login script. The Profile object allows for the setting up of a network environment for a group of users rather than using the IF MEMBER OF GROUP login script command.
- **Print Queue.** Hold print jobs. Printers are assigned to a queue; users can print to a queue or to a printer object.
- **User.** Holds user account information such as name, the rights for that user, and any account restrictions.
- **Volume.** The object that stands for volumes on a server. Maintains statistics about that volume.

Figure 3.23

The NDS creation of new objects screen.

Bindery Compatibility

Compatibility is provided between the NDS and the previous Novell bindery through bindery emulation. This gives NetWare 3.11 server users and bindery-based third-party utilities access to leaf objects such as users and printers. (Leaf objects on the NDS tree are objects that do not contain other objects.) The parties requiring access to bindery information are not able to see container objects because they do not exist within the bindery world.(Container objects such as organizations or servers contain other objects.)

Bindery emulation is through a Read Write replica of the NDS stored on the server for which bindery emulation is operational. During install, a bindery context is created that can be changed in the SET mode or through SERVMAN. This bindery context is how the items look to the non-NDS world.

NetWare 4.x Disk and File Management

Another set of features that make network management easier with NetWare 4.*x* is the disk storage set of features. Disk compression allows for more efficient use of disk space on the network. Another feature that makes for more efficient use of disk space is the ability to store more than one file in a storage block. This allows for better use of disk storage space by not wasting space. Under the older method of storage a 1 KB file would occupy a whole 4 KB storage block. With larger storage blocks being more efficient means of storing larger files, sub block allocation allows multiple smaller files to occupy large storage blocks. This would be especially helpful with Windows 95 user profile replication with its less than 1 KB shortcut or link files.

NetWare 4.*x* also has data migration, which is its foundation for Hierarchical Storage Method (HSM). HSM provides for off-loading older or less often used files to a less expensive storage media but without the user having to be aware of this transfer. HSM leaves a stub file by the original file name, and the HSM software monitors the call to the stub and fetches the file for the user from the secondary storage media. HSM is not itself part of NetWare 4.*x*, but the data migration foundation is.

The point here is that to take advantage of all the NetWare 4.*x* features, the workstation client software must be able to successfully log on to the NDS-based server in the NDS mode. Until Microsoft provides NDS support to its Microsoft Client for NetWare and until Novell publishes its NetWare Client 32, the only option for the administrator is the real mode IPX and VLM software. This real mode choice means sacrificing significant administrative features available in the Microsoft Client for NetWare.

NetWare Real Mode Protocol and Microsoft Client for NetWare

Microsoft has also identified situations in which the use of the NetWare-supplied real mode IPX protocol is more useful than the 32-bit IPX/SPX-compatible protocol. These situations are those in which memory resident programs are run that take advantage of the IPX/SPX protocol or are loaded into memory after the IPX/SPX but before the NetWare client shell is loaded. These programs include the following:

- Dosnp.exe
- LAN Workplace
- Netv.exe
- The Reachout/Networks' remote access components are used, such as RCHIPX, RCHNETB, RCHBANV, RICHSAP
- VPCTCP
- Winfax Pro for Networks and Netw.exe

These and other such situations will be updated by Microsoft in the Netdet.ini file that is part of the Windows 95 distribution files.

Installing Microsoft's IPX/SPX-Compatible Protocol and Microsoft Client for NetWare

Microsoft Client for NetWare is a protected mode 32-bit client that works with a 32-bit adapter card driver and the Microsoft IPX/SPX-compatible protocol. Many of the networking management features available with Windows 95 are based on the use of this client. A significant feature of this client is that it uses no real mode memory. Microsoft claims that in moving large amounts of data across the network cable, this client can be up to 200 times faster than the VLM configuration with Windows 3.1.

The Microsoft Client for NetWare that first ships with Windows 95 only supports NetWare 3.*x* and the bindery emulation of NetWare 4.*x*. Microsoft has promised that within a short period after the debut of Windows 95, there will be a version of Microsoft Client for NetWare that fully supports NetWare 4.*x* NetWare Directory Services.

Microsoft Client for NetWare supports some important Windows 95 innovations such as client-side caching for network information. Unlike previous versions of Windows, which support file caching of only local disks, the Windows 95 implementation of the client treats the client for NetWare as a file system driver that utilizes the same 32-bit cache used by all other Windows 95 file system drivers. The client also supports the new long file-name support, which allows more humanlike naming of the user's data files such as "November 1995 Status Report" rather than the older format "Nov95st.rpt." The long file names could be up to 255 characters versus the older 8.3 character format.

Another significant innovation supported by this client implementation is the automatic reconnection for lost server connections. If a server is either brought down or crashes, Windows 95 Microsoft Client for NetWare retains the connection so that when the server is brought back up the connectivity will still be there, even if the application halts and the application or its virtual machine needs to be closed. What is especially significant is that the workstation that loses the network connection will not have to be rebooted the way that current DOS-Windows–based workstations respond to the loss of the network.

The network traffic side of this implementation of the IPX/SPX-compatible protocol supports two fairly recent NetWare innovations: the Packet Burst protocol and the Large Internet Packet protocol (LIP).

Packet Features in the Microsoft IPX/SPX-Compatible Protocol

A simple description of message packets shows that a packet has an address section, a protocol section that reminds the nodes how to communicate, the message section, and an error checking section (see fig. 3.24). The error checking process can slow down the transmission of data from one computer to another; the Packet Burst process tries to address this.

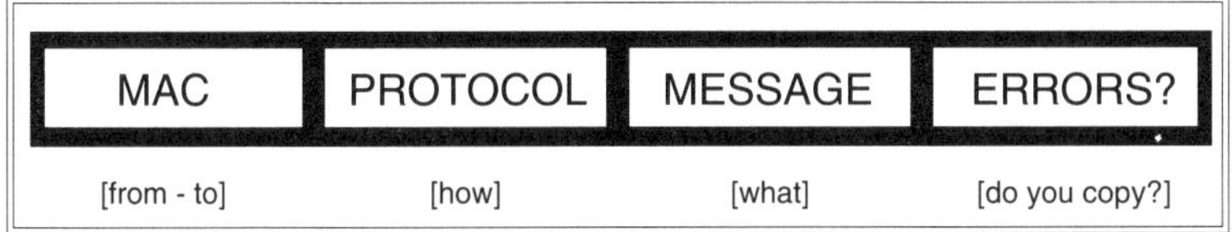

Figure 3.24
The simplified network packet structure.

The process of the transmission and receipt of the IPX protocol packet has its drawbacks. Error checking is built into the packet and is based on the CRC (cyclical redundancy) or checksum process whereby a calculation is created based on the number of binary 1s and 0s contained in the packet. This calculation is passed to the recipient of the packet, which does its own calculation. If both agree on the calculation, the receiver sends a positive acknowledgment packet to the sender. If they disagree, the receiver asks for the sender to retransmit. This process provides error checking, but creates traffic and is not efficient.

Packet Burst protocol support allows the sender to send up to 64 KB worth of packets in a machine gun-like burst of packets without the receiver needing to respond to each packet. The receiver tracks all the packets and might have to ask the sender to repeat specific packets out of the 64 KB worth of packets. Thus, the Packet Burst protocol can be more efficient for large amounts of data transmission.

LIP support changes the nature of the IPX packets when they arrive at a network router. Older technology was like a large freight truck arriving at the router, which could not bear the weight of the full load. The freight had to be offloaded to smaller vehicles to get through the router, and the large truck was brought down to a weight that could get through. On the other side of the router the large truck was reloaded and went on its way. The IPX packet had to be stripped down to smaller size units to pass through the router, and reassembled on the other side. This was not a router issue, but a limitation of the IPX packet. The LIP process allows the IPX packet to pass through without the downsizing process.

The Windows 95 IPX-compatible protocol supports the Packet Burst protocol and the LIP protocol, which are the most recent NetWare developments.

Microsoft Client for NetWare also is capable of using the NetWare MS-DOS Application Program Interfaces and the related set of NetWare Dynamic Link Libraries listed earlier in the discussion of Dynamic Link Library support for the VLMs.

User Profiles and System Policies Supported by Microsoft Client for NetWare

Another element of Windows 95 innovations that is supported by Microsoft Client for NetWare is the capability to create, maintain, and manage user profiles and system policies across the network. Chapter 4, "Managing the Workstation and User," discusses this feature in greater detail. What you need to know here is that the capability to manage users and workstations centrally is a major feature for the NetWare administrator. He or she will have much more control over the network through these features, most of which are not be available if the user and workstation are using the real mode NETX or VLM implementations.

Microsoft Client for NetWare also supports the use of bindery-based peer-to-peer security on workstations that are set up to share their directories and printers. You can offer shared directories and printers on workstations on a user access level rather than the traditional peer-to-peer resource password system. You can also take advantage of a 32-bit implementation of a remote print server that Microsoft offers as a replacement for the NetWare remote printer program RPRINTER.

The 32-bit Microsoft Client for NetWare requires the following files on the workstation or in the NetWare search path for server based Windows 95 stations:

- **Netware.drv.** A Microsoft file replacement for the NetWare file of the same name. This file provides compatibility for NetWare-aware applications that look for this file.
- **Nwlink.vxd.** Provides the NetWare IPX/SPX protocol 32-bit protected mode for Windows 95.
- **Nwnet32.dll.** Provides NetWare networking features for Nwnp32.dll and Nwpp32.dll, which are network provider and printer support files.
- **Nwnp32.dll.** Provides access to NetWare resources for the user through Windows 95 features such as Windows Explorer and Network Neighborhood.
- **Nwpp32.dll.** Provides 32-bit printing support. Printing can be done through the Windows 95 Spools.dll print router instead of NetWare printing resources.
- **Nwredir.vxd.** The client piece that gives applications 32-bit file system access to file server files through NetWare's NetWare Core Protocol calls to the server for file servicing.

32-Bit Processing of the NetWare Login Script

Nwlogin3.exe and Lscon.exe provide the protected mode 32-bit logon support for the Microsoft Client for NetWare. These files are necessary because logons take place in protected mode. If they did not exist, Login.exe of NetWare would be run in a DOS VM. The problem for the administrator is that some TSRs are set to run immediately after login, or some real mode programs might even be executed from the login script.

When the Windows 95 workstation is being tested for the compatibility of the login script with this new environment, you might want to use the PAUSE command frequently for each area of the login script. In testing an existing script process for a network, an error message may appear stating that an illegal operation has been asked for. If this script isn't examined, it leaves the user in limbo.

Through this pause process, you can determine that a problem might be caused by a program that ran fine in a DOS-Windows 3.1 workstation. For example, if you use Norton Utilities Network Administrator from a login script to test the disk drive of each networked workstation, and then report the status of each station to the administrator, the problem of illegal operation goes away when the PAUSE command is remarked out of the login script. The Norton program does not work with the Windows 95 disk structure.

Symantec now has a version of its Norton Utilities for Windows 95, and probably will have a Network Administrator set in the near future. This set may even address this real mode and disk structure incompatibility.

The NetWare Client 32

Novell is developing NetWare Client 32, which will replace the 16-bit client with the VxD support. The 16-bit client is now older technology that has been found to slow network access time and create system instability. A 32-bit client for both DOS and Windows, which is in the testing phase, promises to deliver as much as twice the performance of existing real mode clients. Among the features are access and return of machine resources on the fly, releasing users from complex configuration and optimization issues. Client side caching of network files and auto-reconnect technology is promised along with full support of NetWare 4.*x*'s NDS. NDS also offers a single name and password for accessing all NetWare network resources.

The NetWare Client 32 offers the user a NetWare logon icon on the Windows 95 desktop after the user is in protected mode Windows. By double-clicking on that icon, the user then ties into the NetWare Directory Services where a three-level login script capability already exists:

- The administrator-written SYSTEM login script
- A middle layer profile script that offers a group structure of login script settings
- The user's own personalized login script

The logon process authenticates access to servers, creates drive mappings, captures printer ports, and gathers applications into a folder or group from which the user is able to launch or start applications. This last feature is called the NetWare Application Launcher (NAL).

NetWare Application Launcher

A new feature, the NetWare Application Launcher (NAL), is based on NetWare Directory Services and its object structure. Instead of just assigning directory and file rights for application files to user objects or group objects, NAL builds connections to the program in Windows as objects and icons. These objects are then presented to users in their desktops.

NAL and Effective Icons

One of the problems inherited from Windows 3.*x* is that of providing a unique desktop to every user so that he or she can do their job properly. This issue becomes more critical when users move around among workstations. There are solutions to this problem for Windows 3.*x* and, with Windows 95, Microsoft has provided the ability to replicate the user's menu and desktop to the network as a means of making such access tools available on all workstations. This section explores Novell's solution, which will be part of their NetWare Client 32 for Windows 95.

The concept of NAL can be called "effective icons," which is a play on NetWare's notion of effective rights. *Effective rights* are the total or bottom line rights that a user has on a network. For example, John has Write rights to a directory as a member of the Write group; Mary has Read rights to a directory as a member of the Read group; and George is a member of both groups. George's rights add up to both Write and Read rights, and his effective rights are both Read and Write. If John is in a sales group he might need access to a set of icons for sales applications; if Mary is in the accounting department, she might need access to payroll. As the manager of the Sales group, George may need access to both sales applications and sales commissions that are kept in payroll programs. In Windows 3.1 you can provide John access to a copy of the sales group Progman.ini and give Mary access to accounting's Progman.ini, but would have to create a special Progman.ini for George.

To avoid having to manage the Progman.ini for every user on the network, many administrators of Windows 3.1 on the NetWare network turn to third-party menu type systems, such as Saber, Net Tools, or LAN Escort, that evaluate the user's status on the network at login and make effective icons available to the user. In the case of George, these menu applications evaluate the network's logic, which might say, "If George is a member of group Sales, display the sales icons; and if George is a member of the Accounting group, display the accounting icons." George effectively gets the icons he needs for every group membership he enjoys. NAL builds on this concept of effective icons and promises a system fault tolerance that maintains the application connection pending the reestablishment of server connection.

NAL and Intelligent Update of User Desktop

In addition to taking advantage of other third-party vendors that write their own sections of the Msbatch.inf or similar files, and to be included in the Windows 95 setup process, an "Intelligent Update Process" is expected from the NetWare programmers. This process will add new login script commands that check the workstation for the latest version of NETX, VLMS, and Microsoft Client for NetWare, and will, if necessary, install the latest updates of these programs. Further, given the dynamic nature of 32-bit software, this NetWare Client 32 will make the administrator's tasks easier by dynamically tuning such items as IPX sockets and the number of shell connections that used to be statically set in the Net.cfg file.

The Client 32 will be run either as a DOS TSR or as a Windows 95 VxD. Novell is in the process of developing client-side NetWare Loadable Module features for the desktop. Known as NetWare ISO Subsystem, NIOS loads as a VxD in the Windows 95 Registry. Among the features that can be loaded on the workstation will be Network Management Instrumentation Agents supporting the industry standard Simple Network Management Protocol (SNMP). This type of management protocol allows communication with management applications such as NetWare Management System, HP OpenView, and SunNet Manager.

In addition to all these features, NetWare Client 32 supports the Windows 95 long file-name feature and the NetWare RSA security feature of the VLMs. NetWare RSA adds security to the packets sent from the workstation and returned from the server to the user by adding signatures to the packet. This of course adds overhead to the packets but provides additional security to restricted areas of the NetWare system.

Comparing NetWare Client 32 and Microsoft Client for NetWare

If you want to decide between the use of NetWare Client 32 or Microsoft Client for NetWare, you need to answer the following questions about the NetWare Client 32 when more information is available or when the Client is itself available:

1. Microsoft Client for NetWare sets up global DOS VMS drive mappings as if it had a Windows 3.*x* System.ini [NetWare] section setting equal to "NWShareHandles-true". What is the default setting for NetWare Client 32 and is it changeable?

2. NetWare Client 32 supports long file names, but how will it handle user profiles that involve the use of long file names in the profile such as "Network Neighborhood" or "Start menu," which are Windows 95 features?

3. Microsoft Client for NetWare enables you to update the User.dat file and the \\server\sys\mail*user_id* copy automatically, along with copying profiles from that directory to a workstation if automatic updating is set. Is there such a Windows 95 profile within Client 32? Will NetWare Client 32 provide for such updating of both the user.dat and the menu and desktop profiles?

4. Windows 95 does not have specific Novell NetWare Drv Control Panel icons for NetWare items. What will Client 32 provide for fine tuning? Will this be controllable by the administrator using tools such as Remote Registry and system policy settings?

5. Is there administrative control over any user change to NetWare Client 32, such as that which is available with profiles, User.dat, and Microsoft Client for NetWare?

6. In NetWare Client 32 is there any parallel for file and printer sharing that allows bindery-based user level access control for local workstations? If not, is there any support for the Microsoft feature that otherwise requires the Microsoft Client for NetWare?

7. Is there a Novell NetWare equivalent to the Microsoft Mspserv.exe as a 32-bit replacement for real mode RPRINTER? Mspserv.exe requires the use of the Microsoft Client for NetWare, and RPRINTER the use of the real mode NetWare protocol and client.

8. What will be the NetWare Client 32 equivalent of Net.cfg and its settings? Will there still be a real mode configuration file or will there be a special Ini text file or a set within the Windows 95 Registry? If these settings are in the Registry, they would be available in the Registry Editor and Remote Registry services, but what about the Microsoft System Policy Editor? Will there be a NetWare Remote Registry changing piece of software instead?

These questions are posed as considerations for the NetWare administrator who might prefer the idea of a NetWare 32 client, but wants to know about its ability to provide administrative features such as those available with the Microsoft Client for NetWare.

The importance of these questions for the NetWare administrator is that Microsoft has built a set of services and administrative tools upon the prerequisite use of the Microsoft Client for NetWare. Novell, on the other hand, is building its set of NetWare Client 32 features to support the NetWare 4.*x* foundation of NetWare Directory Services. The choice of which 32-bit protected mode client to use will depend upon the features that the administrator needs for best supporting the NetWare connectivity and providing the most appropriate administrative features.

Microsoft's File and Print Sharing Services for NetWare

With Windows for Workgroups 3.1 and 3.11, Microsoft introduced peer-to-peer networking into the Windows environment. In moving from its version 3.1 of Windows for Workgroups to version 3.11, Microsoft improved the protocol problems caused by a NetBEUI characteristic of not being routeable from segment to ring to another segment or ring. The peer-to-peer features of Windows for Workgroups include the ability to designate workstation directories and printers as being shareable across the network by other Windows for Workgroups workstations. This sharing can be restricted by passwords, which are set for either read-only or full access or both. In Windows for Workgroups 3.11 there is also a way of disabling this file and print sharing feature on a workstation by explicitly running the Admincfg.exe program on the workstation, which creates the binary workgroups workstation configuration file, Wfwsys.cfg.

Windows 95 introduces two significant administrative features:

- Registry control over the peer-to-peer file and print sharing.
- Two mutually exclusive means of providing security for workstation resource sharing. These means are the resource security sharing that is the full access or read-only password basis of Windows for Workgroups 3.11, or the user-level security basis that depends upon the security system of the NetWare server(s) or the Windows NT server(s).

NetWare Bindery-Based Peer-to-Peer Security

The two different ways to control access security to a specific Windows 95 workstation are share-level security and user-level security. As in Windows for Workgroups 3.11, share-level security requires you to designate whether you want to password protect access to share directories or printers. With directories you can establish two levels of passwords: free access and read-only access. The password is then the same for all users for each level of shared access.

With Windows 95, there is a user-level security that is based on the user type security structure of either Windows NT or NetWare. In either of these user-based approaches the user list and validation is conducted at the more secure server: the Windows NT domain controller server or a designated NetWare server. This discussion focuses on the use of a NetWare server as provider of user-level security.

On Windows 95 workstations that run Nwredir.vxd (Microsoft Client for NetWare), you can establish file and printer sharing for NetWare networks as the means of controlling access to that workstation's files and attached printers. This file and printer sharing for NetWare networks is supported by Nwserver.vxd (dee fig. 3.25), which requires Nwredir.vxd to be installed and functioning. Nwredir.vxd cannot be run on the same machine that is using the Server Messaging Block (SMB) of the Microsoft Client for Microsoft networks and the Vserver.vxd, which is the file and printer sharing for Microsoft networks.

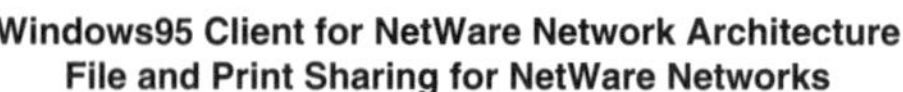

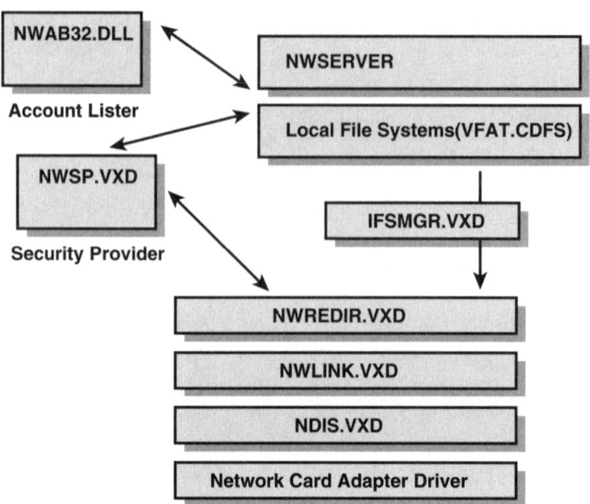

Figure 3.25
Windows 95 architecture supporting NetWare file and print sharing page.

The file and printer sharing for NetWare networks is established in the protected mode with the Nwserver.vxd, which is supported by the Nwsp.vxd, the virtual device driver that handles the security for the Windows 95 workstation sharing of its files and printers. Because the file and printer sharing for NetWare networks depends on the bindery security lists from the NetWare server, an additional function is necessary to read the Netware server's bindery. This function is provided through the Nwab32.dll, which is responsible for reading the NetWare server's bindery account list.

File and printer sharing for NetWare networks is a "service" that is added through the Network icon in Control Panel or during the setup process (whether during the manual process or during the automated Msbatch.inf process). When installing file and printer sharing for NetWare networks, you designate a NetWare server that will be used to authenticate the user and the user's access to the Windows 95 workstation resources. On multiple server networks, this need not be the user's logon or preferred server. You might even designate one server to be the authenticator for all users of Windows 95 workstation-based resources. Users do not have to be actual users of the designated NetWare authenticating server; they must only be established users who might be members of groups on that server.

The designated server will have a Windows pass-through account through which the user accounts are checked and validated. This Windows pass-through account is not itself protected with a password.

The designation of the directories and printers to be shared is something that is done on the user level on the workstation. After the file and printer sharing for NetWare networks is established on the workstation, the rest is up to the user. As discussed in Chapter 4, "Managing the Workstation and User," file and printer sharing for NetWare networks is something that can be restricted by the administrator.

In the Windows 95 Explorer, which shows the workstation's directories, the mouse is right-clicked to select the directory, and then the user clicks on the Sharing option in the Explorer menu, and then provides a share name to the directories. The icons for the drive or folder that is already shared will have a hand over the items, as if offering the item to others (see fig. 3.26). If the Windows 95 workstation owner wants to allow access but not have all users see the share, a dollar sign ($) should be appended to the end of the share name during the designation of the shared directory by the user. Thus, the C:\data directory is established as the Data$ share directory. Only users who know about this data directory and designate it directly will be able to access it; it will not show up during any browsing for shared directories on that workstation.

Figure 3.26

An example of a shared drive.

The process can also be achieved through the My Computer icon, which enables you to view the drives and folders on the local machine. There is a sharing choice on the My Computer File menu. The user enters the share name if the share level is by user level, and then clicks on the Add button to access the bindery names on the referenced server. User-level access can be **R**ead Only, **F**ull Access, or **C**ustom (see fig. 3.27).

Figure 3.27

An example of the use of the bindery for access security.

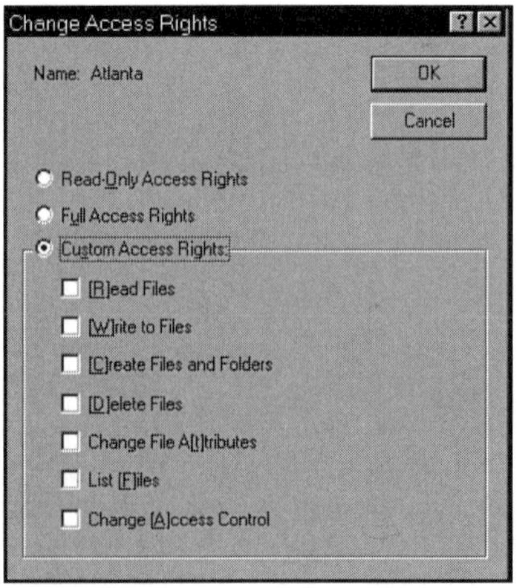

When file and printer sharing for NetWare networks is established a NetWare file server is designated as the reference server. The Add Users Screen indicates that the designated server is shown with the screen label "Obtain list from" and then the server name. On the left side of the screen are the users and groups as listed in that server's bindery.

When working with specific directories, the access rights can be customized beyond the basic read-only or full access categories. Note in figure 3.28 that you can use more NetWare security-like categories of action.

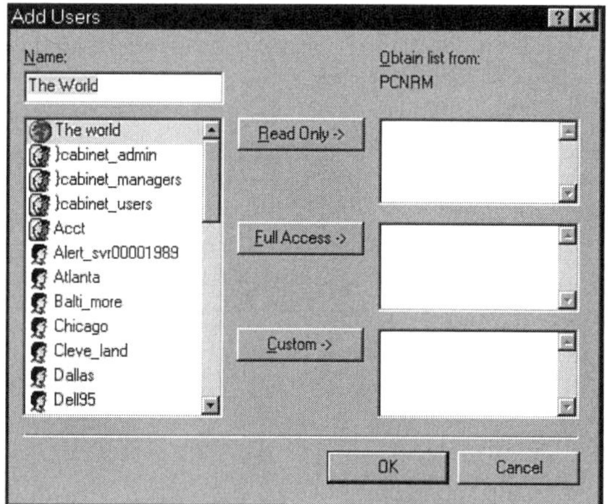

Figure 3.28
Customized user-level access referencing the bindery rights access control categories.

For restrictions beyond the full access or read only categories, you can apply Read, Write, Create, Delete, Change file attributes, list files, and change access control rights for particular users or groups of users established in the bindery.

NetWare Protocol Support for Microsoft File and Print Sharing

When file and printer sharing for NetWare networks is added as a service on the Windows 95 workstation, user-level security is installed with the authenticating server indicated. Nwserver.vxd supports the NetWare NetWare Core Protocol (NCP). NCP is what the workstation uses on top of the NetWare client to make file and print requests to the server. NetWare's Service Advertising Protocol (SAP) is established on the workstation to make the workstation known to the network. NCP and SAP support NetWare utilities such as FILER, RIGHTS, SYSCON, MAP, SLIST, VOLINFO, PCONSOLE, and CAPTURE, which can be used with the Windows 95 workstation that is running file and printer sharing for NetWare networks.

Significant advantages exist for a NetWare network with users who need peer-to-peer sharing of a Windows 95 workstation or more than one station. The IPX/SPX protocol can be used so that others can access either the NetWare servers or the file and printer sharing for network's Windows 95 workstation. The Windows 95 workstation can also take advantage of the co-opting of the NetWare server-based bindery security system. You can use NetWare administrative tools such as VOLINFO to monitor disk drive space, or FILER to manage file and directory structures.

Practically speaking, the workstation appears and works as a NetWare server except for logons, although a VLM user already logged in to a NetWare server can log on using the /Ns switch or use the logon button in NWUSER. The NETX user can, however, use the ATTACH command to get to the Windows 95 NetWare server. The Windows 95 station running file and printer sharing for NetWare networks appears as a NetWare server for a user who uses the SLIST command at the DOS prompt or who uses the File Manager of Windows 3.*x* (see fig. 3.29).

Figure 3.29

Windows 3.1 and the NWUSER VLM showing the shared drive on a Windows 95 workstation.

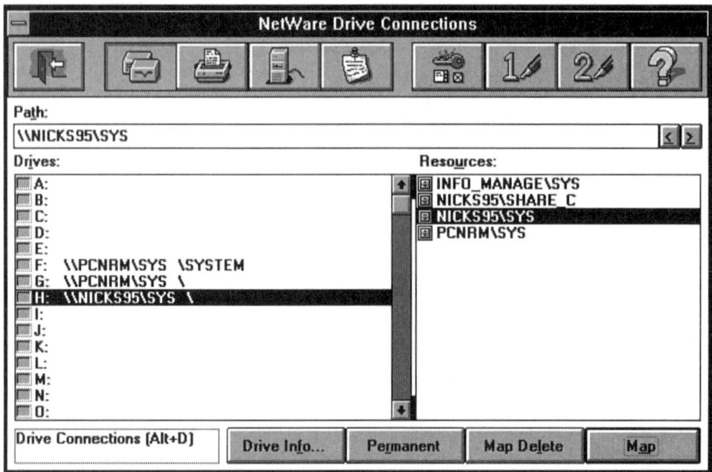

A user on the NetWare network need not be running Windows 95 Microsoft Client for NetWare or even be running Windows 95 to access a Windows 95 workstation that is set up as providing shared files and printers. The NETX or VLM client running DOS or Windows can access the Windows 95 NetWare server workstation and access the directories and print queues of that server workstation. The shared directory can be accessed as it if were a volume on that user's station, so that John's database directory would appear as johns\database. The Windows user can reference that share as \\Johns\database using the Microsoft-created Universal Naming Convention (UNC). Within UNC, the NetWare server shows up as \\server\volume without the NetWare ":" associated with the server volumes.

Network Performance Concerns for File and Print Sharing

If you are entertaining the idea of running file and printer sharing for NetWare networks, you should be familiar with the NetWare protocol structure beyond IPX/SPX and must also be familiar with the NCP and SAP protocols. The use of file and printer sharing for NetWare networks means utilization of NCP with the option of using SAP. When you set up file and printer sharing, you have two options for deciding how users will be able to see the Windows 95 NetWare server: the workgroup advertising mode or the NetWare-based SAP protocol. Both have network traffic consequences.

Although some NetWare network traffic scenarios need to be considered, there are some practical implications regarding the choice of Workgroup or SAP methods. With the Workgroup method, only Windows for Workgroups 3.11 or Windows 95 stations would see the shares offered on the network. With the NetWare Service Advertising Protocol active, the Windows 95 NetWare server will appear on the SLIST run by the traditional NetWare client workstation.

In terms of network traffic, real NetWare servers use the Service Advertising Protocol to identify themselves to the network—especially to the other NetWare servers—for identification and routing purposes. Whenever numerous NetWare servers are on a cable or enterprise backbone, SAP chatting can cause real concerns. Servers are, by default, set to send out SAP messages every 60 seconds on the network, creating network traffic. The Microsoft Windows 95 Resource Kit contains the following notation with regard to SAP-based browsing to see what shares are available on the network:

> SAP browsing has a theoretical limit of 7,000 systems for browsing, and a practical limit of 1,500 systems. Therefore, SAP browsing will not work in a peer networking environment that consists of a larger number of computers. For a large peer network, use Workgroup Advertising.

You should be alerted to the possibility of a Windows 95 workstation SAP being the nearest server to a workstation's NetWare client attempting to "GetNearestServer." Two suggestions need to be explored. The first suggestion is the use of a preferred server in the workstations Net.cfg or the Windows 95 network setup. The second suggestion is to make sure that the Windows 95 workstation running the SAP has a directory called NWSYSVOL\LOGIN with a Login.exe file located there. This stub file redirects the logon to a real NetWare server.

As an administrator, you also need to consider traffic of Workgroup Advertising methods, especially the number of stations of your network that provides peer-to-peer servicing.

Interesting Possibilities for File and Print Sharing

Network administrators have some interesting tools and features for their use on a networked Windows 95 workstation running file and printer sharing for NetWare networks and the required Microsoft Client for NetWare. These tools and features include the following:

- A workstation that appears as a NetWare server without the cost of a copy of the extra NetWare software.
- A peer-to-peer workstation that has user security features. This includes the user being logged on to at least one real NetWare server.
- A workstation that can be set to only allow a user access to the local hard drive and operating system if that user is validated at logon time as a NetWare user in a real NetWare server's bindery.

Even the administrator who does not want to allow peer-to-peer sharing might come up with appropriate network uses for these features listed above.

Some DOS TSRs that run on the non-Windows 95 network duplex write to the server and another location. These TSRs might be able to take advantage of the other location being a Windows 95 workstation with a large disk drive for such fault tolerant programs.

Organizations that need access to older files and large files such as CAD or desktop publishing applications might consider storage servers consisting of a user security-based Windows 95 workstation. Such a workstation would be available for accessing data files, but just accessing data files would not require the caching capability of the NetWare server. Obviously, running applications from this server would not be advised as this is not a recommended use of peer-to-peer functionality.

Another option for such a Windows 95 file and printer sharing for NetWare networks workstation would be as a CD-ROM server or even a print server.

Microsoft's Print Server for NetWare Versus NetWare's RPRINTER

With the introduction of NetWare 3.*x*'s RPRINTER and NetWare 4.*x*'s NPRINTER implementation, Novell provides the NetWare administrator with a free TSR memory resident program to provide the local workstation's printer ports to the NetWare server. This remote printer function allows for printers remote from the server to service print queues on the server (see fig. 3.30). The administrator sets up a printer in PCONSOLE and designates it with a printer number, printer name, and the remote printer port designation. The printer is then assigned to a print queue, and the channel is created between the established print queue (which can then be used with the CAPTURE command) and the printer setup. By running RPRINTER with its

NetWare 4.*x* NPRINTER parallel, the administrator establishes the connection between the printer port on the workstation and the numbered printer created in PCONSOLE.

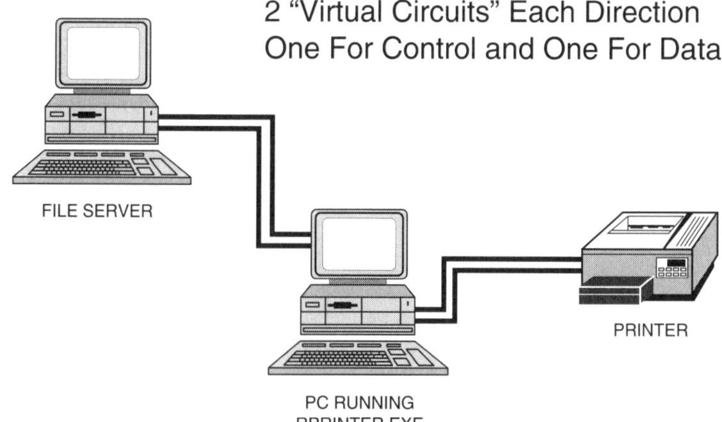

Figure 3.30

The real mode RPRINTER process using the SPX protocol.

RPRINTER Problems

Although based on a workable concept, RPRINTER presents the NetWare administrator with no end of problems because of the nature of how it works both as a memory resident TSR and as a NetWare program.

As a memory resident TSR, RPRINTER takes up workstation real mode memory and disappears from memory when the workstation is rebooted, either intentionally or when the workstation hangs while running Windows or anything else. RPRINTER is best loaded when run as part of a batch file that first unloads RPRINTER in case the workstation was rebooted and the connection to the server has been lost.

You need to unload RPRINTER first to avoid the server telling you that the print queue requested is slotted to another workstation. You should then account for the time it sometimes takes to connect to the server by building in an on error and loop statement to work through any experienced time delays in making the connection. An example of such a set of lines in the batch file follows:

```
:Loop
RPRINTER Print Server Printer # -r : remove the numbered printer connection
RPRINTER Print Server Printer # : load the printer IF Errorlevel goto loop : if
➥rprinter does not load right away
```

On a Windows 3.*x*-based computer, an RPRINTER batch file like the sample shown here can also be placed in the Winstart.bat file. By placing RPRINTER here, it is unloaded and then reloaded in Windows global memory where it does not take up any real mode memory, but is available to the workstation and hence to the network. Because RPRINTER disappears when Windows is unloaded, administrators often put the printer lines in the batch file that starts Windows on that workstation, unloading and then reloading the connection when the workstation is back in DOS mode. This approach resolves the RPRINTER and memory resident problem also for Windows 95 workstations that run the real mode NetWare clients.

Another level of RPRINTER problems is created by the way the program works as a NetWare client workstation application communicating with the server. RPRINTER creates a virtual channel between the server's print server NLM, PSERVER.NLM (or NetWare 4.*x*'s version NPRINTER.NLM) and the printer port on the remote workstation. This virtual channel is supported by the SPX part of the IPX/SPX protocol. IPX is "general delivery" and only requires acknowledgment of correct receipt of the packet; SPX is sometimes referred to as a "guaranteed delivery protocol" and bases its virtual connection over time.

When the server sends an SPX packet to the workstation, it waits for a response from the workstation within 540 workstation tics or about 27 seconds. If a response is not received within this time, another packet is sent in the form of an "are you still there?" query that expects a response within only a few seconds. If the sender receives nothing as a response, it assumes the non-presence of the receiver. For the RPRINTER process, a non-presence assumption breaks the connection between the print server on the server and the RPRINTER workstation, causing the print job to remain in the print queue on the server.

Changes can be made to make the RPRINTER accomodate the often busy nature of the network. The network administrator might try changing the small default settings of SPX timing in the workstation's net-oriented Net.cfg file. In that Net.cfg file, you might set the SPX timing settings to between 2,000 and 3,000 tics. This setting provides between two and two and a half minutes per SPX process or close to five minutes of grace period in the communication process between the server's print server and the workstations printer port. These new settings eliminate common problems with RPRINTER, but require the change to be made in the real mode NET.CFG file that is not used by the Microsoft Client for NetWare.

Another set of issues facing the real mode NetWare client is the matter of the print header and print tail settings. The default settings of 64 bytes for the print header and 16 bytes for the print tail are used by the network shell, NETX, or the VLM Netx.vlm. The problem is that these lengths are often not enough to contain full messages between the printing software and the printer. In the print header the shell truncates the message so that the printer does not get the full message or set of printing instructions. The print tail is a set of instructions that might be sent to reset the printer to its default settings.

To determine if truncation is the problem, check to see if the printer flashes the light showing receipt of the print job. If nothing happens, you have a problem. The solution is to set these values to print header = 255, and print tail = 64, to make sure that the job gets the proper instructions to both set up a complex job and to reset the printer afterward. These settings are established in the Net.cfg file, which modifies the real mode client settings.

Now that you know RPRINTER's weaknesses and the problems it can cause, you may be interested in a replacement. The Microsoft Client for NetWare includes a 32-bit replacement for RPRINTER, known as the Microsoft Print Server for NetWare (Mpserv.exe). This is a "service" that you can add to the workstation to provide remote workstation servicing of the server's printer server print queue (see fig. 3.31). The service is not subject to RPRINTER's real mode limitations.

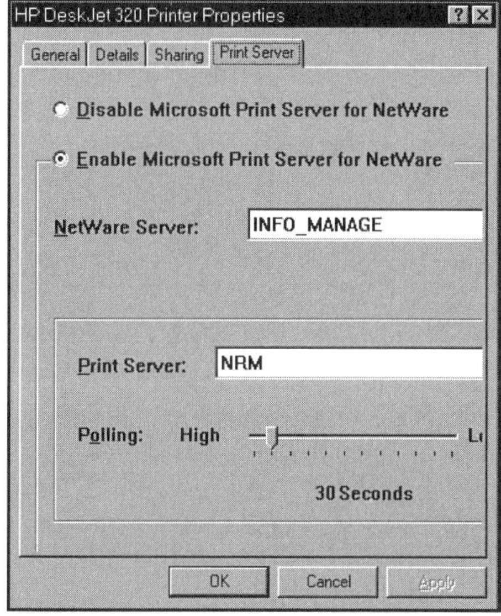

Figure 3.31

The Mpserv.exe 32-bit replacement for RPRINTER.

The Microsoft Print Server for NetWare enables a Windows 95 workstation to receive print jobs from a server's print server. To install the Microsoft Print Server for NetWare, click on Network icon and choose Add, then Service. Click on the Microsoft icon, and then specify the disk or PRTAGENT directory where Msperv.exe and Mspserv.inf are located. Click on OK and the Microsoft print agent for NetWare networks will appear. Click on OK again, and the item will be installed.

To access these print services, you can use the Network icon in the Control Panel. Click on add a network component, then choose the list of "services" as opposed to adapter, protocol, or client. Next, choose the "have Disk Option" and type the path name to the location of the CD-ROM \ADMIN95\NETTOOLS\PRTAGENT directory. This directory can be placed on the server in a similar structured directory set.

To activate the Microsoft Print Server for NetWare, click on the Printers icon in Control Panel and then double-click on the printer installed on the workstation. This will bring up the print management screen for that printer. Choose Properties from the Printer menu. The tab choices are General, Details, Sharing, and Print Server. Click on Print Server and enable Microsoft Print Server for NetWare. This will then allow the choice of a NetWare file server and a NetWare print server running on that file server. These settings allow the workstation to service the remote queue for that Pserver.

Because Mspserv runs in the workstation's background it uses no resources except when it periodically polls for data packets at a designated interval. The program uses the NetWare Queue Management Services (QMS) Application Program Interface, which enables it to attach to a print queue. Receiving an identity handle from that print queue, allows Mspserv to poll the NetWare print server periodically to print jobs. The default polling period is set at 30 seconds.

The polling process timer is adjustable for different workstation and network traffic considerations. For those workstations that will be serving multiple applications and have a high load on them, you might want to use a long period of time between polling—three minutes or greater. This lengthy interval between polling might also be required for busy network segments. If the workstation is not heavily used or if you would like to make network print jobs available as quickly as possible, polling can be set for as often as every 15 seconds.

When notified of a job coming to it, Mspserv will receive print job information in the form of a header. These instructions include any print banner text or number of copy information. The data is then sent to the workstation from the print server and the Mspserv receives the print job and uses win-32 calls to deliver the job to the local printer port and printer. Upon completion of the job, Mspserv notifies the NetWare print server that the job is completed.

Summary of Integration Options

You must choose the protocol/client option that best fits the workstation or network. These choices revolve around the real mode services used and the need for NDS support. Other factors are the features of the Microsoft Client for NetWare and ways of dealing with the DOS global drive mapping issue.

- **Option One:** Running the real mode Ipx.com or IPXODI protocol along with the real mode NETX or VLMS client shell.

  This option is required when you need 16-bit real mode connectivity and network management software. This option, however, does not allow for long file names that support much of the user profile pieces.

- **Option Two:** Running the real mode IPXODI with the Microsoft Client for NetWare.

  This option supports any IPXODI-related TSRs that can be loaded before logon and that can provide support to both Windows and DOS applications. The drawback is the need for conventional memory.

  Microsoft Client for NetWare still provides the long file name support, reconnection when servers go down and come back up, and file system-supported client-side caching of network files.

- **Option Three:** Running the Microsoft "IPX/SPX-compatible protocol"—their 32-bit implementation of the IPX protocol—along with the 32-bit Microsoft Client for NetWare.

  This option is not useable for the NDS client or for workstations needing real mode TSRs. Otherwise, this option provides support for long file names, user profiles, file and printer sharing for NetWare Networks, and the use of the 32-bit Mspserv.

- **Option Four:** Running the Novell NetWare Client 32, which is a protected mode 32-bit implementation of both the IPX/SPX protocol and the former NETX/VLM client shell.

  As of this writing the NetWare Client 32 is still being developed and tested by Novell. When released, it will be an attractive alternative to the Microsoft Client for NetWare, especially when NDS is required.

Whatever decisions you make in regard to the client and protocol being used, these choices can be modified as changes are made by the vendors of real mode pieces, NetWare's Client 32, and the NDS support from Microsoft Client for NetWare 4.*x*.

Managing the Workstation and User

In the network environment there are many criteria used to evaluate Windows 95 and its impact on the end user productivity (which is the business of the network and should be the focus of the network administrator). Among the considerations are the advantages of Windows 95 over the existing Windows 3.*x* systems, and the costs of any hardware upgrades that must be done to upgrade computers to be viable foundations for running Windows 95.

For the network administrator, the criteria is focused more on the ability to manage the network. Most specifically, the network administrator is concerned with the ability to deliver the end user's requirements for business productivity on a networked Windows 95 workstation. This chapter focuses on the Windows 95 provisions for managing the user and the workstation.

Establishing Levels of Control

When a user sits down at a Windows 95 computer on a NetWare and/or Windows NT network, four elements must work together for successful and productive computing: the computer, the user, the network, and Windows 95. The administrator needs to manage these elements in such a way as to provide the user with a dependable computer user interface that will provide access to their applications with minimal problems and downtime.

The network receives a significant amount of attention from the administrator. The Windows 3.*x* environment is single user-oriented and is designed to be managed by the user. As this chapter demonstrates, Windows 95 offers the administrator the ability to manage the user and the workstation across the network.

To provide this optimal environment for the end user, the network administrator needs to establish a system of controls. These controls involve these elements:

- Understanding the elements of the Windows 95 Control Panel
- Limiting or controlling user access to the Control Panel icons
- Controlling or minimizing the need for support calls
- Controlling or minimizing support time
- Anticipating and monitoring problems

These controls enable the integration of hardware and software elements with the user and his or her corporate responsibilities. These controls are means of administrating and of fine-tuning the system. Management means establishing or understanding the control elements, and deciding how to implement or tune these control elements.

In both Windows 3.*x* and Windows 95 the Control Panel enables the user to manage the workstation's configuration. These versions differ, however, in the amount of control that the administrator has over the user's ability to manage the workstation by adjusting matters in the Windows Control Panel.

In addition to these elements of control, the administrator is concerned with controlling his or her own use of time. Experience teaches the administrator the types of Windows 3.*x* issues that take up the most support effort and time, and this learning goes into the establishment of controls and techniques or third-party software implementation that gives the administrator more control over how time is spent managing the network.

Among the elements or ingredients that administrators have adopted in the control over their administrative time are the software applications that either give remote control over the end user's workstation or distribute software and text file changes to the end user's workstation without the administrator having to physically go to it.

A final element of control is the putting into place these elements that enable the administrator to monitor elements of the system and to take appropriate actions when alerted to potential problems.

Improved Management with Windows 95

Windows 95 enables you to configure the workstation and the user's environment to maintain connection with the network so that the user can access applications and data. All of the necessary configurations are established through the Windows 95 Registry.

By contrast, on the Windows 3.*x*-based NetWare client workstation, seven or eight text files must be managed to create the user's networked Windows environment. These files are: the computer's Config.sys and Autoexec.bat files, the network component's Net.cfg file, possibly the Microsoft Network Device Interface Specification Protocol.ini file, and the four Windows' initialization files (Win.ini, System.ini, Progman.ini, and Control.ini).

Figure 4.1 illustrates the factors that the administrator must balance when managing the Windows 3.*x*-based network client. These factors include the following:

- Managing seven or eight distinct files
- The relationship between the network security and the program icons in the Progman.ini file
- The difference between hardware and user configuration files
- The time spent managing these configuration files

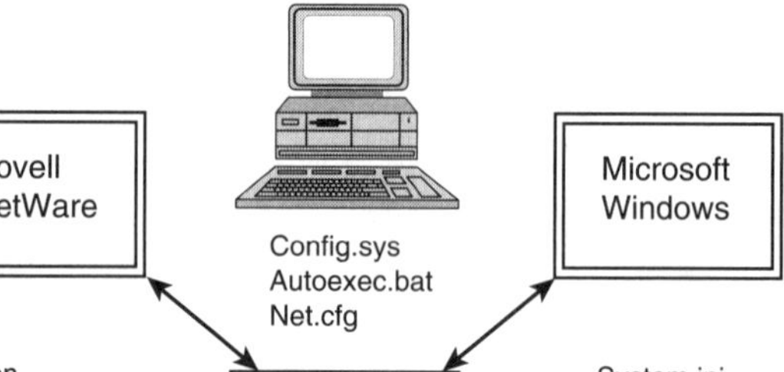

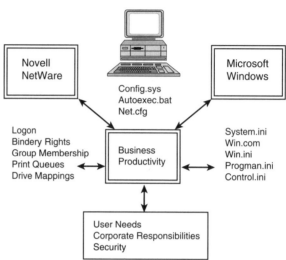

Figure 4.1
The Administrator's toolbox—the Windows 3.1/NetWare configuration files.

Reducing the Number of Configuration Files

This discussion stengthens your understanding of the contributions that Windows 95 makes to your ability to manage the user and the workstation. One of these major contributions is the elimination of these configuration files and their replacement by a singular Registry structure. Table 4.1 describes the configuration files that must be managed.

Table 4.1
Windows 3.*x* Network Workstation Configuration Files

File Name	Description
Config.sys	Loads devices and sets environment
Autoexec.bat	Sets paths and loads TSRs and variables
Net.cfg	Configures network card, protocol, and client shell
System.ini	Loads device drivers
Win.ini	Maintains user preferences
Control.ini	Keeps color schemes and screen saver passwords
Progman.ini	Data file for Program Manager, which serves as the Windows user menu

Although you must learn much about the structure and language of the Registry, having one location for the configuration issues, and having the ability to access this file across the network, makes the management of the user and the workstation significantly easier.

Controlling User Access to Programs

In the Windows 3.*x* and network environment you must work at the relationship between the network's user security system and the Windows Progman.ini file. Progman.ini is the data file for Program Manager, the Windows menu program. Figure 4.2 illustrates the relationship between the network security system and the user's desktop program access icons controlled by Progman.ini.

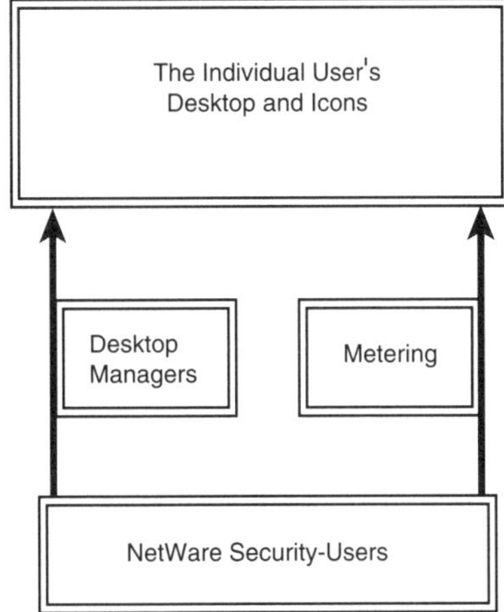

Figure 4.2

Making the user's desktop control - lable through NetWare group membership.

In the network environment, you have the following three levels of control of users accessing programs on the network (in ascending order):

1. **Security-level control through the NetWare bindery or NetWare Directory Services.** Here, you grant users access to the file listing or scanning, read, write, create, and delete rights, along with the rights to modify file attributes like names, and to modify the other users' rights to the files. NetWare blocks access to files and directories unless you specifically grant the rights mentioned.

2. **Application or software metering.** This allows a certain number of users to access files to which they have security rights, but denies that access to users after that certain number of licenses has been used.

3. **Menu or icon access to the application.** The challenge within the networked Windows platform is shaping the user's desktop without giving everyone the same icons or having to manage each desktop by itself.

Solutions for what the user can access in the Windows 3.*x* platform vary, but revolve around a concept similar to NetWare's concept of *effective rights.* Under effective rights, if George gets access to Lotus 1-2-3 because of his membership in the finance network security group, and access to WordPerfect because of his membership in the WordPerfect network security group, and e-mail because of his membership in the network security group "everyone," then you can say that his effective rights are "Lotus123, WordPerfect and Email." Actually, effective rights might be seen as a total of every right the user has in every directory on the network. The variation on the security rights theme would be "effective icons," which would display the icons of a particular application, depending on the user's membership in a particular network user group.

Common solutions to this icon problem include "if member of group 'xxx' then" statements in the login script, or third-party software, such as Saber, Net Tools, and LAN Escort, that evaluate the user's group membership for each part of their icon menu structure and display icons appropriate for the user's membership, or effective icons. These approaches enable the administrator to customize the desktop for the user and provide the icons the user needs to fulfill corporate responsibilities. Some of these approaches require the replacement of Program Manager as part of the solution.

In the Windows 95 environment, the Program Manager is replaced with the Start menu structure. Progman.ini is replaced by the directory structure of the new menu. Whereas Progman.ini is based on the listing of groups of icons, the Start menu structure is based on the presence of the application's Lnk file, which is an object linking and embedding link file pointing toward the application's executible file in the application's folder or directory location. Whereas the Grp file that contains the Windows access icons is a binary file, the Windows 95 Start menu structure is an open structure. These differences make the Windows 95 menu structure more accessible to the administrator than the Windows 3.*x* menu structure.

You can control the user's menu and desktop icon access through the Registry and System Policy Editor structure of Windows 95. You can establish such control by restricting access on the user's desktop to only menu folders and icons that are located in read-only directories on the network servers.

Managing User Versus Hardware Configuration Files

A significant administrative problem exists in the Windows 3.*x* network environment when users move from one computer to another. The five Windows files listed in figure 4.3 need to be in place when Windows starts, but problems exist if the wrong system or hardware files are used.

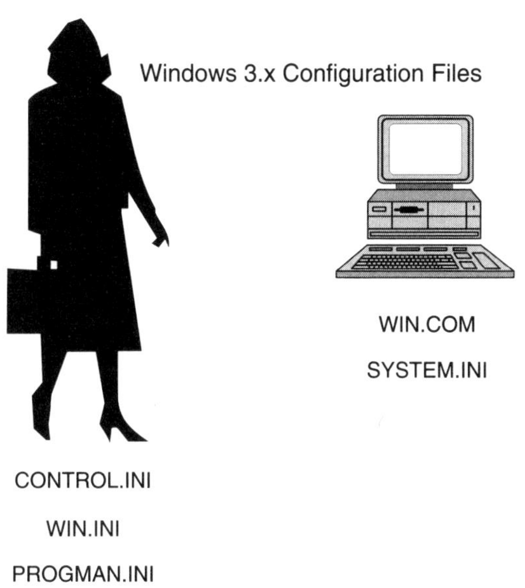

Figure 4.3
Windows 3.x user versus hardware files.

Although the split is not clean, the System.ini and Win.com files are workstation-related and the other Ini files are user-related. Network administrators have been ingenious in working out schemes to make sure that users have their own files copied to the local machines before they start Windows, or to make sure that the workstation hardware files for the current workstation are copied to the user's Windows subdirectory on the network. Some organizations programmed their own scripting or used scripting, such as the INIScriptor by ComputerKnacks, to merge workstation and user configurations at Windows startup and then split them out after the Windows session ended.

The Windows 95 Registry combines two aspects at run time, the System.dat and the User.dat. These two binary files cleanly maintain the two components. Windows 95 will always use the System.dat file of the workstation, but will either use the default User.dat of the workstation or the specific User.dat related to the user. Because each user must log on to the Windows 95 GUI, the Windows 95 system is able to attempt to match the logon user's name with a user's list on the workstation. If the user has been on that station before, a copy of the user's User.dat is stored on that workstation. In a network environment, Windows 95 will even store a copy of the User.dat on the network server, in the user's home directory (Windows NT) or the user's mail directory (NetWare). Windows 95 will even manage the synchronization of the local and server copies of User.dat, updating both at the end of each session of the network user's use of Windows 95.

Remote Management of the User and Workstation

A significant amount of the network administrator's time is spent managing the Windows 3.*x* network computer's configuration files. As shown in figure 4.4, network administrators have turned to both remote control and configuration file management applications to lessen the time spent managing the workstation.

Figure 4.4

Remote configuration management issues—remote control versus e-mail.

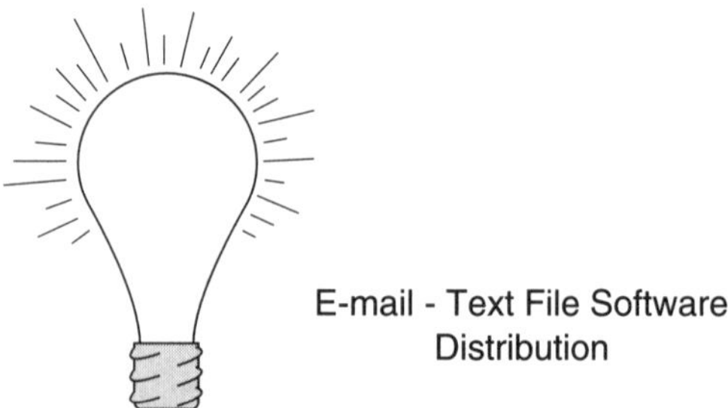

- Using either e-mail or program that runs at logon and checks for distributions for the user
- You can set up jobs on your own time and users receive jobs on their time
- It means you don't have to go there!

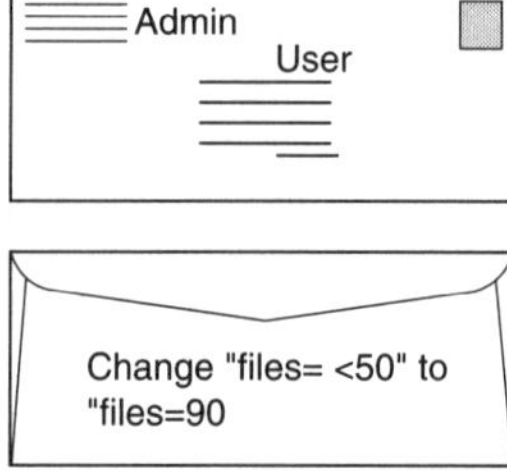

The seven or eight configuration text files are administrative nightmares. It would be a fair estimate to say that the average text file change would take you, the administrator, some 20 minutes per workstation—at least so long as you encounter no surprises and your users don't turn to you with the pleading words, "While you're here, will you please..." Multiply that figure by the number of workstations and very quickly that time becomes full days of text file changes. One step beyond running around to the workstations is using remote control software, which loads as a real mode TSR on the workstation, and which you activate over the network. Going to the workstation by foot or by TSR means negotiating with the user for an appointment and keeping records.

Many administrators have turned to third-party packages—such as Frye Computer System's Software Update and Distribution System, Norton Administrator for Networks, Winstall, and LAN Escort—to distribute text file changes.

These applications enable you to create a distribution on your own time and choose recipients by name, network group, or specifications of computer workstation, hardware, or installed software. These applications perform text file "search and replace" operations by criteria and track who gets and doesn't get the successful job distribution. These text file distribution applications save incredible amounts of time, and therefore money, for organizations that adopt them.

Windows 95 enables you to manage the Registry through the Registry Editor or through the System Policy Editor. Remote Registry editing is made possible through the user of the protected mode network service Remote Registry, which makes the workstation's Registry available to the administrator over the network. The System Policy Editor is used to establish Registry entries for specific workstations or specific users or groups of users. With the System Policy Editor, any changes are made when the user logs on to the network server.

Controlling the User's Activities

With Windows 3.*x* there were some efforts to control the user's ability to change the environment. The Sysedit.exe program file was kept out of the program icons given to the user during the installation program. This program allowed direct editing of the System.ini, Win.ini, Config.sys, and Autoexec.bat files. There were also restrictions that could be placed on the users to prevent them from making changes to the Program Manager configuration.

The Windows User's Group Network System Engineer program is an example of third-party applications that are availble to make Windows more understandable to the administrator. The screen provides the settings that can be made directly to the Progman.ini file to restrict the user's ability to access and change Program Manager settings.

Another problem facing the Windows 3.*x* NetWare administrator is the ASCII text file nature of the configuration files that sometimes leads users to modify their own files, thereby creating support problems. This ASCII text file nature also means the administrator cannot always take advantage of the restrictions in the Progman.ini file. You can set restrictions in the [Restrictions] section of Progman.ini to prevent users from accessing File, Run in Program Manager, or from using Options, Saving Settings on Exit. The problem is that users can edit Progman.ini and remove the administrator restrictions. The administrator who tries to prevent this by attributing the file as Read Only is greeted by the startup message that announced to the user that Windows is being started in read-only mode.

Windows 95 gives you better control over what changes the user can make on the Windows 95 workstation by not only providing detailed restriction categories, but also through the nature of the Registry files User.dat and System.dat. These files are binary files and are not accessible to the user through text editors. You can even remove the Regedit.exe file from user access.

In summary, Windows 95 addresses administrative matters that are problems to the management of the Windows 3.*x* environment on the network. Windows 95 provides the administrator with both a structure and management tools to work with that new structure. Although there will be third-party tools available to add to that ability, network administrators will appreciate the design of Windows 95 management, which took into consideration the feedback that Microsoft received from network administrators.

The Registry Structure

Windows 95 is organized around a central directory-like hierarchical structure, called the Registry. Other than for backward compatibility, Windows 95 no longer needs any of the "traditional" seven or eight configuration text files—much of their content transfers to the Registry. Figure 4.5 provides an overview of the Registry structure.

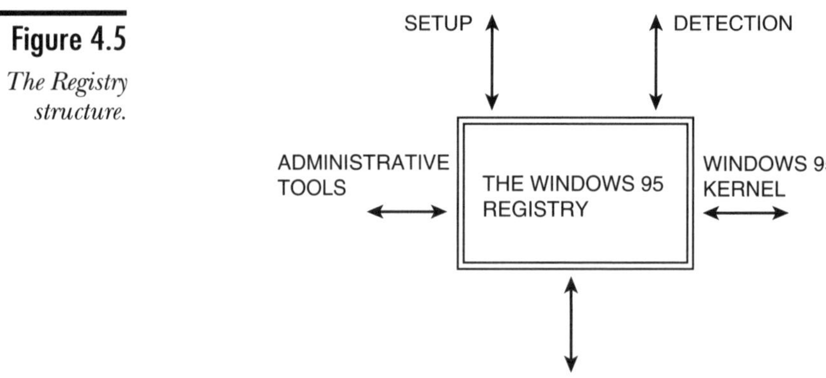

Figure 4.5
The Registry structure.

Microsoft has created a structure that provides you with the tools to manage workstations and users across the network, by replacing the multiple text file Ini structure with the Registry. Developers have benefited from Windows NT and its registry structure to build a basis for network management. Although the full benefit of this structure is only now becoming available for workstations running the Microsoft Client for NetWare, parts are available for the real mode NetWare client as well.

Another feature that significantly eases managing users and workstations on the network is the clean split between workstation and user data. In Windows 3.*x*, you had to manually divide the files between the workstation-related Win.com and System.ini files, and the user-related Win.ini, Control.ini, and Progman.ini files. Network administrators worked out batch files that copy files so that users had their user files copied to the local workstation or the hardware files copied over to their file server directories. Windows 95's Registry divides the User.dat and System.dat files, copies files back and forth to the server, and updates User.dat after a session, maintaining current copies on both the workstation and the server. These files are not accessible through text-file editing.

The Registry Editor

Using the Registry Editor (see fig. 4.6) is the best way to study the Registry, because you can key around the terrain and view the structure. Be advised, however, that you should neither leave the Registry Editor within range of the typical end user nor, usually, use it to modify the Windows 95 workstation.

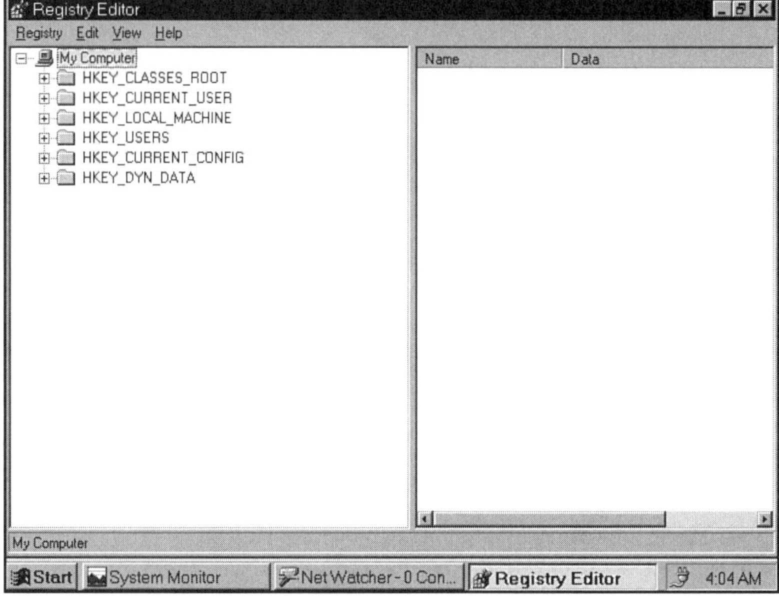

Figure 4.6

The Registry Editor shows the directory-like structure of the Registry.

The Registry is a directory-like structure that has six divisions organized around the structure of keys and named starting with the Hkey expression. The following six areas form the first level of the hierarchical structure:

- **Hkey_Local_Machine.** This Registry section (see fig. 4.7) houses specific computer and workstation configuration matters and maintains serial port and modem communication information. It enables you to track multiple configurations. Bus enumerators build the Registry hardware structure or tree, providing unique identifiers for disks, monitors, and Plug and Play devices. Hkey_Local_Machine maintains network logon information, and tracks some installed software information as well. Additionally, it is the source of the System.dat configuration file.

Figure 4.7

Registry Editor view of the Hkey_Local_Machine.

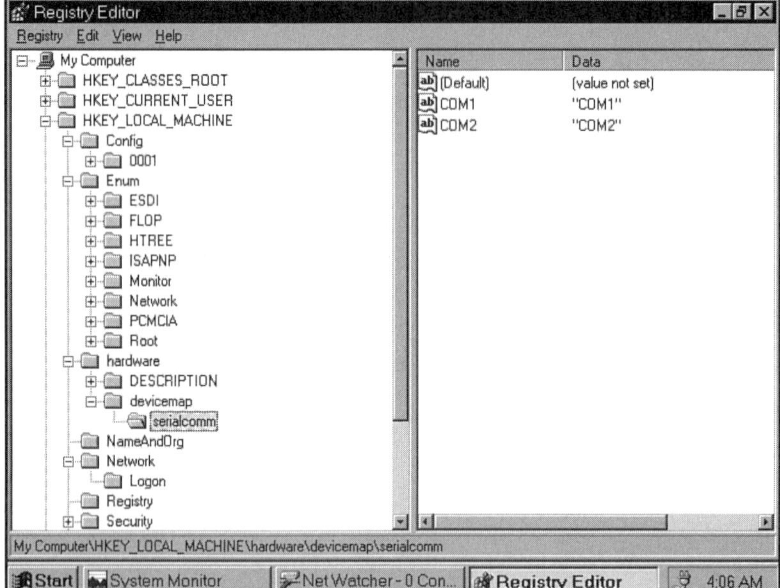

- **Hkey_Classes_Root.** This section (see fig. 4.8) maintains object linking and embedding data with association mapping to support drag-and-drop operations. It also tracks aspects of the Windows 95 user interface, including shortcuts. Shortcuts are actually OLE objects that create links between their graphic representation and the programs. Additionally, this section provides for the compatibility with Windows 3.1's registration database, Regit.dat.

- **Hkey_Users.** Windows 95 maintains information about default users and specific users who log on to the workstation. This section (see fig. 4.9) stores user settings and desktop configurations, and tracks matters including AppEvents, Control Panel, keyboard layouts, network, and most-recently used applications. *AppEvents* are sound bytes maintained for specific system events and then made audible. The data here is partially provided by the System Profile Editor, which is used to create and delete user profiles.

- **Hkey_Dyn_Data.** This area (see fig. 4.10) houses dynamic status information for devices and provides support for the new Plug and Play features. This data is cached into workstation RAM for incidents in which Windows 95 needs fast modification and retrieval. Windows 95 refreshes the data during every system startup and any changes made so that the memory data is always current.

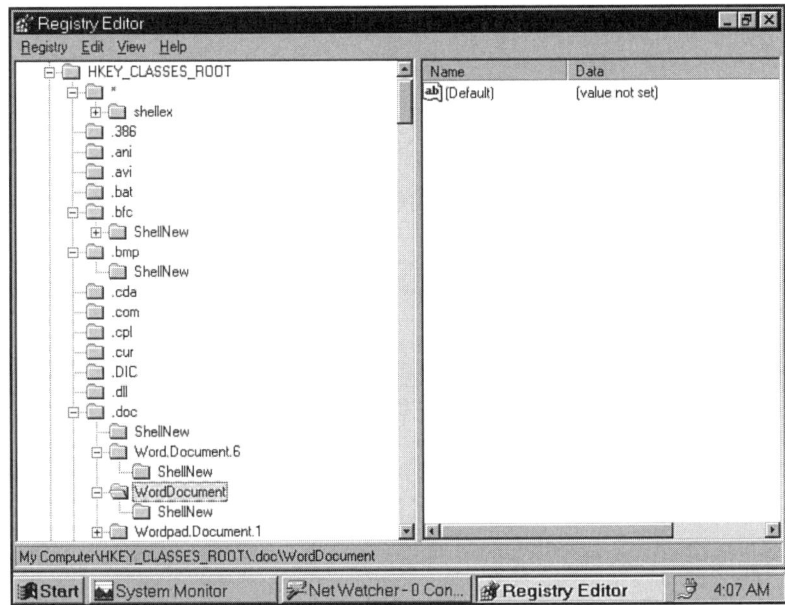

Figure 4.8

Registry Editor view of Hkey_Classes_Root.

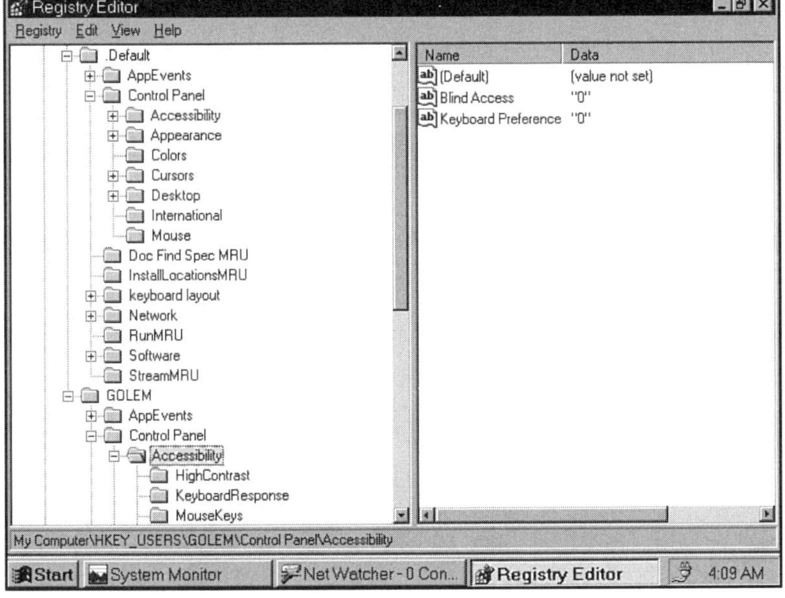

Figure 4.9

Registry Editor view of Hkey_Users.

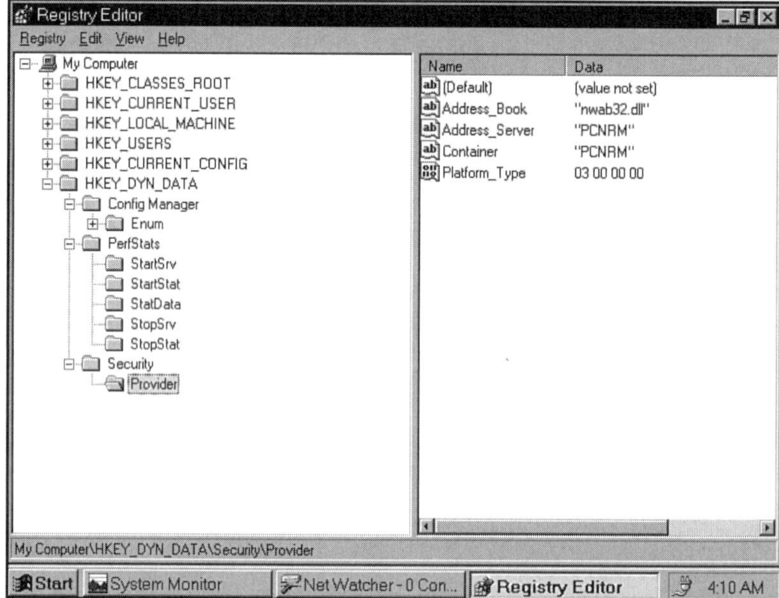

Figure 4.10

Registry Editor view of Hkey_Dyn_Data.

- **Hkey_Current_Configuration.** This section (see fig. 4.11) maintains data about the current session's hardware configuration.

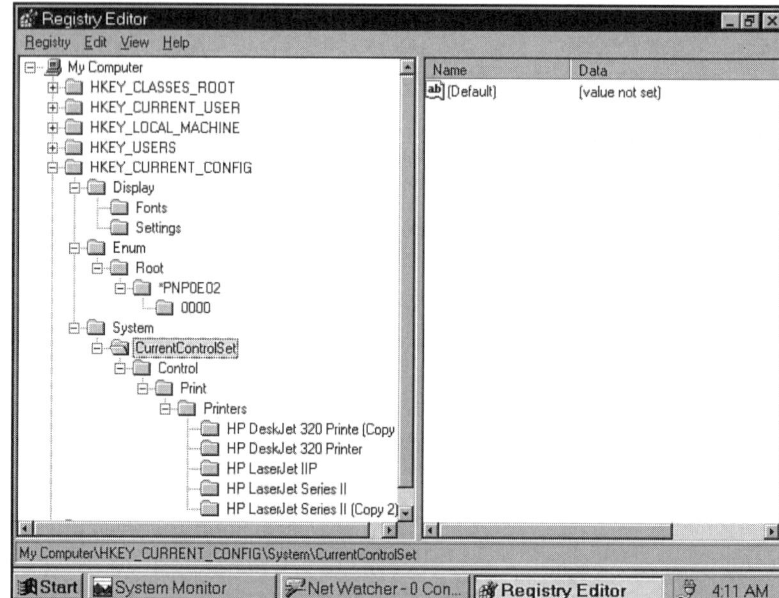

Figure 4.11

Registry Editor view of HKey_Current_Configuration.

- **Hkey_Current_User.** This section (see fig. 4.12) maintains the current user's configuration and provides user preferences in much the same manner as did Win.ini in Windows 3.*x*. It keeps information on the current user such as application preferences, screen colors, security access permissions, and environment variables. Although some settings are maintained elsewhere, this section is rather current-user oriented, containing such information as most-recently used applications (RunMRU) and most-recently used documents or shortcut keys (StreamMRU). This section makes this data available to Windows 95 for fast access and response.

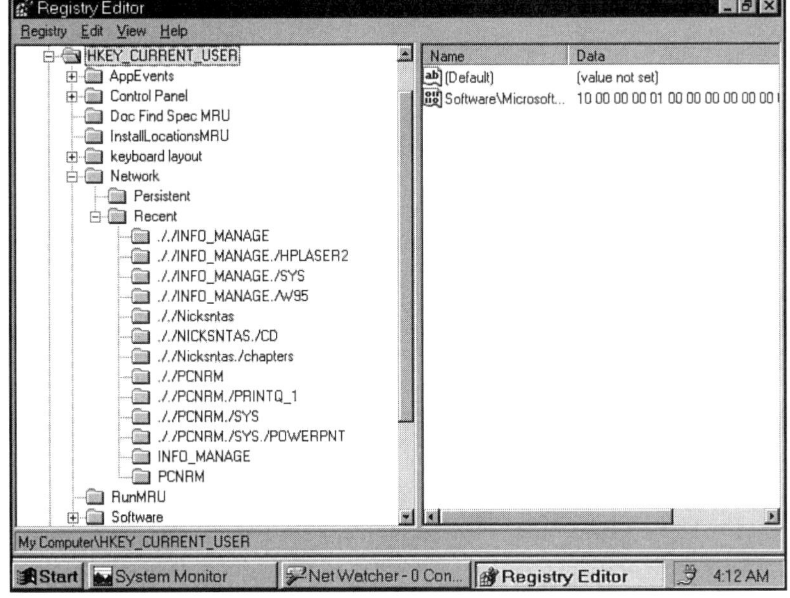

Figure 4.12
Registry Editor view of HKey_Current_User.

The Registry differs from the Ini structure in a number of ways, as follows:

- It's a single structure, whereas Windows 3.1 depends on four files: Win.ini, System.ini, Control.ini, and Progman.ini.

- It's hierarchical, whereas the Ini file is flat and based on single-line entries.

- It's a single structure at run time, but cleanly divisible otherwise into two classes of configuration: user and system, each of which has its own data structure (User.dat and System.dat, which you can control in a number of ways, but which the Registry reassembles at run time).

The Registry structure can be maintained in the following ways:

- **The Control Panel.** The Control Panel in Windows 95 operates similarly to the Control Panel in Windows 3.*x*: it serves as the user's front end to user and system configurations in the Registry.
- **The Registry Editor.** The Registry Editor is similar to the text editing approach used with the Ini files in that it allows direct editing of the Registry.

  The Remote Registry (see fig. 4.13) enables you to edit the Registry of another Windows 95 workstation without having to sit at its keyboard or disturb the user of that workstaton.
- **The System Policy Editor.** The System Policy Editor is more structured and context-oriented, enabling you to maintain settings or policies for individual users or groups of users, and for individual workstations.

You should keep users away from the Registry Editor program (Regedit.exe). One way to do this is to remove the users' access to Regedit.exe on the workstation and from the shared Windows 95 server directories.

Another approach is to use the System Policy Editor setting that restricts user access to the Registry Editor. The option is "Disable Registry Editing Tools."

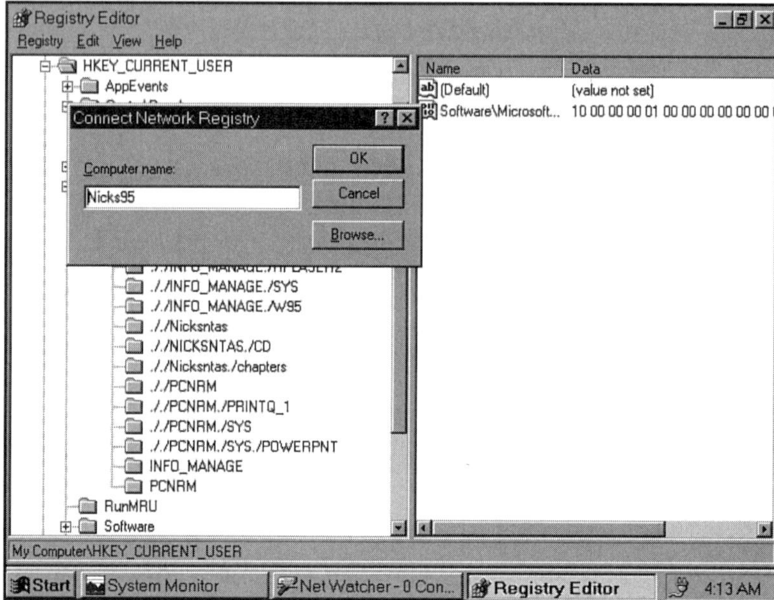

Figure 4.13

Connecting to a remote computer's Registry through the Registry Editor.

Windows 95 provides the capability to use Remote Procedure Calls (RPCs), which you might also call "name pipes." RPCs enable you to remotely manage the Registry if the remote Registry service is enabled. This remote Registry service is loaded on top of the network adapter, protocol, and client, and enables you to use a set of Registry Application Program Interfaces (APIs) to modify the workstation Registry remotely to modify hardware and software components from other workstations on the network.

For the NetWare workstation client, this activity is conducted directly in real time over the IPX protocol through Windows Sockets or processes. As shown in figure 4.14, this direct real-time access can also be performed through the System Policy Editor.

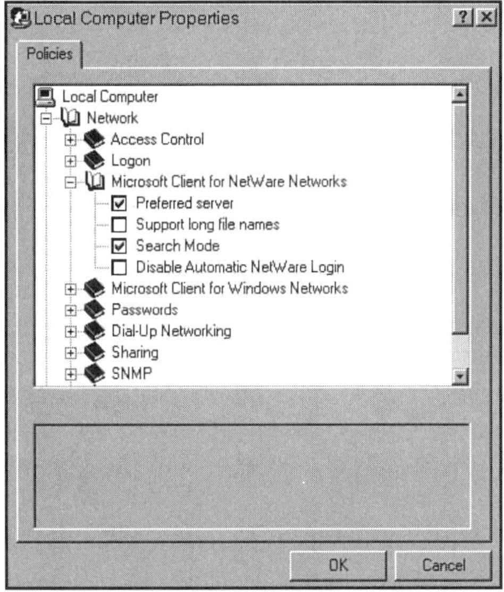

Figure 4.14

Registry access points through the System Policy Editor.

The System Policy Editor (Poledit.exe) allows either direct real-time access to the Registry of another computer or the establishment of a policy change for that workstation and/or user. Such a policy change would be implemented when the user logs on to the network for his or her changes, or when anyone logs on to the network from that workstation for workstation policy changes. In either case, part of the logon process conducted by Windows 95 is to check and update the Registry against other copies or a referenced Config.pol file that is created by the System Policy Editor.

System.Dat, User.Dat, and User Profiles

The Registry consists of workstation and user information. Singular data for the workstation is stored in a binary nontext format, called System.dat. Individual data for the user is stored in a User.dat file associated with the particular user. Beyond the user's specific configuration and your possible restrictions for the user is the user profile. The structure of the user profile consists of the User.dat Registry information and other matters that appear in the directory structure \Windows*profiles**username*\ and includes recent document accesses, menu information, and program data, such as the shortcut indicated by an icon.

Whereas Windows 3.*x* forces the administrator to be inventive in the manipulation of user and hardware initialization files, Windows 95 presents the administrator with the technology to make sure that the workstation always has its appropriate System.dat and the latest User.dat information and full user profile (see fig. 4.15). Windows 95 provides the logic required to either create a local profile or choose between the local and the server copy to ensure the latest version for the user.

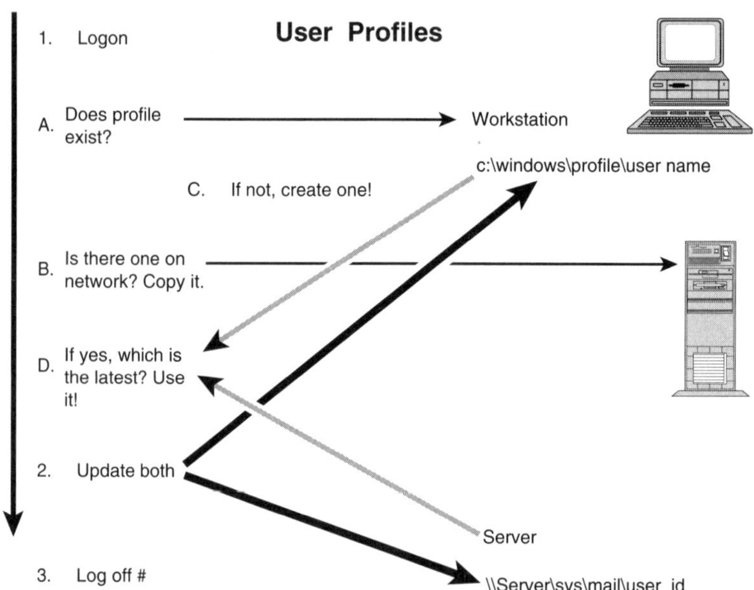

Figure 4.15
The network logon process and the creation of user profiles.

The foundation for the user profile is the shortcut. The shortcut is a form of object linking and embedding (OLE) that creates a connection between a symbol, usually marked with the arrow symbol, and the underlying program. The shortcut improves the speed of accessing the program. The shortcut is a safer form of accessing the program than the folder approach, which displays the icon of the program command file. A user who deletes the shortcut icon destroys only the link. But a user who deletes the program icon wipes out the underlying program file as well.

The user profile is actually the combination of the User.dat Registry file and a duplication of the Start menu structure, populated with the shortcuts appropriate to the user. Under the user's \windows\profiles\username directories are the items that appear on the menu. Fortunately, the structure was cleverly devised by the Microsoft programmers to get past a problem with Windows 3.*x* program icons and groups. The Grp files were nonaccessible binary files that could not easily be modified except by opening up the groups and adding or deleting icons. The Windows 95 menu system is built and maintained by placing the shortcuts into the menu directory structure.

The following is the overall structure of the user profile replication of the application menu and shortcut locations:

```
c:\windows\profiles\username\desktop
```

Contents: Shortcuts that appear on the desktop rather than the menu.

```
c:\windows\profiles\username\nethood
```

Contents: Shortcuts to resources that appear in Network Neighborhood, including shortcuts to shared printers. You should not place folders in Network Neighborhood. This is not supported, and results of doing so are unpredictable.

```
c:\windows\profiles\username\start menu
```

Contents: Shortcuts and options appearing on the Start menu and defined using the Taskbar command from the Settings menu.

```
c:\windows\profiles\username\start menu\programs
```

Contents: Shortcuts that appear in the programs group in the Start menu and in the submenu structure or folders.

```
c:\windows\profiles\username\start menu\program\startup
```

Contents: Programs or batch files that are in the startup group.

The following is a partial listing of files in the user profile subdirectories created through the use of the DOS DIR/S command. The listing is for the local user Golem who will also show up shortly as the NetWare bindery User_ID 13000027. Note the display of files and directories that use the ~ (tilde) character for DOS view of long file names, and then the description of the file, with dates of file and file size so forth. Each of the Lnk files is a link file that, when viewed from within the Windows GUI, will show up as a graphical icon.

```
Directory of C:\WINDOWS\Profiles
GOLEM        <DIR>    01-20-94 1:27p Golem
GOLEM000     <DIR>    05-18-95 9:25p GOLEM000
Directory of C:\WINDOWS\Profiles\Golem
DESKTOP      <DIR>    01-20-94 1:27p Desktop
```

```
Directory of C:\WINDOWS\Profiles\Golem\Desktop
WINDOWS9 LNK       268 01-22-94 9:36a Windows 95 Beta Release Notes.lnk
MICROSOF LNK       270 01-22-94 9:37a Microsoft WinNews.lnk
Directory of C:\WINDOWS\Profiles\GOLEM000
DESKTOP      <DIR>     05-18-95 9:26p Desktop
RECENT       <DIR>     05-18-95 9:26p Recent
NETHOOD      <DIR>     05-18-95 9:26p NetHood
STARTM~1     <DIR>     05-18-95 9:26p Start Menu
Directory of C:\WINDOWS\Profiles\GOLEM000\Desktop
MYBRIE~1     <DIR>     05-18-95 9:26p My Briefcase
INBOX  LNK         276 04-14-94 9:20p Inbox.lnk
MICROS~1 LNK       269 04-14-94 9:20p Microsoft WinNews.lnk
SHORTC~1 LNK       289 05-18-95 9:08p Shortcut to Netsetup.lnk
SHORTC~2 LNK       287 05-19-95 6:08a Shortcut to Poledit.lnk
SHORTC~3 LNK       287 05-18-95 9:08p Shortcut to Regserv.lnk
SSM LNK            394 05-05-95 3:03p Ssm.lnk
WINDOW~1 LNK       266 04-16-94 2:33p Windows 95 Beta Release Notes.lnk
Directory of C:\WINDOWS\Profiles\GOLEM000\Desktop\My Briefcase
Directory of C:\WINDOWS\Profiles\GOLEM000\NetHood
Directory of C:\WINDOWS\Profiles\GOLEM000\Recent
AGENDA LNK         322 05-22-95 10:35p Agenda.lnk
MSDOSB~1 LNK       246 05-24-95 5:27a Msdos.bak.lnk
NICK LNK           235 05-24-95 5:33a Nick.lnk
MSPSRV LNK         330 05-30-95 10:53p Mspsrv.lnk
LOCATION LNK       224 05-24-95 5:43a Location.lnk
SYSTEMTO LNK       331 05-23-95 1:19a Systemto.lnk
NETSET~1 LNK       303 05-27-95 1:57a Netsetup.adm.lnk
SHORTC~2 LNK       322 02-07-94 9:11p Shortcut to Alrtview.lnk
TWO LNK            293 06-01-95 3:00a Two.lnk
SHORTC~1 LNK       287 05-19-95 6:08a Shortcut to Poledit.lnk
CONFIG~1 LNK       320 06-01-95 8:05a Config.pol.lnk
WINPAD LNK         322 05-24-95 5:42a Winpad.lnk
THREE LNK          337 04-18-94 8:23a Three.lnk
SHORTC~7 LNK       312 02-07-94 6:47p Shortcut to Novell.lnk
ADMINA~1 LNK       278 06-01-95 7:41a Admin.adm.lnk
FOUR LNK           289 05-23-95 12:50a Four.lnk
CABINETS LNK       308 05-23-95 3:39a Cabinets.lnk
Directory of C:\WINDOWS\Profiles\GOLEM000\Start Menu
PROGRAMS     <DIR>     05-18-95 9:26p Programs
Directory of C:\WINDOWS\Profiles\GOLEM000\Start Menu\Programs
MICROS~1     <DIR>     05-18-95 9:26p Microsoft Tools
ACCESS~1     <DIR>     05-18-95 9:26p Accessories
STARTUP      <DIR>     05-18-95 9:26p Startup
```

```
LOTUSA~1     <DIR>      05-18-95 9:26p Lotus Applications
MICROS~2     <DIR>      05-18-95 9:26p Microsoft Office
COMPAQ~1     <DIR>      05-18-95 9:26p Compaq Utilities
COLLAG~1     <DIR>      05-18-95 9:26p Collage Complete
NOVELL~1     <DIR>      05-18-95 9:26p Novell-NMS
TABWORKS     <DIR>      05-18-95 9:26p TabWorks
COMPAQ       <DIR>      05-18-95 9:26p Compaq
MAIN         <DIR>      05-18-95 9:26p Main
MS-DOS~1 PIF        967 04-14-94 9:20p MS-DOS Prompt.pif
OPENMA~1 LNK        275 04-14-94 9:20p Open Mailbox.lnk
THEMIC~1 LNK        317 04-14-94 9:20p The Microsoft Network.lnk
WINDOW~1 LNK        330 05-23-95 1:05a Windows Explorer.lnk
NORTON~1     <DIR>      05-30-95 12:02a Norton Utilities
Directory of C:\WINDOWS\Profiles\GOLEM000\Start Menu\Programs\Accessories
GAMES        <DIR>      05-18-95 9:26p Games
SYSTEM~1     <DIR>      05-18-95 9:26p System Tools
MULTIM~1     <DIR>      05-18-95 9:26p Multimedia
CALCUL~1 LNK        266 04-14-94 9:20p Calculator.lnk
CALENDAR LNK        297 01-20-94 7:42a Calendar.lnk
CARDFILE LNK        297 01-20-94 7:42a Cardfile.lnk
CHARAC~1 LNK        302 04-14-94 9:20p Character Map.lnk
CLIPBO~1 LNK        272 04-14-94 9:20p Clipboard Viewer.lnk
DIAL-U~1 LNK        416 05-24-95 5:38a Dial-Up Networking.lnk
DIRECT~1 LNK        278 04-14-94 9:20p Direct Cable Connection.lnk
HYPERT~1 LNK        322 04-15-94 12:36a HyperTerminal Connections.lnk
NOTEPAD LNK         275 04-14-94 9:20p Notepad.lnk
PAINT LNK           331 04-14-94 9:20p Paint.lnk
PHONED~1 LNK        272 04-14-94 9:20p Phone Dialer.lnk
WINPAD~1 LNK        346 05-24-95 3:27a WinPad Organizer.lnk
WORDPAD LNK         375 05-24-95 3:28a WordPad.lnk
Directory of C:\WINDOWS\Profiles\GOLEM000\Start Menu\Programs\Accessories\Games
```

The use of individual user profiles is dependent upon the administrator explicitly turning on the workstation's setting allowing user profiles (see fig. 4.16). There are two decision points here: the first to allow a User.dat Registry file for each user, and the second to allow the link shortcuts to be maintained for the user.

You can set a computer-specific policy that controls access to the Password icon in the Control Panel, which in turn gives access to the determination of whether the workstation requires all users to have the identical profiles or allows them their own unique configurations on that machine. If the setting allows for individual user profiles, the Windows 95 software checks for the user's profile in the Registry listing:

```
Hkey_Local_Machine\software\microsoft\windows\current_version\profile list
```

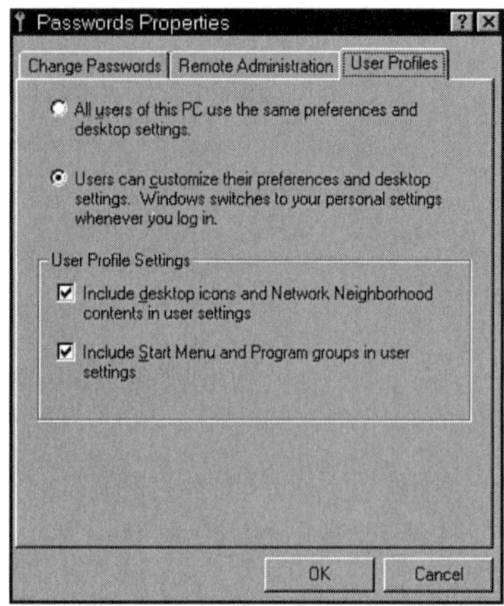

Figure 4.16

The Windows 95 User Profiles options.

If the user isn't at that location, Windows 95 creates a new profile for the user. If you have established a profile for that user on the network in the Pol file maintained on the network, that configuration is copied to the user and a new directory is set and User.dat information is added to the windows subdirectory and local Registry respectively. Alternatively, you can establish group policies that impact the user's Windows 95 environment based on what is established for NetWare groups of which the user happens to be a member.

There are some conditions that form the basis for use of user profiles:

- Enable user profiles on the workstation.
- Install and use a Microsoft 32-bit protected mode network client on the workstation. This is either the Microsoft Client for NetWare or the Microsoft Client for Microsoft Networks.
- Establish long file-name support on the NetWare server. This is required because Windows 95 folders such as the Start menu or the Network Neighborhood are actually seen as long file names. Windows NT Server already supports long file names.
- Make sure that home directories exist for users on the Microsoft Windows NT Server for the storage of the user profiles. On a NetWare server the storage location is the \server\sys\MAIL\user_Id directory that is created when a user is created.
- On each computer that will support profiles, make sure that the directory for Windows 95 has the same directory name so that the profiles subdirectory will

be in the same named directory on each workstation. Note: C:\WINDOWS is not the same as D:\WINDOWS. Each Windows 95 workstation must have the same windows directory structure and Windows subdirectory name to enable ease of downloading of user information at each logon time.

When the workstation allows individual profiles and the preceding set of conditions listed are met, a copy of the users User.dat file is stored on the network server. For NetWare, the network copy is stored in the \mail\user subdirectory, with the user, of course, referred to not by name, not even by logon name, but by 8-digit bindery object identification. At Windows 95 startup—NetWare Logon—if a copy of the user's User.dat exists on the workstation, it is found by Windows 95 and compared to the network server copy. Windows 95 uses the latest copy and at logoff time updates both copies so that they are identical.

After users are established as users who log on to the network from a workstation that fulfills the preceding requirements, they get a copy of their profile copied to the server. You can determine that a given user cannot have his or her own unique settings regardless of what the workstation allows this user in terms of customizing. You copy a User.dat appropriate for the specific user to that user's NetWare mail directory or the Windows NT Server home directory and, in the process, rename it to User.man. This creates a mandatory configuration that prevents the user from saving any changes back to the workstation or the network.

One practical consideration is that the bindery, and the NDS user identity used for the \mail\user directory, are not obvious. NetWare arbitrarily creates the 8-digit ID. (see fig. 4.17). Thus the profiles for the network user Golem are stored under the users \mail\13000027 directory.

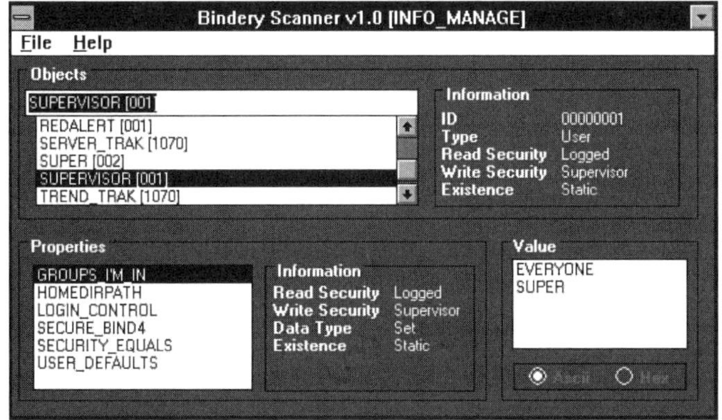

Figure 4.17

Third-party Bindscan illustrating the binary IDs.

The NetWare administrator up until now has not had to deal with the security IDs on a practical basis. The information is not readily available from the NetWare utilities, so you must make constant trips to the NetWare 3.*x* SYSCON or the NetWare 4.*x*

NWADMIN program to get that information for each user. Many administrators will be turning to third-party network management packages, such as Auditware, Bindview, or Frye's NetWare Management program (see fig. 4.18) for an online list or printout of the users and their NetWare user identities for the purpose of working with User.dat, User.man, and the user profiles.

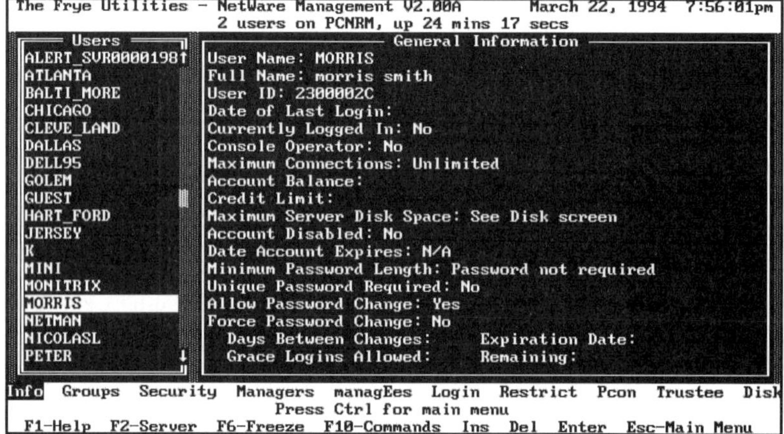

Figure 4.18

Frye's NetWare Management's bindery reporting package.

The following listing shows the structure (as seen through NetWare's NDIR) of the \mail\user_id entries that Windows 95 makes for the user profile on the network. You can see the extra load this places on what has been a relatively simple and empty file structure. \mail\user has been the location for NetWare-specific e-mail and the repository of the user-specific NetWare login script sections, and a storage location for any user-specific print job configurations.

For the particular user "bindery id 13000027," Windows 95 maintains 17 subdirectories under \mail\13000027. The partial listing below stands in contrast to the graphic view (see fig. 4.19) in Windows 95 under the user name 000 with folders for Nethood, Recent, and Startmen.

Windows Explorer is a quite useful tool that provides a graphical user interface view of the file and directory structure. Within the Windows Explorer view, the directories are viewed as folders and the files are viewed as icons.

This abbreviated listing, replicated under the user's mail directory on the NetWare server, reflects NetWare security items such as inherited rights and ownership. At the end of the listing is the actual file size total along with the actual storage space that the files take up on the NetWare server.

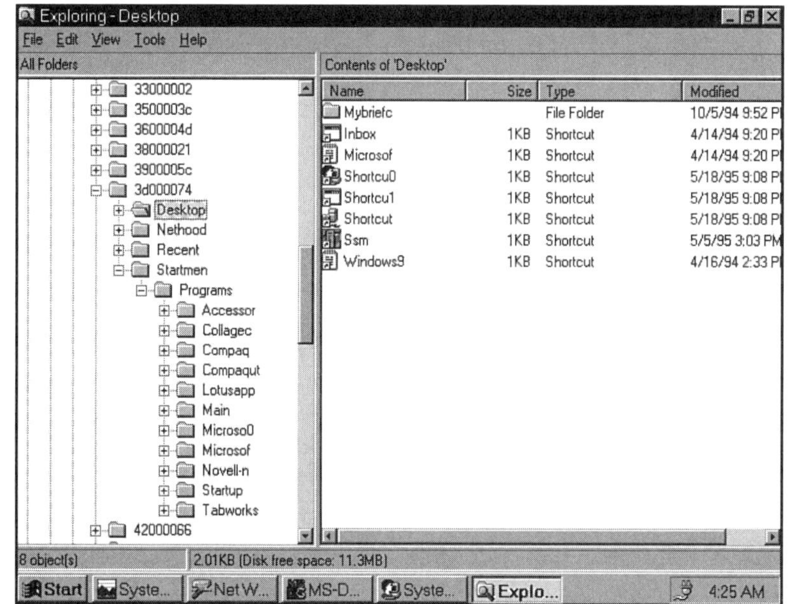

Figure 4.19

Windows 95 Explorer view of the NetWare user's mail directory link files.

```
PCNRM/SYS:MAIL\13000027
Files:         Size    Last Updated      Flags              Owner

LOGIN                  0 1-20-94 1:19p    [Rw-------------] SUPERVISO
LOGIN       OS2        0 1-20-94 1:19p    [Rw-------------] SUPERVISO
USER.DAT     o   106,664 6-02-95 2:54a    [Rw-------------] GOLEM
          Inherited  Effective
Directories:   Rights     Rights    Owner     Created/Copied

DESKTOP      [SRWCEMFA] [SRWCEMFA] GOLEM     4-04-94 4:25a
NETHOOD      [SRWCEMFA] [SRWCEMFA] GOLEM     4-04-94 4:25a
RECENT       [SRWCEMFA] [SRWCEMFA] GOLEM     4-04-94 4:25a
STARTMEN     [SRWCEMFA] [SRWCEMFA] GOLEM     4-04-94 4:42a
   106,668 bytes in  4 files
   114,688 bytes in  28 blocks
PCNRM/SYS:MAIL\13000027\DESKTOP
Files:         Size    Last Updated     Flags     Owner
------------- ------------ ------------ ------------ ------------
INBOX    LNK         276 4-14-94 9:20p [Rw-A-------------] GOLEM
MICROSOF.LNK  o      269 4-14-94 9:20p [Rw-A-------------] GOLEM
SHORTCU0.LNK  o      287 5-19-95 6:08a [Rw-A-------------] GOLEM
```

```
SHORTCU1.LNK  o      287 5-18-95 9:08p [Rw-A--------------] GOLEM
SHORTCUT.LNK  o      289 5-18-95 9:08p [Rw-A--------------] GOLEM
SSM      LNK         394 5-05-95 3:03p [Rw-A--------------] GOLEM
WINDOWS9.LNK  o      266 4-16-94 2:33p [Rw-A--------------] GOLEM

   145,127 total bytes in  113 files
   561,152 total bytes in  137 blocks
```

Some differences exist between maintenance of this profile on the local drive versus on the network, and in the way different utilities show the profile items. The directory list by the NetWare NDIR utility doesn't recognize long file names in the directory name. Therefore, it shows Startmen\Programs\Nortonut, whereas in the Windows 95 workstation listing you see the DOS view Start Menu\Programs\Norton Utilities. In the DOS or Windows 95 DOS Virtual Machine listing, you can see a description that NDIR doesn't support. The NetWare NDIR utility also reports some aspects that DOS doesn't, however, namely storage space used by network files.

Note the NetWare 4 KB storage block in the NetWare 3.11 setting, with the 4.*x* subblock allocation, which means that these 113 link files kept in the relatively simple profile for this user use 561 KB of network space. This gives you an idea of the hidden expense of the use of long file names. If you have a hundred users, this would represent 5,6115,200 bytes, (5.6 MB) of server space.

```
Directory of C:\WINDOWS\Profiles\GOLEM000\Start Menu\Programs\Norton Utilities
.         <DIR>     05-30-95 12:02a .
..        <DIR>     05-30-95 12:02a ..
DISKED~1 PIF        967 05-30-95 12:03a Disk Editor.PIF
DISKED~1 P          967 05-30-95 12:03a Disk Editor.P
NORTON~1 PIF        967 05-30-95 12:13a Norton Diagnostics.PIF
NORTON~1            967 05-30-95 12:03a Norton Diagno
NORTON~1 LNK        460 05-30-95 12:03a Norton Disk Doctor.LNK
RESCUE~1 LNK        465 05-30-95 12:03a Rescue Disk.LNK
SPACEW~1 LNK        450 05-30-95 12:03a Space Wizard.LNK
SPEEDD~1 LNK        448 05-30-95 12:03a Speed Disk.LNK
SYSTEM~1 LNK        456 05-30-95 12:03a System Information.LNK
NORTON~2 LNK        474 05-30-95 12:03a Norton System Doctor.LNK
UNERAS~1 LNK        452 05-30-95 12:03a UnErase Wizard.LNK
IMAGE  LNK          455 05-30-95 12:03a Image.LNK
INFODE~1 LNK        519 05-30-95 12:03a Info Desk.LNK
    13 file(s)      8,047 bytes
```

The Registry, System Policy Editor, and Config.pol

In designing the centrality of the Windows 95 Registry with its System.dat and User.dat, Windows 95 developers also created muliple means of establishing and managing the Registry settings (see fig. 4.20). The user can modify settings in the Control Panel if granted access to it; the administrator can modify individual settings in the System Policy Editor. Although the user can also use the Registry Editor, it is not a recommended option.

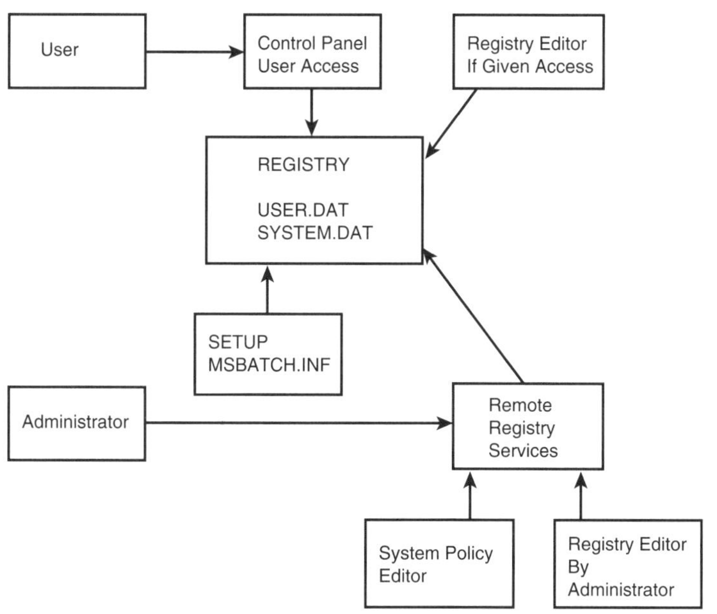

Figure 4.20

The various ways of changing the Registry.

You can use the Msbatch.inf file or another such file to establish these Registry configurations. After you complete the workstation setup, you can establish a default user and a default computer configuration on that workstation.

These settings are in effect unless you notify Windows 95 otherwise. If the profiles aren't allowed on the workstation, these default settings are in effect. If a user has a set of profile information on the network, it overrides the default settings during that user's session.

In maintaining the user or workstation configuration aspects of the Registry, you should use other administrative tools rather than the Registry Editor—namely the System Policy Editor. The System Policy Editor is geared to help and provide warnings, more so than the more text-oriented Registry Editor. This multiple approach to editing and maintaining the configuration is far superior to the Windows 3.*x* text file editing. Bear in mind that unlike the Ini files, the Registry isn't a text file and, as a binary file, you cannot edit unless you use the Registry or System Policy Editor (or, the as-of-yet unannounced third-party applications).

You can use the System Policy Editor to connect over the network to the workstation's Registry if the Remote Registry service is installed on the workstation. The System Policy Editor, however, perhaps serves more effectively to modify the Config.pol or other designated Pol files placed in the NetWare server's public directory where you can use Windows 95 to access it to modify the user's profile and the named workstation. You must give Windows 95 workstations unique names during setup, although you can change those names later on.

You have two choices in terms of user control for the user-related items: the mandatory profile or the specific user profile. The mandatory profile is based on setting up the ideal user structure that would not be changeable by the user, and saving or copying it to a User.man file in the user's mail subdirectory. You must copy the files explicitly to each user's mail directory, but the choice of User.man or User.dat or system profile is made for each NetWare user of a Windows 95 workstation. When a user is controlled by the User.man file, he or she can make changes during the session, but those changes will not be made to the master User.man file.

If you choose the system profile approach for specific users, on the other hand, you can set controls for both the computer and the user. You use these controls to set restrictions or allow choices for the user item by item. Changes you make within the user configurable settings are saved to the User.dat file, and Windows 95 automatically updates that file on both the workstation and the file server.

In the Pol file, you also can create special configurations and limitations on the workstation by identifying that workstation with the name given it when Windows 95 is set up on that workstation. Any number of people might use the company's front desk receptionist desktop or the shipping desktop at the back of the plant, so you should restrict the modifications that users can make to those machines. You should set up the workstation from the network and from the shared program installation directory so that you can register the system by name to the Windows 95 master system policy database.

User Profiles and System Policies

When you establish policies for users and workstations, you should consider the following three policy layers, each of which you can manage in detail over the network:

- Default user and computer
- Group policies for server-based groups
- Specific user or specific computer policies

You can control users, default or specific, in the following five areas:

- Control Panel access
- Desktop
- Network
- Shell settings
- System settings

You can check, clear, or fill most settings:

- **Checked.** Implements.
- **Cleared.** Does *not* implement.
- **Filled.** Gives the user some choice.

For administrative ease, you might consider establishing a system-wide default for user and workstation and provide for specific instances as exceptions rather than creating each item from scratch. You can use the System Policy Editor to add or edit default or specific users or systems. Here, you need to decide what freedoms or limitations you want to apply to users. You can establish multiple groups according to Windows 95 literacy, for example, and as users develop skills and needs, move them into a more advanced level group.

The groups already established on the preferred server or groups created there just for Windows 95 configuration control can be used in place of specific users where a user can fit into a group pattern. If there is a user profile, any group profile containing that user will be ignored. As in the system administration of the server, you, the administrator, are well advised to consider doing all the work on a group level, which gives much greater flexibility. The group policy feature is not established in the default configuration, but must be added through several steps in the Windows 95 workstation. The process involves copying a Grouppol.dll file to the Windows 95 workstation, and then after adding the groups to the System Policy Editor process, you order them from the lowest to highest priority. The way the group profile process works, the highest priority group wins by being loaded and reviewed last and therefore has precedence over other groups. This means that members of multiple groups receive the highest priority settings here.

Through the server and logon process, you can establish a process of maintaining and upgrading user profiles for the Windows 95 user and workstation. This process involves the downloading of a profile, which is either the Config.pol or a policy file with a different name that is advisedly given the Pol extension.

When the user logs on to the Windows 95 workstation NetWare client, the user can be shown the NetWare logon screen with the user logon name and preferred server shown, and then the user provides the password. This is still at the front end of the logon and session startup process. When the logon process is authenticated by the NetWare server, Windows 95 checks for the existence of the user's User.dat file on both the workstation and in the user's preferred NetWare mail directory, uses the latest profile, and after the session updates both automatically.

You can use the System Policy Editor, Config.pol, or any other Pol file to create new users and update existing users. You can set up a process for downloading the configurations during logon—to be done automatically or manually during each logon session. The automatic process depends on workstation settings and the presence of the Config.pol file in the preferred NetWare server's public directory. You can use the default system configuration and default user on the workstation to have the automatic download process bring the special configuration to the user at logon.

You can set up a manual proccss that uses a configuration file other than the Config.pol in the public directory. Manual processing overrides the automatic process and enables you to place the configuration in a directory other than public. You need to set up the workstation to handle manual downloading of files. Microsoft Client for NetWare supports the automatic process, whereas only the manual process supports the real mode NetWare NETX or VLM client. The automatic process also requires that Microsoft Client for NetWare be the Primary Network Logon client, and a Preferred Server is specified.

For the real mode NETX or VLM NetWare client, automatic downloading of user profiles and system policies is not available. Therefore, you must configure the manual updating of these policies. You must enable the local workstation for remote update, then from the settings for remote update choose manual and specify the system policies file to download from the file server. For the NETX or VLM user, you must place the policy on a mapped drive, and designate the location of the system policy file.

Customizing the User's Environment

You should take into consideration that for the user you can set profile settings for five aspects of the Windows 95 environment: Control Panel, desktop, network, shell, and system. Within the shell, you can customize the following five sets of features for users (in addition to the restrictions you can set):

- **Directory structure**, which is where the user menu and desktop items are located. You can modify the default settings to other locations such as network directories where the items can be set as read only.
- **Executable files** that enable the direct running of applications.
- **Batch files**, which are used to build up aspects of the environment before the application starts.
- **Documents** that can be clicked on to start the related application, which then opens that document.
- **Shortcuts**, which are examples of what can appear in customized folders.

You can customize the user's environment by placing items in special locations rather than underneath their user name under \windows\profiles, as you saw earlier in this chapter when you looked at the profile on the local disk and then on the network server in the \mail\user_id directory structure. The following list includes the customizable settings along with their default locations. By referencing these custom locations to which you can copy items, you can control the user's desktop. Read-only network directories can be pointed to in these settings so that they are accessible to the user but are not changeable.

1. **Custom Program Folder**

   `c:\windows\profiles\username\start menu\programs`

   Contents: Shortcuts that appear in the Programs group on the Start menu.

2. **Custom Desktop Icons**

   `c:\windows\profiles\username\desktop`

   Contents: Shortcuts that appear on the desktop rather than on the Start menu.

3. **Custom Startup Folder**

   `c:\windows\profiles\username\start menu\program\startup`

   Contents: Programs or batch files in the startup group, similar to the startup group in Windows 3.*x*.

4. **Custom Network Neighborhood**

   `c:\windows\profiles\username\nethood`

   Contents: Shortcuts to resources that appear in Network Neighborhood, including shortcuts to shared printers.

5. **Custom Start Menu**

   `c:\windows\profiles\username\startmenu`

   Contents: Shortcuts and options that appear on the Start menu and that are defined using the Taskbar command from the Settings menu.

User and Workstation Control and Restrictions

Windows 95 enables you to control the settings for both the user and the workstation (see fig. 4.21).These settings, which are discussed below, can be set for either default or specific users or workstations by name.

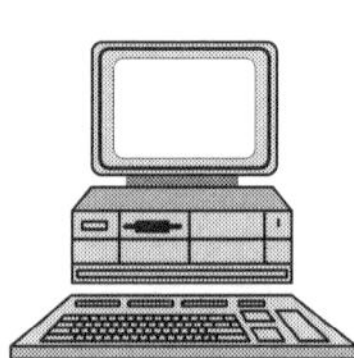

Figure 4.21
Administrative controls and options in Windows 95.

The settings that can define the user and workstation profiles are divided into the following categories:

User-Specific

1. **Control Panel**

   Restrict Network Control Panel Access

   You can disable the Network control preventing access to the network option, Hide identification page, which is the identification property sheet, and hide the security user-share level access control page.

   Restrict Printer Control Panel Access

   You can hide the General and Details property sheets, prevent the deletion of printers, and prevent the installation of new printers.

   Restrict System Control Panel Access

   You can hide the Device Manager property sheet, the hardware profiles, the File System button, and the Virtual Memory button.

   Restrict Password Control Panel Access

   You can prevent access to the Passwords option, hide the Change Passwords page, prevent remote Registry administration, and prevent access to the user profiles page.

2. **Desktop Settings**

   You can restrict users to specific wallpaper graphics that are delivered or downloaded at logon. The wallpaper file can be titled in the background of the desktop, and the user's color scheme can be specified.

3. **Network Settings**

   You can restrict users' file and print sharing abilities so that they cannot change existing setups for these features at the workstation.

4. **Shell Settings**

   You can prevent access to the Run command, remove the Find command, hide the drives showing in the My Computer windows, hide access to Network Neighborhood, keep users from saving settings on exit, remove the Taskbar on Start menu, and remove Folder from the Start menu.

5. **System Settings**

   By disabling Registry editing tools, you can prevent access to the system-altering Registry file, which is highly technical and beyond the average user and at times the experienced administrator. You can limit the list of Windows-based applications that the user can run. You can disable the MS-DOS prompt, preventing access to the system through DOS.

You can, and probably should, limit access to the MS-DOS mode. The MS-DOS mode is configured for a specific application that cannot be run within the Windows 95 environment. Clicking on the MS-DOS-designated application causes Windows 95 to shut down and reboot the workstation under the older MS-DOS operating system to run the application. When the application completes, the workstation reboots to the Windows 95 environment. In the process of rebooting, network connections are lost. Due to the nature of this process, it is a feature that should be used wisely.

Computer-Specific

6. **Computer-Specific Network Settings**

   Enabling or disabling user-level security determines whether a NetWare server will be used for pass-through security that provides bindery-based user and or group assignments for accessing directories and printers on the local workstation. In the logon process you can require server validation before the user can get into Windows 95 itself, and you can create a logon banner to be shown during the logon process.

   Among the network settings are configuration matters dealing the 32-bit network client for either NetWare (see fig. 4.22) or the Microsoft Network–Windows NT Server.

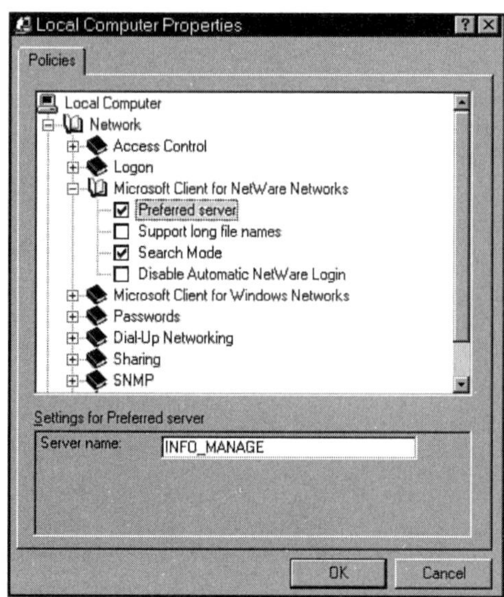

Figure 4.22

Microsoft Client for NetWare setting options in Policy Editor.

For Netware Client you can specify the preferred server, whether long file names are supported, the NetWare Search Mode, and whether or not there is automatic NetWare logon. You can also specify password features such as the use of asterisks, whether passwords are cached to be saved on the station and entered for the user to avoid retyping for each network logon, and the length and alphanumeric nature of passwords.

Simple Network Management Protocol settings, dial-up networking, and file and print sharing are other network settings that are workstation-related. Update polices determine whether or not system policies can be updated remotely, and if so whether this is automatic or manual.

7. **Computer-Specific System Settings**

   You can enable or disable the user profiles on the local workstations, define a network location of the Windows 95 setup files and designate this through the \\server\volume\path Universal Naming Convention, designate the programs that you want to run at logon once only or with each logon, and define the services you want to run at system startup.

Remote Monitoring and Administration

This section focuses on the last of the control issues mentioned at the beginning of the chapter: the ability to anticipate and monitor items that can present problems and the need for support. To address this point, Microsoft introduced the following innovations to enable you to remotely monitor and administer the Windows 95 workstation:

- Remote Registry
- System Monitor
- NetWatcher

These tools, along with the System Policy Editor, give you more control over the desktop and user. Although the System Policy Editor enables you to modify the user and the desktop and distibute these changes at the startup of the user session of Windows 95, these tools enable you to manage the workstation during the user's Windows 95 session.

The Remote Registry Service

The Windows 95 workstation's connection to the network is like any other network node dependent upon a network interface card and driver, a protocol, and a network shell or client. With the 32-bit protected mode adapter, protocol, and client, Microsoft has introduced the 32-bit network services that can be added to the workstation. These services provide the means of connecting to the workstation that is running the service agent in somewhat the same way as the memory resident TSR provided such connectivity with the real network clients, except that these new services are virtual or protected mode programs.

Among the services provided is the Remote Registry service, which enables you to connect to the user workstation as one means of managing the workstation and user configuration.

System Monitor

The System Monitor is a substantial addition to the network administrator's toolbox of support aids. Whereas Windows 3.*x* provides only the Program Manager's Help, About Program Manager screen with limited information about memory and system resources, the Windows 95 System Monitor provides a long list of measurements that can alert you to potential problems.

The System Monitor is provided as three files: Sysmon.exe, Sysmon.cnt, and Sysmon.hlp. These files are not put out on the workstation during the setup process, but must be extracted from the distribution disks or CD-ROM. You can find these files and the associated help files by searching the CD-ROM for the win95 subdirectory. Windows 95 is distributed in a new format of disks formated to 2 MB. On each disk is a numbered "cabinet" file that contains compressed files. These cabinet files are also the form that is used for distribution on the CD-ROM. You use Extract.exe to expand the files from their compressed format within the cabinets. The following command:

```
Extract /d cabinet name
```

provides a list of the names of files within that cabinet file. `Extract /d` is for display only; the *`cabinet name`* is in the format such as Win95_02.cab; and the file name can be searched for such as Sysmon.*. The whole command then reads:

```
Extract /D WIN95_02.CAB SYSMON.*.
```

On the CD-ROM set or the disks in the 13th and 17th cabinet sets of files are the Sysmon.* files. You can copy the cabinets from the CD-ROM to a DOS hard disk and then extract the files. To locate files, run the Extract command.

The Extract command is used to decompress the files contained in the cabinet files. The files can be extracted manually as a set of specific names. Typing **extract/?** at the command line gives you a list of all the extract options.

For the workstation, the System Monitor gives you measurements about the file system, kernel, and memory manager (see fig. 4.23). For the networking piece, the System Monitor gives you measurements about server performance of the Windows 95 workstation in peer-to-peer mode, the IPX/SPX protocol, and Microsoft clients for both Microsoft Networks and NetWare Networks. You can connect to the remote workstation and view the system performance matters without being able to eavesdrop on the actual work of the user.

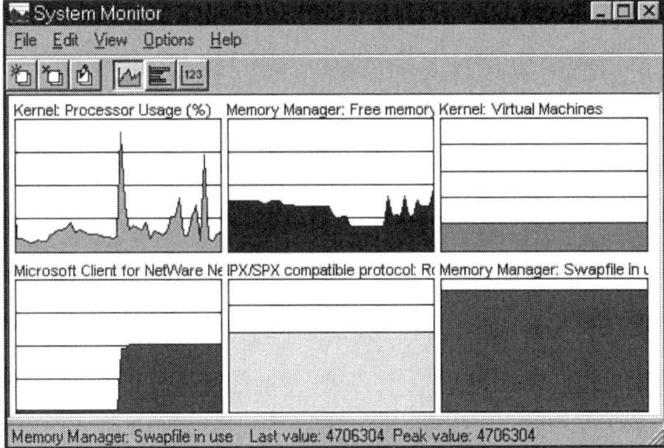

Figure 4.23

The System Monitor.

The categories of system measurement in the System Monitor are listed below with their subheadings. When choosing the items that are to be added to the visual screen for charting, you can click on the subheading and get a brief explanation. (It's too bad these items are not in the System Monitor's help topic index.) The items listed below are presented with both the Windows 95 help explanation and general networking and system explanations:

- **File System.** These items deal with the reading and writing that is done on the workstation.

  Bytes read/second

  Bytes written/second

  Dirty data

  Reads/second

  Writes/second

- **IPX/SPX-compatible protocol.** These items deal with the traffic to and from the workstation using this protocol.

  IPX packets lost/second

  IPX packets received/second

  IPX packets sent/second

  Open sockets

  Routing Table entries

  SAP Table entries

  SPX packets received/second

  SPX packets sent/second

- **Kernel.** These items relate to the computer's CPU and the threads of programs being used, as well as the number of virtual machines active.

  Processor Usages (%)

  Threads

  Virtual Machines

- **Memory Manager.** These items refer to the various memory usages on the workstation, including the swap file. Note that Page Faults refers to the times when data needs to be swapped out to provide real chip memory locations to other items.

  Allocated Memory

  Discards

  Disk cache size

  Free memory

  Instance Faults

  Locked Memory

  Maximum disk cache size

  Minimum disk cache size

  Other Memory

  Page Faults

  Page-ins

Page-outs

Swapfile defective

Swapfile in use

Swapfile Size

Swapable memory

- **Microsoft Client for NetWare.** These items refer to the 32-bit client shell for NetWare. Note here the two "bytes in cache" measurements indicating the ability to cache network reads and writes.

  BURST packets dropped

  Burst receive gap time

  Burst send gap time

  Bytes in cache

  Bytes read/second

  Bytes written/second

  Dirty bytes in cache

  NCP packets dropped

  Request pending

- **Microsoft Network Client.** These items refer to the activity of the client for Windows NT Server.

  Bytes read/second

  Bytes written/second

  Number of nets

  Open files

  Resources

  Sessions

  Transactions/second

- **Server.** These items refer to the activities of a Windows 95 workstation that has file and print sharing enabled.

  Burst packets dropped

  Bytes read/second

Bytes throughput/second

Bytes written/second

Cache memory

Packets dropped

Threads

Total Heap

Transactions/second

NetWatcher

With the NetWacher utility (see fig. 4.24), you can connect to Windows 95 and determine how that workstation is being used on the network.

Figure 4.24

The NetWatcher utility.

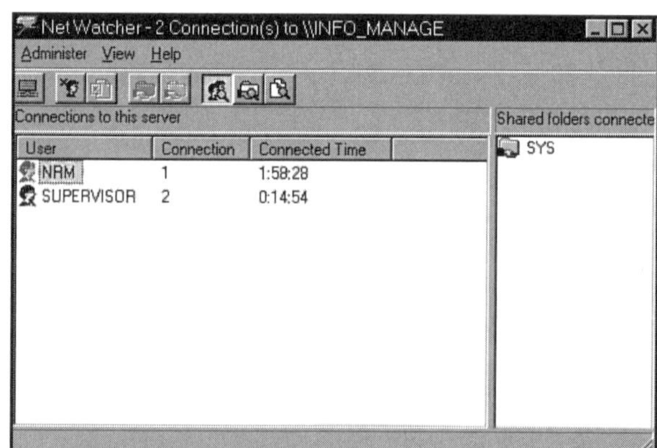

NetWatcher enables you to determine peer-to-peer networking matters such as the following:

- Who is connected to the network
- The shared folders
- The open files in use by others
- The properties of shared folders, such as who has what rights to these folders

The user of the workstation or the administrator can also disconnect a user and view shared file folder properties.

Like the System Monitor files, the NetWatcher files are not extracted during the setup process, but can be found using the extract process described for the System Monitor files. The NetWatcher files, Netwatch.exe, Netwatch.cnt, and Netwatch.hlp, are located in the distribution cabinet files.

Other Remote Management Tools

There are other remote management tools that add to the network administrator's ability to better manage the networked Windows 95 workstation. Additional remote management tools will continue to be developed. Among these other tools are the following:

- **The Microsoft Simple Network Management Protocol Agent.** SNMP is a means of monitoring the status and traffic of a workstation by a monitor station. Status is compared to a database of accepted or normal status measurements called "MIBs," or records in a management information-base database.
- **The Microsoft DMTF Agent.** The Desktop Management Task Force is an industry group that is evolving standards for monitoring and reporting on the status of desktop computers, software, and other matters of concern for the network administrator.
- **Microsoft's System Management Server.** This is part of the BackOffice suite of applications that run on the base of a Windows NT Server. The following are some of the features that this set offers:

    Integrated and centralized management

    Hardware inventory

    Software inventory

    Software distribution

    Remote control

    Troubleshooting of PCs

    Management of shared applications

    Software metering

    Network protocol analysis for remote diagnostics

Vendors such as Symantec, McAfee, Frye, On Demand, and Lanovations will be providing other tools for the Windows 95 workstation. These are some of the vendors who have been providing such support for the Windows 3.*x* environment.

Planning for User and Workstation Management

In summary of this chapter, Windows 95 provides a powerful set of tools with which to control the workstation and the user. What you must now do is carefully think out how these tools can and should be implemented in the workplace environment.

You should list and evaluate each workstation on the network to determine which of the workstation policies should be implemented.

Next, each of the Windows 95 users should be listed and evaluated for the policies that should be implemented for the specific user or network server groups that can be used for policy assignments.

The users then need to be evaluated in terms of the desktop set of applications and tools that each should have. You can then decide which if any should have preset menu items and desktop shortcuts assigned to them, and make these assignments in that user's Registry of custom locations.

You should become familiar with the typical activity of a Windows 95 workstation and establish some baseline performance measurements for guidance when reviewing the System Monitor tools provided.

The items listed above give you a good start in the planning and implementation of a system of managing the user and the workstation in the Windows 95 environment.

Location Issues: Server or Workstation

As you consider the location of the Windows 95 program files and the Windows application files, you must take two perspectives into account. The first perspective is that of the management of the network on which the Windows 95 workstation will operate. The second perspective is the structure of the Windows 95 system itself.

The location of Windows 95 and the Windows applications will have an impact on the network. Windows 95 program files and the files for Windows applications that are run from within the Windows 95 environment can be placed on and run from either the local workstation or the file server. From a network management perspective, there are some advantages for the location of these files on the network server and some disadvantages in terms of the location's impact on the performance of the file server and the traffic load on the network. This chapter examines the location of the Windows 95 and application files in terms of the the workstation, the server, and the traffic load of the network.

The design of the Windows 95 system provides a level of complexity to the question of the location of the Windows 95 program files. The

Windows 95 system is designed to boot to and run within protected mode. The Windows 95 system provides 32-bit network client connection to the network server, allowing the user to log on to the network from within the protected mode Windows 95 GUI. Running Windows 95 from the server requires real mode connection to the server before the switch can be made into the protected mode Windows 95 GUI. This real mode versus protected mode network connectivity requires some clarification, which is provided in this chapter.

The Windows 95 Location Options

You must decide where to place the Windows 95 program files (see fig. 5.1). This decision involves the placement of the files and the location from which the Windows 95 program will be run.

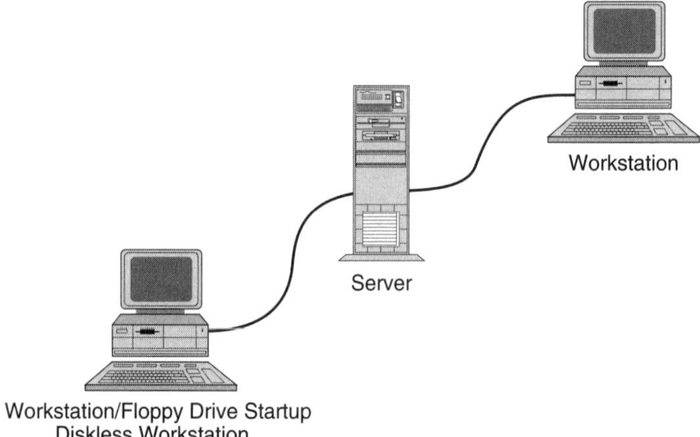

Figure 5.1
Where to put Windows 95 files—server or workstation.

The following are the options you must consider for the running of Windows 95:

- Windows 95 fully installed on the local workstation
- Windows 95 booting from the local hard disk but running from the server installation
- Windows 95 booting from a floppy drive and running from the server installation
- Windows 95 booting from a remote boot prom of a diskless workstation and running from the server installation

You need to examine the choice of the boot file location and the location of the Windows 95 program files in terms of the Windows 95 system. This chapter contains a technical discussion of the nature of the Windows 95 boot process as well as an analysis of some of the implications of the choice of whether to use the floppy drive, the hard disk boot, or the remote boot prom method when electing the server-based Windows 95 option.

The Windows 95 and Application File Location Considerations

From a network management perspective, the location question for either or both the Windows 95 files and the Windows application files revolves around the overhead involved on either the network or the network administrator (see fig. 5.2). If all the Windows 95 program files and application files are placed on the file server, the overhead will be on the file server and the network cabling. If all the Windows 95 files are placed on the workstation, the overhead will be on the network administrator.

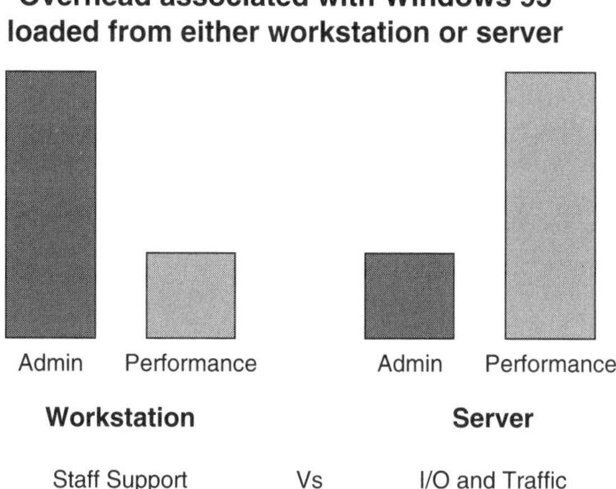

Figure 5.2

Choice of overhead, server/network versus administration.

The practical options facing the network administrator are as follows:

- Running both Windows 95 and applications from the workstation
- Running both Windows 95 and applications from the server
- Running Windows 95 from the workstation and the applications from the server

As many administrators did with the Windows 3.*x* client-based network, it is expected that administrators will split the locations of the Windows 95 program files and the Windows application files, placing the Windows programs on the workstations and the Windows-based applications on the file servers. This combination is seen by many network administrators as giving the performance advantage of the local workstation location with the central configuration advantage of having the applications installed on the server.

A key factor to consider is the set of remote administration and management tools that are now part of Windows 95. These tools, such as remote registry editing and system policy management, give you the advantages of centralized management that many network administrators desired in the Windows 3.*x* environment. It is that desire for centralized management that lead network administrators to either place the Windows user files on the network or turn to third-party applications. These administration and management tools are discussed in detail in Chapter 4, "Managing the Workstation and User."

As a network administrator, you often must strive to achieve a practical balance between what would be ideal and what is realistically possible. Although you might prefer the workstation setup rather than the file server option, or vice versa, organizational factors might mitigate against the choice in any given situation. Budgetary considerations, for example, might prohibit upgrading the server to handle an increased load, or a recent set of expenditures on cable structure might prevent considerations of a server-based installation process. Thus the question of Windows 95 and its applications revolves around both technical and political matters. After some technical discussion about Windows 95 install options and the Windows 95 boot process, this chapter explores matters that deal with server and network health as factors in the location of the Windows 95 files and the overall well being of the Windows 95-based network.

Types of Installation Options

Table 5.1 summarizes the differences between a shared server directory install and a workstation upgrade install or a new Windows 95 installation, in terms of the impact on the workstation and the work that you must perform.

Table 5.1
Windows 95 Installation Options

Installation Option	Actions and Impact
Upgrade from Windows 3.*x* to Windows 95	Transfers the System.ini, Win.ini, and Protocol.ini settings into the Windows 95 Registry. Moves application settings into the Registry. Upgrades the network client to Microsoft network client. Windows 3.*x* program groups become program folders within the Windows 95 Start menu structure. Program icons become "shortcuts" on the Start menu.
Install to New Directory	All Windows-based applications must be reinstalled so that they become part of the new Windows 95 menu structure. Desktop settings and application shortcuts must be created manually. Dual boot options are provided automatically, allowing the user to choose the old DOS version rather than Windows 95.
Shared Server Directory Install	Places boot and network connectivity files on floppy drive, hard drive, or remote boot prom location source. Places user and workstation data on server locations. Creates a home directory for the workstation for its system configuration files, and places the user files in the user's Windows NT Server home directory or the NetWare user's mail directory. Places shared server program directories locations in the Registry and boot configuration files.

Server-Based Shared Installations

Windows 95 provides the you with some positive options when a full local disk installation might not be possible or the ideal option (see fig. 5.3). You must do the server-based or shared server directory install on diskless machines (machines that don't have a hard drive), on machines that boot from a floppy, and on machines that boot remotely through an NIC-installed remote boot prom. Another machine for which the server-based install might be less obvious is the workstation that has limited disk space for the Windows 95 files and/or the swap file.

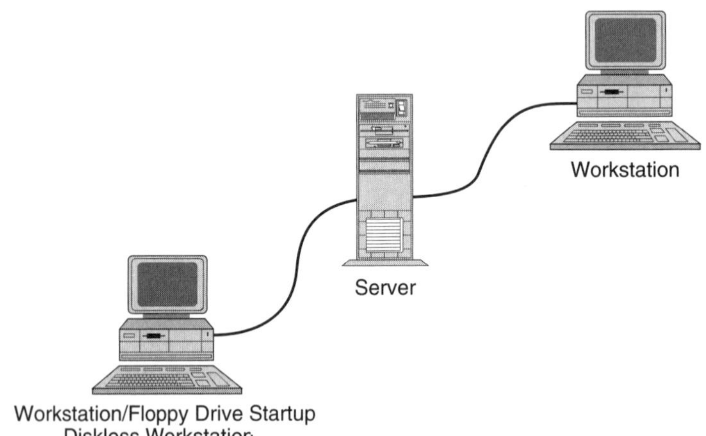

Figure 5.3
Installation choices including the shared server-based Windows 95 options.

The server-based option also might be ideal for the novice user, for example, or in situations in which you don't want to impact the working configuration of a non-Windows 95 workstation but *do* want to provide a Windows 95 environment for the user. This approach gives the user a means of becoming familiar with Windows 95 without losing his or her working environment. A Windows 95 boot floppy allows the workstation to boot to the Windows 95 environment and proceed from there to the network without disturbing the workstation's hard disk, which remains under the previous DOS version.

As will be mentioned in the context of the full workstation install, this Windows 95 shared server directory mode does not allow for the user to transit the MS-DOS real mode that might be required to run some DOS applications because the network connection would cease when the Windows 95 workstation reboots to run that special MS-DOS mode.

Windows 95 Startup Process
PROTECTED MODE OPERATING SYSTEM WIN.COM - checks and loads
Windows 95 Graphic User Interface Session
STATIC VIRTUAL DEVICE DRIVERS - VMM32.VXD or Executible Virtual Machine Manager
Normally from the Registry, but with the System.ini and Win.ini for older programs
MS-DOS DRIVERS and TSRs - Config.sys and Autoexec.bat
Config.sys for modifications of the default environment set up in the IO.SYS. Autoexec.Bat for Real Mode settings
BOOTSTRAPPING
Windows 95 IO.SYS or its Real Mode Operating System to start the computer
MSDOS.SYS - Other settings-Locations

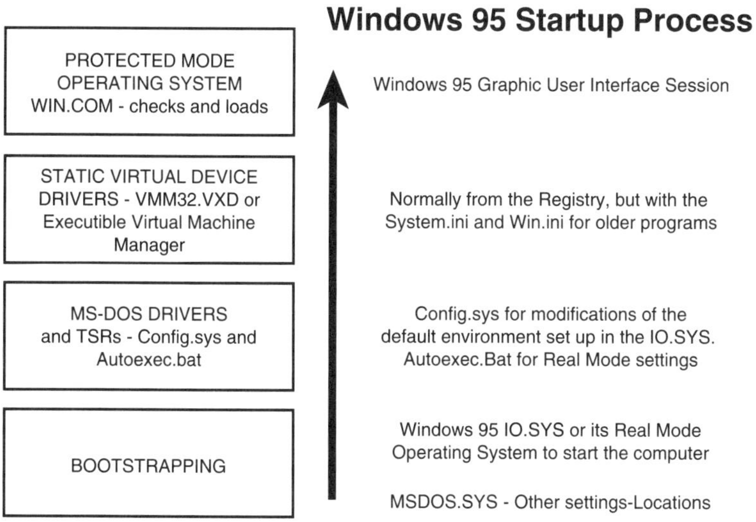

Figure 5.4
The Windows 95 startup process.

The Windows 95 Boot Process

In considering the server-based shared installations, you need to be aware of the Windows 95 startup process (see fig. 5.4). This process takes place during the startup of Windows 95 whether it is run from a full local disk installation or from a server-based installation. What makes this discussion relevant here is that the process becomes more complicated when the workstation is booted to Windows 95 and must transition to real mode to access the server and then back to Windows 95 to run the GUI.

Upon booting, Io.sys determines Windows 95's status and invokes Command.com, which activates the Config.sys and Autoexec.bat; these files should include commands for starting up the network. On real mode clients, network logon includes the user name and password, and on protected-mode clients, logon uses a generic user name. After logon, Windows 95 searches for System.dat in the home directory and sets a variable to Home\System.dat. Io.sys, then starts up Windows 95, and the transition is made to the protected-mode Microsoft Client for NetWare or Microsoft Client for Microsoft Networks.

To make it possible to use a floppy disk to boot to the Windows 95 system, the required files should fit on a 1.2 MB floppy disk that you can remove after bootup and Windows 95 startup. You can make copies of the startup floppy and use it on identically configured workstations, which makes administration that much easier. You can make the files on the floppy, as well as the floppy itself, read only, to prevent users from modifying or reformatting the disk.

Because the floppy disk and remote boot process use a hardware detection process, these methods should not be used unless you know that Windows 95 will detect the workstation's network card. These methods will not work with PCMCIA cards that need to have a driver loaded in the Config.sys file. The methods work best with established standard network cards or those that support the Windows 95 Plug and Play standard.

The following list of Windows 95 workstation files includes the required files for shared directory or server-based installations, the specific user configuration files that would be in the Windows NT Server's user's home directory or the NetWare server's \mail\user_id directory, and the workstation configuration files that would be in the workstation's home directory on the server. The list also indicates the files that provide for workstation bootup and network access to get to the full Windows 95 shared files.

Windows 95 also uses many of these files in the boot process of the full workstation installation, or remote boot prom install, so these files are discussed here in some detail. You should become familiar with the Windows 95 boot process that goes on behind the startup Windows 95 logo.

Pressing the F8 key as the Windows 95 system boots causes the system to offer a number of menu items including the Step by Step Confirmation option, which steps through the startup process, asks for confirmation of each step, and allows you to follow the startup process in detail.

- **Io.sys.** Real mode operating system that replaces the DOS system previously installed with DOS. Windows 95's installation program renames the previous version, Io.sys or Ibmbio.com, to Io.dos. Himem.sys and Ifshlp.sys are loaded by default with Io.sys, as well as Setver.exe, and, if either is on the disk, Dblspace.bin and/or Drvspace.bin.

The following is a list of the default devices loaded and the settings of the internal Config.sys file:

- **DOS=High,Umb.** Loads DOS into high memory area and makes upper memory blocks available.
- **Himem.Sys.** Opens up the memory areas above the 640 KB base memory to the session.
- **Ifshlp.sys.** Installable File System helper. This helps the system make file system calls and helps make the network part of the workstation's file system for client-side caching.
- **Setver.exe.** The DOS set version device that allows you to strategically misinform (in other words, lie to) the applications about the version of the operating system.
- **Files=60.** The default number of files open on the workstation. Can be overwritten by a Config.sys file setting.
- **LastDrive=z.** The last DOS drive setting Windows 95 uses to allow remapping of DOS drives for persistent connections.
- **Buffers=20.** Sets up buffers for applications that might need them.
- **Stacks=9,256.** Number and size of stack frames, included for applications that might need them.
- **Shell=Command.com /p.** Sets up DOS shell as permanent.
- **Fcbs=4.** File control blocks for DOS, in case older programs might require such a setting.

- **Msdos.sys.** A Windows 95-specific hidden read-only system file that establishes specific system settings, including the location of critical Windows 95 files, and provides compatibility with applications that seek the former Msdos.sys. Windows 95 renames the previous Msdos.sys file Msdos.dos. During installation on an established workstation, Windows 95 renames Command.com to Command.dos, and renames Config.sys to Config.dos.

The following are the other files you need to boot into Windows 95 real mode and then switch to protected mode:

- **Himem.sys.** Memory loader
- **Ifshlp.sys.** Installable file system

- **Ndishlp.sys.** Network Device Interface Specification (NDIS) driver
- **Protman.dos.** Protocol Manager device
- **Autoexec.bat.** Startup batch file
- **Protman.exe.** Protocol Manager executable file
- **Snapshot.exe.** Captures the memory and sets up for later reloading under protected mode
- **Net.exe.** Network executable for starting the real mode Windows 95 network
- **Net.msg.** Network message text
- **Neth.msg.** More network text
- **NDIS 2 Adapter Driver.** Real mode NDIS card driver

Remote boot workstations that boot from a remote prom on the NICs require that the following additonal files be on the server:

- **Bootdrv.com.** Executable file for booting
- **Nwrepltrm.com.** NetWare remote driver
- **Ramdrive.sys.** RAM driver for remote connectivity
- **Rplboot.sys.** Remote boot driver

When the shared server based install options are chosen the workstation accesses files on the server for configuration information (see fig. 5.5).

The shared Windows 95 server directory installations boot from the floppy or hard drive, or pull their boot files from the server. They then run real mode network drivers to get to the server and then pull their system information from one location and their user information from another location. These locations on the server are in addition to the actual shared Windows 95 program files.

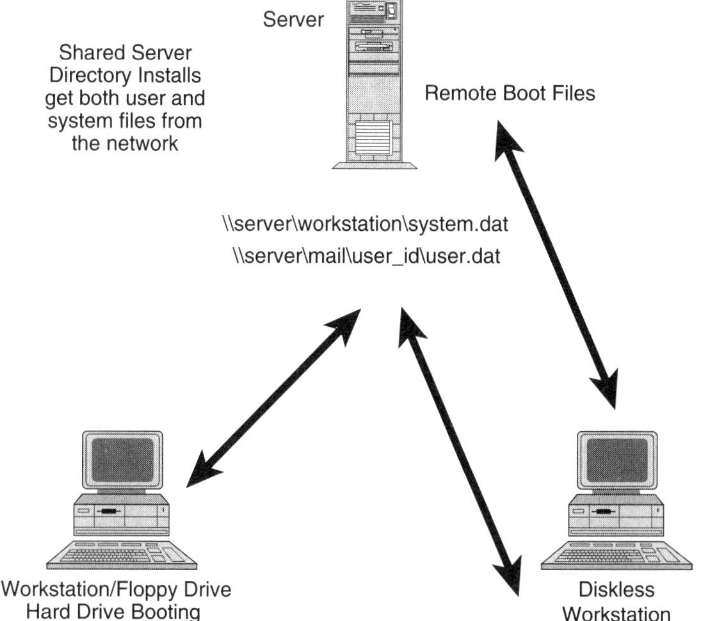

Figure 5.5
Shared directory Windows 95 installations.

Local Workstation Full Installations

A full workstation install places not only the GUI Windows 95 files and programs on the local drive, but as with the shared server directory installs, modifies the boot files to boot into Windows 95 protected mode status. All files, including the virtual memory swap file, are set up on the local drive. Any workstation that runs Microsoft Client for NetWare must run the Config.sys and Autoexec.bat files if backward compatibility is needed, and then the switch to protected mode and the protected mode logon to NetWare. This installation is the obvious choice for notebooks and workstations that must provide Windows 95 access even when the network might not be operational. All 30–40 MB of program and supporting files are self-contained at the workstation.

Perhaps not so obvious is that this full install mode is the only mode you can use to run those legacy DOS applications that require a full DOS real mode environment and cannot run in the Windows 95-based virtual DOS machine. The user would choose the shutdown option on the Start menu and then elect to have the workstation restarted in DOS real mode. Computers that depend on the server files lose contact with them during shutdown and restarting in DOS real mode.

When you, as administrator, install the full Windows 95 on a workstation, you must make a decision: install over an existing Windows 3.*x* installation or create a new and separate installation on the hard drive. Although it might appear to be as simple as whether to use or recycle space, it's far from being that simple.

Updating Windows 3.*x*

Installing Windows 95 on a workstation requires an estimated 30–40 MB as a new install, 20–30 MB installed over Windows 3.1, and 10–20 MB installed over Windows for Workgroups 3.11.

You run Setup for installing Windows 95 from the Windows GUI interface, whether you use a full existing copy or a miniset that Windows 95 Setup creates for the occasion. Whether you install from floppies, a CD, or a shared Windows 95 setup directory on the network, Microsoft recommends you do so on top of Windows 3.*x* or Windows 3.11 for Workgroups.

Installing on top of a previous Windows interface offers a few advantages for you, the administrator, as well as for other users. Setup utilizes many of the existing files, so it uses less new space on the disk. Another plus is that the process converts all existing Windows program groups into folders and shortcut icons, installing existing applications from Windows 3.*x* as programs in Windows 95 on the Start menu with the Programs option.

The potentially undesirable consequence of installing over the existing Windows installation is that Windows 95 becomes the only operating system on the workstation. The alternative, installing Windows 95 into its own directory structure, leaves the workstation with a dual boot option that lets the user press F4 during bootup for the workstation to boot to the former DOS version, or F8 to obtain a number of boot options, including that original DOS version. The downside of this alternative, however, is that you must reinstall all applications, including those from the disk's existing versions of Windows, before anybody can run them in the new Windows 95 system.

To provide a Windows 95 workstation with dual boot capability, make a bootable floppy from workstation a DOS 5 or higher version using FORMAT/S. This instructs DOS to create an Io.sys and an Msdos.sys file. Attribute them from their hidden system file status to non-hidden and non-system files and copy them to the root directory of the Windows 95 workstation as Io.dos and Msdos.dos, respectively. Copy the Command.com of the floppy disk to the root directory as Command.dos.

Windows 95 Boot Options

When the user pushes the F8 key during the startup process, the system provides a menu of options (see fig. 5.6). If there is a dual boot capability, the option of booting with the previous DOS version will appear.

Windows 95 Boot Options

- Normal
- Logged (bootlog.txt)
- Safe Mode
- Safe Mode with Network Support
- Safe by Step Confirmation
- Command Prompt Only
- Safe Mode Command Prompt Only
- Previous DOS Version

Figure 5.6
Windows 95 boot options.

These boot options exist to provide flexibility. If you have a problem starting up Windows 95 and its GUI, or loading items in one of the backward compatibility configuration files, you can run the boot process line-by-line, as in earlier versions of DOS. If, on the other hand, you want to copy files at a DOS prompt, you still can do so working with the protected mode DOS.

Workstation Versus Server-Based Installations

Being able to install Windows 95 fully to the local workstation or use one of the shared Windows program directories on the server lends flexibility to planning and implementing the Windows 95-based network client and network.

Having greater control over the user and the workstation than in earlier versions of Windows also provides you greater flexibility in planning and implementing the Windows 95 based NetWare client and network.

As you take advantage of this flexibility, you need to exercise the highest network management principles. The three areas of the greatest concern are as follows:

workstation or asset management, server management, and network traffic management. Before discussing these in detail and how each in its own way contributes to the location question, suffice it to say: You need the local disk space for Windows 95 and swap file or to make sure that the server has enough memory and processing power for the server-based load, and that the network cabling and devices can adequately handle the increased traffic of a shared server directory-based Windows 95 and NetWare network.

The Microsoft Windows 95 Resource Kit lays out the benefits of each type of installation. The benefits of installing Windows 95 on the local hard disk of a computer include the following:

- Superior performance
- User-customizable system
- Server-independent system
- Reduced network traffic

The benefits of a shared installation include the following:

- Easier to customize and manage multiple desktops
- More secure (each user must log on to the network to use the computer)
- Easier to upgrade, especially for multiple computers
- Safer for novice users, because access to system files is controlled
- Requires less computer power and has other lower system requirements

Server-based installs are easier to control and manage, while performance is far better with local workstation installs. Security is better on the server, but traffic loads are greater.

Although many of the same issues were true of the Windows 3.*x* user interface, the details are significantly different. Windows 95 requires a greater amount of disk space on the workstation, and also requires more space on the server for server-based installs. Installing, configuring, and implementing the server-based installations requires far more effort than in the Windows 3.*x* framework.

To position yourself better for making the right decision for the right reason in dealing with the location issues for the purposes of managing the network, you need to approach the network from three perspectives: the workstation, the server, and the network traffic/cable structure.

Workstation Perspectives

One of the decisions you must make is the standard that will be used for the workstation that will support Windows 95 on the network. This includes such items as processor, memory, video card, disk space, and network card. After these minimums have been established the existing workstations need to be inventoried to determine if these workstations meet the standard.

Workstation Disk Space Considerations

Although workstation disk space availability may not be an issue for new workstations coming in the door with 500 plus MB disk drives and with Windows 95 preinstalled by the vendor, it might very well be a significant issue for the large number of installed workstations on the network (see figure 5.7). You will have to test for space availability on individual workstations.

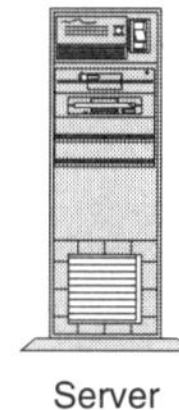

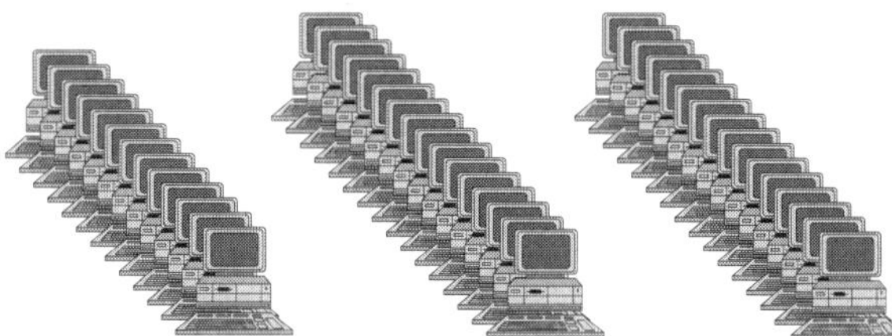

Figure 5.7
Space considerations for Windows 95 installations.

Deciding where to put Windows 95, based on space (or real estate) considerations is one workstation or asset management issue. The server-based installation requires 70–80 MB of space, along with the required configuration files for both the user and the workstation (an estimated 3 MB of files), whereas the full workstation install is approximately 40 MB without taking the virtual memory swap file into consideration.

If there is not enough free disk space on the workstations, then either the workstations need to be upgraded or disk cleared for Windows 95 or the decision will be needed to run Windows 95 from the server for any particular workstation. On the other hand, you might decide that it would be more financially realistic to run Windows 95 from the server than to upgrade a particular workstation or group of workstations.

Windows 95 starts out as any other software application in terms of workstation inventory or asset management. You must determine the standard for the Windows 95 workstation in terms of processor, workstation memory, and disk space—total and available. You also should evaluate the workstation on the basis of current network software versions, and even network cards. (Microsoft suggests updating the network card whenever possible to current versions that might be more efficient.)

Among the significant matters for determining, not only if you can run Windows 95 on a particular machine, but also from that machine's own copy, is the disk space available on that workstation. You can physically go to each workstation on the network with a pad of paper and a pencil, start up each machine, and run DIR to see the amount of free space on the computer, or you can run a copy of Microsoft's MSD (see fig. 5.8) to get a more detailed picture of the workstation. Better yet, you might run a workstation inventory program, such as the Norton Administrator for Networks' inventory module.

```
File  Utilities  Help
                          Disk Drives
Drive  Type                                  Free Space  Total Size
-----  ------------------------------------  ----------  ----------
  A:   Floppy Drive, 3.5" 1.44M
         80 Cylinders
  C:   Fixed Disk, CMOS Type 55                   7696K         99M
         287 Cylinders, 14 Heads
         512 Bytes/Sector, 51 Sectors/Track
       CMOS Fixed Disk Parameters
         934 Cylinders, 14 Heads
         51 Sectors/Track
  D:   Fixed Disk, CMOS Type 0                     120M        428M
         1023 Cylinders, 15 Heads
         512 Bytes/Sector, 63 Sectors/Track
       CMOS Fixed Disk Parameters
         306 Cylinders, 4 Heads
         17 Sectors/Track
  E:   Floppy Drive
         1 Cylinders
                              OK
Disk Drives: Displays disk drive types and sizes.
```

Figure 5.8

Microsoft's System Diagnostics disk drive data.

The MSD program also can produce a flat ASCII text file. For smaller networks that lack funding for network management and workstation inventory software, you can collect and evaluate the flat files one by one for disk drive space and other important matters, such as memory, network configuration, and so forth. The following text taken from the MSD report file shows the drive data needed to evaluate disk space available:

```
Drive Type Free Space Total Size
 A: Floppy Drive, 5.25 1.2M
 80 Cylinders, 2 Heads
 512 Bytes/Sector, 15 Sectors/Track
 B: Floppy Drive, 3.5 1.44M
 80 Cylinders, 2 Heads
 512 Bytes/Sector, 18 Sectors/Track
 C: Fixed Disk, CMOS Type 1 2472K 50M
 102 Cylinders, 16 Heads
 512 Bytes/Sector, 63 Sectors/Track
 CMOS Fixed Disk Parameters
 269 Cylinders, 16 Heads
 63 Sectors/Track
 D: Stacker Drive 123M 155M
 Actual Free Space 49M
 E: Fixed Disk, CMOS Type 0 68K 81M
 166 Cylinders, 16 Heads
 512 Bytes/Sector, 63 Sectors/Track
 CMOS Fixed Disk Parameters
 306 Cylinders, 4 Heads
 17 Sectors/Track
```

Many network administrators turn to any of numerous vendors for workstation inventory management modules or packages. One such package is the Norton Administrator for Networks (see fig. 5.9), which has an inventory module that takes a hardware and software inventory of the workstation NAN is typical of these inventory packages, which execute a real mode program during the network logon script, and in doing so, go out to the logon machine and capture data about the memory, bios, network, physical and logical drives, video, system board, and other such details.

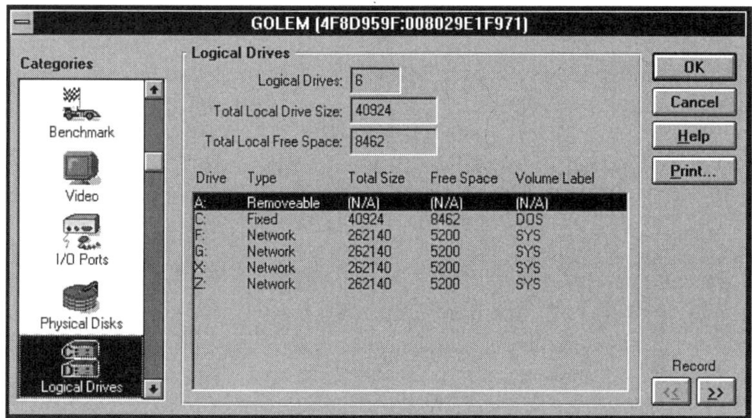

Figure 5.9

Norton Administrator for Networks inventory for logical drives.

Norton Administrator for Networks captures the individual workstation data when you run Nainv.exe from within the logon script. After it captures the data, it is available in the inventory module. You then can page through a particular workstation for a variety of information, including disk space on drives. Note the forward and backward buttons at the lower right corner on-screen. You use these buttons to wander through the database of workstations, looking at various records through the Logical Drive screen view.

Workstation Network Card Matters

The typical workstation inventory package gathers information into a network database that can then be searched for specific information. One of the relevant pieces of data beyond disk space availability is information specific to network cards (see fig. 5.10). These inventory packages can identify the network card or driver being used without the administrator having to open the workstation case and physically identify the network card.

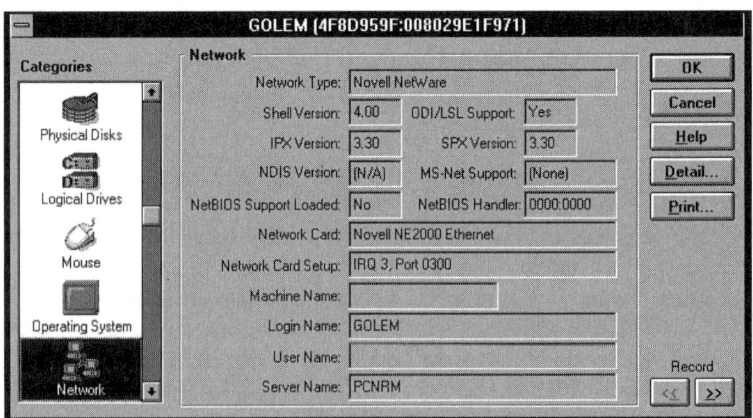

Figure 5.10
Norton Administrator for Networks network card information.

Network interface cards are a matter to which you must give careful attention. Microsoft identifies a number of manufacturers for which you need special network card configuration files, including DEC, 3COM, HP, IBM Token Ring, and Novell/Anthem ne2000+. You can find a set of network card configuration files in the *.inf file collection in the \Windows\INF directory. What you want to do here is identify all the network cards that require such attention so that at Windows 95 setup time you can properly address these matters.

Using Norton Administrator for Networks and its inventory module can facilitate finding similarly configured or equipped stations (see fig. 5.11). The inventory database can be searched for particular items either by querying the database or by using some type of filtering process such as used by the Norton Administrator for Networks Inventory Module.

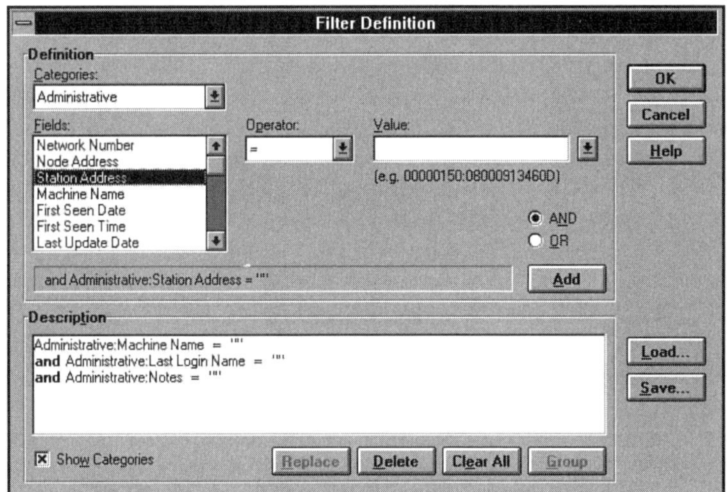

Figure 5.11
Norton Administrator for Networks inventory filtering.

To better manage the network workstation and query the network nodes for those equipped and configured to support Windows 95 and that possess enough available disk space, the typical workstation inventory management application enables you to search the database according to criteria you specify.

In any event, the local workstation needs to be able to support not only the Windows 95 program files, but the swap file as well. Further discussion of the swap file follows at the end of this chapter on location of files and applications as a special aspect of this location question. Unless a workstation has enough space to support the 30–40 MB of Windows 95 program files and drivers and roughly another 10 MB for the Virtual Memory Win386.swp swap file, you need either to upgrade or perform a Windows 95 shared server directory installation. The swap file dynamically grows and expands according to need. The Windows 95 swap file is discussed later in this chapter in the "Virtual Memory or Swap File Location Issues" section.

Overhead Versus Performance

Windows 95 involves overhead on the network. The issue facing you is just where that overhead will occur (see fig. 5.12). Will the overhead be on the server with increased activity caused by access of the program files from workstations using the shared Windows 95 directories or shared Windows applications, or will the overhead be on the administrator who will need to support Windows 95 on the workstations, along with Windows applications distributed on the workstation?

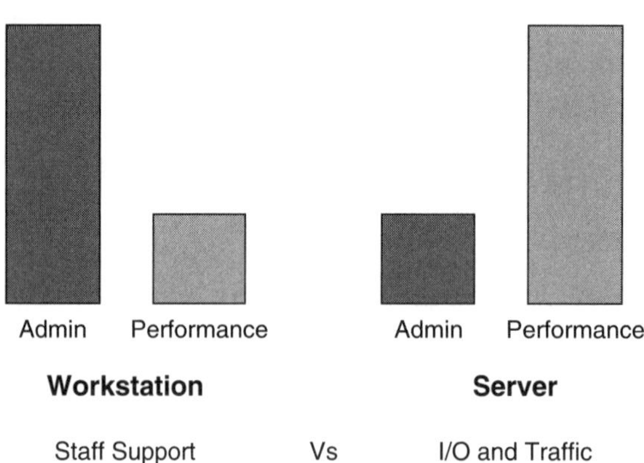

Figure 5.12
Choice of overhead, server/network versus administration.

In Windows 3.*x*, the issues were server location, with its increased use of server cache memory for open files, increased server space usage, and network traffic versus time and effort required to walk to each workstation to modify the configuration text files; and other administrative tasks that concerned the eight text files: Config.sys, Autoexec.bat, Net.cfg, Protocol.ini, System.ini, Win.ini, Control.ini, and Progman.ini.

In the long run, the Registry, with its remote registry management, will be the focus of all configuration matters, users, applications, and hardware. In the short term, text file configuration still will be required for the older applications and even the use of real mode network drivers.

Until vendors create 32-bit protected mode workstation agents, the administrative overhead might be even more than with Windows 3.*x*. As discussed in Chapter 2, "Key Issues Networking with Windows 95," the memory resident programs that a number of programs use for the distribution of configuration file changes are not available in Windows 95.

The following discussion assumes these four basic premises:

1. You will choose between the local workstation install and the server-based shared directory install.

2. Vendors will over the first six months or so after the release of Windows 95 have protected mode client versions of their network management software.

3. Remote management software will become available to inventory, configure, and meter both hardware and software, as well as remote software install management applications.

4. Although traffic will occur in the remote management of the workstations, it will occur less than by running Windows 95 from the server.

Server Performance Issues

One truism that carries over from Windows 3.*x* experience is that putting Windows and/or Windows applications on the server does indeed increase its load, CPU utilization, memory usage, and need for communication packer receive buffers. Over the years, however, server capacity has grown rapidly to match this overhead. A typical server today might, for example, have 16–32 MB RAM with a minimum 1.2 GB hard drive.

This dicussion of the NetWare file server stems from two primary factors:

- The health of the server, or the willingness and capability of the organization to pay attention to this matter and budget for the necessary upgrades
- The need to closely monitor server performance to ensure successful operation of the Windows 95-based NetWare network

Consider this discussion a brief lesson in network management that focuses on the centrality of the file server. This section utilizes a number of management packages to fill out some areas and tell about some tools currently on the market. This is in the spirit of Microsoft pointing toward the management aspect of the network.

The health of the file server, which essentially is the center of the network with its network operating system (NOS), is a fundamental area of concern in the mission to keep the networks functional. File servers work best under optimum circumstances, and will fail when limits are reached. Although network servers, such as Novell NetWare, provide some monitored statistics, LAN administrators must turn to third-party vendors for software that provides more features and longer tracking periods than does the NOS.

The NOS runs on a server that contains the RAM and disk space to service the system's users and support the operating system software. You need to consider hardware and software matters that impact the server. Your concern is not only performance but disk space usage, memory, and network traffic.

Server Architecture and CPU Performance

If you want to beef up the server, you need to utilize all resources. CPU speed is one obvious issue. Many systems now are being installed on the newer architecture EISA and local bus system boards. Under local bus and other new technologies, the peripheral cards can run faster and can offload processor responsibilities from the CPU for refreshing the video, accessing disks, and handling network messaging packets. This increased performance of the CPU means that it will use less processor cycles to complete tasks. This means that the CPU will appear to be less active or busy (see fig. 5.13). CPU utilization is a key measurement that network administrators need to track to determine the health of the network server.

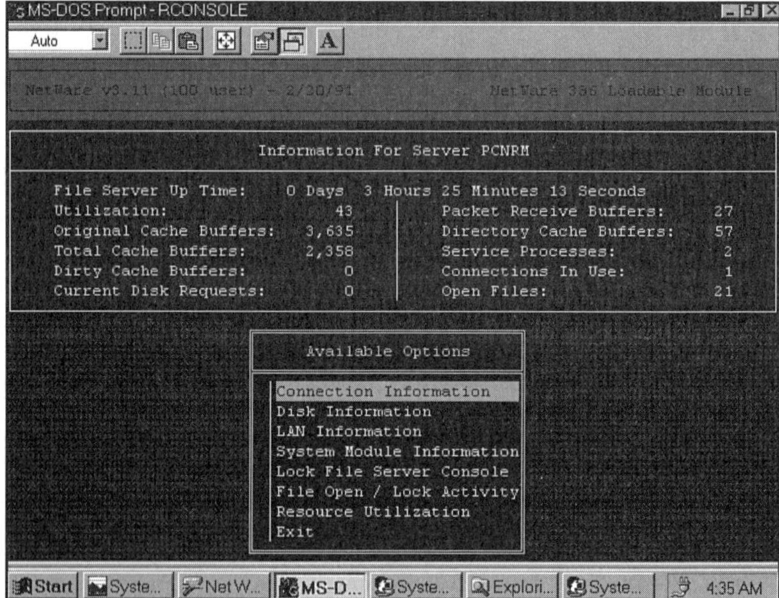

Figure 5.13

NetWare Server MONITOR NLM as seen through Windows 95 running RCONSOLE.

Novell offers the MONITOR NLM, which resides on the server. Within the Novell NetWare environment, you can run the Remote console (RCONSOLE) from workstations on the network and choose the server you want to observe. The MONITOR NLM readings are momentary measurements that do not indicate trends, which are much more important. One such measurement that you need to monitor over a period of time is server utilization, which is the measure of just how busy the server's CPU is over a given period of time.

Because the NetWare server only provides glimpses of the utilization in the Monitor screen, the you might want to use third-party server monitor applications such as Saber's Server Manager (see fig. 5.14), or similar applications from Frye, InTrak, Netmagic, or Hawknet.

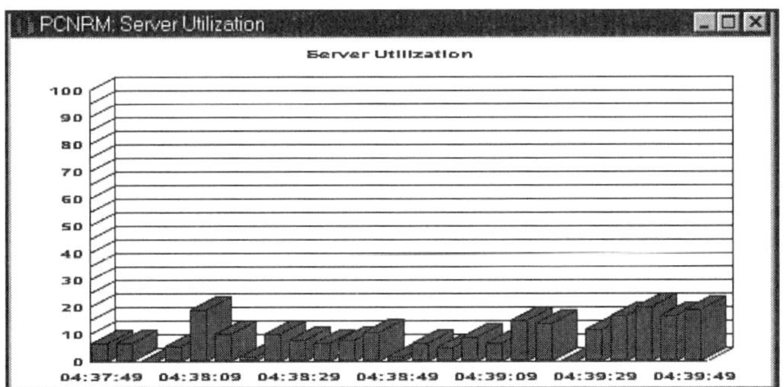

Figure 5.14

Saber Server Manager showing server utilization trends.

Server utilization basically is a percentage figure:

> % CPU Utilization = (100) × (1-(Polling Loop/Max Polling Loops)), as quoted in the *Saber Server Manager* software manual

Simply put, you calculate the amount of times per a polling period that you could talk to the server. You try to talk to the server a number of times over a period of time, and if the server fails to respond 40 percent of the time, then you say that it's operating at 40 percent utilization.

Changing from the traditional ISA to the EISA could cut the server utilization considerably, as could the newer Computer Peripherial Interface (CPI) system boards. Also, because of the way server utilization currently is calculated, certain NetWare Loadable Modules (NLMs) might significantly throw off server utilization measurements. If the server utilization is constantly in the high range of 80 percent, you might want to check out the possibility of NLM causing the constant high reading.

Server Memory Issues

Two measurements show up on the monitor screen, the Original Cache Buffers and Total Cache Buffers. The Original Cache Buffers are the 4 KB buffers that exist on the server in RAM after the server starts up and the Server.exe loads during the server's 640 KB DOS session. Thus, in the server illustrated in figure 5.13, the 3,600 cache buffers registering as original represent the approximate 14.5 MB that the server can use out of the 16 MB RAM that actually exists on the server system board.

After the File Allocation Table (FAT) and Directory Entry Table and programs or NLMs load into memory, the server illustrated in figure 5.13 has a Total Cache Buffer measurement equal to about 40 percent of the Original Cache Buffer figure. If your server had this ratio, you and the users would notice slow server performance. The watershed mark is 50 percent, and to keep server memory healthy, you should make sure that the Total Cache buffers available are significantly higher than the 50 percent mark.

Memory use is a concern with NetWare 3.11 and its Alloc memory on the server that you need to set properly for NLM memory to be released for reuse. Also keep in mind with smaller servers that you can remove DOS on the server required to load Server.exe, which facilitates remote rebooting of the server because the server exits, not to the DOS session, but to a reboot, because that DOS session isn't available.

Although information is available in the monitor's process screen, more useful information is available from one of the network management tools available for managing the NetWare server (see fig. 5.15) and for analyzing traffic on the network, namely the NetWare Management System. Such applications either provide more information than the server utilities or provide the information in more meaningful ways.

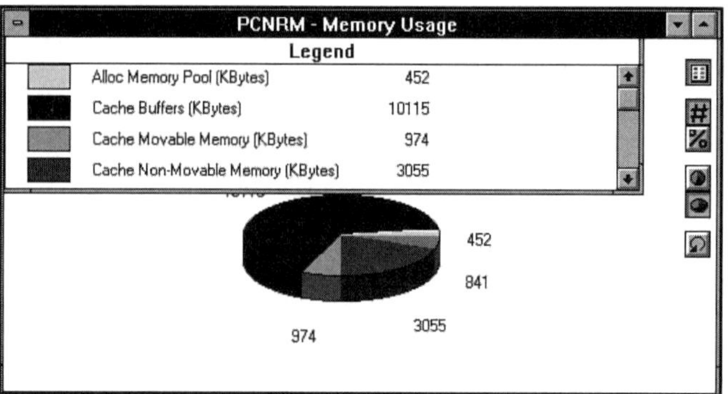

Figure 5.15
NetWare Management System's server memory.

Memory on the NetWare 3.*x* server is reflected in the image above from the NMS monitoring capability. This graph and its legend shows cache memory and then permanent as well as alloc memory. These memory pools reflect long-term versus short-lived items. What is vital to management of 3.*x* servers is the nature of this short-term memory.

With NetWare 3.*x*, simply running the network server can use up memory such as the alloc or short-term memory. When this happens, the server steals memory from file caching memory with no intention of returning it. File caching memory is used to hold open files in server memory to make them available to other users. The solution actually is to give it more memory to start out. This solution is worked through by monitoring this memory pool and increasing the starting size out of the experience with it. This tracking of specific memory is available in such representations as illustrated in figure 5.15. Fortunately, this issue is not present with NetWare 4.*x*, which handles memory far more efficently.

Another useful example of the use of third-party applications for monitoring and managing the server is the examination of server-based NLMs (see fig. 5.16). Although you can type **Modules** at the server console prompt for a listing of these loaded NLMs, applications such as the NetWare Management System provides more useful listings including memory use of these modules.

NetWare Management System - [PCNRM - NLMs]

File Edit View Fault Performance Configure Security Tools Cheyenne Window Help

LM Name	Description	Total Memory Used (Bytes)	Ve
'AGENT.NLM	Network Management Specific Agent for	105682	1.
DEWIND.NLM	NetWare 386 Instrumented OS Emulator	303276	1.
IAGENT2.NLM	Generic Agent 2	161415	1.
IAGENT.NLM	Network Management NLM	41207	1.
NZCTL.NLM	NetWare LANalyzer Agent (v1.00), Contr	44534	1.
NZSM.NLM	NetWare LANalyzer Agent (v1.00), Stati	59208	1.
NZFCB.NLM	NetWare LANalyzer Agent (v1.00), Filte	53404	1.
NZHIS.NLM	NetWare LANalyzer Agent (v1.00), Histo	41125	1.
NZAEL.NLM	NetWare LANalyzer Agent (v1.00), Alarm	33112	1.
NZDI.NLM	NetWare LANalyzer Agent (v1.00), Multi	110273	1.
NZLIB.NLM	NetWare LANalyzer Agent (v1.00), Libra	15390	1.
NZMEM.NLM	NetWare LANalyzer Agent (v1.00), Memor	304307	1.
NZSU.NLM	NetWare LANalyzer Agent (v1.00), Start	11086	1.
PLANZ.NLM	NXPLANZ	158116	2.
PIP.NLM	TCP/IP for NetWare	169920	2.
PIPX.NLM	NXPIPX	366312	2.
PMEM.NLM	Net Explorer, Memory Manager	226266	2.
TXPLOR.NLM	NETXPLOR	55764	2.
2000.LAN	Novell NE2000	8533	3.
2100.LAN	Novell NE2100	9432	3.
HERTSM.NLM	Novell Ethernet Topology Specific Modu	6998	2.
M.NLM	Novell Generic Media Support Module	11508	2.
PPLUS.NLM	Netware 3.11 NXPPLUS, Network Explorer	20256	1.
MP.NLM	SNMP Agent	64554	2.
TER311.NLM	NetWare 3.11 Forward Compatibility Sup	34262	3.
THLIBC.NLM	NetWare C NLM Runtime Math Library (fp	14107	3.
I.NLM	NetWare Transport Level Interface (TLI	11000	3.

03/23/94 06:56:36 PM

Figure 5.16

NetWare Management System: NetWare Loadable Modules listings.

This NLM format is attractive for NetWare developers because it enables applications to be run on the NetWare file server appearing to be part of the operating system in figure 5.17. The developers write their applications to hook into the software bus shown as the T-shaped form to which the different functions and NLMs are attached.

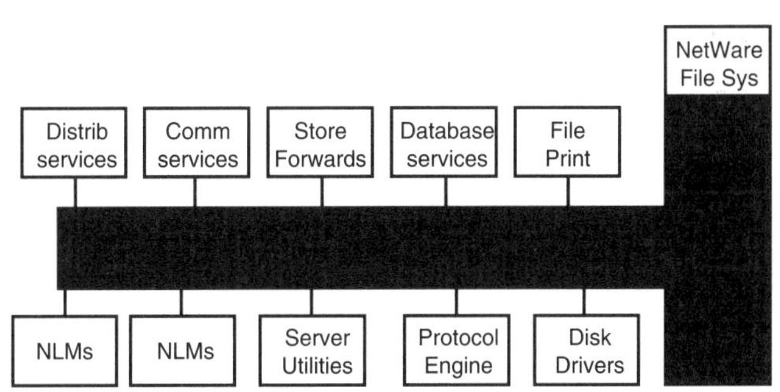

Figure 5.17

Novell NetWare's NLM structure.

Novell 3.*x* and 4.*x* are built on a basic NetWare kernel and modules that the operating system, the manager, or other NLMs can load and unload as they require. The NLMs are written to appear and behave as if they were part of the operating system and thus function more effectively.

You should guard against overloading the network server with these NLMs. The NLMs take up memory on the server even as they work for the benefit of the server, the network, or the users. If they take up too much memory, they can cause degradation to the server's performance or even lead to the crashing of the server when it runs out of memory .

Disk Channel Issues

A disk channel capable of clearing current disk requests in a timely manner is a mark of a healthy server as opposed to a channel that acts as a server bottleneck. Check the number of current disk requests over time for patterns, for information about the file activity on the server. *Dirty cache* refers to memory that houses files that have changed but have not yet been written out to disk.

Dirty cache and pending writes reflect the server's capability to write changes to disk. The speed and health of the disk controllers and the disk drives also are reflected by this measurement. You need to keep in mind that speed is determined for the user by how long it takes to get data from the server. The hidden aspects of disk writes and actual saves to disk are important measurements.

High measurements in dirty cache and pending writes are signals that you need to pay attention to the disk channel, just as a consistently high CPU utilization rate tells you that you're placing too much pressure on the CPU for performance and need a more potent CPU or a second server, or perhaps to check for NLMs that might be eating at the CPU cycles.

When is a saved file saved? Not when the user thinks, but rather, when NetWare flushes out the dirty cache buffers to disk. By default, NetWare has 3.3 seconds to write the data to disk. The maximum wait time is 10 seconds. You can make the server more efficient in terms of disk reads by increasing the time from 3.3 seconds to a larger time wait—at the risk of crashing and losing changes sitting in the dirty cache buffers.

System Fault Tolerance—Disk Issues

System fault tolerance is a critical issue to network and server management, because it provides a margin of safety for data protection and integrity. What makes system fault tolerance relevent here is the tension between the read and the write functions on the network. Users somehow trust you, the administrator, to provide saved files when they need them again, but are less than tolerant when it comes to accessing their files from the network. Who can be patient when the network is slow?

As you work through the ability to provide a safety net on the network, you need to consider network performance issues. You can improve the speed of access to program files and data files and also provide data file integrity. Novell distingushes between levels of system fault tolerance as follows:

- **Level one.** Read after write verification
- **Level two.** Disk mirroring or duplexing
- **Level three.** Duplicate servers

This books confines its discussion to levels one and two.

Read After Write Verification

The most basic form of fault tolerance starts with concern about the operation of the electromechanical disk drives that develop bad sectors over time. In the DOS world, the expression is "read after write verification." The NetWare term for the same thing is "hot fix." When you create a disk partition you save 2 percent of the disk for a safety zone. When NetWare performs a read after write verification and cannot verify the write, it dynamically adds the storage location to the bad block table and rewrites the data to the redirection block area, which ensures the integrity of the data.

Novell was a pioneer in the read after write verification of data files to maintain the integrity of data, but you do accrue an overhead when you maintain this hot fix system fault tolerance level 1. NetWare expends a certain amount of effort to verify the disk writes. Considering the capability of any of today's disk controllers to perform read after write verification, you can go ahead and turn off this operating system feature, lifting this burden from the Novell server's shoulders.

Requiring the hardware to perform read after write verification allows the server software to better attend to reading user program and data files, which provides users the Windows 95 programs and data files more efficiently and quickly than if it had to do the read after write verification itself.

Protecting Against Disk and Controller Failure

You must also be concerned about the failure of the disk itself and the disk controller (see fig. 5.18). A positive aspect of this protection is that providing two distinct channels, controller and disk, can actually speed up server performance for the user by allowing faster reads from disk. While one channel is writing, the other can be used for reads, which is how the users judge the network performance anyway.

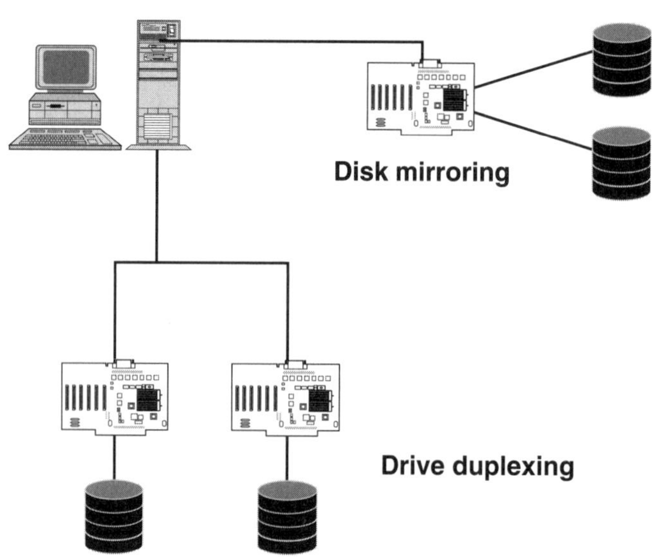

Figure 5.18
System fault tolerance level two.

Level two fault tolerance protects in the event of failure of the whole disk drive by configuring the system with two disk drives so that one can stay up if the other crashes. This is called *mirroring* if you use one disk contoller, *duplexing* if you use two disk contollers, one for each disk. Duplexing also means that the operating system can determine which disk will provide the faster disk read at any moment to better serve the users.

An advanced form of system fault tolerance level two is what is called RAID (see fig. 5.19). This arrangement of multiple disks is finding its way into the server market especially where up time for the servers is critical.

The newest form of fault tolerance is RAID, or Random Array of Inexpensive Disks, which provides disk striping as a means of improving speed by writing and then reading data across the number of disks, and data integrity by writing parity data across the disks as well. Under RAID level five, for example, you can pull out the bad disk and replace it with a new disk, and RAID then rebuilds the lost disk data onto the new disk.

RAID Technology

RAID Level 5

- **Both Data and Parity striped across entire array**
- **Offers on-the-fly fault tolerance by replacing drives**
- **Any drive may fail - no Single Point of Failure!**

Figure 5.19
RAID disk arrangement.

Disk Storage Block Size

When Novell loads the server, the FAT loads into server's RAM to track all parts of the server files. With a default storage block size of 4 KB, a 2 MB file will have 512 entries in the FAT. Considering the many multimegabyte data files, especially as graphics files grow, you might want to increase the disk storage block size and reduce the number of FAT entries required. This not only reduces the FAT's RAM requirements, but provides faster access to data in these files because fewer FAT entries have to be searched. The problem with pre-4.*x* servers is that a 1 KB file wastes more space, but 4.*x* suballocation lets you put 512 byte file pieces in the larger disk blocks. All versions let you set the disk block size for each volume and have volumes with 4 KB for word processing and 16 KB for big data use.

NetWare 4.*x* makes adjustments for large file size by basing its block size on the size of the volume created. It can use these larger block sizes because of the subblock allocation scheme that allows multiple files to be stored within one storage block.

Volume Size	Storage Block Size
1–31 MB	4 KB
32–149 MB	8 KB
140–499 MB	16 KB
500–1999 MB	32 KB
2000+ MB	64 KB

With Windows 95 and the profile Lnk files stored in the \\server\mail\user_id directory, the NetWare 4.*x* subblock allocation often proves to be a tremendous space saver because these files are quite small.

Server Network Traffic Issues

You must also be concerned with the server itself as a source of network slow down or bottleneck. Here, you need to consider the network card on the server and the packet receive buffers on the server.

The Server Network Card

The server requires network cards that are good at handling packets coming in and buffering them on their way to CPU attention. The newer 32-bit bus mastering local bus cards take advantage of the new higher speed system boards. Multiple network cards on the server allow multiple party lines so that users have a better chance of fighting network traffic. More on this traffic configuration later in this chapter.

The Communication Packet Receive Buffers

A key matter on the server is the ability of the server to handle all the requests that come in from the workstation. The NetWare server allows a certain number of the request packets to accumulate in a memory area on the server that might be called the "waiting room." If there is a buffer available the server will accept the packet and move it into the waiting room; if not, it will not allow the packet into the server, having the server's network card deny access.

To understand the impact of such a refusal, the structure of the NetWare IPX packet needs to be reviewed (see fig. 5.20). You need to consider the structure that provides such data as the source and address of the packet, the protocol information, the message content itself, and a means of providing error checking.

Figure 5.20

IPX packet simplified.

Simplified Message Packet

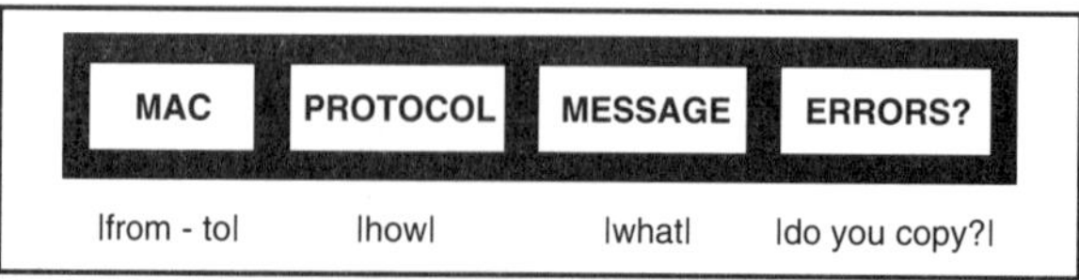

When you send a packet, you wait for response from the recipient: This message is based on the error checking performed using the sender's "I am sending you so many 1s and so many 0s" with 1s and 0s being the machine-level way communicated over networks. The sender expects one of two responses: Received as sent or retransmit! Machines not getting either response go into IPX Retries for the default of twenty times until a response or a time-out, whichever comes first. Packets not getting read by the intended recipient die on the wire, die of old age on Token Ring, and are killed off by the end of the cable terminator on Ethernet. Computers whose packets are lost resend until receiving response or timing out.

Network traffic to the server needs to get in the server or it generates more traffic as the workstations go into IPX retry mode. When traffic to and from the server increases, you need to create more waiting room seats, or communication packet receive buffers. If you have too few of these buffers, the server network card refuses to even look at the packet for error checking. If there is room, the NIC reads the error checking. You then want to increase the buffers so they are adequate for the traffic load. Keep in mind that in Windows 3.*x*, and now in Windows 95, increased numbers of packets go to and from the file server. The modular nature of Windows, Dynamic Link Libraries, and virtual device drivers all contribute to increasing traffic.

The following list provides rough guidelines for setting the proper amount of buffers:

- For every network card in the server, provide 10 buffers.
- For every file server directly on the network cable, provide 10 buffers.
- For every external bridge, gateway, router, or brouter on the network, provide 10 buffers.
- For every shared printer on the LAN, provide two buffers.
- For every logged-on user, provide one buffer.

The default settings for the Startup.ncf files are 10 buffers, which come right out of the cache buffers available on the server. The server, by default, allows a tenth of a second to seat the incoming packet before it must create another buffer by stealing the memory from the cache buffer memory on the server. It creates an 11th, a 12th, and on up to 100 buffers, which is the default maximum specified in Autoexec.ncf. Following the guidelines given in the preceding list, you might set the maximum much higher to accomodate these traffic factors or to meet the configuration needs of communication processes such as TCP/IP or SNA gateways. The settings in the Startup.ncf hold for the server up time session, you can adjust the settings in Autoexec.ncf upward. Note that the MONITOR server program shows the current numbers of Packet Receive buffers and File Server Processors (FSPs).

The discussion of the network traffic load that follows might lead to segmenting the network or increasing the number of network cards in the server to create new Ethernet segments or Token Rings to spread out the traffic load and reduce the load per cable. If an extra network card is placed in the server for load balancing of network traffic, you need to worry about the impact on the communication packet receive buffers the system needs (see fig. 5.21). Increasing the network cards in the server generates more packets arriving at the server, which then need to be met with packet buffers and serviced by file server processors.

Layers to deal with increased server utilization

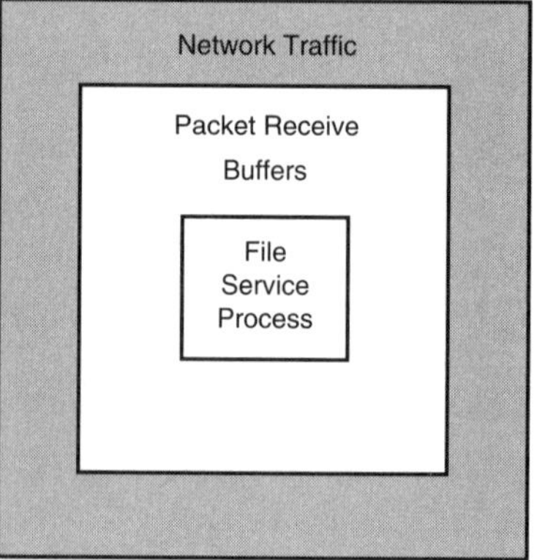

Figure 5.21

Packet buffers, traffic, and file server processes.

Figure 5.21 notes the outer and inner spaces dealt with. The buffers and the file server processors use server memory to do their jobs. The buffers are set at the 1 KB size of Ethernet or the 4 KB size of Token Ring. FSPs are set at roughly 1 KB larger than the buffer size. You use server set commands to increase the minimum and set the maximum of these items.

Note You need to be aware of the kinds of concerns that accompany the location question of Windows 95 and Windows applications. Before you even consider the server location for server-based shared Windows 95 program installations on the server, you need to be able to evaluate server health using the previously outlined server concerns. If you find that your servers do not pass these basic health requirements or that you cannot build up the server functionality to support this extra Windows related load then you cannot even consider the server location as an option.

Network Traffic Issues

Network traffic is impacted by the location of Windows 95 shared program directories on the server and/or Windows applications on the server, be they the 16-bit or new 32-bit Windows programs. These programs and their components, such as the many Dll files, cause the creation of significantly more message packets going to and from the file server.

Traffic on a network is both a necessary evil and a problem. Without traffic, the need for a network disappears, but too much traffic can bring a network screeching to a halt. Traffic and packet analyzers enable you to monitor whether traffic is too much or might owe to problems concerning NICs or cables.

The following poetic description of the packet provides some insight into the function and activity of network traffic.

> Consider the packet. A figment of the network imagination, the packet serves as a digital drone traversing your network at the speed of light. Day and night millions of packets cycle through your well-laid rings, backbones, and switches—colliding, reconciling, presenting their digital IDs to watchful routers, then continuing on their way. Your network pulses with these transient voyagers, in fact your business depends upon them.

John Battle, "The Big Picture," *Corporate Computing*, June 1993.

Figure 5.22 shows the four basic components of the packet, which serves as an envelope for network requests and data transmissions. The MAC (Media Access Control) piece contains the network card addresses, the protocol or language of communication shared by the nodes, the message or data section, and the basic error checking for the correct number of 1s and 0s—the basic language unit of the computer.

Simplified Message Packet

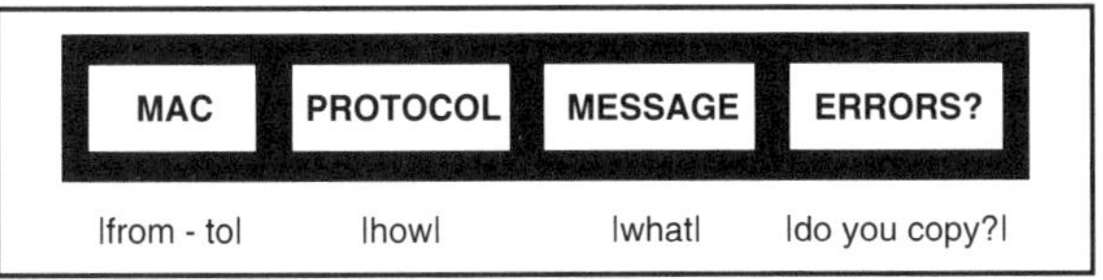

Figure 5.22

The network packet simplified.

Traffic

Traffic is generated by the transmission of the packet, usually originating as a request or message from the application layer of the OSI tower (see fig. 5.23). The message or request travels down the seven layers, picking up baggage or additional information at each level. In an office environment, this would be similar to being printed out, placed in an envelope, then in an "interoffice" envelope, then in a mail bag, then in a mail truck that delivers it to the second office location. The highway is the cable and upon arrival at the other location, the message arrives at the "application" level after coming out of the mail bag, "interoffice" envelope, its own envelope, and placed on the recipient's desk.

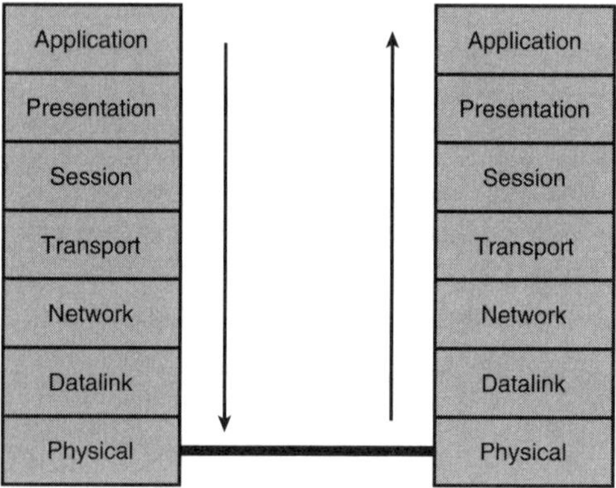

Figure 5.23
OSI networking layers.

Primary Methods of Traffic Control

Traffic or the movement of packets needs to be controlled on the cable. The primary means of controlling traffic on your networks break down to Ethernet or Token Ring and ARCnet.

Ethernet

Traffic control in Ethernet is based on the principle of silence: I transmit only when I don't sense any one else on the cable. Known more formally as CSMA/CDCA, Ethernet came about as a means of developing a one-cable solution for a variety of networking protocols. Its original sponsors include Digital, Intel, and Xerox, whose initials became the name of the original thick Ethernet cable connector, the DIX connector.

Token Ring and ARCnet

Although differing significantly, Token Ring and ARCnet control traffic using a token, where you transmit only when you hold the token. The token is controlled on the cable by one of the stations functioning as an "active monitor." This station makes sure that the token always is fresh and active. Token Ring networks are characteristic of shops that have IBM Main Frames or System 36 and AS/4000 platforms, because until a few years ago, IBM did not support Ethernet networks.

Secondary Methods of Traffic Control

Beyond the cable controlling methods, you can add other levels of control. You can extend the engineered lengths of cabling, which supports the Ethernet method. You can prevent messages from going beyond the cable segment by using filtering bridges or targeting the next step for the packet using routers. You now can turn to switches to increase the bandwidth of the cable systems, using sophisticated traffic management techniques that split the cable into segments and then pretend that each has the full bandwidth of the cable, so four segments seem to increase the bandwidth of the cable 400 percent.

As network management expands its horizons, intelligence is being built into these secondary method devices. Hub or concentrator vendors are providing Windows-based applications that enable you to manage these network devices remotely. Narrowly defined, network management can mean specifically the management of these devices. Vendors often use Simple Network Management Protocols (SNMPs) to monitor their devices. Vendors then write Management Information Base records (MIBs) for their devices and their device-specific management applications. Vendors who write SNMP management consoles enable these consoles to add device-specific MIBs to the database of the console.

Protocols

Protocols are standards that establish the ways the computers can communicate. NetWare uses the Internet Packet eXchange (IPX) protocol. Unix operating systems have established the Transmission Control Protocol/Internet Protocol (TCP/IP) brand of standards for intercomputer communications. Microsoft and IBM have been using the NetBIOS or NetBEUI (NetBIOS Extended User Interface) protocol. Apple Macintosh computers might use the AppleTalk Protocols. Windows 95 can use IPX or NETBEUI and also run TCP/IP along with either protocol.

Network Management and Analysis Concepts

This section discusses tools that are used in the measuring of traffic, which is a concern for two reasons. The first is the consideration about where to place Windows 95 and the Windows applications, knowing that when placed on the server, running Windows 95 and applications can generate traffic. The question is whether the network cabling and structure can sustain this extra load without degredation of performance. The second area of concern is the monitoring of traffic patterns so that the network does not become saturated and present problems for the user and the network administrator.

SNMP and RMON Standards

Simple Network Management Protocol (SNMP) is one of the most widespread standards for establishing messaging between computers, hubs, routers, printers, and even UPS power sources, and a centralized management computer console. SNMP is a system of "standard" behavior for elements for comparisons during polling by the console, and "traps" or alerts coming from the agents on the nodes or devices.

Coming into the LAN from the Unix environment, SNMP has the following three basic components:

- Central management console
- Agent residing in a device, such as a personal computer, network card, bridge, router, hub, gateway, or Uninterrupted Power Supply
- MIB

The MIB is a set of database records establishing, within reason, the predictable behavior of the agent's device.

RMON (remote monitoring) is a subset of the SNMP MIB, sending reports across the network in TCP/IP packets or SNMP packets. Agents are placed on the LAN segment to be monitored. RMON collects and analyzes the data and then reports its findings to a central management console.

Under the traffic monitoring of the SNMP and RMON standards are areas and concepts used by traffic analyzers and monitors to measure traffic and alert the network manager about potential problems.

Statistics

This aspect tracks the number of packets traveling on the network and calculates the bandwidth utilization and errors that occur on the network segment during a specific period of time.

History

For analysis purposes, you can maintain a set of statistics for a period of time so that you can review and graph them for study. This enables you to respond to current trends and plan for future needs.

Alarms

You can set the monitoring threshold to send alarms to the network manager when traffic packet numbers or bandwidth utilization exceed preset measurements that seem to make sense for the specific network. You can use the history you collect to establish the benchmark for setting the alarm-tripping threshold.

Hosts

This process referred to as the number of hosts collects statistics for each network node identified by the media access control identity of the network interface card. The manufacturer burns the identity into the card.

Hosts Top N

When you review network statistics, this aspect lets you sort the top *N* number of nodes on the network by any of the statistics you gather, such as number of packets or bytes received or transmitted.

Traffic Matrix

Network managers at times need to review statistics that concern the traffic that passes between two specific nodes on the network. Such capability can be useful when traffic between two nodes might be the subject of a search for faulty traffic on the network.

Filter

Filtering the packets allows for more focused analysis. In multiple protocol networks, you might want to limit the specific protocols that you review. So, you might want to capture and review specifically the IPX, AppleTalk, or IP traffic. Another use for the filter might be to filter "bad packets" when you suspect them and then analyze them to determine the faulty network card by address.

Packet Captures

This is the facility for capturing a given number of packets or the size of the buffer in which to capture and store the packets for analysis. After you capture the packets, you can review them for source and destination, and type of traffic or protocol transaction.

Event

An *event* takes place when the traffic exceeds alarm thresholds and traps are sent to the network management console for response from you, the network administrator. Events are logged and might also serve to set off reactions by the management application. Among the reactions might be a beeper page.

Network Analysis Platforms

The platforms used to utilize the RMON standards and procedures vary from the larger Unix or mainframe platform to software run on your PC or workstation. The applications available vary in scope from LANdecoder/e, the dedicated Ethernet protocol analyzer, from Triticom to Hewlett Packards' Openview, which runs on the Unix platform and can work with Ethernet and Token Ring and a variety of networking protocols.

The Novell NetWare Management System

Novell's NetWare Management System (NMS) is an umbrella application into which other vendors' software should fit or snap in. You will see that it has some real strength for the manager in the traffic and packet analyzer module, which is similar to the LANalyzer for NetWare, the Windows-based program (see fig. 5.24).

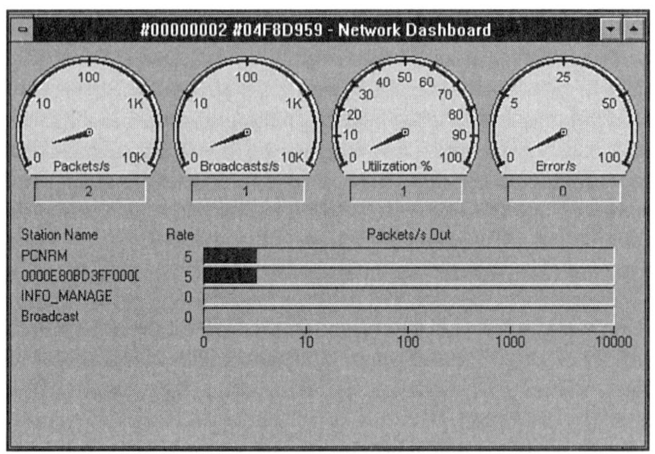

Figure 5.24
NetWare Management System's Network Dashboard.

NMS is based on an Explorer module and a LANalyzer module running on a server, and a console station on a Windows-based machine. The station acting as an NMS station activates a Network Explorer module, which reads some server and network information into an NMS database. If you click on a specific network segment, you can see the LANalyzer screen shown in figure 5.25. The icons can then be used to choose monitoring functions such as traffic metering, packet capturing, or checking for most active network nodes. All these icons represent functions listed above as aspects of SNMP and RMON monitoring.

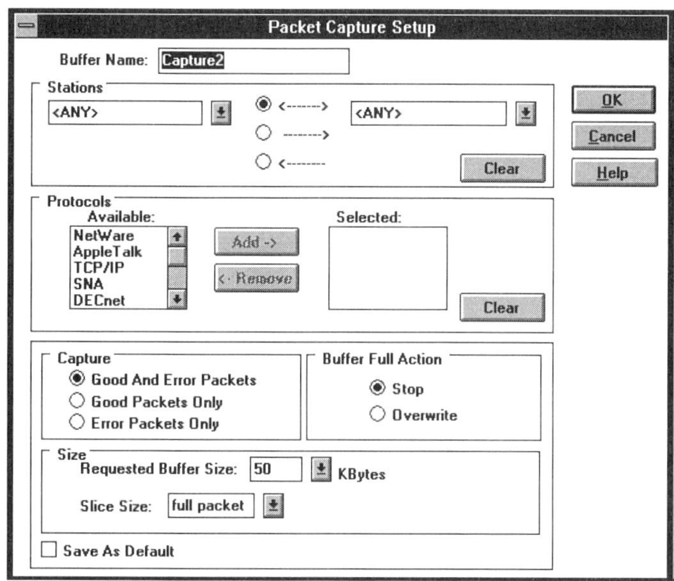

Figure 5.25

NetWare Management System's Packet Capture Setup screen.

You can then capture packets as described in figure 5.26. After you define the packets, you capture them before you analyze them. Please note that on the Packet Capture Setup screen illustrated in figure 5.25, you can choose NetWare, AppleTalk, TCP/IP, SNA, DECnet protocol packets to monitor.

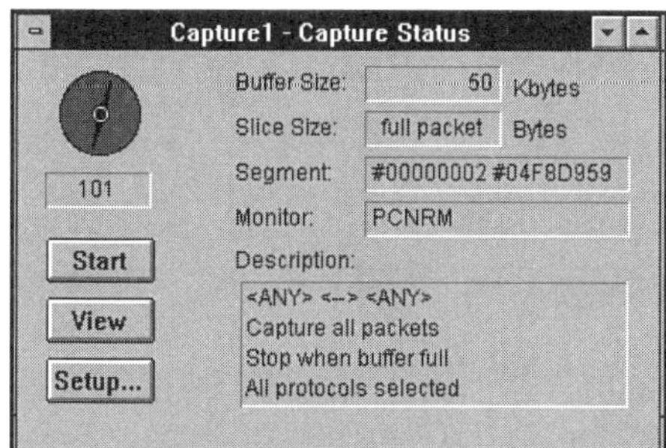

Figure 5.26

NetWare Management System's Capture Status screen.

Generally, you capture a given buffer file size worth of packets to analyze and work with. You can then analyze the packets by calls to the NOS and servers. Another use of the analyzer is to see who creates the traffic and see if that makes sense. A word processing station shouldn't generate much traffic, but an accounting station or database report writing station might. Once captured, the packets can be analyzed for patterns and unusual activity (see fig. 5.27). The captured packets in this program will display the to and from nodes, the type of protocol being used, and a summary of the request or reply being carried by the packets.

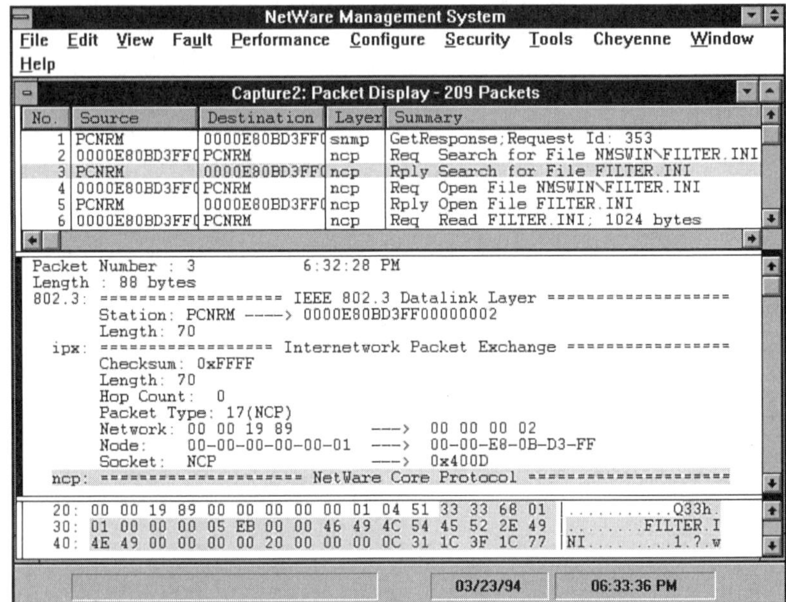

Figure 5.27
NetWare Management System's captured packet display.

You can review the captured packets one by one or you can have the packet capture setup choose only the bad packets so that you can determine the stations involved in that type of traffic. Note in figure 5.27 that the packet information first provides a summary set at the top of the screen, a viewing of the structure mid-screen, and a hex dump at the bottom. Users can resize the screen pieces to better view an item.

The summary section shows source and destination by server name and network card address, the protocol layer and then the summary of activity. The first three packets captured here are SNMP packets, which show the normal polling process of Get Request and Get Response. The next three packets are at the level of NetWare Core Protocol, which is the application layer calls at the server, wherein the client has asked for a close file action, and then once that was replied to, an open file request.

Another major concern within traffic analysis is the review of the top traffic producers (see fig. 5.28). This enables you to review the nodes that create the most traffic on the network.

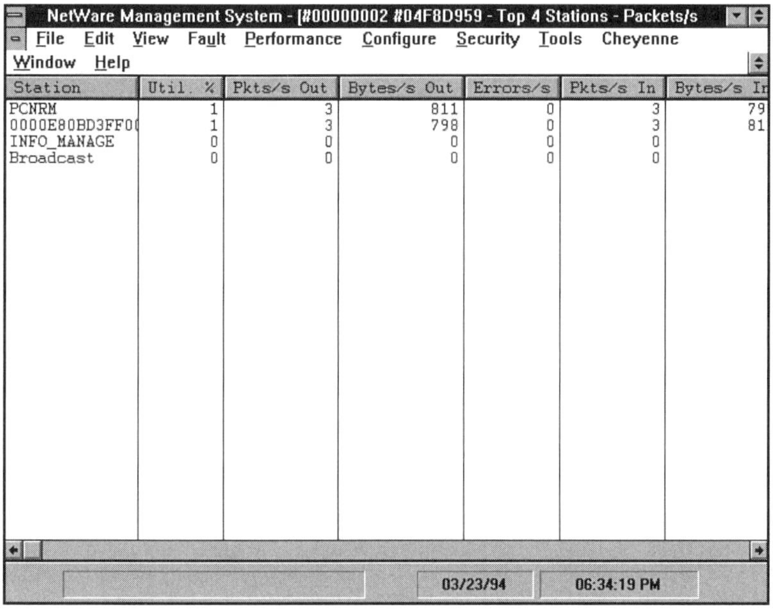

NetWare Management System - [#00000002 #04F8D959 - Top 4 Stations - Packets/s

File Edit View Fault Performance Configure Security Tools Cheyenne

Window Help

Station	Util. %	Pkts/s Out	Bytes/s Out	Errors/s	Pkts/s In	Bytes/s In
PCNRM	1	3	811	0	3	79
0000E80BD3FF0(	1	3	798	0	3	81
INFO_MANAGE	0	0	0	0	0	
Broadcast	0	0	0	0	0	

03/23/94 06:34:19 PM

Figure 5.28
NMS's top packet producing stations.

As previously mentioned, the HOST TOP N measurement exemplified in the NMS top packet producing report screen, is a process that involves sorting out nodes by traffic produced to check for problems in the network. Clearly, you then can determine whether such active status is appropriate for a particular node. If inappropriate, you can track that station or device down and do some specific troubleshooting.

The Intel LANDesk Traffic Analyzer

Intel offers two versions of its traffic monitoring and analyzing software, one a stand-alone that comes in both DOS (see fig. 5.29) and Windows flavors, and the other a version integrated into the LANDesk Manager package. The LANDesk Manager version is Windows-based and not as full-featured as the stand-alone model.

The LANDesk program also enables you to review the captured packet (see fig. 5.30). This provides more insight into the traffic patterns on the network.

First, capture the packets, then analyze or decode them. The software enables not only analysis, but also the ability to generate traffic for testing purposes. Note the packet seen in figure 5.30 is the NetWare Server Advertising Protocol (SAP), which represents the server announcing itself every 60 seconds to the network as being present and available for activity and routing.

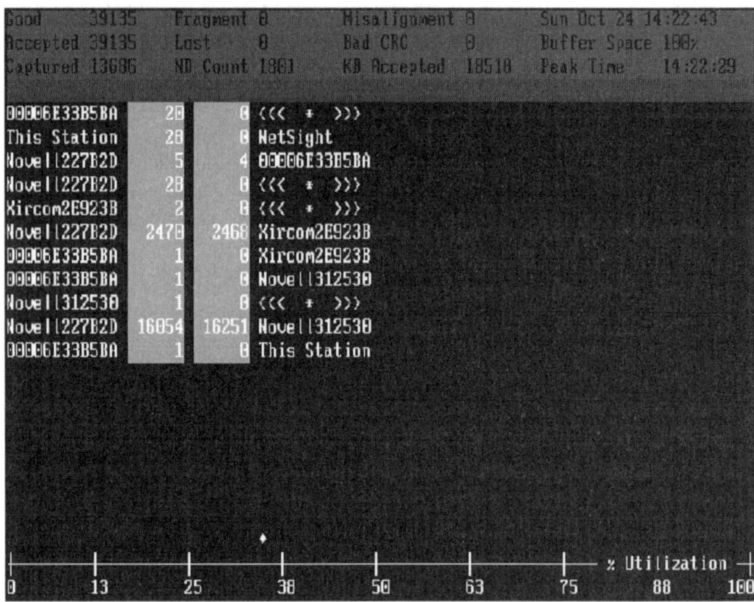

Figure 5.29
LANDesk Traffic Analyst for DOS.

Figure 5.30
LANDesk Traffic Analyst frame decoder.

```
LANDesk Traffic Analyst(tm) V2.00                          Sun Oct 24 14:23:25
                         Full Decode of frame 1
  ========== Service Advertizing Protocol Services 2 Bytes at Offset 44
SAP:
SAP:    Sap Type: Service Advertise (0002)
SAP:
  ========== Server Identification Packet 64 Bytes at Offset 46 =======
SIP:
SIP:    Server Type: 023A (Unknown Server:)
SIP:    Name: INFO_MANAGE
SIP:    Network: 00000006
SIP:    Node: 000000000001
SIP:    Socket: 0000
SIP:    Hops: 0002
                              Hex Decode
0000:  FFFF FFFF  FFFF 0000  6E33 B5BA  0160 FFFF  |  ........n3...`..
0010:  0160 0000  0000 0001  FFFF FFFF  FFFF 0452  |  .`.............R
0020:  0000 0001  0000 6E33  B5BA 0452  0002 023A  |  ......n3...R...:
0030:  494E 464F  5F4D 414E  4147 4500  0000 0000  |  INFO_MANAGE.....
0040:  0000 0000  0000 0000  0000 0000  0000 0000  |  ................
0050:  0000 0000  0000 0000  0000 0000  0000 0000  |  ................
0060:  0000 0006  0000 0000  0001 0000  0002 0004  |  ................
0070:  494E 464F  5F4D 414E  4147 4500  0000 0000  |  INFO_MANAGE.....
```

The Intel LANDesk Traffic Analyst has a Windows version (see fig. 5.31) that adds come clarity to the process of reviewing the network traffic through its more graphical interface.

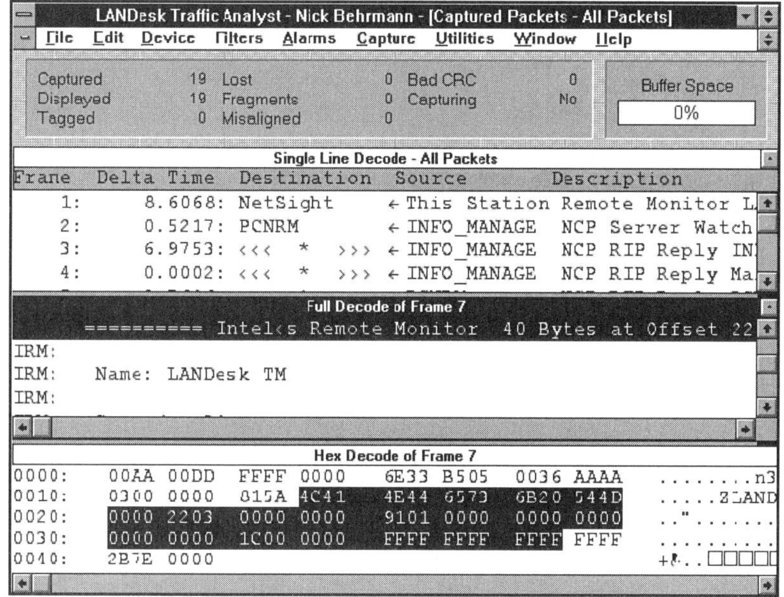

Figure 5.31

LANDesk Traffic Analyst for Windows.

The Windows version not only is easier to read, but provides more information. Note the different types of packets you can track and monitor. The monitor process here tallies the bad packets, defined as lost, fragments, misaligned, or failing the simple checksum or Cyclical Redundancy checking error checking to make sure that the right numbers of 0s and 1s are transmitted and received. You note in this packet set the RIP protocol. RIP (Routing Information Protocol) is usually a request for directions to the server, or "how do I route my packet to find the network segment where you are?"

Figure 5.32 presents two different views of packet rates on your network. LANDesk uses the thermometer metaphor for packet rates, percentage of utilization, and error rates. You also see the history over a period of time and a set of counts for particular packet types. Notice that LANDesk handles NetWare, TCP/IP, and AppleTalk packets.

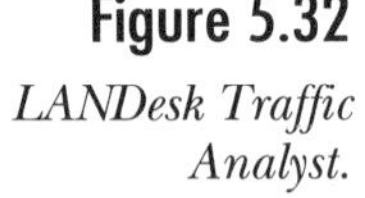

Figure 5.32

LANDesk Traffic Analyst.

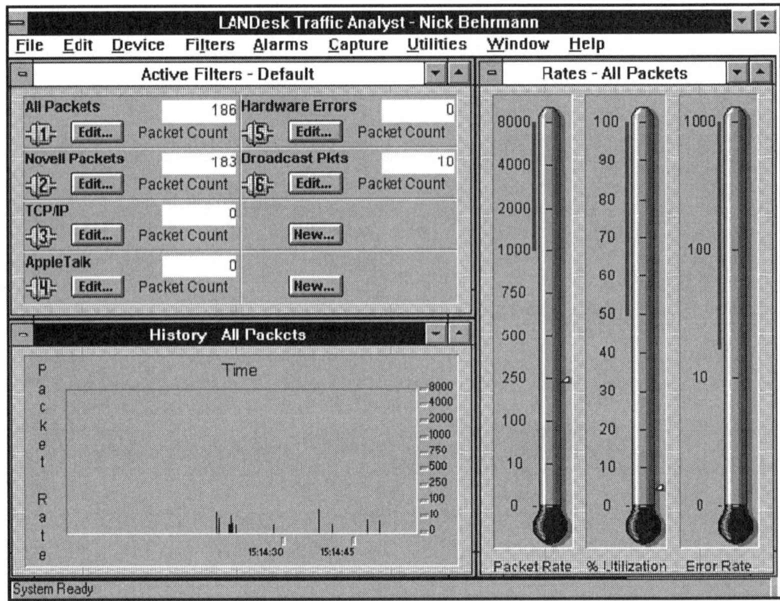

Frye's NetWare Management and Node Tracker

Frye Computer Systems provides two modules that feed information about traffic on the network: the NetWare Management module (see fig. 5.33) and the Node Tracker module (see fig. 5.34). These items not only enable you to view network traffic issues differently than the applications present previously, but they also allow discussion about other network aspects as well.

From a manager's workstation, you can see who's on the NetWare network and observe some statistics regarding the protocol and the client shell. You see the up time of the workstation and observe the type of traffic being generated. IPX and SPX statistics differ in the type of use for the packets. IPX is the standard packets, while SPX is for packets when you need confirmation or guaranteed connections, such as in NetWare's Rprinter, where use of a network shared modem or using the remote console RCONSOLE to run server commands from your workstation, using RSPX.

After you log on to the network, you can use Frye's Node Tracker to access the workstations (access, that is, in terms of over-the-wire monitoring of network issues). Here, you can see the protocol and shell data along with the DOS version and setup of the network card on the node, which can help you with troubleshooting issues.

IPX is the protocol used between the workstation and the NetWare server. Traffic analysis involves wanting to know about the performance of the workstation's packets on the network. The IPX statistics reflected in figure 5.34 tell you about the capability of the packets of this machine to reach their destination and be responded to by the server. If the server does not accept the station's packets, these packets would be recorded in the packets lost or no ECB, or no Event Control Block, items.

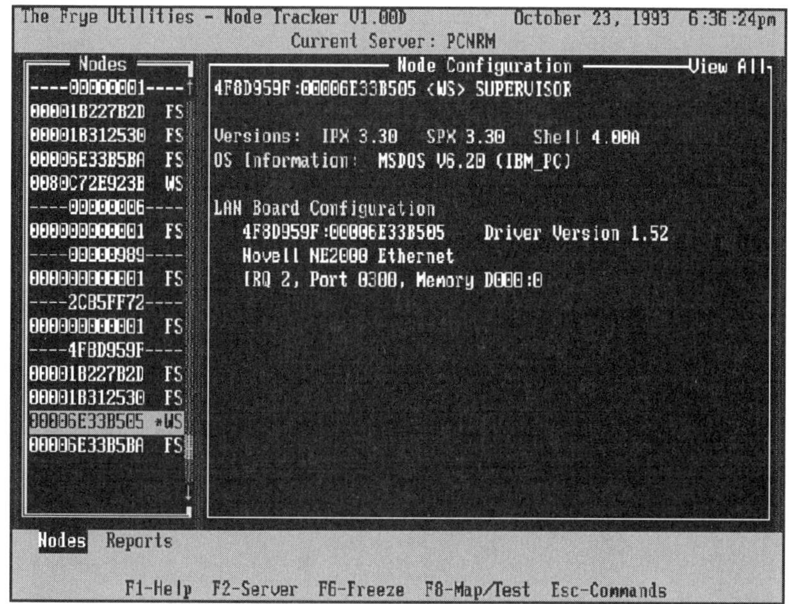

Figure 5.33

Frye's NetWare Management nodes statistics.

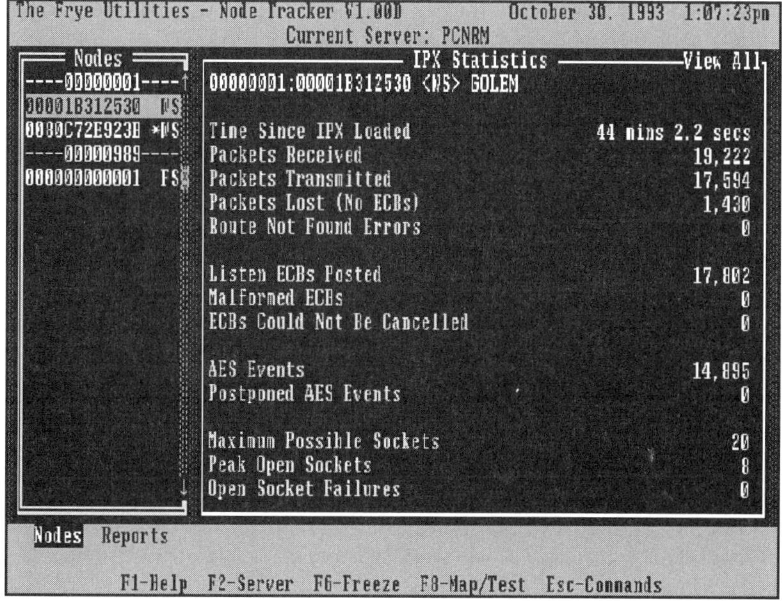

Figure 5.34

Frye's Node Tracker IPX Statistics screen.

SPX is the protocol used in the NetWare arena when you want to ensure two-way communication between nodes, such as between the server and the workstation when the workstation serves as a remote printing device for the server, or using modem-sharing software on the network. The SPX protocol could be characterized as almost always constantly checking to make sure of connections. This activity is reflected in the statistical items tracked in figure 5.35.

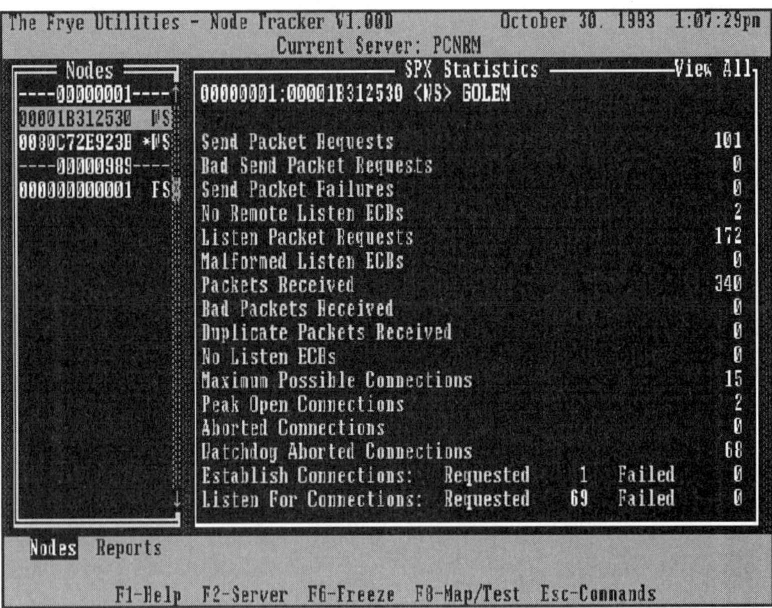

Figure 5.35
Frye's Node Tracker SPX Statistics screen.

As with thc scrvcr issucs dealing with Windows 95 and Windows applications, unless you are able to deal with these traffic issues and the increased number of packets that will be created because of the server location, then the server location is not a positive option. Companies concerned about network traffic should not place the program or application files on the server.

Also as with the server performance issues, the administrator of the Windows 95-based NetWare network is well advised to monitor the traffic measurements for insuring the properly functioning network.

Virtual Memory or Swap File Location Issues

The Windows swap file is virtual memory for Windows. *Virtual memory* is used here to mean memory that is used in place of or as a holding location for real physical chip memory. This virtual memory often proves to be a critical component in the successful Windows environment, providing for an inadequate amount of real memory chip locations. When Windows finds that it needs an otherwise used real chip memory location, it issues a page fault and searches for contents of a real chip memory location that it can move to the virtual memory location or swap file.

Virtual memory or swap file space is a poor substitute for real chip memory. Network managers find that workstation Windows performance significantly improves when you add real chip memory. Another important consideration for performance of both the workstation and the network is in the location area of the swap file. Network locations are not good replacements for local disk locations because of the distance that the packets carrying swap file content has to travel from the workstation to the server and back again. Network locations for swap files also cause increased traffic that as the contents of memory is moved to the server location of the swap file and then brought back as needed.

The Freezing of RAM Memory

The theory behind virtual memory is that when attempting to load, or return to, an application running under Windows in protected mode virtual machines, Windows checks to see if there is enough real chip memory space to accommodate that application. If not it issues a page fault and needs to move items from real chip locations to a disk swap file. It then checks the LRU (least recently used) list to move the oldest untouched data to disk. There not only is no guarantee that the items will be brought back to the same location, there is a certainty that it will not happen. This becomes a problem with some DOS applications that might require you to maintain their chip space, cutting down the ability of Windows to do its thing efficiently by shuffling items around. You might even be able to imagine an application needing disk data and having part of itself swapped to disk as LRU, and then needing that part to deal with what it is asking for from the disk.

Windows 3.*x* Swap File Types

Whether to swap is not really the question; rather, the question is whether to create a permanent or temporary swap file. You obtain the best performance using a permanent swap file, not only because you don't have to create it for each Windows session, but also because it's built on contiguous disk space, so that you don't have to travel all over the disk to recapture the swapped data.

The Permanent Swap File

These are the criteria for the more efficient type of swap file and the names of the files associated with this process. The permanent swap file is created on the local disk that is controlled through the workstation's BIOS and is created out of continguous storage blocks on the disk. This use of storage blocks that are arranged next to each other allows for faster write and reads as the disk drive head does not have to travel all over the disk to access disparate disk locations.

There are two files associated with the permanent swap file: Spart.par and 386spart.par. Spart.par is a read-only pointer to the physical location of 386spart.par, which is the hidden system file that is the actual permanent swap file. Within the System.ini file will be the following structure to the reference to the permanent swap file:

```
System.Ini
PermSwapDOSDrive=C
PermSwapSizeK=10240
```

The Temporary Swap file

A temporary file is created each time Windows 3.*x* is started, which adds to the startup time. Like any other file that is created, it might be spread out over the entire disk if the disk is fragmented. The movement to and from the temporary swap file is slowed down by the necessity of writing to and reading from storage blocks all over the physical disk.

When you cannot have a permanent swap file because of your disk space being on a fragmented drive, or must use a network drive or even a compressed drive, you have to use a temporary swap file. The Win386.swp file by default is created in the directory from which you start Win.com, unless you specifically instruct Windows otherwise in the [386enh] section of System.ini.

Windows attempts to grab 50 percent of what it sees as available disk space for this temporary swap file, which can be a problem on a large shared network disk drive. On a NetWare 3.*x* and NetWare 4.*x* drive, this is created as a sparse file, meaning that while within Windows it can be up to the size Windows wants, it is not set up as allocated space, but grows as the user uses the space. Smart LAN administrators use the MaxPagingFileSize setting, which you write into System.ini, to limit the temporary swap file size on the network.

You can use the paging directory setting in System.ini to set up temporary swap files on compressed drives, although you cannot set them up using the Control Panel. The following entry from the System.ini file designates the use, location, and size of the the temporary swap file:

```
System.ini:
[386enh]
PagingFile=d:\WIN386.SWP
MaxPagingFileSize=10240
```

Watch out on NetWare drives for the sparse file phenomena that finds disk space disappearing as users ramp up their Windows use with temporary swap files created as sparse files. Windows 3.*x* swap files on the network are created as sparse files, meaning that they have a beginning of file mark and an end of file mark and nothing in between. Sparse files can grow as needed and compress when their contents are released. Also note that Windows does not see the bindery-based space limitation set up by the administrator; it only sees the available disk space on disk. Interesting and unpredictable results may happen.

Windows 95 Swap Files

Swap files on Windows 95 are more efficient and dynamic than with Windows 3.*x*. They expand and contract like the temporary files but take up some space like permanent swap files. In the Windows 95 environment, these files are called by the Win386.swp file name of the temporary swap files of Windows 3.*x*. The Windows 95 swap file can be placed on fragmented drives without the performance problems of the Windows 3.*x* swap files.

Because swap files take up space and can be placed either on the workstation drives or on the network, you must be concerned about space issues. The good news for the network administrator is that the full workstation installed Windows 95 can only place the swap file on the workstation through the Control Panel, but they can be placed on a compressed drive, usually at the end of the drive where there is some expansion space. The only requirement with a compressed drive is that it be controlled by the Drvspace.vxd, the protected mode driver. Only the network shared directory installations offer a choice of locations for the swap file through the Control Panel.

In Windows 95 the status and changes of the swap file are maintained in the Control Panel under the System settings icon. After you click on that icon, click on the

Performance tab to see figure 5.36, and then once again to maintain the virtual memory settings (see fig. 5.37).

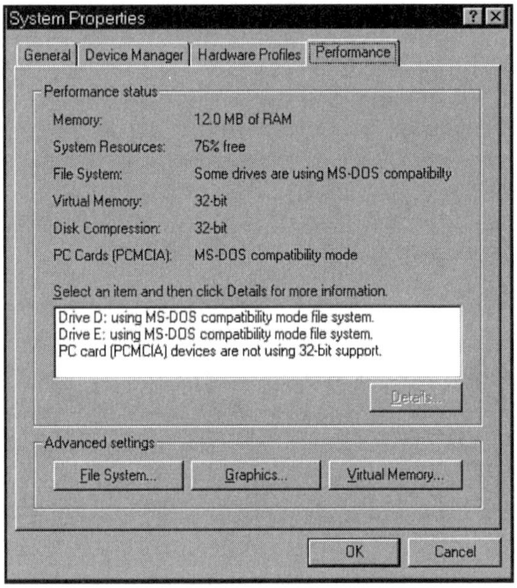

Figure 5.36

Windows 95 Control Panel System performance settings.

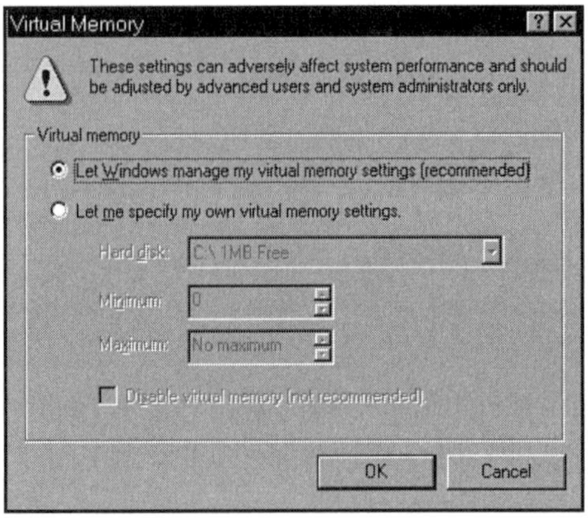

Figure 5.37

Windows 95 Virtual Memory options.

Windows 95 gives you the following virtual memory options:

- Windows 95 control over the optimization of the swap file (recommended)
- User control over the minimum and maximum size (sometimes dictated by space considerations at the cost of optimization)
- None (not recommended)

If you venture from the recommended usage, you need to exercise caution and monitor closely. You can remotely monitor swap file settings and counters (see the system monitor options discussed at the end of Chapter 4).

If you want to learn more about the operation of the swap file, you might want to use one of the new utility programs, such as the Norton Windows 95 utilites to observe and monitor the swap file or virtual memory functions. You can set it up as one of the meters on that program's screen of meters, or single it out.

You might want to track the history of size and activity of the swap file, because it's a dynamic file growing as needed, and contracting as use diminishes. You then can determine whether you need to add more real chip memory to the workstation.

Summary of the Location Issues Discussion

In summary, Windows 95 raises the same location issues as did Windows 3.*x* versions, with some slightly different twists. You need to address these location questions and their answers in network management terms, using the best available network management tools. You can use these same management tools to ensure the ongoing well-being of the Windows 95-based NetWare network.

Installing Windows 95

Microsoft designed Windows 95 to be easy to use and powerful. The first place you get a taste of these features is during the Windows 95 installation process. You get a chance to use Windows 95's new wizards to guide you through the process, making the installation process relatively painless. You also get a chance to witness how Windows 95 uses its strength as a 32-bit operating system to control your entire system, replacing MS-DOS as your basic operating system.

Although the Windows 95 installation process is relatively easy, there are some problems that you may run into. For this reason, you'll want to prepare yourself and your computer for some potential problems during this stage. This chapter helps you make these preparations and walks you through the Setup program for an individual PC.

The following elements are covered in this chapter:

- Reviewing the features of Windows 95 setup
- Understanding the requirements of Windows 95
- Windows 95 installation options
- Preparing your computer to install Windows 95

- Starting Windows 95 setup
- Testing your Windows 95 installation

Looking at the Windows 95 Setup

There are a couple things you need to do when you start installing Windows 95. First, you need to decide if you want to keep your previous operating system, such as Microsoft Windows 3.11 or MS-DOS, installed. Second, you'll need to be patient. The Windows 95 installation process can take some time to install, usually between 30 and 60 minutes. If you need to prepare your hard disk or decide to customize the set up, don't be surprised if you invest two or more hours to ensure everything is properly set up. (If you run into massive problems, don't be surprised to find yourself working on it at 3:00 in the morning!)

Windows 95 is a new operating system and with it comes a new installation process. Many of the options and customization procedures you had to perform with older versions of Windows are now automatically included during Windows 95 setup. Some of these improvements are given in the following list:

- Windows 95 uses installation wizards to guide and interact with users. Although wizards are designed to help beginning and novice users, advanced users still can select and modify options during setup. For the most part, the wizards do not get in the way of what advanced users need to do to customize their installation and computer environment.

- Automatic detection of hardware during setup frees users from having to configure all their hardware devices after the setup stage. Many network adapters are detected during setup to ease the burden of the administrator.

- Compliance to the Plug and Play technology standard helps facilitate hardware setup.

- A smart recovery system is used in case of interrupted setup process. Windows 95 knows when a previous installation has failed and returns to the point of interruption to continue setup. Great for those times when the power glitches or lightening strikes.

- Windows 95 creates a setup log to verify the system is set up properly. Administrators can view the setup log to ensure all components are installed properly, or use it to diagnose problems.

- Windows 95 provides improved network setup, including use of batch installs across LANs.

Examining Windows 95 System Requirements

Windows 95 is a robust operating system that has greatly improved over previous versions of Windows. Some improvements include support of long file names (file names up to 255 characters long), enhanced resource cleanup after an application has crashed, preemptive multitasking for 32-bit applications, and better memory management. Because of these features, you need to make sure your computer can handle the demands of Windows 95.

This section discusses the requirements for installing Windows 95, specifically in terms of the following elements:

- Operating system
- PC system
- Hard drive setup

Operating System Needs

First you'll need to make sure your current PC has an operating system in order to install Windows 95. The recommended choice is to have Windows 3.*x* or Windows 3.11 for Workgroups installed. Windows 95 is designed to upgrade these systems.

If you do not have Windows 3.*x* or Windows for Workgroups, you must have MS-DOS 3.2 or higher installed. If your primary operating system is Windows NT or IBM OS/2, you still are required to have DOS installed in a bootable partition. Unfortunately, you cannot install Windows 95 straight from OS/2 or NT.

If your system has a version of DOS but not MS-DOS 3.2 or higher, make sure your DOS version can exceed the 32 MB partition limit, which Windows 95 supports. Some OEM versions of DOS do not meet this standard. Check your system manuals to make sure your version of DOS does. If you do not know what version of DOS you have, type **VER** at the command prompt for this information.

Make Sure Your System Can Handle Windows 95

You should find that a computer that currently runs Windows 3.1 or 3.11 without many performance problems should be adequate for Windows 95. If your system is slow under Windows 3.*x*, it will be *very* slow under Windows 95. A good way to judge your PC against one that will perform well with Windows 95 is to open three to four applications and check the system resources. You can do this by selecting **H**elp, **A**bout Microsoft Windows in the Windows 3.*x* Program Manager and looking at the system resources used by your system.

If you can run three to four applications simultaneously and keep the system resources above 50 percent, you should find your system adequate for Windows 95. If, on the other hand, you see your resources dropping below 50 percent with only three or four applications running, consider upgrading your CPU or memory, or both.

Table 6.1 lists the minimum system requirements that Microsoft publishes. For a more realistic set of requirements, see table 6.2, which contains the recommended requirements for running Windows 95. These are the recommended requirements for running Windows 95.

Table 6.1
Microsoft's Minimum System Requirements

System Components	Windows 95 Requirements
Processor	80386 or higher
Hard Drive	30 MB of free disk space for a compact installation; 40 MB for a typical installation
Memory	4 MB
Input Device	Mouse
Floppy Disk	Required for installation from floppy disks
CD-ROM Drive	Required for installation from CD
Monitor	VGA
Fax/Modem	Required to use Microsoft Network, Remote Access, HyperTerminal (included in Windows 95), Microsoft Fax, and Phone Dialer

Although Windows 95 is a powerful operating system, it is designed only for Intel x86-based processors. You cannot, for instance, run Windows 95 on a RISC-based system. Windows 95, moreover, differs from Windows NT in that Windows 95 does not support multiple processors.

Another processor limitation you need to be aware of is that Windows 95 cannot install on a 386-based B-step processor. A B-step processor has an ID of 0303; this can be determined from your system documentation or by using a utility such as Microsoft Diagnostics from MD-DOS.

Table 6.2
Recommended System Requirements

Components	Recommended Status for Windows 95
Processor	80486/33 or Pentium
Hard Drive	50 MB of free disk space
Memory	8 MB minimum; 16 MB recommended for running four or more applications
Input Device	Mouse or trackball
CD-ROM Drive	Quad-speed for multimedia applications
Monitor	Super VGA with 256 color capabilities
Fax/Modem	14.4 bps; 28.8 bps for Internet connectivity

When your budget allows for a system upgrade or replacement, try to settle for nothing less than a Pentium processor, 16 MB of RAM, a 500+ MB hard disk, and a quad-speed CD-ROM. You also should look for a system that includes Plug and Play devices and a Plug and Play BIOS.

When you run Windows 95 Setup, you need to decide if you want to install Windows 95 on top of your existing Windows 3.*x* installation. If you choose to install in a new directory to preserve your old setup (so you can have a dual-boot environment), you must reinstall all your applications to work with Windows 95. This means that each must occupy space again on your hard disk if you plan to use the same application under Windows 3.*x* and Windows 95. For this reason, a hard disk with lots of free space is necessary. For most computers connected to a network, copying over your previous installation of Window 3.*x* should be fine. The only time you won't want to do this is if you have not fully tested Windows 95 in your specific environment, or if one of your users employs a DOS- or Windows-based application that doesn't work under Windows 95.

Requirements of Your Hard Drive

Not only do you need plenty of room on your hard disk to install Windows 95, you must always make sure your hard disk is prepared to handle Windows 95. A later section entitled "Preparing Your System for Windows 95" shows you how to optimize your hard disk before you install Windows 95. This section discusses how Windows 95 uses partitioned drives and compressed drives.

Windows 95 and Partitioned Drives

Many users use partitioned drives to organize files (to get around the 512 file single-root directory limitation) or to install another operating system on the same hard disk. Because Windows 95 does not support HPFS (High Performance Files System) or NTFS (NT File System) partitions, you must have a FAT (File Allocation Table) partition on your hard disk. As you install Windows 95, Setup writes information to the master boot record and reads most partitioning schemes, such as those set up by FDISK in MS-DOS.

Windows 95 installs over existing MS-DOS FAT partitions as long as you have enough space in the partition for Windows 95. You also need at least 5 MB for the Windows 95 swap file, which you will read about in the "Recommended Task: Delete the Windows Swap File" section. Windows 95 recognizes partitions set up by third-party schemes, including Disk Manager DMDRVR.BIN and SSTOR.SYS from Storage Dimensions SpeedStor.

Many users like to install Windows 95 on a clean hard disk by running FDISK and "starting over." If you do this, remember to back up all your data, device drivers (save those CD-ROM drivers!), and system files. Keep in mind that during the partitioning stage, you lose all the data on the hard disk and will need to reload MS-DOS on your hard drive before you can run the Windows 95 Setup.

If you want to delete the partitions on your hard drive, delete them in the following order:

- Any non-DOS partitions
- Any logical drives in the extended DOS partition
- Any extended DOS partition
- The existing primary DOS partition

To delete a partition or logical drive:

1. Run FDISK and from the FDISK Options screen, press 3, and then press ENTER. The Delete DOS Partition Or Logical DOS Drive screen appears.
2. Press the number as shown on the screen for the kind of partition you want to delete, and then press Enter.
3. Follow the directions on the screen, and repeat the steps for deleting any additional logical drives or partitions.

If FDISK cannot delete a non-DOS partition, quit FDISK, delete the non-DOS partition by using the software used to create it, and then restart FDISK.

If you have IBM OS/2 installed on your system, you must have MS-DOS installed as well to start the Windows 95 Setup program. Windows 95 must run from MS-DOS if OS/2 is in your primary partition, which usually is the case when running OS/2 to take advantage of the OS/2 dual-boot feature.

As indicated earlier, Windows 95 does not recognize the NTFS system that can be set up for Windows NT. If you are running NTFS, you can install Windows 95 on a FAT partition if enough disk space is present, and then use NT's multiple-boot feature to boot into Windows 95. If you do not have a FAT partition set up, set up one and then perform the Windows 95 installation.

Windows 95 and Compressed Drives

Windows 95 supports many compression applications, such as Microsoft DriveSpace or DoubleSpace. Before you start Windows 95 Setup, check to make sure you have enough free space on an *uncompressed* drive for a Windows 95 swap file to be built. Swap files cannot be set up on compressed drives.

Generally, you need 14 MB of *total* memory on your system to run Windows 95. Your total system memory can be figured by adding the amount of physical memory you have to the amount of virtual memory you have (this is your swap file size). If you have 4 MB of memory in your system, for example, you need a swap file that is at least 10 MB. Free up that amount of uncompressed disk space before running Windows 95 Setup.

For information on freeing up uncompressed disk space, consult your DOS documentation or the documentation that comes with your compression software.

Windows 95 includes built-in support for Microsoft DriveSpace and is compatible with DoubleSpace, both of which are provided with versions of MS-DOS 6.*x*. Windows 95 compression uses a 32-bit virtual device driver to give it better performance over the 16-bit product available in MS-DOS 6.*x*. The 32-bit driver also frees up conventional memory so MS-DOS–based applications have access to this free memory. If you currently use DoubleSpace or DriveSpace with DOS 6.*x* or with Windows 3.*x*, you do not need to make changes to the compressed volume file (Cvf) that these applications currently are using. Except for freeing up enough space for a swap file (as pointed out earlier), you do not have to change any settings or instruct Windows 95 to install over the compressed drive. Windows 95 does it automatically.

Examining Your Windows 95 Installation Options

Windows 95 provides you with several different installation options from which to choose. Depending on aspects of your system's configuration (such as do you currently run a previous version of Windows or just DOS), you can choose to apply one of the following setup options:

- Install Windows 95 from DOS
- Upgrade Windows 3.*x* to Windows 95
- Choose from Custom, Typical, Portable, or Compact install
- Install Windows 95 from across a local area network
- Create a customized and automated installation
- Maintain or update an installation

If you do not have Windows 3.*x* installed on your system, you can install Windows 95 from DOS. Windows 95 first installs a mini version of Windows on your system. The Windows 95 Setup program is a 16-bit, Windows-based application.

You cannot run install from an MS-DOS prompt from within Windows 3.x. Exit from the DOS prompt to start Setup from Windows.

Upgrading Windows 3.*x* to Windows 95

The preferred installation method is to install Windows 95 from Windows 3.*x*. When you do this, Windows 95 migrates your System.ini, Win.ini, and Protocol.ini configuration settings and your Windows 3.*x* Registry associations into the Windows 95 Registry. The Registry entries in your Windows 3.*x* configuration are file and program associations. You need to conserve these to make your applications work under Windows 95.

Another conversion that takes place during the Windows 95 setup is that Windows 3.*x* Program Manager groups are converted to Windows 95 *folders*. Folders in Windows 95 have replaced program groups and directories. You access program folders from the Start button in Windows 95.

By default, Windows 95 installs over your existing Windows 3.*x* system. When this occurs, applications installed are automatically updated. If, however, you decide to keep
your existing Windows 3.*x* setup, you need to reinstall all your applications under Windows 95.

Choosing the Install Type

You can choose from four installation types: Custom, Typical, Portable, or Compact. Each of these give you the flexibility you need to configure your computer as necessary:

- **Typical Setup.** Designed for the average computer user who does not want to interact a great deal with the Setup routine. A Typical install performs most installation steps automatically.
- **Custom Setup.** Enables you to choose many of the installation options offered by Windows 95, such as application settings, network settings, and device configurations. If you are an experienced user, use this setting to get more control over the type of utilities and applications that Windows 95 installs. In the Custom Setup, for instance, you can choose the type of applets that Windows 95 installs.
- **Portable Setup.** Designed particularly for mobile users with laptop computers. During Portable Setup, Windows 95 automatically installs the Briefcase application and support for Direct Cable Connections, a Windows 95 feature that enables you to connect to other computers through parallel or serial ports. The Briefcase is a Windows 95 application used to synchronize files that you transfer between your mobile computer and stationary one.
- **Compact Setup.** If you have limited disk space on your computer, use the Compact Setup option. This Setup option installs only those files necessary to run Windows 95 (note: the space needed still ranges from 10 to 30 MB of hard disk space).

How do you know which is the best Setup option for you? Table 6.3 lists the files that install during different installation procedures.

Tip

If you decide to install or remove a component after Windows 95 is installed on your system, you can use the Add/Remove Programs application in Control Panel. This is a Windows 95 wizard that walks you through the process of installing or uninstalling applications.

Table 6.3
Files Installed During Windows 95 Setup

File Type	Typical	Custom	Portable	Compact
Accessories	Yes	Yes	No	No
Backup	Yes	Yes	No	No
Bitmaps	Yes	Yes	Yes	No
Briefcase	No	No	Yes	No
Compression Utilities	Yes	Yes	Yes	Yes
Dial-Up Networking	Yes	Yes	Yes	No
Direct Cable Connection	Yes	Yes	Yes	No
Games	Yes	Yes	No	No
HyperTerminal	Yes	Yes	Yes	No
Multimedia Files	Yes	Yes	Yes	No
Maintenance Tools	Yes	Yes	Yes	Yes
Paint	Yes	Yes	No	No
Screen Savers	Yes	Yes	Yes	No
Windows 95 Tour	Yes	Yes	No	No
WordPad	Yes	Yes	No	No

The following items also are available, but must be selected during the installation process or added after Setup:

- Internet Mail Service (you must acquire Microsoft Plus! to obtain this service)
- Microsoft Exchange
- Microsoft Fax
- Microsoft Network
- Network Administration Tools
- Online User's Guide

Maintaining or Updating a Windows 95 Installation

Sometimes you may encounter a situation that prematurely stops the Windows 95 installation process. A number or events can trigger this, such as power outages, installing Windows 95 during a lightening storm, or a system glitch. If you encounter an error during Setup and you restart the installation process, you do not have to start all over again. Windows 95 automatically starts the Safe Recovery utility to pick up where you left off if the Setup wizard detects a previous unsuccessful installation. Safe Recovery skips over the problem that was previously encountered and continues with the installation.

Even if everything goes well during the installation, it's okay to decide later to update your installation, and Windows 95 provides you with several ways to do so. The applications you use to add, remove, or configure Windows 95 are part of the Control Panel options and are usually wizards. This means users of all experience levels can feel comfortable adding components such as printers, modems, and other options to their configurations.

The following list summarizes these applications:

- **Modem.** Enables you to install and configure printers.
- **Mouse.** Enables you to configure and set up a new mouse
- **Add/Remove Programs.** Enables you to install options that you didn't install during the Setup procedure. You also can create a startup disk from this wizard.
- **Add New Hardware.** You can install new hardware by starting this application. This wizard walks you through installing hardware device drivers.
- **Display.** Enables you to install and configure display drivers.
- **Fonts.** Enables you to add and remove fonts from your system. You also can view a sample of a selected font.
- **Network.** Enables you to install and configure network components on your system.

Using the Windows 95 Dual-Boot Feature

As mentioned earlier, you can install Windows 95 into a separate directory from your previous Windows 3.*x* installation. This gives you the capability to boot into either Windows 95 (which is the default boot) or your old DOS version. You may want to keep Windows 3.*x* on your system if a particular application is known not to work under Windows 95. Another reason to keep Windows 3.*x* on your machine is in case you have problems with Windows 95 installing properly. In situations where Windows 95 does not work, you can boot into Windows 3.*x* and fix the problem or totally remove Windows 95 and restart the installation—a much easier and quicker solution than rebuilding your computer system from the ground up.

Dual boots work by displaying a message on your screen during the boot process. When you see the message `Starting Windows`, you can press F4 to bypass the Windows 95 boot-up and boot into your old version of DOS. From DOS, you then can start Windows 3.*x*.

Preparing Your System for Windows 95

Keep in mind that installing Windows 95 is a major upgrade to your computer. The Windows 95 installation process will go much smoother if you do a few pre-setup tasks—described in this section—before you launch Windows 95 Setup.

Recommended Task: Back Up System Files

As a system administrator, you know that one of the most overlooked and taken-for-granted areas of computing is back-up procedures. Many users don't take the time to back up their data and only think about it when they lose some critical data. (And then come running to you to complain about the network destroying their data!) Before you run the Windows 95 installation program, however, make sure users back up all the files that they don't want to lose. It is better to assume that you will lose something as opposed to thinking you won't.

Another valuable lesson to learn is to always have a boot disk on hand. A boot disk enables you to boot your system from a floppy in case you have a major problem during the Windows 95 installation process. To create a boot disk in Windows 3.*x*, place a floppy disk in the floppy drive from which your system boots, which usually is drive A. Next, in Windows File Manager select **D**isk, **M**ake System Disk and click in the **M**ake System Disk check box. Click OK. Store this disk in a safe place and don't copy over it. In DOS you can make a system disk by using the Format command, such as FORMAT A:/S.

As a place to start, have users back up the files shown in the following list. Back up these files onto a tape backup system, recordable CD-ROM, a network backup system, floppy disks, or other backup media. Users should not back these files up on their local hard disk if that's where you are installing Windows 95.

- **Ini Files.** Make sure all Ini files are backed up. Not all Ini files are stored in the same directory, so you'll need to go looking for them. A quick way to locate all your Ini files is to run a search for *.Ini in Windows File Manager.
- **Documents.** Often overlooked during back up procedures, personal documents, such as memos, spreadsheets, drawings, and so on, should be backed up. Any templates that are customized should be backed up as well. In short, anything you don't want to spend time re-creating needs to be backed up.
- **Autoexec.bat.** As Windows 95 installs, it modifies the current Autoexec.bat file to include Windows 95-specific instructions. If a problem occurs during the Windows 95 install process, you may need to reboot into the old configuration. Having a backup of Autoexec.bat will speed up this process.
- **Config.sys.** As it does with the Autoexec.bat file, Windows 95 modifies Config.sys during installation. A backup copy of it will save you time and headaches if you need to restore your original system.
- **Group Files.** Group files tell Windows 3.*x* what to display in groups in Program Manager. Group files, denoted as Grp, are in the WINDOWS directory.
- **Network Files.** Back up all the network-specific files already deployed on systems, including startup files and any batch files that may run during the logon process.

Recommended Task: Turn Off TSRs and Time-Out Features

As Windows 95 installs, it goes through several phases that are being processed in the background. Your machine may appear to pause or not work during these times in which Windows 95 is preparing system files and checking your existing system configuration. For this reason, if you have power-down features, such as those in laptops or newer "Green PCs", turn off these features so that the installation process is not terminated prematurely.

Disable TSR programs (terminate-and-stay-resident programs) and screen savers that may turn on during the install process. You need to clear out all but necessary device drivers and batch files from memory. You can do this by REMing out appropriate lines in your Autoexec.bat and Config.sys files (after you've backed them up, of course). Do not, however, delete settings for the following drivers: network drivers, CD-ROMs, video cards, and the mouse.

You should not delete device settings for network adapters, CD-ROMs, video cards, and for the mouse. Also, do not turn off TSRs that are used for partitions or hard disk controls.

Recommended Task: Delete the Windows Swap File

Windows 3.*x* and Windows 95 differ in the way swap files are managed. In Windows 3.*x*, you can use a temporary or a permanent swap file. Windows 95, however, uses a dynamic swap file. A *dynamic* swap file changes as needed by the system. Your old permanent swap file is no longer needed by Windows 95, so you can remove it to give you additional hard disk space.

Before removing your permanent swap file, read this! If you choose to have both Windows 3.*x* and Windows 95 on your computer, do not delete the swap file from your system. You'll still need it for Windows 3.*x* to run.

Required Task: Defragment Your Hard Disk

After you back up files and delete files from your hard disk, you need to run a disk defragment utility to clean up your hard drive. When you run a disk defragment utility, the hard disk reorganizes files so that you get optimal performance from the drive. As you use your computer—copying, deleting, and creating files—your hard disk becomes fragmented, increasing disk-access time. A disk defragment utility cleans up your disk and eliminates fragmented files.

Microsoft DOS 6.0 and higher versions include a disk defragment utility called DEFRAG. To run it, exit Windows 3.*x* and type **DEFRAG** at the DOS prompt. Follow the instructions on-screen to optimize your hard drive. Other programs, such as Norton Utilities and PC Tools, include defragment programs as well.

During the Windows 95 installation process, Windows 95 automatically runs a disk defragment utility called ScanDisk to check your drive. Unfortunately, if you have a problem that ScanDisk cannot fix (which occurs many times), you may have difficulty cleaning up the problem in DOS. The reason for this possible difficulty is because long filenames are created on your hard drive during the initial part of the Windows 95 install (even before ScanDisk is executed). If ScanDisk reports a hard disk error it cannot fix, the Windows 95 install stops and you are returned to your old Windows 3.*x* or DOS setup. Then, when you try to run a disk defragment utility, such as DEFRAG, to correct the problem ScanDisk found, you get an error when the software encounters the long filenames that Windows 95 placed there. You have to delete those files manually if this occurs.

Another utility you should run is CHKDSK. CHKDSK, which you run from the DOS prompt, is used to analyze and fix any surface-level problems with your hard disk. If CHKDSK encounters errors or bad files, it asks you if you want CHKDSK to fix them or leave them for you to fix. You should let CHKDSK fix them in most cases.

After you prepare your system for Windows 95, you are ready to run Setup.

Starting Windows 95 Setup

After you prepare your computer for Windows 95, you can start the Windows 95 Setup program. Setup is located on the Windows 95 installation disks or CD-ROM. (You'll find that running Setup from a CD-ROM is much faster than running it from floppy disks because you won't have to keep feeding disks to the computer.) The Windows 95 Setup program uses the Setup wizard to guide you through installing Windows 95 on your system.

Be sure to read all the README files and similar files on the Windows 95 installation disk. You'll find valuable information that may pertain to your specific system hardware, software, or network.

Taking Your System's Inventory

Before you start Setup, make a note of the following items on your system:

- Video card and monitor type
- Mouse type
- Network configuration, including network operating system, protocol, and mapped drive specifications.
- Printer type and port
- Modem type
- CD-ROM
- SCSI adapter, if installed

You also should make sure you have the Windows 95 identification number that is included with your floppy disks or CD-ROM. You will need this number during the installation process.

Examining Special Setup Switches

Windows 95 Setup is designed to be used by users of all experience levels, including novice, intermediate, and advanced. No setup utility, however, can satisfy every user's needs and special system configuration. Windows 95, therefore, includes command line switches to control the installation process. If you want to use these switches, add them to the end of the SETUP command line when you start Setup. The following list describes each of the switches you can use to customize the Setup procedure:

- **/?.** Displays help on using Setup switches, and also shows the syntax of each switch.
- **/ih.** Instructs Setup to run ScanDisk in the foreground so that you can see the results. Use this switch if the system stalls during the ScanDisk check or if an error results.
- **/nostart.** Directs Setup to copy only the required Windows 3.*x* DLLs (Dynamic Link Librarys) used by Windows 95 Setup. After Setup copies these files, it exits to DOS without installing Windows 95.
- **/iL.** Instructs Setup to load the Logitech mouse driver, if you have a Logitech Series C mouse.
- **/iq.** Directs Setup to bypass the ScanDisk quick check when running Setup from DOS. Use this switch if you use compression software other than DriveSpace or DoubleSpace.
- **/is.** Directs Setup to bypass the ScanDisk quick check when running Setup from Windows 3.*x*. Use this switch if you use compression software other than DriveSpace or DoubleSpace.
- **script_file.** Directs Setup to use the custom script files you create to automatically install Windows 95.
- **/d.** Directs Setup not to use your existing version of Windows 3.*x* during the first part of Setup. You should use /d when you experience problems with Setup due to missing or damaged Windows 3.*x* files.
- **/C.** Directs Windows 95 Setup not to load the SmartDrive disk cache.
- **/id.** Directs Setup to bypass checking of the required minimum disk space to install Windows 95. For most users, you shouldn't use this switch unless you attempted to install Windows 95 and it failed but Setup copied some files to

your hard disk anyway. When you restart Setup, use the /id switch to bypass the part of Setup that checks for required disk space. This way you do not get an "Out of Disk Space" error during your next attempt of running Setup.

- **/t:tempdir.** Specifies the directory in which Setup is to copy its temporary files. This directory must already exist, but any existing files in the directory are deleted after Setup finishes installing Windows 95.

For most situations, you do not need to use the preceding Setup switches when you install Windows 95. If, however, you encounter a problem with Setup, look at this list to see if any of these switches can help you overcome the problem.

Launching Windows 95 Setup from Windows 3.*x*

Use the following steps to install Windows 95 from Windows 3.*x*. If you install Windows 95 from DOS, see the next section, "Launching Windows 95 Setup from DOS."

1. Start your computer and run Windows 3.*x*. Make sure all applications are closed before running Setup.

2. For installation from floppy disk, insert the disk labeled Disk #1 in the floppy drive. Or, if you are installing from CD-ROM, place the CD-ROM in the CD drive.

3. From Program Manager, select File, Run. In the Run dialog box, type the letter of the drive containing the disk or CD-ROM, a backslash (\), and the command SETUP (see fig. 6.1). The following command, for example, starts Setup from a floppy drive labeled A:

   ```
   A:\SETUP
   ```

4. Click on OK. Setup starts and the Windows 95 installation wizard initializes and begins installing Windows 95. See the section "Collecting Information for Setup" for the next step in the Windows 95 installation process.

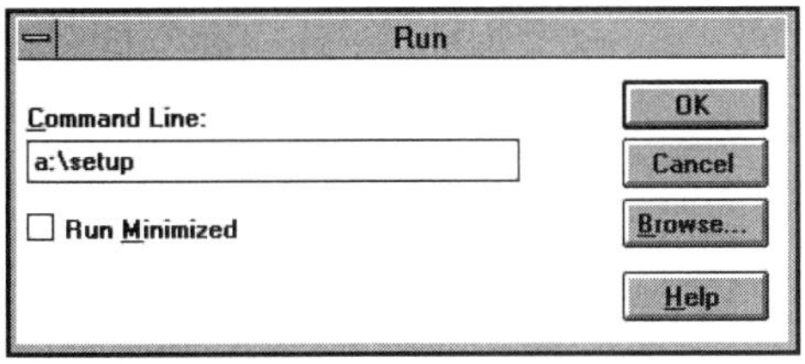

Figure 6.1

Start the Windows 95 Setup program from the Windows 3.x Program Manager.

Launching Windows 95 Setup from DOS

To start Windows 95 Setup from DOS, use the following steps:

1. Start your computer.

2. For installation from floppy disk, insert the disk labeled Disk #1 in the floppy drive. Or, if you are installing from CD-ROM, place the CD-ROM in the CD drive.

3. At the DOS command prompt, type the letter of the drive that contains the setup disks, a backslash (\), and the command SETUP (see fig. 6.2). The following command, for instance, starts Windows 95 Setup from a floppy disk in drive A:

   ```
   C:\A:\SETUP
   ```

4. Press Enter. Setup starts and the Windows 95 installation wizard initializes and begins installing Windows 95.

Figure 6.2
You can start Windows 95 Setup from the DOS prompt using the SETUP command.

Working with the Setup Program

When Setup starts, a Welcome screen displays (see fig. 6.3) telling you that Windows 95 is ready to start installing Windows 95 and that the process may take 30 to 60 minutes to complete. Click on OK.

Windows 95 Setup gathers most of the information it needs automatically during the installation process. There are, however, some items you need to provide manually, such as the directory name in which to install Windows 95 and the type of Setup you want to perform. Windows 95 by default installs into your current directory of Windows 3.*x* if it is installed, but you can change this directory if you want to run Windows 95 and your current Windows 3.*x* installation.

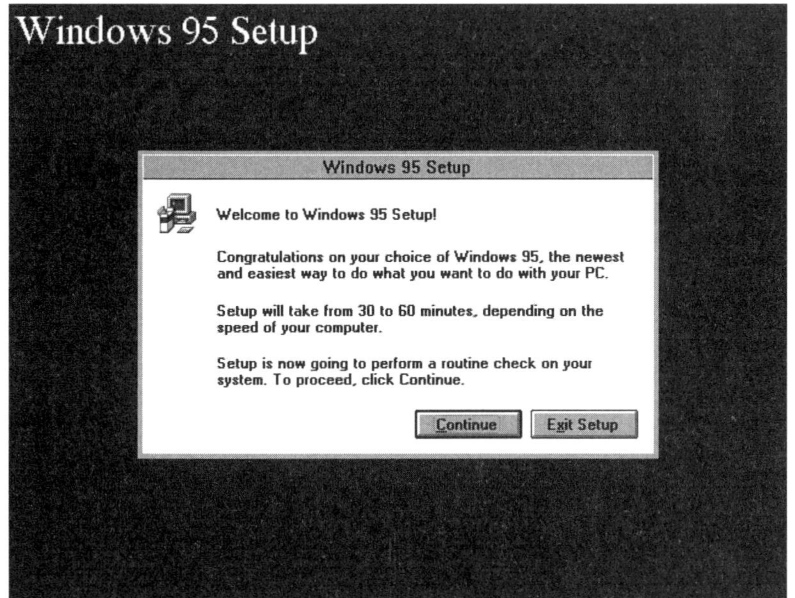

Figure 6.3

The initial Windows 95 screen you see after you start Setup.

Use the following steps to continue installing Windows 95:

1. Click on **C**ontinue on the Setup Welcome screen. Windows 95 checks your system for available disk space, possible hard disk problems, and other system setting information.

If Setup detects a hard disk problem, an error message appears. Be sure to read the message and perform the recommended actions. In most cases, Setup advises that you run ScanDisk prior to restarting Setup. Click on OK to leave Windows 95 Setup and return to DOS or Windows 3.*x*. Setup does not let you continue with the installation process if an error is found.

2. If Setup does not detect a problem during its routine check, it moves to the next stage of the installation process. This stage prepares the Setup wizard, which guides you through the rest of the installation.

3. After the Setup wizard starts, the Windows 95 Software License Agreement appears. Read the license agreement and click **Y**es if you accept the terms of the agreement. If you do not accept the terms, click **N**o and Setup exits, ending the installation process. You must accept the terms of the agreement to install Windows 95.

As mentioned earlier, you should close all applications before running Setup. If you do not, a warning message displays advising you to do so (see fig. 6.4). Task switch to the other application and exit from it. Do not exit from Program Manager, however.

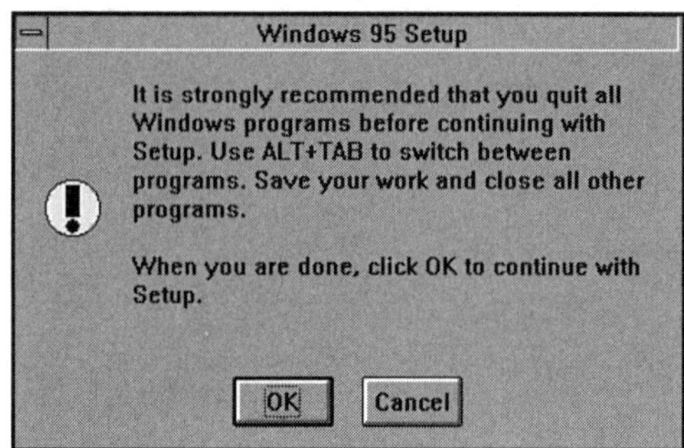

Figure 6.4
Setup displays a message telling you to exit from other applications before continuing with the installation.

4. Click on OK when you are ready to continue with Setup.

Starting the Windows 95 Setup Wizard

The Windows 95 Setup wizard appears on screen. This is your hands-on guide to installing Windows 95 on your system. The wizard screen (see fig. 6.5) lists the three major parts of the Windows 95 setup procedure:

- Collecting information about your computer
- Copying Windows 95 files to your computer
- Restarting your computer and finishing setup

Each of these parts are described in the following pages.

Note A note at the bottom of the wizard screen informs you that Windows 95 replaces your existing DOS and Windows versions. Don't worry, by following the procedure provided later in this section, you can instruct Setup to install Windows 95 in a separate directory from DOS and Windows 3.*x*, enabling you to keep your previous version installed.

Click on Next to advance to the next wizard screen. The Choose Directory screen displays (see fig. 6.6). This is where you must decide to keep or install over a previous version of Windows or DOS. Make sure the C:\WINDOWS option is selected and click on Next to replace Windows 3.*x* with Windows 95. If you want to install Windows 95 into a separate directory and keep your previous version of Windows 3.*x*, click the Other directory radio button and click on Next.

Figure 6.5

The Setup wizard helps you navigate through the Windows 95 installation process.

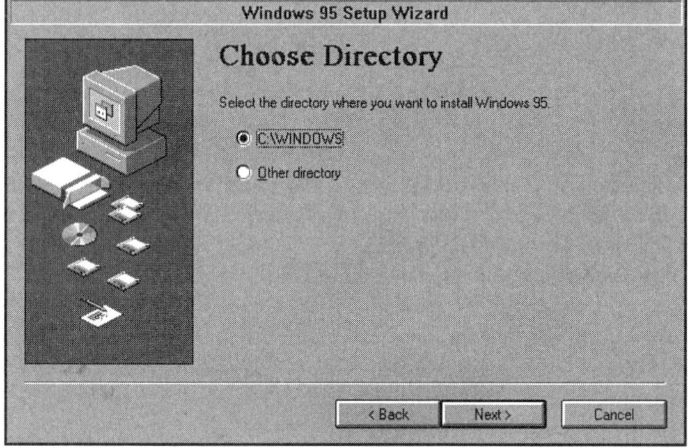

Figure 6.6

The directory in which your current version of Windows is installed may differ from the one shown in this figure.

If you choose to install Windows 95 to a separate directory, the Change Directory screen will display (see fig. 6.7). This is where you name the directory for Windows 95. Although Setup advises that only advanced users and system administrators should modify this directory, you must change the directory name to retain your previous version of Windows.

In the text box, type the new directory name (C:\WIN95, for example). The new name must be unique and no more than eight characters. Click on Next when this box is filled out. At this point, Setup displays a screen that warns you that you must reinstall all your applications. Click Yes to continue or No to return to the Change Directory screen. The Preparing Directory screen appears.

Figure 6.7
You must give a new directory name in which to install Windows 95 if you want to keep your previous version of Windows.

If you did not choose to install to a new Windows directory, Setup bypasses the preceding step and displays the Preparing Directory screen instead.

The Preparing Directory screen informs you that Windows 95 is creating your new directory or preparing your existing Windows 3.*x* directory for Windows 95. After the directory is prepped and ready, the Setup Options screen appears (see fig. 6.8), in which you select the type of installation you want to perform. To set up Windows 95 on a computer that has adequate hard disk space (35–50 MB), make sure the **T**ypical option is selected. The Typical install assumes that you do not want to customize the components that Windows 95 installs. As you see in the section called "Windows Components" you can modify the options that install, although it is not necessary to do so with the Typical install type. For control over the components and options that are installed, select **C**ustom install. This is highly recommended if you want to minimize the number of frivolous items that Windows 95 installs, such as wallpaper and screen savers.

Click on Next when you are ready.

When the User Information screen displays, enter your name and company name. The company name is optional, but you must fill in a user name. Click on Next.

The next screen, the Product Information screen, is used to input the serial number of your Windows 95 disks (see fig. 6.9). This number is unique to your disks and is used for product support and for registering your software with Microsoft Corporation. You must input this number to successfully install Windows 95. Click on Next after you enter the ID.

Figure 6.8

From the Setup Options screen you can select the type of Windows 95 installation Setup performs.

Note Click on the **A**dvanced button on the Product Information screen to install Windows 95 in a networked environment. To install Windows 95 in a networked environment, you must have purchased a group license. This license number is included in the dialog box that displays when you click on the **A**dvanced button.

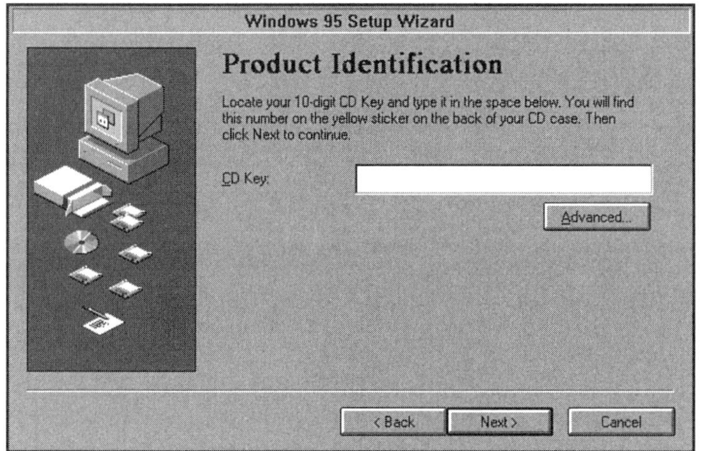

Figure 6.9

Enter the product identification number of your Windows 95 disks or CD-ROM discs.

Waiting... Windows 95 Analyzes Your Computer

The Setup wizard checks your computer's hardware. You can select to have Windows 95 check for hardware items automatically (this is suggested), or you can select the hardware manually. In figure 6.10, the Analyzing Your Computer screen is shown, displaying the choices from which you can select specific hardware devices. In this example, the only choice is Network Adapter. If you have a network interface card in your system and you want Windows 95 to search for and configure it, make sure this option is selected. Depending on your system, other options may appear in this screen, such as CD-ROM. Select the appropriate ones for your system.

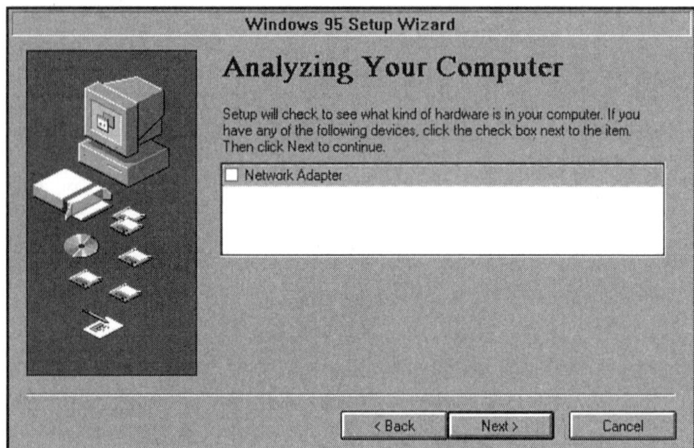

Figure 6.10
The Analyzing Your Computer screen.

Click on Next to have Windows 95 analyze your system. This process may take a few minutes to complete. You might notice that the on-screen Progress bar moves rapidly through the first 90 percent of the process and then seems to quit. This is normal and you should not reboot your PC at this point. Give Setup some time to complete this part. It's a good practice to let it sit for at least twenty minutes before you attempt to recover your computer.

If, after a long period of inactivity (watch your hard drive light on the front of the computer for activity), your system seems to have crashed, reboot the system by pressing Alt+Ctrl+Del. Start Setup again and use the Smart Recovery program, which starts automatically if Setup can salvage anything from the previous installation attempt.

Selecting Online Options

Windows 95 provides built-in support for many electronic and online services, including e-mail (using Microsoft Mail), the Microsoft Network, and Microsoft Fax services. After the Setup wizard analyzes your system, you need to select the types of services you want Setup to automatically configure. The Get Connected screen (see fig. 6.11) enables you to select the service or connection you want Setup to install automatically. You can select any combination of choices or pick none. If you are not sure if you want to install one of these choices now, you can bypass them now and install them manually after Windows 95 is installed by using Add/Remove Programs in Control Panel.

Figure 6.11

Select the type of online and electronic mail connections you want.

Remember to read the fine print. If you don't read the Setup wizard screen for this option closely, you may overlook an important point. If you install one or more of the Get Connected options, Windows 95 automatically installs Microsoft Exchange. Exchange is Microsoft's new electronic mail and communications client that acts as a universal inbox and outbox for your e-mail and faxes.

Exchange requires 4.6 MB of hard disk space by itself. If you install all three Get Connected options, the total hard disk space required is over 12 MB. You also need at least 8 MB of RAM to run Exchange and Microsoft Fax. The Microsoft Network also demands a large amount of memory. You should have at least 8 MB minimum and 16 MB recommended.

After you make your choice(s), click on Next. The screen that displays shows you the Windows 95 components that you can install on your system.

Selecting Windows Components

The Setup wizard now gives you a choice to modify the list of components to install on your system. The default setting installs the most common Windows 95 components, but you can change the list by selecting the Show me the list of components so I can choose option (see fig. 6.12).

For most users, the default list of components is recommended, especially if you are a new user and are not familiar with Windows 95 components, many of which are available in previous versions of Windows. If you change your mind later about an option, you can add additional components or remove any by using Add/Remove Programs in the Control Panel after Windows 95 is installed. Click on Next to continue with Setup. The Startup Disk screen displays.

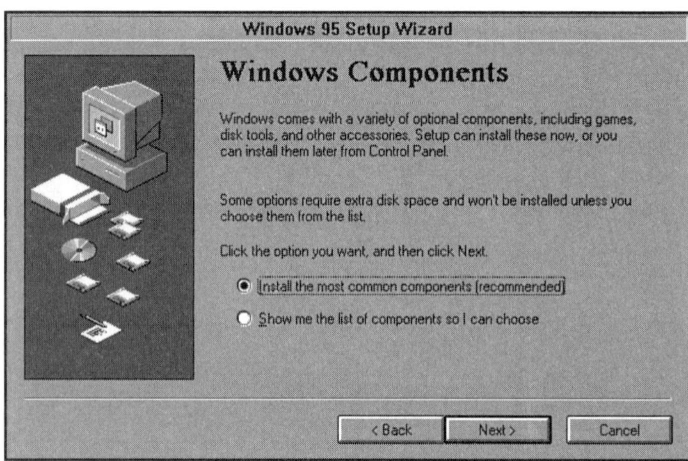

Figure 6.12

Select the types of components to install.

To choose specific components, click the second choice from the list of setup types and click on Next. The Select Components screen appears (see fig. 6.13).

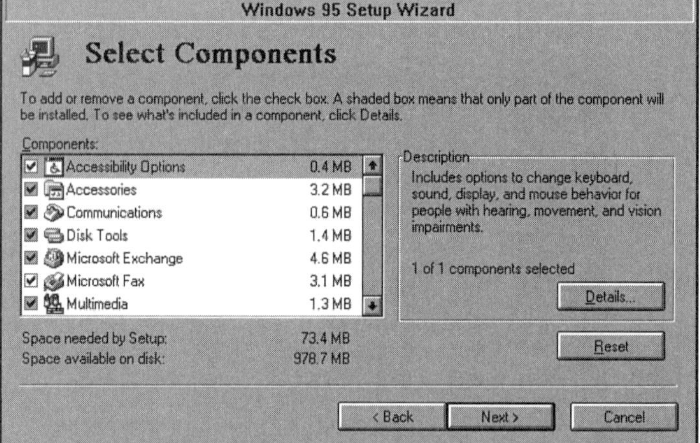

Figure 6.13

You can modify the list of components Setup installs from this screen.

Recommended Task: Creating a Startup Disk

When you go boating, you take a life preserver with you. You don't expect to fall overboard, but you know that sometimes bad things happen to good people. Well, the same is true when you are installing Windows 95. Regardless of how well things are going up to this point, you may run into some stormy waters ahead. For this reason, when Setup asks if you want to create a startup disk, say **Y**es. The startup disk is your life preserver in case you experience problems with Windows 95 after it's installed. By taking a few minutes now and using one floppy disk, you insure yourself against potential problems down the road.

To make a startup disk, you'll need one floppy disk that can be reformatted when the startup files are copied to the disk. Because you will lose all the data on this disk, make sure it does not contain anything important. The floppy disk must be one for the floppy drive from which your PC boots, which usually is drive A.

Many older PCs have 5 1/4-inch floppy disk drives as drive A. Many users, however, have abandoned the use of 5 1/4-inch floppy disks. If your drive A is the 5 1/4-inch drive, you must use this size floppy disk as your startup disk. You cannot change Setup to create a startup disk on drive B.

The startup disk is a bootable floppy disk that stores several system files (over 1.2 MB) on it. If you need to use the startup disk, place it in your floppy drive and reboot your machine. You are presented with an MS-DOS command line that provides utilities and maintenance instructions to help you recover your installation.

The startup disk has some limitations. It cannot, for instance, be used to provide access to a CD-ROM device or to a network connection. You need to clean up any problems associated with your installation to recover from these problems.

The files Setup copies to the startup disk are shown in the following list:

- **Attrib.exe.** Sets file attributes, such as hidden and read-only.
- **Chkdsk.exe.** Checks a disk and displays a status report of it.
- **Command.com.** Starts a new copy of the Windows Command Interpreter, which is the primary operating system file for MS-DOS.
- **Debug.exe.** Runs Debug, a testing and editing tool program.
- **Drvspace.bin.** Runs the DriveSpace disk-compression utility.
- **Edit.com.** Text editor in MS-DOS.
- **Fdisk.exe.** Configures a hard disk for use with MS-DOS.
- **Format.com.** Formats a hard disk or floppy disk for use with MS-DOS.
- **Regedit.exe.** Starts the Registry Editor.
- **Scandisk.exe.** Starts ScanDisk.

- **Scandisk.ini.** Stores system configuration settings for ScanDisk.
- **Sys.com.** Copies MS-DOS system files and command interpreter to a disk you specify.
- **Uninstal.exe.** Starts utility for recovering deleted files

After Windows 95 installs (and assuming everything functions correctly), consider loading other files onto your startup disk. These might include Autoexec.bat, Config.sys, Win.ini, and System.ini. Other Ini files may come in handy as well.

To instruct Setup to create a startup disk, make sure the top choice in the Startup Disk screen is selected and click on Next.

Finally! Copying Files

Setup now has gathered enough information to begin copying files to your hard disk. In figure 6.14, Setup displays a message telling you that it is ready to start copying the files. Click on Next to continue.

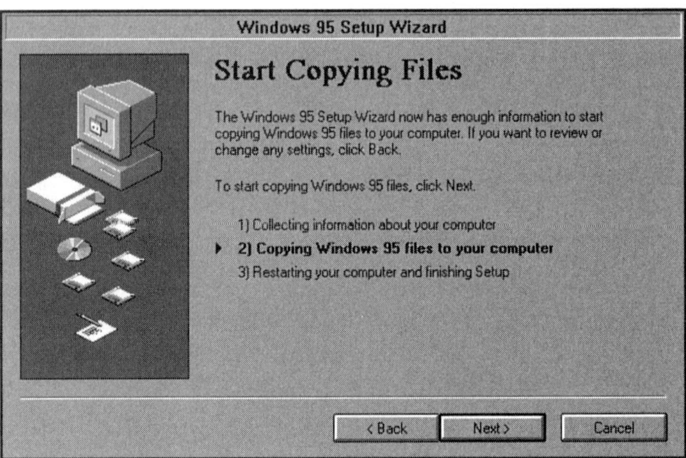

Figure 6.14
Setup starts copying files to your system.

Setup begins copying files to your hard disk and displays a meter showing the progress of the action. If you selected the choice to create a startup disk, Setup instructs you to insert this disk when the progress meter hits about 20 percent. Insert the floppy disk and click on OK. After the startup disk is created, Setup displays a message telling you to remove the floppy disk from the drive. Do this now and place it in a safe place. Setup continues installing Windows 95. As it copies files, Windows displays screens that describe key features of Windows 95.

Completing Windows 95 Setup

When the Setup files finish copying onto your system, Setup begins the third and final phase of installation: the Finishing Setup phase. This part restarts your computer and configures your hardware and software to work with Windows 95.

Not to scare you, but even though you've made it to this point in the installation process, you still are not "home free." Many installation errors occur after the Windows 95 Setup restarts your computer and starts configuring your system. One of the primary problems that occurs is when the Plug and Play configuration part of Windows 95 tries to locate incompatible devices.

Some of the tasks that Windows 95 performs during this final stage include these:

- Adds a new system file (Io.sys) to replace the old MS-DOS Io.sys and Msdos.sys. These old files are renamed Io.dos and Msdos.dos.
- Copies System.dat to System.dao and System.new to System.dat. This is the primary system database that the Registry reads.
- Combines all the virtual device drivers (VxDs) to create Vmm32.vxd, which is the 32-bit virtual device driver.
- Renames Arial.win, User32.tmp, and Logo.sys files used by Setup.

Click on Finish to finish setting up Windows 95. This last stage typically takes several minutes to complete.

Note: If your PC does not restart after a reasonable times, such as twenty minutes or more, then reboot your system manually. You may be able to boot into Windows 95. If not you may be able to boot into Windows 95 in Safe Mode, which you can select from the Startup menu. Safe Mode is used to start Windows 95 with only the default driver so that you can diagnose and fix basic installation problems. Beware that network and CD-ROM drivers do not load during Safe Mode startup.

After your computer restarts and everything acts normal, Windows 95 starts and then runs your Autoexec.bat and Config.sys files. You'll see the Windows 95 opening screen flash on-screen for a few seconds, and then the DOS screen displays. This is normal. You'll see the following message in DOS:

```
Please wait while Setup updates your configuration files.
This may take a few minutes...
```

Your PC may appear dormant for several minutes, but be patient. After the configuration files are updated, Windows 95 reappears on-screen and starts to run through setting Run-Once options. These options include PCMCIA and MIDI devices, printers, Time Zone, Microsoft Exchange, Windows Help, programs on the Start menu, and Control Panel setting. Other hardware devices also can be configured at this point. A screen displays that lists these options as they are being set up.

Many of the items on the list configure automatically, such as the Control Panel and programs on the Start menu. Some, however, require user interaction. When Setup runs the Time Zone option, for instance, you must select the time zone in which you live. Click on the list on the Time Zone tab and select your time zone. To modify the time and date, click on the Date & Time tab. Click on Apply to save these settings, then click on Close when you are finished.

Configuring Microsoft Exchange

Next, Setup configures Microsoft Exchange on your system. If you did not select a choice in the Get Connected screen earlier (see "Getting Connected" earlier in this chapter), Setup does not perform this task. You can proceed to the "Starting Windows 95" section.

Setup displays the Inbox Setup wizard, which guides you through setting up Microsoft Exchange's universal mail inbox. This box is also used to receive e-mail and faxes and to connect to the Microsoft Network, if you selected this option earlier. Use the following steps to configure Exchange:

1. If you've never used Exchange on this system before, make sure No is clicked when the Setup wizard asks if you have used Exchange before. Otherwise click on Yes. Click on Next.

2. In the next screen, you are prompted to select the services you want to use with Exchange, such as Microsoft Mail, Microsoft Network, and Microsoft Fax. These are the options you selected earlier during Setup.

   By default, the items listed are selected and the Use the following information services radio button is selected. If you want Setup to automatically configure these services (which is recommended for most users), click on Next.

Note You may want to manually configure some of the Exchange settings, such as the default profile name (MSEXCHANGE) if you have other Exchange settings set up on your network. To modify the configuration of the services, select the Manually Configure Information Services option. Any configuration setting can be changed later by using the Add/Remove Program option in Control Panel.

3. When you choose to let Setup automatically configure Exchange, the Location Information dialog box displays. This box configures the way in which your phone calls are dialed. In this box, you need to set the country in which you live, area code, any special dialing codes to get an outside number (such as 9), and

the type of phone system you use, either tone or pulse. Click on OK when you have this dialog box filled out.

4. The next Inbox Setup wizard screen that displays sets up your Microsoft Fax connection, if this is one of the selections you picked earlier. You are given two choices when installing Microsoft Fax. First, you can set up Fax so that it runs from your local computer. Click on the Modem connected to my computer option to use Fax only from your computer.

   Second, you can set up Microsoft Fax so that others can share it across a network. To do this, you must connect a fax modem to a networked computer and use it as a fax server. Click on Next.

For in-depth coverage of configuring and using Exchange, see *Inside Windows 95* published by New Riders Publishing.

Detecting a New Modem

If you have a modem installed, Windows 95 can automatically detect it and set it up for you using the Install New Modem wizard. Before working through the Install New Modem wizard, make sure your fax modem is attached to your computer and that it is turned on and hooked to a phone line. If you need to install an internal modem first, skip over this section and finish Setup first. Then install your modem (you'll need to shut down your computer to do this) and start the Add Hardware option in Control Panel to configure the modem.

If your modem is turned on and ready to be configured now, use the Install New Modem wizard. Unless you want to select your modem manually, click on Next. If you want to specify your modem type, click on the Don't detect my modem; I will select it from a list option and click on Next.

Configuring Your Printer

After Setup sets up Exchange and other online connections, it sets up the printers you have connected to your computer. If you do not want to set up a printer now, you can set one up later by selecting the Printers folder from the Start, Settings menu. Double-click on the Add Printer icon to start the Add Printer wizard.

During Setup, you need to specify whether the printer is located locally or on a network. You also need to tell Windows 95 Setup the manufacturer of the printer, such as Hewlett Packard, and the printer name, such as HP LaserJet IIIP. Click on Next to have Setup install the printer drivers on your system. If Setup detects a driver from a previous installation, you can elect to keep it or use an updated one from Windows 95. Select the option and then click on Next.

The next screen prompts you for the port or connection to which your printer is connected. Select the appropriate connection and click on Next. Windows asks you to name the printer, and gives you a default name such as HP Laserjet IIIP. Keep or change this name as necessary and click on Next.

Setup then displays a screen that asks if you want to print a test page on your printer. If your printer is set up to your machine or network, it's a good idea to do this. This way Setup can diagnose any problems you may have with your printer now. Click on Finish. After your text page prints and you respond that everything is fine, tell Setup that the page printed correctly. If your printer does not print correctly, click on the No button when Windows 95 asks if your printer printed correctly. Then, follow the on-screen Help that Windows provides.

Congratulations! Setup is now finished setting up Windows 95.

Starting Windows 95

After Setup finishes installing Windows 95 and configuring Exchange, your printer, and other options, Windows 95 starts. Figure 6.15 shows the initial Windows 95 screen, with a Welcome screen that includes helpful suggestion for navigating Windows 95.

Figure 6.15

Welcome to Windows 95!

Does It Work?

Before you start using Windows 95 and loading up tons of applications, you should test to see if it is properly installed. To do this, shut down Windows and restart it by clicking on the Start button at the bottom of the screen (this is called the Taskbar) and selecting **S**hut Down. The Shut Down Windows dialog box displays (see fig. 6.16). Make sure the **S**hut down the computer? option is selected and click on **Y**es. This begins the Windows 95 shutdown procedure, which you must do whenever you want to exit Windows 95.

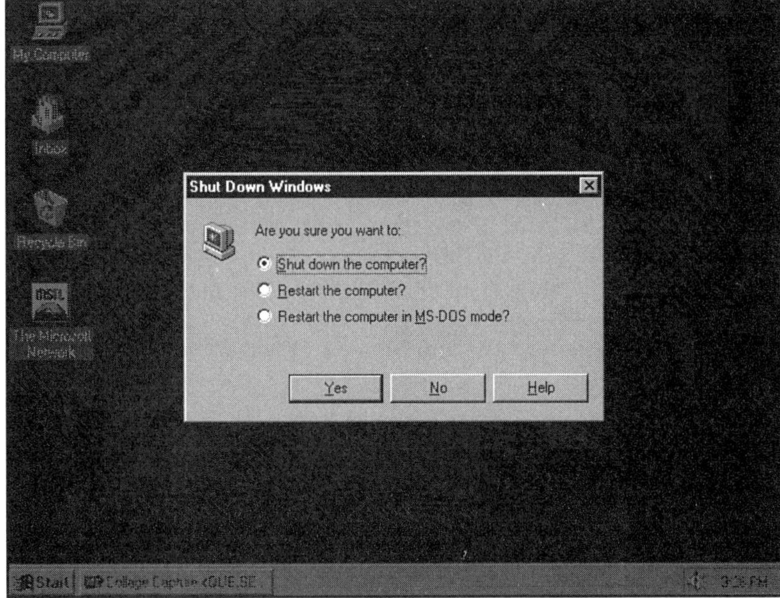

Figure 6.16

Become friends with the Shut Down procedure. You'll be using it every time you turn off your computer.

When a message appears on your screen telling you it's OK to turn off your machine, press the reset button on your computer. As your PC reboots, watch the screen to see if you notice any errors. If Windows 95 starts, your system probably is working fine and you can start using Windows 95.

If it doesn't start or if you get a DOS screen, your setup has encountered some problems. You can start Windows 95 in Safe Mode and fix the problem.

Running Windows 95 in Safe Mode

Your computer should start and you have no problems running with your new Windows 95 installation. Many times, however, Windows 95 encounters a problem (such as a Registry setting missing or corrupted) during startup that it cannot fix. When this happens, you need to run Windows in Safe Mode from the Startup menu.

You can display the Startup menu by pressing F8 during the boot process. Press F8 when the text `Starting Windows` displays on-screen. This usually appears after your system checks the internal RAM on your system. Windows 95 also starts Safe Mode automatically if it detects a problem with the startup files.

The Startup menu provides you with the following options from which to choose. Depending on your specific setup, you may or may not have the same settings.

- **Normal.** Enables you to start Windows 95 in its normal start up manner, loading all device drivers and Registry settings. If Windows 95 automatically displays the Startup menu, choosing this selection probably will not do anything except return you to the Startup menu. Choose this option only if you want to watch what happens on-screen during the failed startup.
- **Logged (\Bootlog.txt).** Creates a file called Bootlog.txt in your root directory that contains a record of the current startup process. This file is created during Setup and shows the Windows 95 components and drivers loaded and initialized, and the status of each. You can view this file in Notepad.
- **Safe mode.** Starts Windows 95 but bypasses startup files and uses only basic system drivers. Because Safe mode is intended only to be used as a way in which you can diagnose and fix problems in the WIndows 95 environment, many devices are not available—such as the Add New Hardware utility in the Control Panel. You also can start Safe Mode by pressing F5 during boot-up or typing **WIN /D:M** at the command prompt.
- **Safe Mode with Network Support.** Starts Windows 95 but bypasses startup files and uses only basic system drivers, including basic networking. You can also start this option by pressing F6 or typing **WIN /D:N** at the command prompt.
- **Step-by-step confirmation.** Enables you to confirm each line in your startup files, including Autoexec.bat and Config.sys. Answer Y to lines you want to run; answer N to lines you want to bypass. You can also start this option by pressing F8 when the Startup menu is displayed.
- **Command prompt only.** Starts MS-DOS (Windows 95 version) with startup files and Registry settings, displaying only the MS-DOS command prompt.
- **Safe mode command prompt only.** Starts MS-DOS (Windows 95 version) in Safe Mode and displays only the command prompt, bypassing startup files. Same as pressing Shift+F5.
- **Previous version of MS-DOS.** Starts your previous version of MS-DOS if you have a multiboot configuration. You must install Windows 95 into a different directory during Setup for this option to be available. You also can start this option by pressing F4 during startup. This option is only available if `BootMulti=1` in the Msdos.sys file.

When Safe Mode is selected from the Startup menu, it bypasses startup files, including the Registry, Config.sys, Autoexec.bat, and the `[Boot]` and `[386Enh]` sections of System.ini. Table 6.4 shows the files that the three most common Safe Mode options bypass and initiate. As you can see in the table, Safe Mode does not load all the Windows drivers. In fact, during Safe Mode, only the mouse, keyboard, and standard Windows VGA device drivers are loaded. Other drivers, such as Super VGA video drivers or network drivers, are not available in Safe Mode.

TABLE 6.4
Files Loaded During Startup Menu Options

Action	Safe Mode Network Support	Safe Mode Prompt Only	Command
Process Config.sys and Autoexec.bat	No	No	No
Process Registry information	No	Yes	No
Load Command.com	No	Yes	Yes
Run Windows 95 Win.com	Yes	Yes	No
Load Himem.sys and Ifshlp.sys	Yes	Yes	No
Load DoubleSpace or DriveSpace if present (Loaded if Safe Mode Command Prompt Only option is selected)		Yes	Yes
Load all Windows drivers	No	No	No
Load network drivers	No	Yes	No
Run Netstart.bat	No	Yes	No

After Windows 95 starts in Safe Mode, you can access the configuration files, modify configuration settings, and then restart Windows 95 normally.

Help! Using the Windows 95 Startup Disk

If you instructed Windows 95 to create a startup disk during Setup, you can use it to load your previous operating system and display an MS-DOS command prompt. The startup disk also contains utilities for troubleshooting your Windows 95 operating system. To use the Startup disk, place the disk in drive A and reboot your computer. A command prompt appears, from which you can diagnose and fix problems associated with your installation.

If you did not create a Startup disk during Setup, you can create one using a single floppy disk. In the Add/Remove Programs option in Control Panel, click on the Startup Disk tab. Then click on the Create Disk button, and follow the instructions on-screen. You should do this even if you are not having problems starting Windows 95 now. In the future, you may experience a problem that only the Startup disk can remedy.

Windows 95 as a Server

Windows 95 is the product of Microsoft's continued efforts to create an all-purpose operating system. Users in network environments traditionally have required an operating system for the workstation PCs (such as MS-DOS or Windows 3.*x*) and a networking system (such as Novell NetWare or LANtastic).

Windows 95, however, can serve as both a workstation operating platform and a server or networking system, owing to its peer-to-peer networking capabilities, which include file sharing, printer sharing, and access control. Windows 95's 32-bit system attributes allow it to deliver a flexible peer-to-peer network and act as a high performance server that supports a range of clients, including NetWare.

The new features in Windows 95 are well worth exploring. This chapter covers the many steps involved in setting up, configuring, and optimizing Windows 95 as a server on a peer-to-peer network.

Exploring the 32-Bit Network Components

Windows 95 is a 32-bit operating system, and therefore has 32-bit protected mode network components that deliver a higher level of performance than Windows for Workgroups or Windows 3.*x*. Windows 95 loads these components (which have no conventional memory footprint) dynamically as it needs them. Because all these components run only in protected mode, network input/output performance is greatly increased over previous version of Windows. Additionally, the reliability of these components is enhanced because they don't run in real mode, and thereby, aren't subject to real mode memory conflicts. The following list provides and describes the major network components in Windows 95:

- **VSERVER.** VSERVER is a virtual device driver (VxD) that is multithreaded to handle multiple network requests. This is the main server component of Windows 95. The server (VSERVER) accesses the network via the transport level interface.

- **MSSHRUI.** MSHRUI (Microsoft Share Point User Interface) is a DLL (Dynamic Link Library) file that handles the sharing operations that have been initiated by the user. This is the component that adds the share point to the local computer when you share a file or directory.

- **Spooler**. The Windows 95 spooler is comprised of two parts. The first part exists at the application level and accepts print jobs from the applications and passes them to the server (VSERVER). The second part of the spooler is a VxD that accepts the print jobs from the server and passes them to a print device, such as a printer connected to the server.

- **Access Control.** The access control component is also a VxD that controls individual file requests. It uses the *username, password* (if any), and *filename* to verify the users' rights to use a particular file or resource.

- **Security Provider.** The Security Provider component verifies the users' requests for access to the network. It uses the username and password to check and authenticate each request.

- **IFS Manager.** The IFS (Installable File System) Manager routes file system requests from the server (VSERVER) to either the network FSD (File System Driver) or the local FSD. The IFS Manager in Windows 95 offers multiple redirector support, unified cache which enables client side redirector caching, and protected mode use which eliminates real-mode conflicts.

- **VREDIR.** This is a VxD that is the network file system driver. It handles all requests from the IFS manager for files located on network resources.

Preparing to Share Your Resources

Before you can share your workstation's resources on a Windows 95 network, you must enable file and print sharing.

When you install Windows 95, file and print sharing default to "disabled." To enable this functionality, double-click on the Network icon in the Control Panel folder. Figure 7.1 shows the Network property panels.

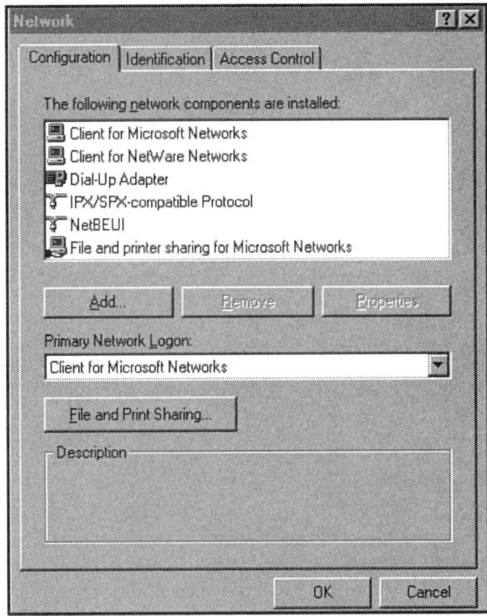

Figure 7.1

Network properties can be changed from this box.

From this screen if you click on the **F**ile and Print Sharing button, you can choose the sharing options that you want to enable.

Figure 7.2 shows the file and print sharing options as they appear on the screen. Place a check mark in the box preceding the option that you want to enable.

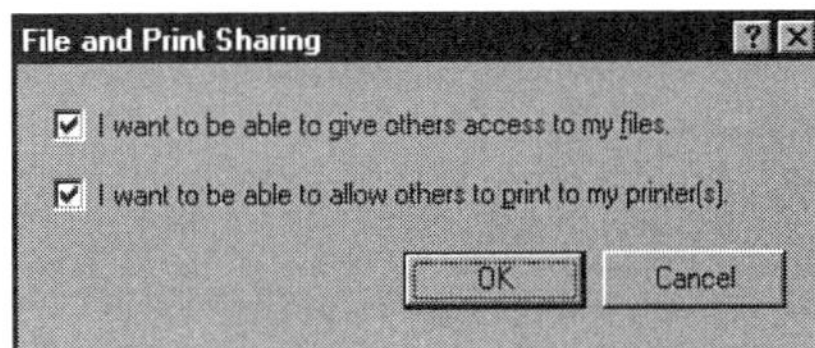

Figure 7.2

Choose the sharing options from this dialog box.

Setting these options prepares your computer to act as a server on a peer-to-peer network. After you choose the file and print sharing options from the dialog box (see fig. 7.2), the network component "File and printer sharing for Microsoft Networks" appears in the network component box on the network configuration panel shown in figure 7.1.

Sharing Your Files, Folders, and Disks

You can use Windows 95's peer-to-peer networking capability to share a file, folder, CD-ROM drive, or entire hard disk. To share a resource with other people on the network, follow these steps:

1. Double-click on the My Computer icon on your Windows 95 desktop, and then select the folder you want to share.
2. Choose **F**ile, **P**roperties (or right-click on the folder and choose **P**roperties). A Properties dialog box appears (see fig. 7.3).

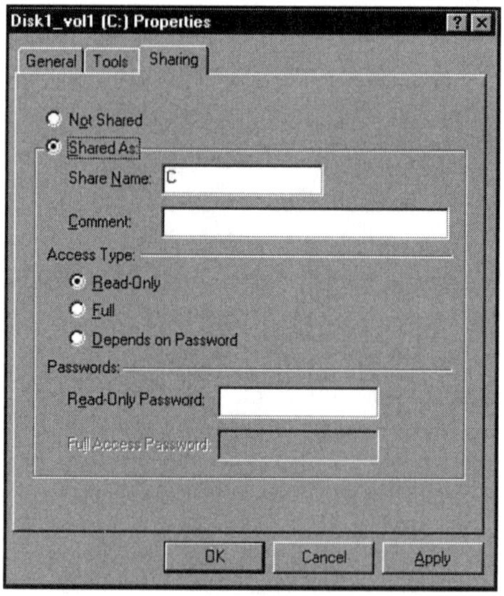

Figure 7.3
The property dialog box for files, folders, or disks.

3. From the Sharing panel, choose **S**hared As.

After you choose **S**hared As, the following options become usable:

- **Share Name.** This is the name of the item you want to share. Other users who browse the Your Computer selection for shared resources see this name.
- **Comment.** Other users also see the Comment field as they scan your computer for shared resources. This field can help further define or describe the shared resource. Other users can use the Details view to see this comment line when they access the folder.

The Access Type options enable you to control the level of access to a particular folder or resource. The access levels are as follows:

- **Read-Only.** Users sharing this resource can read or access the resource, but cannot write, change, or delete it.
- **Full.** Sharing users can Read, Write, and Delete this resource.
- **Depends on Password.** This option allows you to specify a level of access depending on the password entered by a sharing user. With this option, some users can have full access while others can have read-only access.

The following are the two password options that appear on this screen:

- **Read-Only Password.** Here is where you set the password used for read-only access.
- **Full Access Password.** Enter the password used for full access in this box.

Connecting a Workstation to Network Resources

You can use two methods to connect to network folders or drives. One method simply connects you to the resource while the other method *maps* a drive letter to the resource.

The first method creates a temporary connection to the resource that lasts until you disconnect or shut down your system. To temporarily connect to a shared folder, double-click on the Network Neighborhood icon on your Windows 95 desktop. Then double-click on the computer on the network that has the shared folder you want to access.

After you find the folder to which you want to connect, double-click on the folder to make the connection.

The second way to connect to a network resource is to map a drive letter to that resource. Using this method creates a *logical drive letter* on the workstation that refers to the network resource. You can do this, regardless of whether the network resource is a disk or a folder.

You generally should create a logical drive letter for a resource when you plan to use that resource often. If you access the hard drive on another workstation on a daily basis, for example, you should probably create a logical driver letter for that hard disk.

To map a drive letter to a shared drive or folder, follow these steps:

1. In My Computer or Network Neighborhood, click on Map Network Drive on the toolbar. (If your My Computer or Network Neighborhood panel doesn't have a toolbar, choose View and select Toolbar.) The Map Network Drive dialog box appears, as shown in figure 7.4.

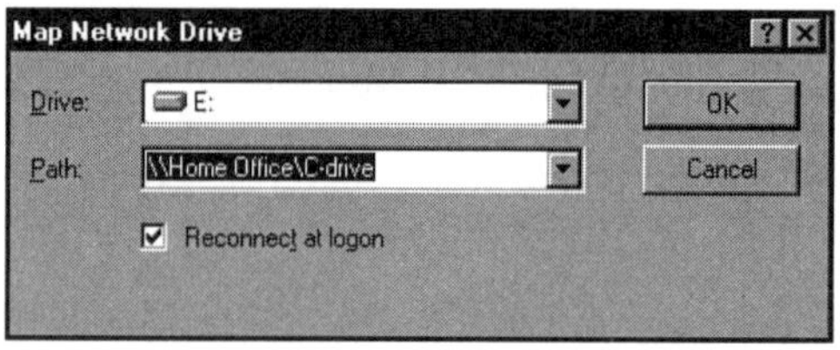

Figure 7.4

Enter the path name in this dialog box.

2. Type the path to the resource in the **Path** text box. For example:

```
\\mainserver\accounting files
```

The preceding example would map a logical drive letter to the accounting files folder on the computer named *mainserver*. Windows 95 prompts you for the password if the folder is password protected.

Disabling a Folder or Drive Mapping

To disconnect a network resource mapped on your workstation, follow these steps.

1. In My Computer, click on the disconnect network drive button on the toolbar to open the Disconnect Network Drive dialog box (see fig. 7.5).

2. Choose the network drive you want to disconnect and click on the OK button.

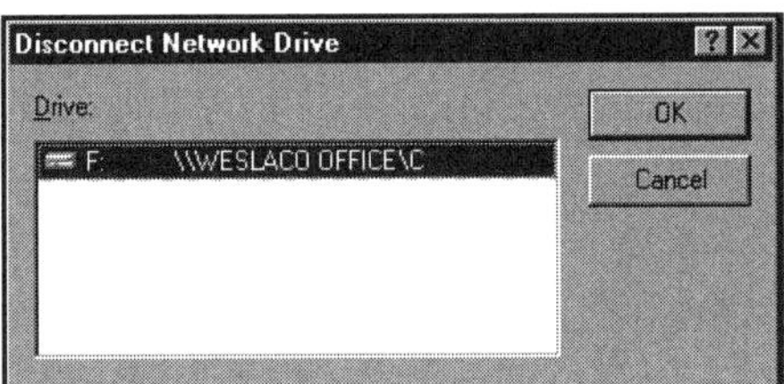

Figure 7.5
Choose the network drive that you desire to be disconnected.

The drive you select no longer is available. If you have any shortcuts for accessing this network drive, you need to change or delete them.

Sharing Printers

Another type of resource you can share on the network are the printers on your workstation.

Before you can share printers, you must enable printer sharing on your computer, as described in the section "Preparing to Share Your Resources" earlier in this chapter.

To share a printer, open the Printers folder. Choose the icon for the printer that you want to share, then choose File, Properties (you also can right-click on the folder for the printer and choose Properties from the menu that appears).

Figure 7.6 shows the settings available on the Sharing panel on the printer's Properties dialog box.

The sharing options available to you in this option box are Not shared and Shared As. The Shared As option box contains the following choices:

- **Share Name.** This box contains the name of the printer that is visible to someone who browses your computer for shared printers.
- **Comment.** This box contains comments that are visible to someone who browses your computer for shared printers. You can use this field to tell the person connecting to this printer what type of paper is in the different bins on the printer. Leaving the comment "Letterhead, bin 1 - Plain White, bin2," for example, might help users sharing this printer ascertain which type of paper is available and which printer bin to select.

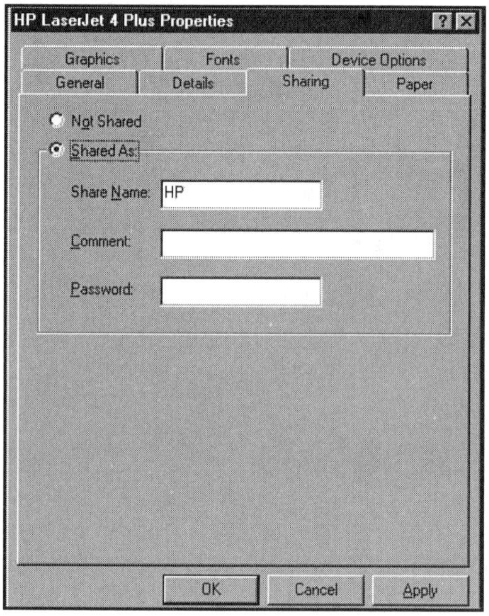

Figure 7.6
The sharing options dialog for a particular printer.

- **Password**. If you want or need to, you enter the password for access to this printer in this text box.

After you enable printer sharing on your workstation, other users can access those printers from across the Windows 95 network.

Connecting to Network Printers

To connect to a shared printer on the network, follow these steps:

1. In Network Neighborhood, double-click on the icon of the computer to which the shared printer you want to use is located.
2. Double-click on the Printer icon in the window that appears.
3. To set up the printer, follow the instructions on the screen. The wizard will guide you through the process.

Disconnecting from Network Printers

At times, it may be necessary to disconnect from a network printer. If the network printer was being removed from the network, for example, you would want to remove the reference to it from your workstation. To disconnect a network printer from your workstation, follow these steps:

1. In the Printers folder, select the printer you want to disconnect.
2. Press the Delete key to remove it from your printer folder.

Printing to a Printer That Is Temporarily Disconnected

A workstation (or portable computer) can print to a printer currently unavailable. This Windows 95 feature can be useful, for example, if a network printer is temporarily out of service (such as out of toner) or if the network is down.

To work with a temporarily disconnected printer, follow these steps:

1. In the Printers folder, click on the icon for the printer you want to use.
2. Choose File, Work Offline.

Now, when you send a document to this printer, it stores on disk until you turn the printer online by choosing Work Offline again.

This feature is also useful, for example, on a laptop or notebook computer that does not always have its printer attached.

Understanding Access Control

The network security system in Windows 95 was designed with two ideas in mind. First, to provide easy-to-use and quick security for the local machine. Second, Windows 95 security enables the local computer (via Windows 95) to participate in a more complex security system.

Because one primary purpose of the Windows 95 security system is ease of use, it is not foolproof. It doesn't provide nearly the same level of security, for example, as Windows NT. The Windows 95 security system is designed to keep honest users honest. It keeps them out of resources that they are not intended to use. However, it does not offer much protection against so-called hackers that might try a more sophisticated break-in.

The security system in Windows 95 contains two types of security schemes, as follows:

- Share-level security
- User-level security

The next two sections discuss each of these two levels of security.

Share-Level Security

With share-level security, each shared resource has a particular set of access rights. These access rights apply to the resource, regardless of which user tries to access the resource. If you have a hard disk that you share with other users and if you set a share-level password of "DANCE," for example, all users who know that password (and only those users) may access that drive. Figure 7.7 shows the Sharing property screen for a hard drive.

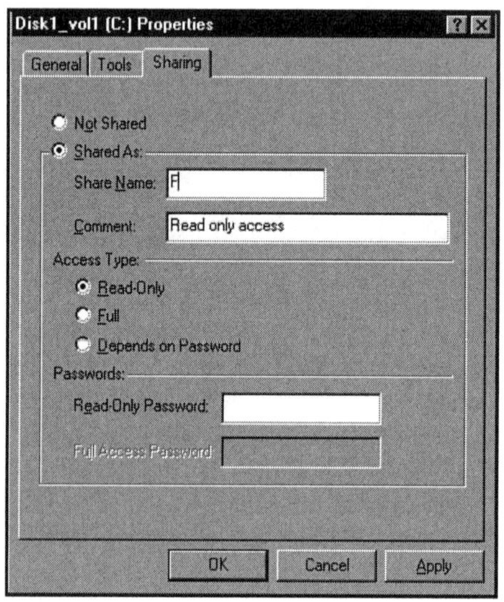

Figure 7.7

The screen that appears when you right-click on a drive icon in the My Computer folder.

With share-level security, each resource is protected by a password. You can usc passwords for read-only access or read-write access.

User-Level Security

User-level security enables you to create a list of users who have access to a particular resource. Before a user can gain access to a resource, he or she must be on this list of users. When a user logs on to the system, you can require a password to assure the user is who he says he is.

You can use user-level security to provide security for a variety of services beyond network access. The following is a list of services that you can control using user-level security:

- File and print sharing
- Backup agent

- Network management
- Dial-up networking

In addition, you can gather users together into groups to make assigning users to a resource easier. Thus, rather than enter twenty user names to the access list, you can add these users to a group called, for example, "secretaries," then add one entry to the access list called "secretaries."

Also, a Windows 95 workstation can adjust the desktop to each user, which enables each user of the workstation to customize the desktop by setting up his or her own icons in a certain way or choosing a screen saver without affecting other users of that workstation. To enable this function follow these steps:

1. Choose Passwords properties in the Control Panel folder.
2. Choose the User Profiles panel.
3. Check the second option—allowing users to **C**ustomize their desktop settings.

Now, the next person who logs on can alter the settings without affecting the other user's settings.

To log off and log on as another user follow these steps:

1. Click on the Start button, then choose Sh**u**t Down.
2. Choose the **C**lose All Programs And Log On As A Different User option.
3. In the Enter Network Password box, click on Cancel. Windows restarts without logging you on to the network.

Configuring the Windows 95 Server

Depending on your particular situation, you might have a few special considerations for setting up a Windows 95 server on a peer-to-peer network. If you have a Windows 95 network and one of the computers on the network acts as the primary depository of files and as the print server, you might want to consider the following:

- Performance settings in Windows 95
- Hard drive choices in the server
- Bus type of the motherboard

Performance Settings in Windows 95

Windows 95 has a few adjustments that can effect the performance of a Windows 95 server, all of which you can find in the Control Panel folder. Figure 7.8 shows the Performance panel in the System Information dialog box from the Control Panel Folder.

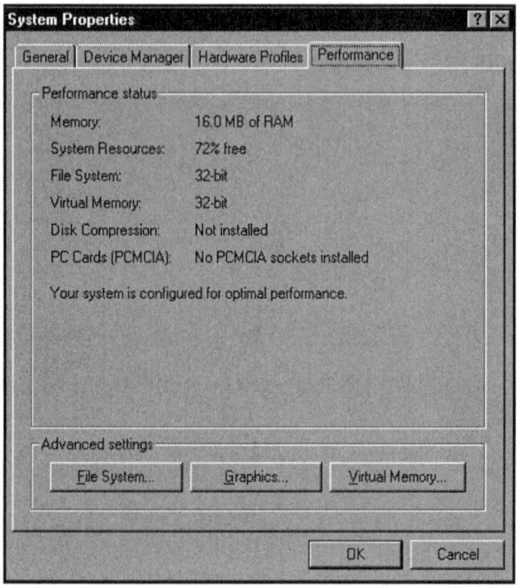

Figure 7.8

Click on the File System button to change disk performance settings.

From this screen, click on the **F**ile System button to go the advanced settings for file system properties. Figure 7.9 shows the settings box.

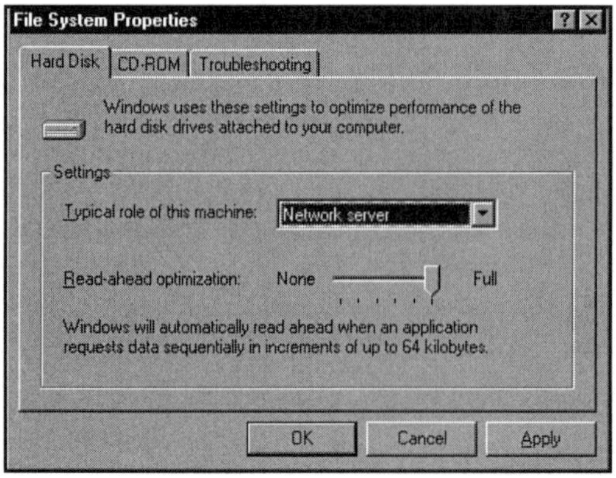

Figure 7.9

The advanced settings box for file system properties.

The File System Properties dialog box contains two settings that effect server performance. The first setting is the Typical role of this machine drop-down list box. You should set this for Network server. The second setting is the Read-ahead optimization slider. Slide the selector all the way to the right for full read-ahead optimization.

Establishing these two settings optimizes your file system as a Windows 95 server.

Server Hard Drive Choices

Because the server acts as a central depository of files and applications, you need to consider a few items that concern the hard drive.

- **Type of hard drive.** You should consider using an Enhanced IDE interface or a SCSI-2 interface hard drive. These drive types deliver a higher data throughput than other drive types.
- **Access time.** The lower the access time rating of a hard drive, the better. This means the hard drive finds the data faster than hard drives that have a higher access time.
- **Capacity.** The larger the hard drive on the server, the better. With hard drive prices currently so low, you shouldn't even consider a hard drive of less than 1 GB for your Windows 95 network server .

Motherboard Bus Type

When you choose a computer to act as a Windows 95 server, you should consider the bus type of the motherboard. Naturally, the most significant consideration in motherboards is the type of CPU (that is, Pentium, 486, and so on). In addition to that issue, however, you have two primary choices for a good performance motherboard.

- **PCI (Peripheral Component Interconnect).** PCI allows the fastest communication possible between a peripheral device and the CPU. You find PCI technology more prevalent among Pentium processor-based motherboards. PCI expansion cards also are becoming very popular and can deliver some of the fastest performance ratings in their respective categories.
- **VESA (Video Electronics Standards Association).** VESA also is referred to as local bus. Local bus motherboards offer a higher rate of communication between peripherals and the CPU than ISA motherboards. The PCI standard, however, delivers a higher performance level. VESA (local bus) is the standard for most 486-based motherboards.

ISA bus motherboards operate on a 16-bit playing field and do not have the capability to offer any performance advantages. Although ISA motherboards are on there way to extinction, VESA and PCI motherboards offer a few ISA type slots that enable you to plug in your older ISA type cards.

Using NetWare Clients with a Windows 95 Server

In addition to sharing files and printers with Windows clients, Windows 95 can share files and printers with NetWare clients, which is useful if you run a Windows 95 peer-to-peer network on top of a NetWare network. You can share expensive printers that you might have attached to a Windows 95 workstation with less fortunate NetWare workstations on the same network.

This feature also can prove useful if you phase out a NetWare network and phase in a Windows 95 network. Both a Windows 95 server and a NetWare server can set up on the same network. Since both servers can share information, Windows 95-based workstations can replace older NetWare workstations one at a time, thus distributing the expense and shock of an all-at-once conversion.

The services that Windows 95 offers to accomplish these tasks are 32-bit protected mode drivers that (like the other network components) have no conventional memory footprint and prevent memory problems associated with real-mode drivers.

To enable Windows 95 to share its files and printers with NetWare clients, perform the following steps:

1. Choose the Network icon in the Control Panel folder. From the Configuration panel, click on the Add button and a Select Network Component Type dialog box appears (see fig. 7.10).

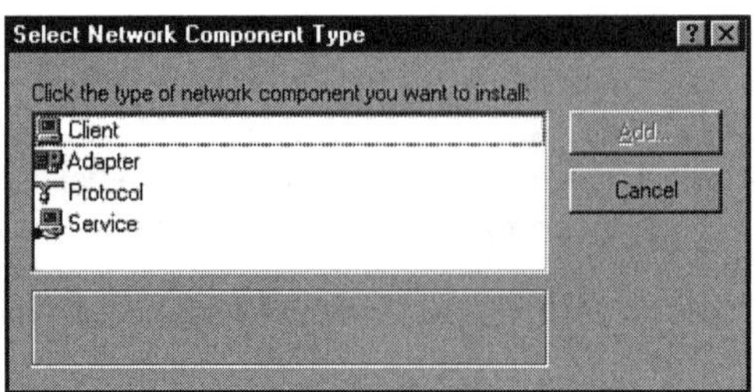

Figure 7.10

Choose the type of component that you are adding from this window.

2. Select Service from the list and click on the **A**dd button. Figure 7.11 shows the Select Network Service dialog box.

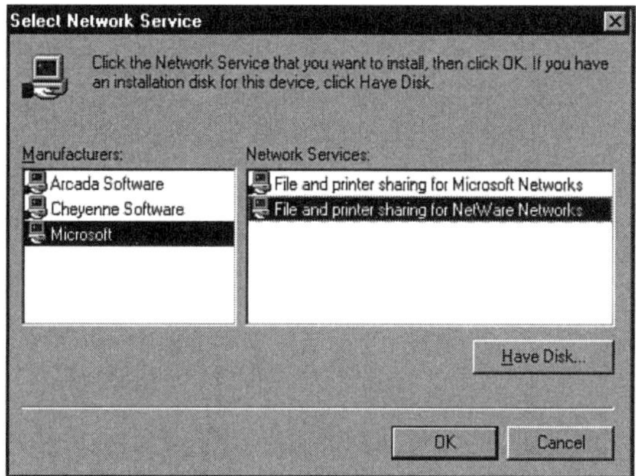

Figure 7.11

Choose the network service that you are installing.

3. From the **M**anufacturers list, select Microsoft; and then from the Network Service list, select File and printer sharing for NetWare Networks.

Assuming you have a NetWare server on the network, Windows 95 now can share its files and printers with the NetWare clients.

Security Issues with NetWare Clients

Share-level security is not supported with NetWare clients, which means that to secure any resources involving NetWare clients, you need to set up user-level security. Windows 95 has a pass-through security model that uses the NetWare server's bindery to pass the validation of users.

Before Windows 95 can use this pass-through security model, it must know where to find the NetWare server. In the Control Panel folder, under the Network icon is the Access Control panel (see fig. 7.12).

In this panel enter the name of the NetWare server in the Obtain list of users and groups from field and click on the OK button. After you do this, you have set up Windows 95 pass-through security, and Windows 95 is ready to share resources with NetWare clients on the network.

Figure 7.12

Enter the name of the NetWare server here.

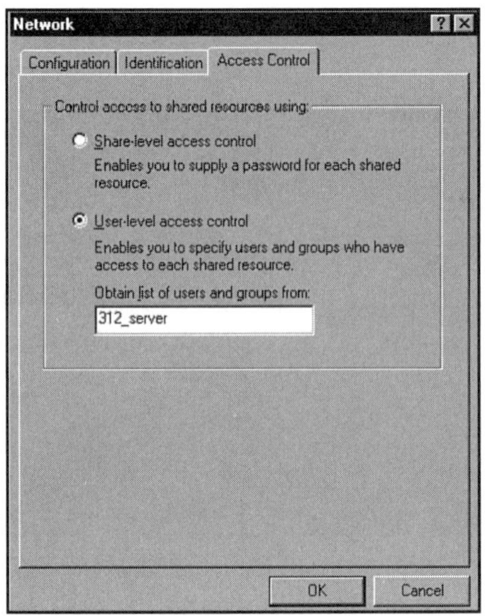

Microsoft Print Server for NetWare

The PSERVER utility is a 32-bit printer service that can despool print jobs from NetWare queues to Windows 95 printers. You can connect a Windows 95 printer directly to a NetWare print queue, via the NetWare queue configuration. After you share the printer on the Windows 95 network, any NetWare print queue can use it.

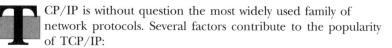

Using TCP/IP

TCP/IP is without question the most widely used family of network protocols. Several factors contribute to the popularity of TCP/IP:

- **Maturity.** Definition of the TCP/IP protocols began in the 1970s to satisfy a requirement of the Department of Defense for a robust wide-area-networking protocol. TCP/IP gained wide distribution when it was written into Berkeley Standard Distribution (BSD) Unix, and has been a standard feature of Unix implementations for a long time. As a result, TCP/IP received thorough field trials when other protocols were in their early developmental stages.

- **Openness.** TCP/IP is the only protocol suite with an open standards definition process. Discussion takes place in the form of Requests for Comments (RFCs) that are posted and debated publicly on the Internet. Proposals and debates are open, not restricted to members of a standards committee.

- **Non-proprietary ownership.** In a real sense, TCP/IP is owned by the user community. Other protocols, almost without exception, are proprietary protocols, owned by vendors. Users have little or no input into these proprietary protocols, and manufacturers must often pay licensing fees to build proprietary protocols into their products.

- **Richness.** TCP/IP is actually a suite of protocols that provides a vast set of capabilities. Little, if anything, a network should do cannot be done with TCP/IP.

- **Compatibility.** TCP/IP is the only protocol suite that runs on almost anything. Computer system manufacturers now regard TCP/IP as a requirement. Name the hardware, and you will probably find at least one TCP/IP implementation for it.

Unfortunately, a single chapter can only skim the subject of TCP/IP, a subject that would require many volumes to cover thoroughly.

Before you can appreciate TCP/IP and understand how to set it up, you need to know something more about how small and large networks work.

Networks and Internetworks

On simple networks such as the one in figure 8.1, delivery of messages between devices is quite simple. Each device is assigned a device address (a numeric name). When device A wants to send a message to device C, device A simply adds C's device address to the message and puts the message on the network. C, like every device on the network, is looking at all of the messages that zip by. If C sees a message that bears its device address, it can retrieve the message. Other devices, such as B in the figure, will ordinarily ignore messages not addressed to them.

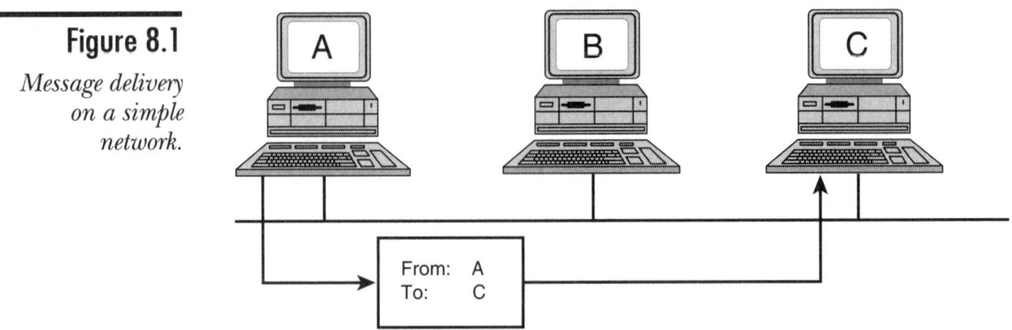

Figure 8.1
Message delivery on a simple network.

Message delivery on a simple network is just like finding your luggage on the conveyor belt at the airport. The baggage handlers aren't aware of where you're standing or even if you're present at all. They just throw your bags on the conveyor, and it's up to you to spot the pieces that have your name on them.

But large networks, and real luggage delivery, are a lot more complicated than simply getting suitcases from the airplane to the owner. Consider what really happens on a long flight with several stops and some plane changes. When you arrive at your departure airport, your bags are marked by a tag that identifies the destination airport. When you change planes, your bags are supposed to change planes with you, and baggage handlers at the intermediate airport must sort through the incoming bags and route them. Each bag is tagged with a destination. Some bags stay at this airport, some go to another airport, and some, whose destination can't be reached directly from this location, need to be routed through another intermediate airport as the next hop toward their destination. If the current airport matches the destination on a luggage tag, the bag needs to go onto the conveyor belt for local delivery. If an item is sent to the wrong airport, a mechanism must be in place to identify the error, discover how to get the item to its correct destination, and start it on its way.

Airport baggage handling is a concrete example of the problems large networks face thousands of times in every second that they operate. Here is a summary of the problems that must be solved to deliver messages through a complex network:

- Each device must have a unique identification on its local network. Imagine if there were two Bill Roberts with the same street address trying to pick up the same luggage with an LAX (Los Angeles International) airport tag.
- Each intermediate and final destination must have an identification. No two networks or airports can use the same identification symbol.
- Procedures must be in place for routing messages between the source and the final destination. Airports use baggage handlers. Networks use routers and routing protocols.
- If an intermediate destination is of a different type from the source and/or destination, all must agree on procedures so that confusion does not arise. Imagine what it would be like flying from New York to Saudi Arabia if every country along the way required you to route your baggage with a completely different procedure.
- When problems occur, as they surely will, mechanisms must be in place to attempt to correct the error.

Figure 8.2 shows a fairly involved wide area network. With this network, a message from A that was addressed to B could hypothetically take several routes to reach its destination. Every place that networks interconnect, devices called *routers* are placed. Routers serve the same function as baggage handlers in an airport; they route packages toward their destinations, hopefully along the fastest route.

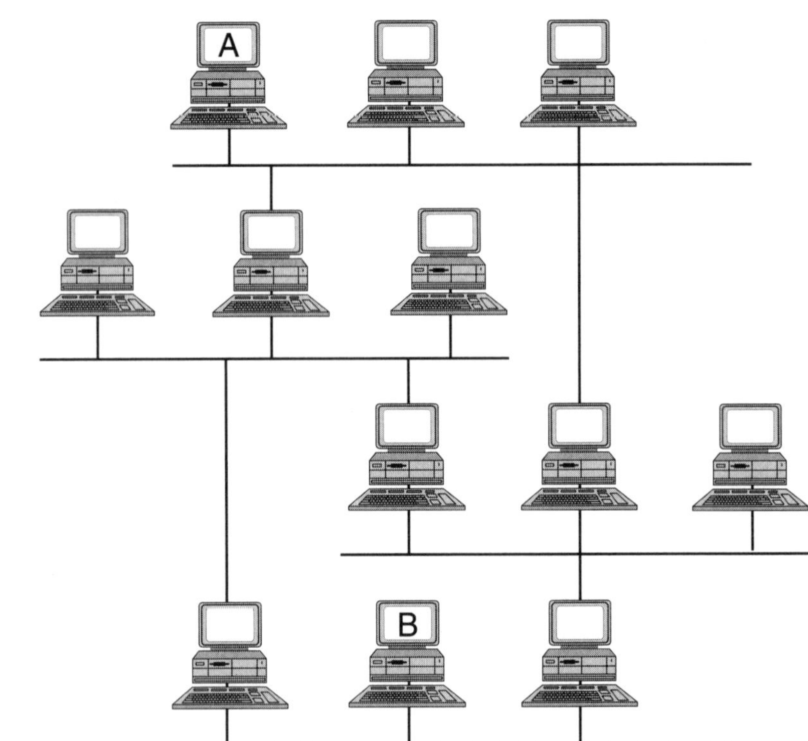

Figure 8.2
A complex network.

The network in figure 8.2 consists of several networks that are interconnected. A "network of networks" is commonly called an *internetwork* or simply an *internet. The* network of networks, a vast, international network that originated from the original Defense Department networks of the late 1970s, is called the *Internet.*

Following are the elements of an internetwork, expressed in somewhat more technical terms:

- **Each device on a network is identified by a unique address, often called a device or node address.** These addresses are frequently permanently coded into the network hardware. Each Ethernet and token-ring card possesses a 48-bit address number that is guaranteed to be unique throughout the world.

- **A local delivery mechanism enables devices to place messages on the medium and retrieve messages that are addressed to them.** Using the OSI reference model, local delivery is performed by the physical and data link layers.

- **A mechanism for delivering messages that must travel through the internetwork.** In the TCP/IP protocol suite, internetwork delivery is the responsibility of the Internet Protocol (IP).
- **A way to determine good ways of routing messages.** With TCP/IP, routing in complex networks is performed by IP, usually with support of a routing protocol such as Routing Information Protocol (RIP) or Open Shortest Path First (OSPF).
- **A way to detect and recover from errors.** The Transmission Control Protocol (TCP) is responsible for error detection and recovery on TCP/IP networks.

TCP/IP isn't the only way of solving these problems, but it is an excellent approach and the approach with the widest acceptance.

TCP/IP and Internetworks

This section looks at how the layers solve the internetwork problems that were introduced earlier.

Local Network Addresses

TCP/IP can use a wide variety of lower layer protocols, including X.25 packet switching, Ethernet, and token ring. In fact, TCP/IP was explicitly designed without data link and physical layer specifications because the goal was to make the protocol suite adaptable to most types of media.

TCP/IP relies on physical addresses to deliver messages on the local network. On LANs, physical addresses are functions of the medium access control (MAC) sublayer of the OSI data link layer. Most LAN standards make provisions for assigning physical (hardware) addresses to cards. Each Ethernet and token ring card has a 48-bit address that is burned into the card's hardware when it is manufactured. A central address registry assigns address ranges to each manufacturer so each card will have a unique address.

Note Computers on TCP/IP networks are called *hosts*. When TCP/IP was being developed, there were no personal computers or workstations. All computers were multiuser computers that were and still are called *hosts*. Today, even a single user computer on a TCP/IP network is called a host.

Local Message Delivery

TCP/IP refers to each local network as a *subnet.* Whenever IP sends a message that is directed to a device on the local subnet, it tags the message with the physical address of the message recipient and sends the message down the protocol stack. The physical layer places the message on the network, where it circulates past all devices on the subnet. The device that matches the physical address retrieves the message.

Routing Messages through Internetworks

When a message is not destined for a device on the local subnet, it must be routed. Each subnet is assigned a subnet address. Each computer is configured with a default router to which it sends messages that must be sent to a remote subnet.

The responsibility of determining how messages should be addressed is one of the tasks of IP, the Internetwork Protocol. IP identifies whether each message is destined for a computer on the local network or whether it should be sent to the default router. The physical address for either the local host or the default router is added to each message that is sent.

IP makes use of addresses called *IP addresses* to logically identify subnets and devices, which are called *hosts* in TCP/IP terminology. IP addresses will be explained later in this chapter, in the section "IP Addresses."

IP receives frames from higher-level protocols. One of IP's responsibilities is to attach to each frame a header containing address information. Once the IP header has been attached to the frame, the combination is generally referred to as a *packet.*

Determining routing paths between routers is usually the responsibility of one of two protocols: Routing Information Protocol (RIP), an older and less-efficient protocol that remains in widespread use, and Open Shortest Path First (OSPF), a newer and more efficient protocol. Thorough discussion of RIP and OSPF is beyond the scope of this book. IP makes use of routing tables built by RIP or OSPF to determine the next router to which a packet should be sent.

Detecting and Recovering from Errors

IP provides what is known as *unreliable network service,* meaning that IP assumes that packets will be delivered correctly and does nothing to verify delivery. Generally speaking, this is insufficient, and a mechanism is required to detect and recover from errors.

Error recovery is the responsibility of the Transmission Control Protocol (TCP), the second protocol that identifies the TCP/IP protocol suite. Among the responsibilities of TCP are the following:

- Fragmentation of large messages from upper layer protocols into *frames* that fit within the limitations of the network. (No network can transmit a 100 MB file in a single chunk because that would monopolize the network for too long a period of time. The file must be broken into smaller units.)
- Reassembly of received frames into messages that are passed to upper layer protocols.
- Error detection and recovery.

When TCP sends a frame, it expects an acknowledgment when the frame is received. When no acknowledgment is forthcoming, TCP assumes that the frame was lost and retransmits. TCP is an extremely robust protocol, enabling TCP/IP to function reliably on surprisingly flaky networks. After all, the protocol was developed with the goal of running critical defense networks when networks weren't all that reliable under normal use, let alone during wartime conditions.

The reliable features of TCP come at the cost of reduced performance. When "best effort" delivery is sufficient, an alternative protocol can be utilized. User Datagram Protocol (UDP) provides unreliable transport service for less critical functions. One use of UDP is to transmit network management information for the Simple Network Management Protocol (SNMP).

IP Addresses

Network addresses, unlike physical addresses, are not burned into any hardware anywhere. Network addresses are assigned by network administrators and are logically configured into network devices.

In addition to logical addresses for subnets, TCP/IP assigns a logical address to each host on the network as well. Although they complicate network setup, logical IP addresses have some advantages:

- They are independent of the specific physical layer implementation. Upper layer processes can use logical addresses without concerning themselves with the address format of the underlying physical layer.
- A device can retain the same logical IP address even though its physical layer may change. Converting a network from token ring to Ethernet doesn't affect the IP addresses.

IP Address Format

IP addresses are 32-bit numbers that contain both a subnet address and a host address. The method used for encoding addresses in an IP address is a bit confusing for newcomers and is the primary stumbling block for TCP/IP newbies.

Following is an example of an IP address. Please commit it to memory.

```
11000001000010100001111000000010
```

It's not that easy to scan, is it? And it's really hard to quickly identify differences between two numbers. Assuming that the two numbers were not nearby on the same page, how quickly could you spot the difference between the previous number and this one:

```
11000010000010100001111000000010
```

That little change makes a big difference in the way the address functions. To make IP addresses easier to work with, the 32-bit addresses are typically divided into four *octets* (8-bit sections):

```
11000001 00001010 00011110 00000010
```

Still not easy, but the next step considerably simplifies things. Each of the octets can be translated into a decimal number in the range of 0 through 255. This leads us to the more conventional method of representing the example IP address:

```
193.10.30.2
```

This format is commonly called *dotted-decimal notation.*

Although IP addresses are most commonly represented in dotted-decimal notation, it is important to keep in touch with the underlying binary numbers. IP functionality is defined by the bit patterns, not by the decimal numbers we commonly use. The vast majority of IP addressing problems result because the network administrator failed to closely examine the bit patterns for the IP addresses that were selected.

If you are among the 99.44 percent of the population that doesn't think it's fun to convert binary to decimal in your head, make use of the Windows Calculator application. Switch it into Scientific mode by checking the **S**cientific option in the **V**iew menu. Then you can use the Binary and Decimal mode buttons to convert numbers from one representation to another.

IP Address Classes

Each IP address consists of two fields:

- A *netid* field that is the logical network address of the subnet to which the computer is attached.
- A *hostid* field, which is the logical device address that uniquely identifies each host on a subnet.

Together, the netid and the hostid provide each host on an internetwork with a unique IP address.

When the TCP/IP protocols were originally developed, it was thought that computer networks would fall into one of three categories:

- A small number of networks that had large numbers of hosts.
- Some networks with an intermediate number of hosts.
- A large number of networks that would have a small number of hosts.

For that reason, IP addresses were organized into *classes*. You can identify the class of an IP address by examining the first octet:

- If the first octet has a value of 0 through 127, it is a *class A* address. Because 0 and 127 in this octet have special uses, 126 class A addresses are available, each of which can support 16,777,216 hosts.
- If the first octet has a value of 128 through 191, it is a *class B* address. 16,384 class B addresses are possible, each of which can support up to 65,536 hosts.
- If the first octet has a value of 192 through 223, it is a *class C* address. 2,097,152 class C addresses are available, each of which can support up to 254 hosts.

The number of hosts that a class address can support depends on the way the class allocates octets to netids and hostids. Figure 8.3 shows how octets are organized for each class.

As you can see, a class A address uses only the first octet for network IDs. The remaining three octets are available for use as host IDs.

Class B addresses use the first two octets to designate the netid. The third and fourth octets are used for host IDs.

Class C addresses use the first three octets for network IDs. Only the fourth octet is used for host IDs.

Figure 8.3

Organization of octets in classes of IP addresses.

Class	Octet 1	Octet 2	Octet 3	Octet 4
Class A	NNNNNNNN	HHHHHHHH	HHHHHHHH	HHHHHHHH
Class B	NNNNNNNN	NNNNNNNN	HHHHHHHH	HHHHHHHH
Class C	NNNNNNNN	NNNNNNNN	NNNNNNNN	HHHHHHHH

N = netid

H = hositd

Technically, the class of an address is defined by the leftmost bits in the first octet:

- If the first bit is a 0, the address is class A.
- If the first two bits are 10, the address is class B.
- If the first three bits are 110, the address is class C.
- If the first four bits are 1110, the address is class D.
- If the first four bits are 1111, the address is class E.

Class D and E are not available for standard network addressing and aren't discussed in this book.

Special IP Addresses

You might have noticed that the numbers don't add up to the subnets and hosts that I indicated a particular address class could support. That is because several addresses are reserved for special purposes. If you set up a TCP/IP network, you will be assigning IP addresses and should keep the following restrictions in mind:

- Any address with a first octet value of 127 is a loopback address, which is used in diagnostics and testing. A message sent to an IP address with a first octet of 127 is returned to the sender. Therefore, 127 cannot be used as a netid, even though it is technically a class A address.

- 255 in an octet designates a broadcast or a multicast. A message sent to 255.255.255.255 is broadcast to every host on the internetwork. A message sent to 165.10.255.255 is multicast to every host on network 165.10.

- The first octet cannot have a value above 223. Those addresses are reserved for multicast and experimental purposes.
- The last octet of a hostid cannot be 0 or 255.

Network IDs and Subnets

The rule for configuring TCP/IP subnets is quite simple: Every host on the network must be configured with the same subnet ID. Figure 8.4 shows an internetwork with three subnets:

- A class A subnet with the subnet address 65.
- A class B subnet with the subnet address 140.200
- A class C subnet with the subnet address 201.150.65

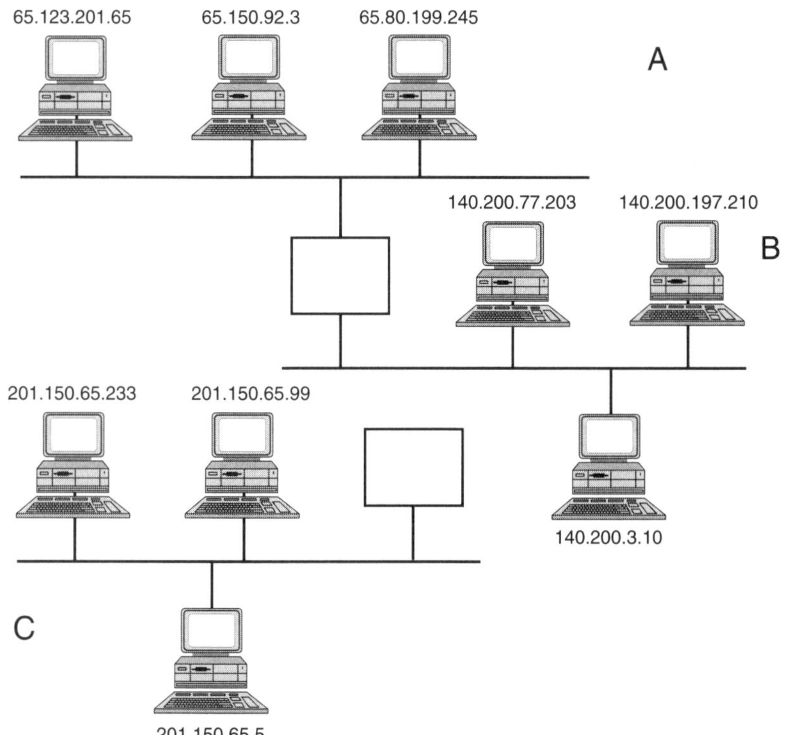

Figure 8.4
An internetwork based on three IP network IDs.

Each host on each subnet is shown with its internet ID. These subnets function in the same fashion. The only difference is that the class A subnet can support many more hosts. The subnets are internetworked with routers.

Actually, you can configure devices on the same cable segment with different netids, and nothing will blow up. However, the devices behave as though they are on different subnets and cannot communicate without a router. As you can see, the netid is the crucial identifier of a subnet, not the cable segment to which the hosts are attached.

Subnet Masks

A *subnet mask* is a bit pattern that defines which portion of the IP address represents a subnet address. Because the octet organization of each IP address class is clearly defined, the purpose of subnet masks is not obvious at first, but subnet masks have good reasons for existing.

Here is a basic example. Consider the Class B address 170.203.93.5. The binary equivalent for this address is:

```
10101010 11001011 1011101 00000101
```

The default subnet mask for a class B address is:

```
11111111 11111111 00000000 00000000
```

As you can see, the subnet mask has a 1 in each bit position that corresponds to a bit in the netid component of the address. When a 1 appears in the subnet mask, the corresponding bit in the IP address is part of the netid of the subnet. Therefore, the netid of this subnet is:

```
10101010 11001011
```

A 0 (zero) in a subnet mask indicates that the corresponding bit in the IP address is part of the host ID.

Like IP addresses, subnet masks are usually represented in dotted decimal notation. The preceding subnet address is 255.255.0.0.

The RFCs do not allow a hostid that is all 1s or all 0s. Similarly, the RFCs do not permit the subnet portion of the netid in an IP address to be all 1s or all 0s.

Subnet masks make it easier and faster for IP to identify the netid portion of the IP address. But subnet masks have another benefit, as well; they permit you to suballocate network addresses.

This capability is particularly important when your network is attached to the Internet. This is because you will be assigned your IP addresses, and you probably won't get all the addresses you would like to have. Internet addresses are getting scarce, and you might not be able to secure enough addresses to assign an address to each subnet. Suppose that you have been assigned one class C address but you need to organize your network with three subnets? That's where subnet masks really come in handy.

Consider the class C network address 205.101.55. The default subnet mask would be 255.255.255.0. It is possible, however, to extend the subnet mask into the fourth octet. Consider this binary subnet mask, which would be expressed as 255.255.255.224 in dotted-decimal notation:

```
11111111 11111111 11111111 11100000
```

This mask designates the first three bits of the fourth octet of the IP address as belonging to the subnet ID. To see how this works, apply the subnet mask to an IP address on this network. The IP address 205.101.55.91 would have this binary address:

```
11001101 01100101 00110111 01011011
```

After applying the subnet mask, the network ID for the subnet is:

```
11001101 01100101 00110111 01000000
```

The host ID consists of the five bits that correspond to zeros in the subnet mask. Therefore, the host ID is binary 11011, which is decimal 27.

The first three bits of the fourth octet of the IP address can have values ranging from 001 through 110. Because 000 and 111 are not valid subnet IDs, a total of six subnets are made available by a subnet mask of 11100000.

The subnet mask designates that hostids in the fourth octet will fall in the range 00001 through 11110, with decimal values ranging from 1 through 30. (Again, 00000 and 11111 are invalid and decimal addresses 0 and 31 may not be used.) This range of host IDs can be reused with each of the available subnet IDs.

The six subnets designated by a subnet mask of 255.255.255.224 would be associated with the following ranges of values in the fourth octet of the IP addresses:

`00100001` through `00111110` (33 through 62)

`01000001` through `01011110` (65 through 94)

`01100001` through `01111110` (97 through 126)

`10000001` through `10011110` (129 through 158)

`10100001` through `10111110` (161 through 190)

`11000001` through `11011110` (193 through 222)

As you can see, the use of the subnet mask has made a considerable number of possible values unavailable. The benefit of creating multiple subnets with a single Class C address must be weighed against the cost in terms of unavailable addresses.

Figure 8.5 shows an internetwork that requires a single class C network ID to implement three network segments. This would not be possible without using subnet masks.

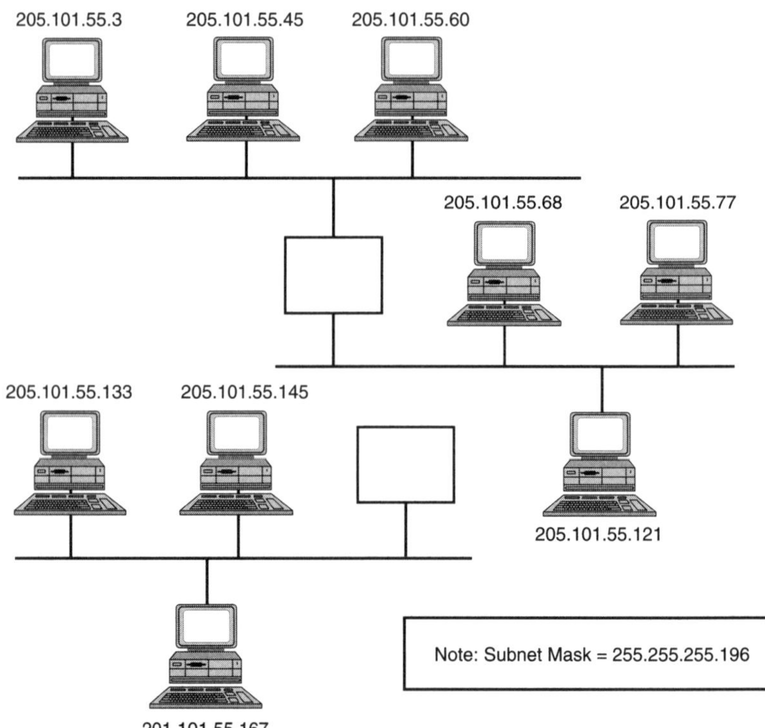

Figure 8.5
An internetwork based on one class C address.

When expressed in decimal form, subnet masks can appear to be somewhat of a mystery. For subnet masks to make sense, you must see them in terms of their binary patterns. Fortunately, subnet masks almost always use adjacent, high-order bits, so there are only eight common subnet mask octets:

Binary	Decimal
00000000	0
10000000	128
11000000	192
11100000	224
11110000	240
11111000	248
11111100	252
11111110	254
11111111	255

Delivering Packets on the Local Subnet

One of IP's responsibilities is to determine whether a packet can be delivered on the local subnet or must be routed to another subnet for final delivery. Subnet IDs make it much easier for IP to make this determination.

Before examining how routing takes place, take a look at the steps IP uses to deliver a packet to another host on the local subnet:

1. IP receives a frame from TCP, the next higher layer in the protocol stack. This frame is addressed to a particular IP address.

2. IP compares the subnet ID of the frame's IP address to the subnet ID of the local subnet. If the two subnet IDs match, the frame can be delivered locally.

3. Before sending the frame on the subnet, IP must determine the hardware address of the device that corresponds to the destination IP address. To get this information, IP utilizes the Address Resolution Protocol (ARP). Given an IP address of a host, ARP can determine the associated physical address for the host.

4. IP adds the following information to the frame, which is now referred to as a packet:

    - The source IP address
    - The source hardware address
    - The destination IP address
    - The destination hardware address

5. IP passes the packet with the address information down the protocol stack to the protocols that actually place the packet on the network.

Because the packet is tagged with the hardware address of a host on the local subnet, the destination host will be able to spot the packet and retrieve it.

Routing Packets to Remote Subnets

But what happens if IP determines that the source and destination subnet addresses don't match? That's a clear indication that the packet must be routed through the internetwork. IP in the local host doesn't perform the routing, but IP sends the packet to a device where it can be routed.

When hosts are connected to an internetwork, each host is configured with the IP address of a *default gateway* or *router.* (*Gateway* is an older term for *router.*) When IP determines that the destination of a packet is not on the local subnet, IP addresses the packet to the default router (or an alternative router if the default router is unavailable).

Figure 8.6 illustrates the routing process. For the first time, the devices that connect the subnets have been labeled as routers. A router is essentially a computer running a TCP/IP protocol stack that is equipped with network adapters on all of the attached subnets. The adapter on each subnet is assigned an IP address that is appropriate for that subnet. Thus, a router is assigned two or more IP addresses and has a presence on two or more subnets.

Routing algorithms can be very simple or very complex. To illustrate the simple approach, assume that the default class C subnet mask (255.255.255.0) is configured on all hosts. Suppose that host 200.1.1.5 is sending a packet addressed to host 197.2.2.10. Using figure 8.6 to illustrate, the simple approach works like this:

1. IP on host 200.1.1.5 determines that the destination host is not on the local subnet because the subnet addresses of source and destination don't match.

2. Because the packet must be routed, IP addresses the packet with the following information:

    - Source Hardware Address: 222
    - Source IP Address: 200.1.1.5
    - Destination Hardware Address: 110
    - Destination IP Address: 197.2.2.10

    Notice that the destination hardware address identifies the default router. The destination IP address matches the ultimate destination of the packet.

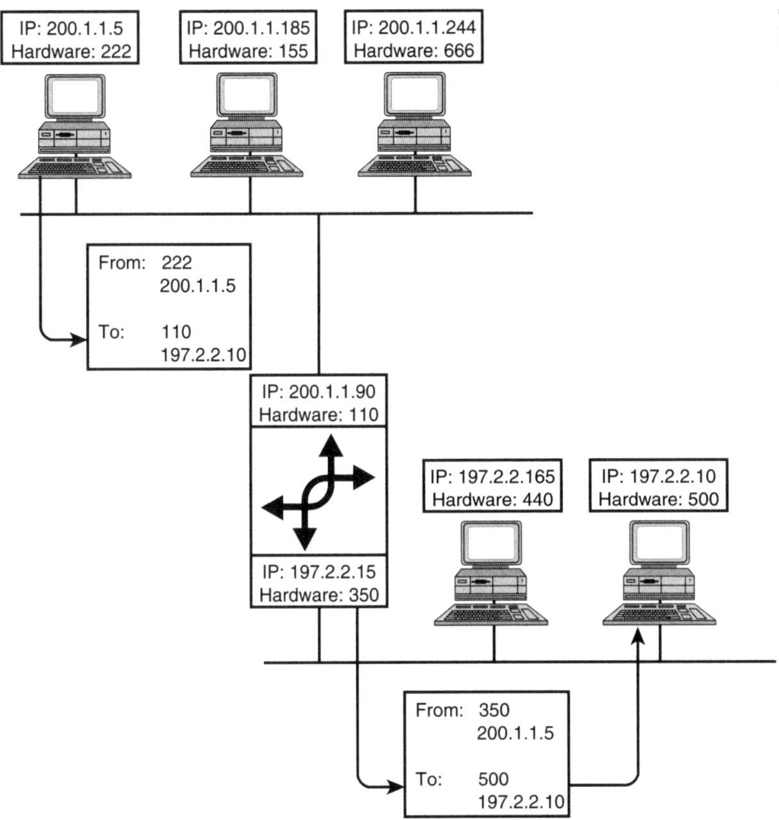

Figure 8.6

Simple IP routing.

3. IP on the router receives the packet from subnet 200.1.1 and determines from the IP address that the packet is addressed to a host on subnet 199.2.2.

4. A local network adapter on the router has been configured with an IP address on subnet 199.2.2. Therefore, IP will use that adapter to forward the packet.

5. If it is not already known, IP on the router uses ARP to determine the hardware address of the destination host.

6. IP addresses the packet with this information and sends it on subnet 199.2.2:

   - Source Hardware Address: 600
   - Source IP Address: 200.1.1.5
   - Destination Hardware Address: 500
   - Destination IP Address: 197.2.2.10

7. When host 197.2.2.10 examines the packet, it determines that the addressee of the packet is itself and retrieves the packet from the network.

Notice two things in the routing process:

- The source and destination IP addresses don't change as the frame is routed. They always represent the original source and the ultimate destination of the packet.
- The hardware addresses change to indicate the host that last sent the packet and the host that should receive it.

Complex IP Routing

IP determines where to route packets by consulting routing tables. To route packets through more complex internetworks, it is necessary to enhance the richness of the routing table information that is available to IP. There are two approaches to building routing tables: *static* and *dynamic* routing.

Static Routing

A router can be configured with a *static routing table* that contains routing information that is manually defined by a network administrator. The term *static* is used because the table is not automatically updated when the network changes. When you reconfigure TCP/IP, a routing table is maintained on the computer.

Each time the network configuration changes, static routing requires you to update the routing table. You can readily see that this could become a time-consuming and error-prone task.

Dynamic Routing

Because maintaining static routing tables is a pain, most networks rely on routers that can use routing algorithms to dynamically maintain routing tables.

Routing algorithms are quite complex, and the details far exceed the scope of this chapter. This discussion, therefore, will be limited to brief descriptions of two algorithms that are commonly employed on TCP/IP internetworks.

Routing Information Protocol

The Routing Information Protocol (RIP) is known as a *distance vector* routing algorithm. If a router knows several routes to a destination, it assigns a cost to the route in terms of the *hops* the route involves. The hop count is incremented each time a packet crosses a router. Each router broadcasts its routing table every 30 seconds. In this way, routers in the internetwork share their routing tables, and routing information gradually propagates through the internetwork.

Distance vector algorithms have a number of practical problems. One, called the *count-to-infinity* problem, has to do with routes that loop back on themselves, causing packets to circulate the network indefinitely. Count-to-infinity is controlled by setting a maximum hop count of 16. Any packet that registers 16 hops is discarded. This limits the maximum number of hops a packet can take to 15 and limits the scope of networks that RIP can manage.

Another problem is that it can take considerable time for a change to propagate through the network. This is called the *convergence* problem.

Finally, because all routers broadcast routing information every 30 seconds, considerable traffic is generated. RIP traffic can really bog down a network, particularly when slower WAN links are involved.

RIP is available in two versions: RIP I and RIP II. RIP II supports the use of subnet masks. Some routers can support both RIP versions simultaneously.

Open Shortest Path First

The Open Shortest Path First (OSPF) algorithm is based on a different approach called *link state.* Each router broadcasts periodic *link state packets* that describe its connections to its neighbors. Using this information, routers build a link state database that is used to identify routes. OSPF enables networks to use costs as high as 65535, enabling designers to build internetworks without the 16 hop limitation.

Link state algorithms do not suffer from the count-to-infinity problem. They also generate much less broadcast traffic than RIP. Link state packets are retransmitted only when the network changes or at infrequent intervals.

As such, OSPF is a significant improvement over RIP and can be expected to become the TCP/IP routing protocol of choice.

Host Names and Naming Services

It would be a real nuisance to have to refer to each host by its IP address. Let's face it, humans don't remember numbers very well. Therefore, a system was developed that enabled users to refer to hosts by name.

Originally, the system involved a file named `hosts`, a text file that was stored on each host that mapped IP addresses to host names. A hosts file might contain entries like this:

```
201.150.63.98....widgets.keystone.com
```

Conventionally, the hosts file is stored with other TCP/IP configuration files on Unix computers in a directory named "etc."

The hosts file must be manually maintained by the network administrator. One of the big hassles of maintaining a TCP/IP network is updating this file and ensuring that the updates make it onto each computer on the network.

Maintenance of hosts files should qualify for mental hazard pay, and would be even worse on really large networks. To get around the problem, you need a naming service.

The Domain Name Services (DNS) protocol was developed to serve as a central repository of names on the Internet.

Connecting to the Internet

More and more private networks are being connected to the Internet, a giant TCP/IP internetwork descended from the ARPANET, a network built by the Defense Advanced Research Projects Agency (DARPA) to connect the Department of Defense (DoD) with educational institutions and defense contractors. The Internet has recently been made public and now interconnects millions of hosts throughout the world.

When you connect your TCP/IP network to the Internet, you enter a larger world with restrictions, risks, and responsibilities. One of your responsibilities is to obtain an IP address for your organization that does not conflict with addresses of other organizations on the Internet.

After you obtain an IP address, you will need to obtain a connection to the internet, usually through a commercial Internet provider.

Obtaining an Internet Address

If you are running a TCP/IP network in isolation, you can use any addresses you choose. On the Internet, however, you need to use an address that is assigned by the Internet Network Information Center (InterNIC).

You can obtain documents from InterNIC by using FTP to connect to `is.internic.net`. Log in as anonymous and transfer the documents you require.

If you don't have Internet access, contact InterNIC at:

Network Solutions
InterNIC Registration Service
505 Huntmar Park Drive
Herndon, VA 22070

Applications and questions can be e-mailed to `hostmaster@internic.net`.

Incidentally, don't expect to obtain a class A or B address at this late date. Class A addresses were used up long ago by the likes of IBM. Class B addresses are rare enough that they have been listed as business assets by companies offering themselves for sale. Very few class B addresses remain unallocated, but few organizations have the clout to obtain one.

All that's really left are class C addresses, and even those are in short supply. In fact, the Internet will run out of class C addresses in a year or two. To fix the problem, a new generation of TCP/IP protocols is being developed. Next-generation TCP/IP should be seeing the commercial light of day in 1996.

Note It's a good idea to obtain addresses from InterNIC even if your network is not currently attached to the Internet. If you do connect to the Internet in the future, you won't have the headache of reassigning all the IP addresses on your network.

Internet Domain Names

Domain Name Services was mentioned earlier as the solution used on the Internet to assign names to IP addresses. DNS was developed as a means of organizing the nearly 20 million host names that are using the Internet. An example of a domain name is `newriders.macmillan.com`.

DNS names are organized in a hierarchical fashion, as shown in figure 8.7.

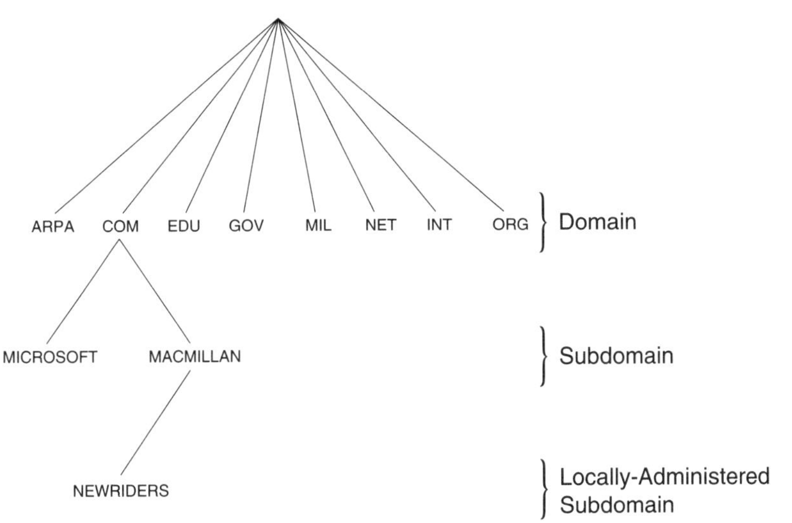

Figure 8.7

The DNS name hierarchy.

The first layer of the hierarchy consists of *domain names* that are assigned by the Network Information Center (NIC). Table 8.1 summarizes the top-level domain names. Each domain is given its own administration authority.

TABLE 8.1
Top-Level Domain Names

Domain Name	Description
ARPA	Advanced Research Projects Agency network (ARPANET)
COM	Commercial organizations
EDU	Educational institutions
GOV	Government agencies
MIL	Military agencies
NET	Network support centers, such as Internet service providers
INT	International organizations
ORG	Non-profit organizations
country code	Two-letter X.500 country codes

Second-level domain names, called *subdomain names*, must be registered with the NIC. The application can be found in the file DOMAIN-TEMPLATE.TXT, which can be retrieved by anonymous ftp from `hostmaster@internic.net`. If you are running a DNS service on your local LAN, register the name even if you are not currently connected to the Internet. When you do connect, you can be sure that the name you want is available.

Third-level domain names usually name a particular host in the subdomain. (You can have as many levels you want, provided that the entire name does not exceed 255 characters.) The NIC only registers domain and subdomain names. Additional levels of the name hierarchy are maintained locally. If you wish to maintain a naming service for hosts, you will need to run a local name service.

Getting Access

Unless you are well-connected with an organization that is already connected to the Internet, you will probably gain access through a commercial provider.

Access can be through a dial-up connection if you don't need your site to be consistently accessible from the outside. You can set up a dial-up connection using the Remote Access Server (RAS). RAS supports dial-up connections through conventional modems using the SLIP and PPP protocols. RAS also enables you to use the high-speed dial-up capabilities of ISDN.

A permanent connection usually means that you will be leasing a dedicated phone line from a local communication provider. This line will connect you with your local Internet access provider. In most cases, you will install a router between your network and the dedicated line to route traffic to the Internet.

When you connect to the Internet, you open your network to the world. There is considerable risk in that because a TCP/IP connection gives outside users significant access capabilities on your network. The Internet is filled with people who know how to infiltrate your system through an Internet connection.

To protect yourself, you should consider installing a *firewall* at your Internet access point. Just as firewalls in buildings slow the spread of fires, a network firewall impedes the ability of outsiders to gain access to your network. NRP offers an excellent book on firewalls named *Internet Firewalls and Network Security.*

Coexisting with OS/2 Warp

There are many reasons for you to be concerned about Windows 95 and OS/2 Warp coexistence. You would not be reading this book if you did not have some reason to learn about the capabilities of the new Windows 95 operating system. You may only be interested in finding out which system is the right one for you, or you may have already made a decision to migrate to Windows 95. In either case, this chapter will help you sort out your installation, coexistence, and migration options.

Because Windows 95 is brand new, you probably have OS/2 Warp on your system today. You will, in all probability, need to have both operating systems installed on your workstation for conversion or migration testing. You probably have a LAN based on one system with workstations based on the other. Although similar in design concept, Windows 95 and OS/2 Warp behave very differently. You need to be aware of the installation "gotchas" and the different usability limitations and incompatibilities between the two operating systems.

This chapter discusses how to install both systems on a single workstation, how to access a LAN from both systems, and how to avoid some potential pitfalls.

This chapter is based on the final Windows 95 beta. The final product may differ in some details.

Using OS/2 Warp and Windows 95 on the Same Workstation

Both Windows 95 and OS/2 Warp have improved user interfaces when compared to DOS or previous versions of Windows. Their new interfaces are significantly different from each other, however.

Coping with the Different User Interfaces

The most obvious difference with switching between Windows 95 and OS/2 Warp are the different user interfaces. You will have no trouble remembering which system is running. Figure 9.1 shows the basic Windows 95 desktop; figure 9.2 shows the basic OS/2 Warp desktop.

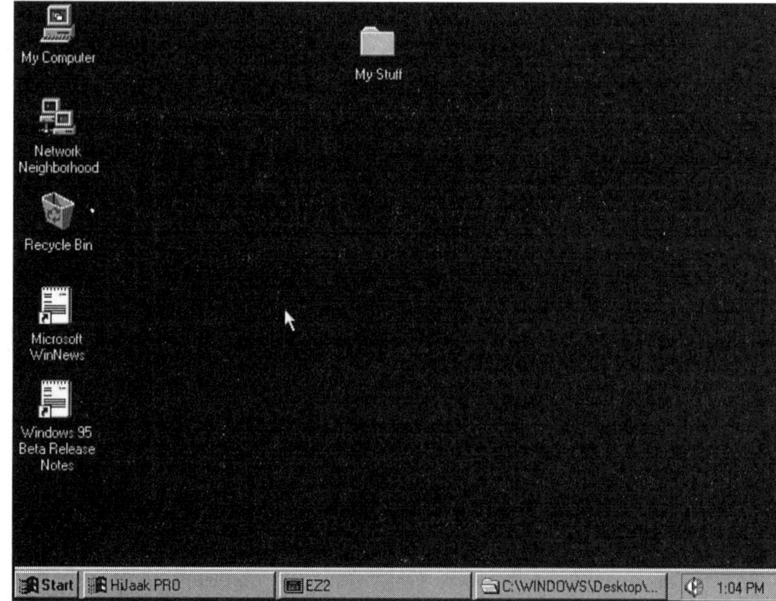

Figure 9.1
The Windows 95 desktop.

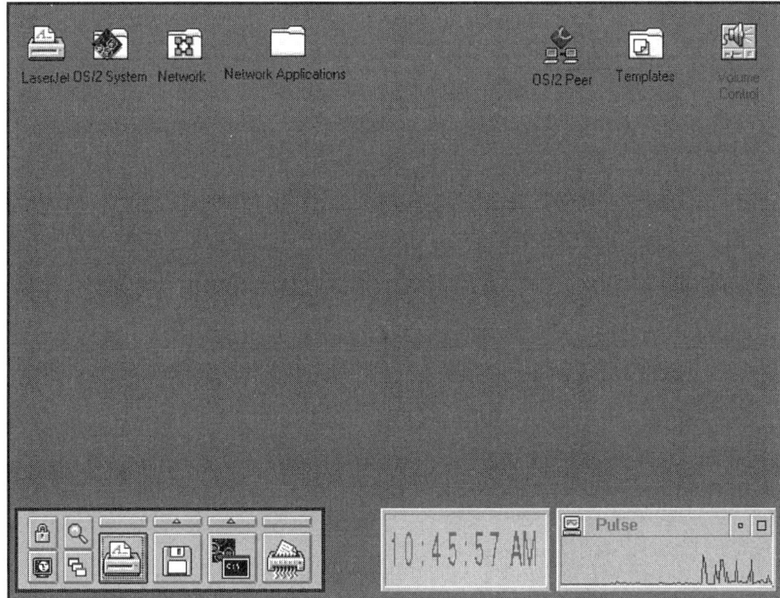

Figure 9.2
The OS/2 Warp desktop.

You will find advantages in each system for doing some specific tasks. The interface you prefer will be as much a matter of individual taste as anything else, but you will agree that the new Windows 95 interface is a great improvement over previous versions of Windows.

An especially nice feature of Windows 95 is the ability to undo a mistake. Although OS/2 does include an undelete command if you accidentally erase a file, you must first enable it by editing the CONFIG.SYS file, and then be familiar with its syntax. Windows 95 puts a Recycle Bin right on the desktop that provides the undelete capability.

One difference that might irritate experienced OS/2 users is the way Windows 95 leaves the keypad in numlock mode. You will be forever hitting the arrow keys to move around the screen, but will be typing numbers instead. Dust off your old utility program that turns numlock off and call it from the Autoexec.bat file.

Experienced Windows users will have to get used to using the right mouse button. The new Windows 95 UI, as the Microsoft documentation calls the user interface, uses the right mouse button much more, as does OS/2, to open the menus that define the properties of programs, folders, and other objects.

There is another quirk that experienced Windows users will have to watch: the use of the Ctrl+Alt+Del keys. In Windows 95, you can use the Ctrl+Alt+Del keys to do a local reboot to kill a stuck session or program. Windows 95 displays a list of running programs and lets you select the program to end. If you get used to doing this under Windows 95, then have a program hang while running OS/2, don't hit Ctrl+Alt+Del: it will reboot the whole system, and it won't ask if you really want to do it.

Using the OS/2 High Performance File System (HPFS)

Both Windows 95 and OS/2 Warp include many advanced features compared to previous versions of both products. These new features can present some problems to you if you are planning to install both systems on your workstation. Microsoft and IBM recognized the need for significant enhancements to DOS and Windows. Since their split in 1992, they have implemented these improvements in vastly different ways.

One example is the way the performance problems, or limitations, of the FAT file system have been addressed. DOS and Windows 95 cannot use the OS/2 HPFS file system. If you plan to share data between both systems, you must sacrifice the performance gain provided by HPFS.

AMOS3 is a shareware program that enables you to read HPFS drives while running DOS. It works with Windows 95 as well, giving you the ability to read data from OS/2 HPFS drives. You are not be able to update or add data to the HPFS drive, however. AMOS3 is a very useful utility if you use both OS/2 with HPFS and Windows 95.

Understanding the Differences in Long File-Name Support

One of the most visible, and most dangerous, enhancements in Windows 95 is the inclusion of long file-name support. Although perceived as a potentially significant convenience compared to the DOS 8.3 file name convention, long file-name support can cause you grief. Probably the only safe way to use long file names is on a LAN. Otherwise, Windows 95 cannot see the files with long names on OS/2 HPFS drives because it can't access the drive, and OS/2 can't see the long names on FAT drives created by Windows 95 because it does not understand how they are stored in the directory. This is also true with Windows NT version 3.1 and earlier. In fact, Windows NT version 3.1 removes the long names.

Also, don't try to copy files with long names between the systems on a floppy disk. With OS/2, the long file name is stored as an extended attribute (in a hidden file in the root directory) and a short abbreviated name is placed in the directory. Windows 95 does not understand OS/2's extended attributes and, therefore, does not display the long name.

If you go the other way and store a file with a long name under Windows 95, OS/2 will not be able to find the long name. Windows 95 lets the long name span multiple directory entries. This has the advantage of not putting an extra file on the disk but can cause trouble with programs that manipulate directory entries directly because they may remove the "unused" entries. Windows 95 includes a utility called LFNBK to remove and later restore long file names.

There is another consideration. Although subdirectories are really files with a special attribute, and can therefore be very large, the root directory is a specially allocated location of the disk. It usually is limited to space for a maximum of 512 entries. If you store files with long names in the root directory using Windows 95, you will not be able to store many files as the long file names may use many of the available directory entries. This is not a problem with OS/2 HPFS because the file names are actually stored in the file system itself.

You will notice another significant difference in the long file-name support between Windows 95 and OS/2. Windows 95 always displays the short file-name in the directory list when you issue the DIR command as shown in the following:

```
Volume in drive H is DRIVE_E
Directory of H:\CCHAMB

.            <DIR>            07-03-95  8:44a.
..           <DIR>            06-30-95 12:25p..
07392c03                   0  06-28-95  7:57a 07302c03
073a0828                   0  06-28-95  7:58a 073a0828
073a6c63                   0  06-28-95  7:58a 073a2c63
073a3806                   0  06-28-95  7:58a 073a3806
073b083a                   0  06-28-95  7:59a 073b083a
0d0c0b24                   0  06-29-95  1:12p 0d0c0b24
CID          <DIR>            05-22-95  1:14p CID
ORG          <DIR>            05-12-95 12:09p ORG
PEGCPUMP OUT               0  06-28-95  7:57a PEGCPUMP.OUT
PEGDRV   OUT               0  06-28-95  7:57a PEGDRV.OUT
PEGDSK   OUT               0  06-28-95  7:58a PEGDSK.OUT
PEGFCMP  OUT               0  06-28-95  7:58a PEGFCMP.OUT
PEGHPFS  OUT               0  06-28-95  7:58a PEGHPFS.OUT
PEGMEMMP OUT               0  06-28-95  7:59a PEGMEMMP.OUT
Prog8-2  EXE          38,508  06-26-95  4:32p PROG8-2.EXE
```

```
this fil               22  06-29-95  8:27a this file has a long name
THIS IS                37  07-03-95  8:45a THIS IS A FILE WITH A REALLY LONG
FILE NAME TO show the display and how caps are maintained by both systems
USERLOGP BAT        2,899  08-17-94  8:44a USERLOGP.BAT
USERLOGP CMD        2,892  05-30-95  1:40p USERLOGP.CMD
        17 file(s)        44,358 bytes
         4 dir(s)        524,288 bytes free
```

OS/2 does not display the short file name in the directory list when you issue the DIR command. It only displays the long file name, as shown in the following:.

```
The volume label in drive H is DRIVE_E.
The Volume Serial Number is E663:A414.
Directory of H:\CCHAMB

 7-03-95   8:44a     <DIR>          0 .
 6-30-95  12:25p     <DIR>          0 ..
 6-28-95   7:57a         0          0  07392c03
 6-28-95   7:58a         0          0  073a0828
 6-28-95   7:58a         0          0  073a2c63
 6-28-95   7:58a         0          0  073a3806
 6-28-95   7:59a         0          0  073b083a
 6-29-95   1:12p         0          0  0d0c0b24
 5-22-95   1:14p     <DIR>          0  CID
 5-12-95  12:09p     <DIR>          0  ORG
 6-28-95   7:57a         0          0  PEGCPUMP.OUT
 6-28-95   7:57a         0          0  PEGDRV.OUT
 6-28-95   7:58a         0          0  PEGDSK.OUT
 6-28-95   7:58a         0          0  PEGFCMP.OUT
 6-28-95   7:58a         0          0  PEGHPFS.OUT
 6-28-95   7:59a         0          0  PEGMEMMP.OUT
 6-26-95   4:32p     38505         49  PROG8-2.EXE
 6-29-95   8:27a        22         35  this file has a long name
 7-03-95   8:45a        37          0  THIS IS A FILE WITH A REALLY LONG FILE
NAME TO show the display and how caps are maintained by both systems
 8-17-94   8:44a      2899          0  USERLOGP.BAT
 5-30-95   1:40p      2892          0  USERLOGP.CMD
       21 file(s)      44358 bytes used
                      684544 bytes free
```

This has a more significant implication: with OS/2, programs that do not have long file name support cannot use files with long file names at all. If they make calls to OS/2 to find files, OS/2 does not even indicate that the files with long names exist.

Windows 95, on the other hand, will return the short file name to these older applications. This greatly increases the utility and safety of the older applications.

Notice also the extra column in the OS/2 directory list. That is the size of the extended attributes. Remember, this directory list was made on an HPFS drive. The directory list for FAT drives (shown below) looks like the old DOS directory list. Look at the OS!2_WAR file. This file would have a long file name on an HPFS drive. In this case, OS/2 has compressed the name to work on the FAT drive.

```
The volume label in drive E is OS2.
the Volume Serial Number is 25BD:B814.
Directory of E:\

OS2           <DIR>       6-26-95   2:17p
PSFONTS       <DIR>       6-26-95   2:17p
SPOOL         <DIR>       6-26-95   2:48p
DESKTOP       <DIR>       6-26-95   2:54p
NOWHERE1      <DIR>       6-26-95   2:54p
IBMLAN        <DIR>       6-26-95   2:55p
MUGLIB        <DIR>       6-26-95   2:55p
CONFIG   EPW        3118  6-26-95   2:54p
CONFIG   SYS        4389  6-27-95   7:46a
ROOTE         <DIR>       6-26-95   3:16p
IBMLVL   SYS        1018  6-26-95   3:01p
NSC           <DIR>       6-26-95   3:01p
README   1ST       38003  4-29-95   4:41p
STARTUP  BAK          99  6-26-95   3:02p
IBMVESA       <DIR>       6-26-95   2:17p
GRPWARE       <DIR>       6-26-95   2:19p
MINSTALL LOG          17  6-28-95  12:26p
OS!2_WAR           26704  2-05-95  11:03p
STARTUP  CMD          97  5-31-95   8:50a
CDFS     IFS       41795 12-12-94   6:25p
MAINTENA      <DIR>       6-26-95   2:26p
NOWHERE       <DIR>       6-26-95   2:26p
OAD           <DIR>       6-26-95   2:30p
MMOS2         <DIR>       6-26-95   2:38p
AUTOEXEC BAT         325  6-26-95   2:41p
IBMCOM        <DIR>       6-26-95   2:45p
MPTN          <DIR>       6-26-95   2:45p
CONFIG   MPT        2634  6-26-95   2:45p
        28 file(s)     118199 bytes used
                    237600768 bytes free
```

Let's take an example. You have an old program that you use often and with which you have become very proficient. You use its file manipulation capability to copy all of the files from a directory onto a disk to send to a friend. Under OS/2, you will not copy any of the files with long names, your friend will not get the critical file that she needs, and you will lose the $2 million you would have made on the deal. With Windows 95, all files would have been copied.

There is one time where you are free to use long file names: on the LAN. Because the redirectors in both OS/2 and Windows 95 understand how to manipulate files with long names, you can use them freely over the LAN. The server stores them and retrieves them properly, and your requester does not know, or care, how they were stored by the server—it will just see the long file name and use it correctly. Your NetWare server must have the optional OS/2 Name Space installed to take advantage of this capability.

If you do decide to use long file names with Windows 95, you need to add the line

```
SHELL=C:\WINDOWS\COMMAND.COM /U:255
```

to Config.sys to increase the size of the keyboard buffer to its maximum size or you will not be able to create long file names from the command prompt. Remember to enclose the long file name in quotes.

One final caution with long file names: the characters that you can use as part of a long file name in Windows 95 include the + (plus), , (comma), ; (semicolon), = (equals sign), and [] (brackets). These are not valid in 8.3 file names. To avoid compatibility problems, they should not be used.

Understanding OS/2 Application Compatibility

Native OS/2 applications will not run under Windows 95. OS/2 family applications, however, will run under Windows 95 correctly. Family applications are OS/2 16-bit native programs that use a subset of the OS/2 programming API. This OS/2 API subset can be converted into DOS, and therefore Windows 95-compatible, programs that can be run in a Windows 95 DOS session by using the BIND utility after they are compiled for OS/2. These programs are subject to the normal limitations of running under DOS. In an OS/2 session, for example, the standard memory function calls such as malloc in the C language can allocate megabytes of memory. In a Windows 95 DOS session, the 640 KB limit still applies.

OS/2 still has an edge in running DOS applications. Its individually tailorable startup files and environment settings eliminate most DOS compatibility issues. Of those that remain, the virtual DOS boot concept, where you actually boot a real copy of DOS in a virtual machine, takes care of all but the most stubborn problem.

Windows 95 has addressed the problem and has improved significantly over Windows 3.*x*. It is still not as versatile as OS/2, however. If you have a stubborn DOS application that you must run, Windows 95 gives you the option to actually suspend the Windows code completely while the DOS program is executing. You can also specify the specific Autoexec.bat and Config.sys files for these programs.

Understanding the Differences in Included Network Support

Windows 95 has a very comprehensive set of built-in networking support, including the following:

- Artisoft LANtastic version 5.0 or later
- Banyan VINES version 5.52 or later
- Beame and Whiteside BW-NFS version 3.0c and later
- DEC Pathworks version 5.0 and later
- IBM OS/2 LAN Server
- Novell NetWare version 3.11 and later
- SunSelect PC-NFS version 5.0 and later
- TCS 10-Net version 4.1 and later

This list should pose no coexistence problems for you as you migrate to Windows 95 because the OS/2 Warp list of supported networks is shorter. In addition to LAN Server, OS/2 Peer also provides access to file, printer, serial, and application resources located on NetWare and Windows NT servers and to resources on DOS systems as long as they are running either Windows for Workgroups, LAN Manager, or IBM DOS LAN Services Version 4.0.

Note If you are using the OS/2 Warp Peer capabilities to share a serial device, you may have a problem. The Windows 95 peer services only support sharing files and printers. Therefore, when you run Windows 95 instead of Warp, the users of your serial devices will lose the use of them until you reboot with OS/2 Warp.

Windows 95 includes significant enhancements to the system management functions. In the past, to change the way your system attaches to a network, for example, you probably had to manually edit the Protocol.ini or Ibmlan.ini file. With Windows 95, you will use the Registry functions to perform these tasks.

Installing Windows 95 and OS/2 Warp on a Single Workstation

This section looks at how to get the two operating systems onto your workstation. This may not be as simple a task as you would expect.

The two systems have different hardware requirements. Windows 95, for example, requires that you partition your hard drive with partitions greater than 32 MB and will not install if your version of DOS does not have that support. This is because the typical installation requires at least 40 MB of free disk space. It is possible (though certainly not recommended) to install OS/2 Warp on a system with the boot disk formatted to less than 32 MB, as you can specify that it load its components onto multiple logical drives. You might run into this situation if you are upgrading older systems and don't want to backup all of their disk data.

As mentioned previously, you cannot install Windows 95 on a system that has only HPFS or NTFS partitions as they are not supported by DOS. This means that you will have to backup your data, reformat the boot drive as FAT, and reinstall the other system before you can install Windows 95.

Understanding Boot Manager

IBM developed the boot manager to allow users to migrate to OS/2. The boot manager is the foundation for your being able to run both OS/2 Warp and Windows 95 on the same workstation without having to resort to technical trickery to switch between the two systems. The boot manager is installed in a separate 1 MB partition on the disk.

The OS/2 FDISK program enables you to configure the drive as you do with DOS, except that you can add entries for up to four partitions, including logical drives, in the boot manager menu. When the system is booted, it is boot manager that actually starts the system. Boot manager displays its menu of bootable logical drives that you created with FDISK and, based on your input, passes control to the user-specified operating system.

Understanding Dual Boot

If you do not install boot manager (probably because you did not reserve space for it when you partitioned your drive), you can use dual boot to switch between Windows 95 and OS/2 Warp. Dual boot is implemented in an OS/2 program (Boot.com) that changes the boot record on the C drive and saves/restores the appropriate Config.sys and Autoexec.bat files for both a DOS and OS/2 configuration. The files are saved in the C:\OS2\SYSTEM directory as Boot.dos or Boot.os2, Config.dos or Config.os2, and Autoexec.dos or Autoexec.os2.

To switch from OS/2 to DOS, and therefore Windows 95, enter the command:

```
BOOT /DOS
```

at the OS/2 command prompt. Then reboot the system. To go from DOS to OS/2, enter the command:

```
BOOT /OS2
```

at the DOS command prompt. These commands install the proper boot record and copy the appropriate Config.sys and Autoexec.bat files from the C:\OS2\SYSTEM directory into the C root directory.

Windows 95 has a simplified version of dual boot. If you specify BootMulti=1 in the [Options] section of the Msdos.sys file, you can start your previously installed version of DOS by pressing the F4 key while the Windows 95 startup message is on the screen. There are two problems with this. On a fast system, you have to be very quick to catch the message in time, and Windows 95 is fussy about what version of DOS it lets you boot. It does not let you boot PC-DOS version 7, for example.

Installing OS/2 Warp

The easiest way to install both Windows 95 and OS/2 on a single workstation is to install OS/2 Warp first. You should start with a clean disk drive. That is, get a new workstation or backup all of your data to tape or the LAN and reformat your hard drive. Doing this lets you install the boot manager that is included with OS/2 Warp. This will greatly simplify the task at hand, which is coexistence of two operating systems that each want to own your workstation.

Partitioning the Disk Drive

If you take this approach, you first boot the OS/2 installation disks. When you are asked whether to take the Easy or Advanced installation path, choose Advanced. You are then asked to select the target disk to hold the OS/2 system. Don't accept the C default. Instead, chose the "Other Drive" option. This starts the FDISK program. You can now install the boot manager program and partition your drive into multiple logical drives. DOS (and therefore Windows 95) must boot from the C drive, which must be the first partition. OS/2 can boot from a logical drive, so you should create at least two logical drives: C as the primary drive for DOS and Windows 95, and D as an extended logical drive for OS/2. For maximum convenience, create three logical drives, reserving the third drive for your data. This gives you the added flexibility of being able to reformat the boot drives without losing any data.

When FDISK completes, you have to reboot if you changed your disk partitions (as the drive letters will have changed). If that is the case, reinsert the installation disk and reboot. When you format the OS/2 boot drive, you will have to decide whether to format the drive as FAT or HPFS. If you want to be able to access the OS/2 drive from DOS or Windows 95, you must choose FAT. If you choose HPFS, then you might want to make the E drive the OS/2 drive, because DOS and Windows 95 will not be able to see it and will not assign it a drive letter. This means that the drive letters of logical drives behind it on the disk will have different drive letters when you run OS/2 and Windows 95.

For example, if you create three logical drives, C, D, and E, and format D as HPFS to install OS/2, you will save your data on the E drive. Booting Windows 95 will shift these drive letters (remember that it can't see the HPFS drive), calling the data disk D instead of E. This can be very confusing. It can also break any programs or Bat files that have drive letters included in them.

The figures in this section show how to partition the physical disk drive into three logical drives to eliminate these problems. Drive C will be the Windows 95 boot disk, with 60 MB. Drive E will be the OS/2 Warp drive with 80 MB. This will be large enough to also hold the LAN server code. Drive D will be the data drive with *X* MB. You need to calculate the *X* value for the D drive. It will be the size of your drive minus 1 MB for boot manager, 60 MB for the C drive and 80 MB for the E drive.

During the OS/2 Warp installation process, which is discussed in the next section, you have the opportunity to partition the disk drive. The FDISK program will be called by the installer. Follow these instructions when the FDISK program is started.

Figure 9.3 shows how the screen looks when FDISK starts if there are already logical drives on the disk.

1. If there are logical drives already configured that are the wrong size, delete them by moving the bar to them one at a time and pressing Enter. From the menu, select Delete partition, as shown in figure 9.4.

   Do this until there is only one entry: FreeSpace, as shown in figure 9.5.

2. Press Enter to see the drop-down menu, shown in figure 9.6, and select Install Boot Manager.

3. At the next prompt, shown in figure 9.7, specify Create at End of FreeSpace.

   This takes you back to the main FDISK screen. Move the bar to the FreeSpace entry, choose Enter to see the menu, select Create partition, and then choose Enter again. Fill in the size for the C drive of 60 MB, as shown in figure 9.8.

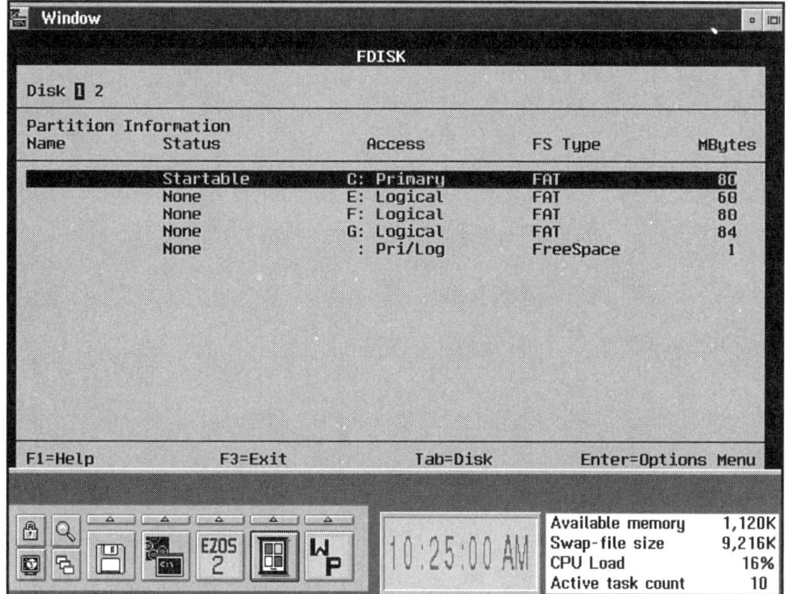

Figure 9.3

The initial FDISK screen.

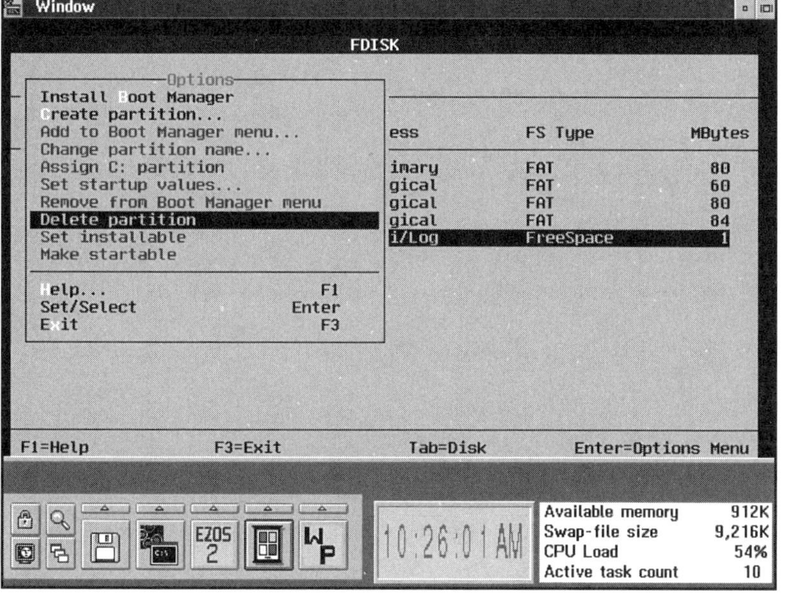

Figure 9.4

The FDISK Delete partition menu.

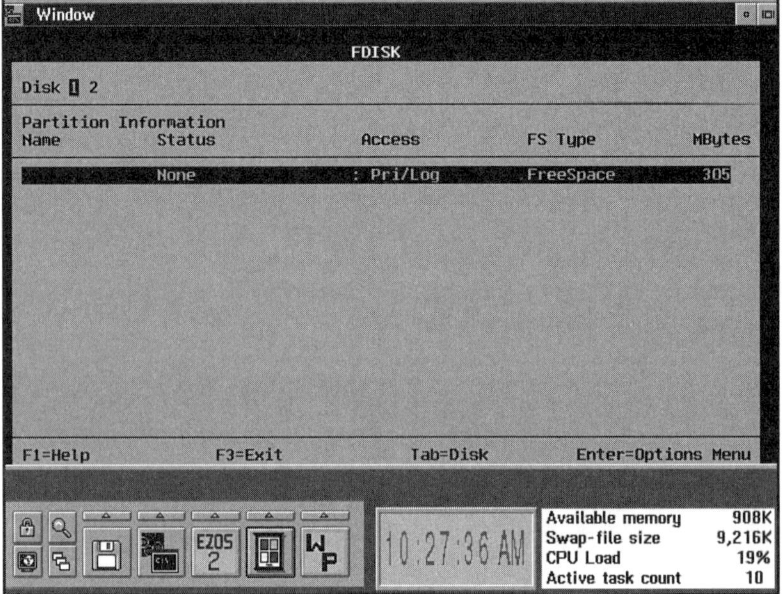

Figure 9.5
The FDISK screen showing an empty drive.

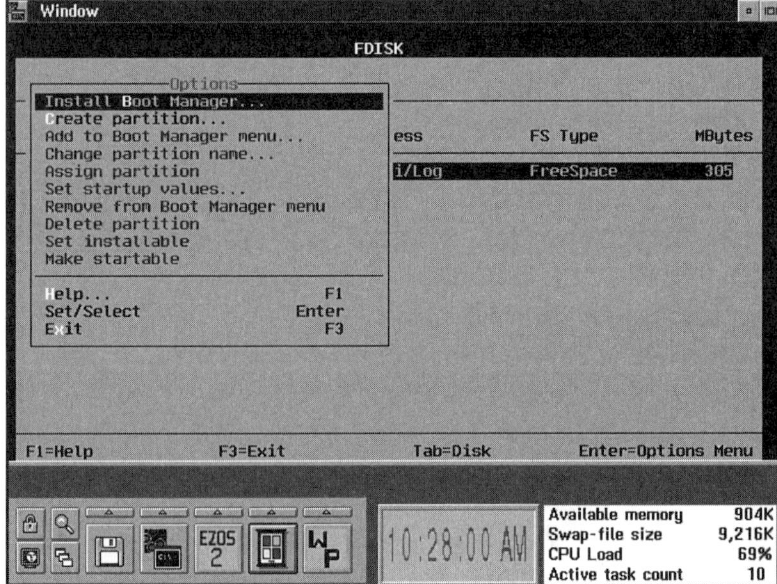

Figure 9.6
Install Boot Manager selected.

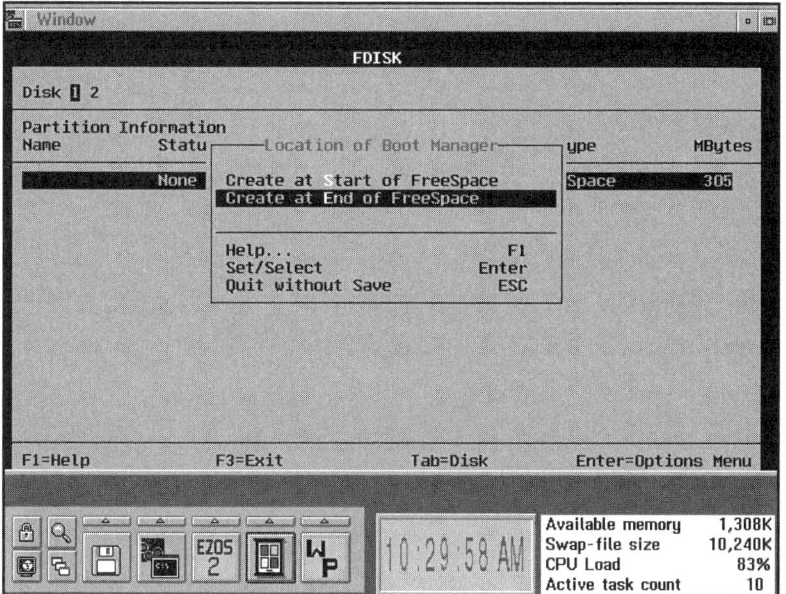

Figure 9.7

Creating Boot Manager partition at end of FreeSpace.

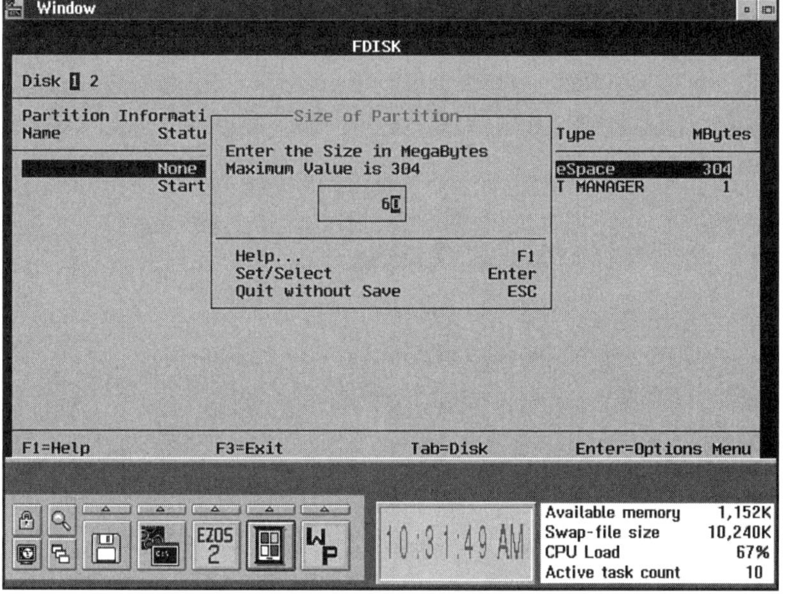

Figure 9.8

The FDISK screen to specify logical drive size.

4. In the Type of Partition box, select Primary Partition, as shown in figure 9.9 and choose Enter.

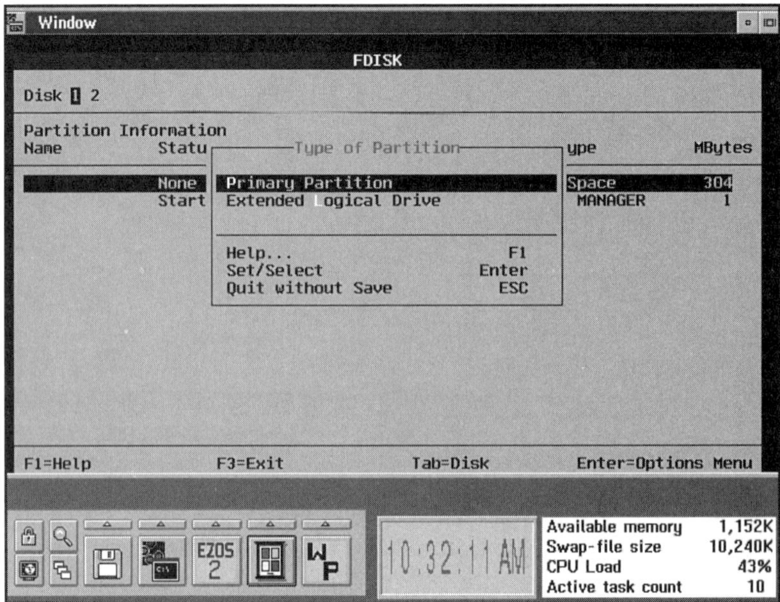

Figure 9.9

Specifying the type of partition.

5. At the Location of Partition box, select Create at Start of FreeSpace and press Enter, as shown in figure 9.10.

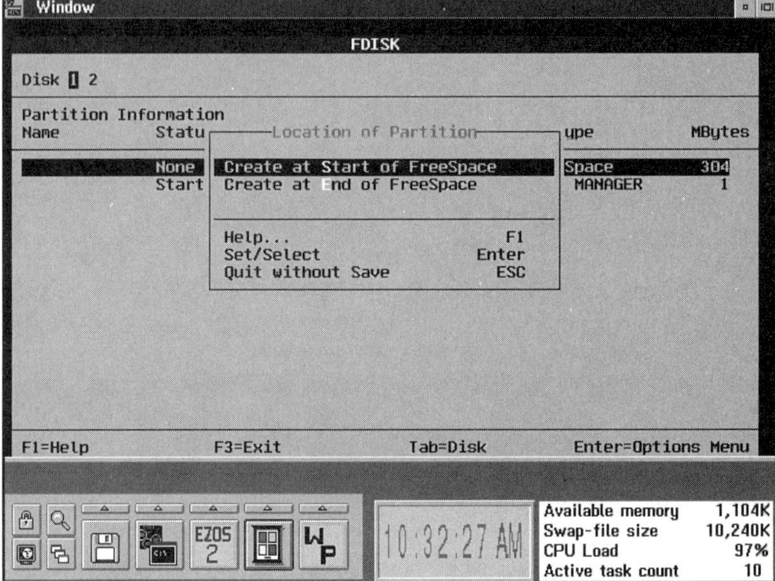

Figure 9.10

Creating the partition at the start of the free space area.

For the next drive (D), follow these steps:

1. Make sure the cursor is on the FreeSpace partition again and choose Enter.
2. Select Create partition and choose Enter.
3. Specify the logical drive size (*X* MB as calculated previously).
4. In the Type of Partition box, select Extended Logical Drive and choose Enter.
5. In the Location of Partition box, select Create at Start of FreeSpace and choose Enter.

Repeat this process for the E drive. Drive letters will be assigned in alphabetical order, beginning with C and going to the end of your list. Be sure to set the E drive as Installable so that you can install your OS/2 Warp system on that drive. (FDISK will display an error message if you forget to do this.)

Installing OS/2 Warp

OS/2 Warp takes approximately one hour to install. If you are on a LAN, you need to know the type of server (LAN Server, NetWare, and so forth) and the type of connection (Token Ring or Ethernet) that you are using. The system will reboot several times as the various components are loaded. After you have OS/2 working, then you can install Windows 95.

You are given the opportunity to specify the target disk after you have inserted disk 1 in the A drive. Be sure to choose the Advanced installation path, and specify a new target drive when asked. This starts the FDISK program. Fill in the partition sizes as discussed in the previous section.

A nice feature of OS/2 Warp's installation program is that it lets you use the system while it is installing. After the first reboot, a simplified desktop is started and you can do productive work while the rest of the system is loading. Just keep an eye on the installation program so that you are not caught with unsaved files when the system does an automatic reboot.

You need to take one more safety precaution before installing Windows 95 if you are going to use dual boot to start both OS/2 Warp and Windows 95 from the C drive. (Actually, this is a good idea under all conditions.) Before you start the Windows 95 installation, create a subdirectory (called ROOTOS2, for example) and copy all of the files from the root of the C drive into that directory. It seems that the Windows 95 installation, at least with the beta release, interferes with the saved files that OS/2 needs to switch the system back to OS/2 mode. Copy the OS/2 CONFIG.SYS file to a backup location also, just to be safe.

Installing Windows 95

You must boot DOS to run the Windows 95 installation program. You cannot run the Windows 95 setup program under OS/2. Also, you should run the command

```
BOOT /DOS
```

first if you are using dual boot, because Windows 95 will overlay the OS/2 boot record.

You must install a version of DOS on the C drive before installing Windows 95. Therefore, you will already have formatted that hard disk before the Windows 95 installation. Remember to make the C drive partition large enough to hold the entire Windows 95 system. According the Microsoft documentation, this is at least 40 MB for a typical installation, although the installation program objected when the free space on the target drive was less than 52 MB.

Windows 95 is designed to be installed in a Windows environment. If there is not already a copy of a previous version of Windows 3.*x* on the system, the installer first installs a "mini" version of Windows to run the setup program. Because the beta code was an upgrade, if it does not find one of the upgrade products, Windows 3.1 for example, it requires you to put the setup disk in the A drive to verify that the installation was a valid system upgrade.

Windows 95 can be installed from floppy disks, CD-ROM, or over a network. This chapter assumes a local installation where the files will reside on the local system. When installing over a network, many of the system files will remain on the server.

The Windows 95 installation process seems faster than the OS/2 process, taking around 30 minutes. The first boot, however, takes a long time so you should allow at least an hour for the entire job.

Windows 95 detects the type of network, if any, you are connected to and automatically installs the proper support software. Microsoft recommends that your current network software be running when you start the installation so that the setup program can properly detect the network type. Because you are adding Windows 95 support to an OS/2 system, you are not able to do this. Windows 95 still seems to be able to detect the network correctly, however. The Client for Microsoft Networks is installed by default. If you need to do so, you can add network support after the system installation. This is explained in the section, "Accessing Your LAN," later in this chapter.

There are several interesting features in the Windows 95 installation program. One of the best, besides the automatic detection of hardware and network configuration, is the ability to get past a problem area. If the installation hangs on a particular hardware test, for example, when you restart the installation, that step will be skipped the next time you attempt the installation. Windows 95 maintains a log as the installation progresses as part of a feature called the Safe Recovery option that allows setup to skip over this type of problem.

Be sure to install Windows 95 into a new directory. The installation program will not migrate any of the OS/2 desktop settings. You have to configure the Windows 95 desktop after installation. This is probably not a problem because the OS/2 and Windows desktop settings are so different. Also, you may have to reinstall your Windows applications to get them to run under Windows 95.

You should back up the root directory again into a directory called ROOTDOS after installing DOS but before installing Windows 95, just to be safe.

Reinstalling Boot Manager

Windows 95 removes the boot manager that you were so careful to install at the beginning of the OS/2 Warp installation process. This is not a significant problem, but it will take a bit of your time to fix. You have to reboot from the OS/2 installation disks one more time and run FDISK again to reinstall the boot manager. From then on, there will be no conflict, and you will be able to easily switch between the two systems.

The Microsoft documentation does not suggest that you install OS/2 Warp after Windows 95 is on a system, but you can do it if you plan ahead. You cannot install boot manager until you do the OS/2 Warp installation, but you must leave room for it when you partition a drive as part of the DOS and Windows 95 installation process. You should leave at least 1 MB of free space on the drive when you create your partitions.

Partition the drive as you normally do under DOS, and install both DOS and then Windows 95 on the C drive. Create a directory to backup your root directory files, just in case.

Your next step is to install OS/2 Warp. Follow the Advanced procedure if you want to install OS/2 Warp on a drive other than C or if you want to install boot manager. Otherwise, the Easy procedure is adequate. The Easy procedure installs OS/2 Warp on the C drive and installs dual boot for you. You are then able to switch back and forth between Windows 95 and OS/2 Warp with the boot command.

Accessing Your LAN

You may need to install additional network support after the basic Windows 95 system installation if the setup program did not completely detect your LAN environment. To do this, open the Control Panel and click on the Network icon. This brings up the screen shown in figure 9.11.

Figure 9.11

The Network configuration screen.

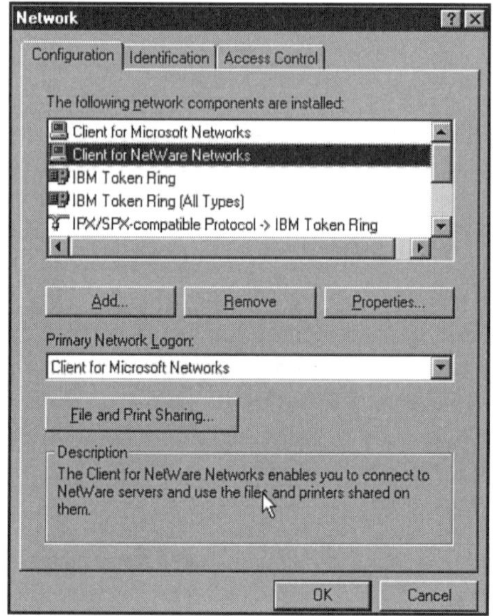

Move the bar to your type of network. In figure 9.11, you see Client for NetWare Networks selected. Double-clicking there brings up the screen shown in figure 9.12 in which you select the component type. In this example, Client is selected. Double-click on this line.

Figure 9.12

The Select Network Component Type screen.

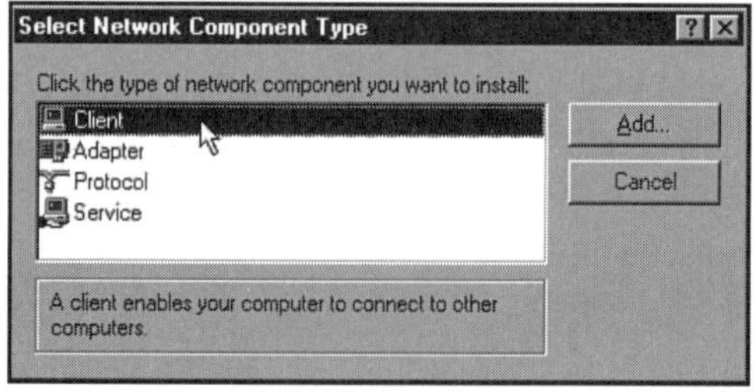

The Select Network Client screen (see fig. 9.13) shows the list of supported networks. Select your network type and choose OK to install the client software. It is interesting to note that the NetWare client was written by Microsoft, not Novell as is the usual case. You can use Novell drivers, but the new Microsoft code all loads into high memory, is all 32-bit, and executes faster than the Novell-written routines.

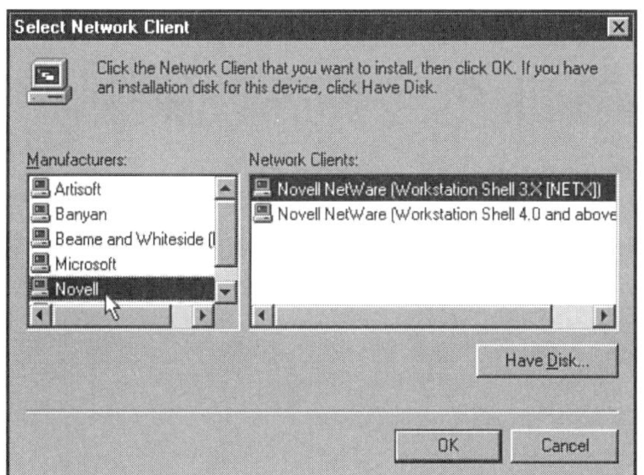

Figure 9.13

The Select Network Client screen.

You also need to install the adapter support. Go back to the Select Network Component Type screen shown in figure 9.12 and move the bar to Adapter. Double-click to bring up the Select Network adapters screen (see fig. 9.14), which has the list of supported LAN adapters. Scroll to your adapter manufacturer to bring up the list of supported adapters. Select your adapter and choose OK.

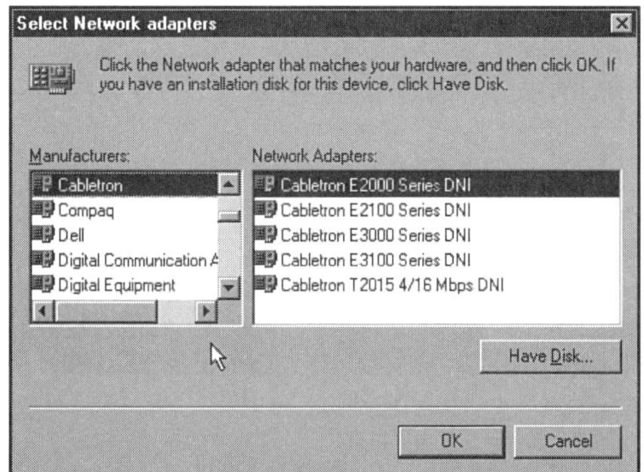

Figure 9.14

The Select Network adapters screen.

Sharing Your Resources

If you are adding OS/2 Warp Connect client systems to a Windows 95 network, you will want to use its peer server capabilities to share resources on the OS/2 systems with the Windows 95 systems. This section describes how to share subdirectory (file) and printer resources on OS/2 Warp Connect workstations.

Sharing Resources with OS/2 Warp Connect

There are many ways to share a device with OS/2 Warp Connect. You can use the GUI, the command line, or the desktop to share local resources. To share a local resource, open the Sharing and Connecting icon, select the Sharing page, and then drag the object's icon onto the Shares page of the Sharing and Connecting notebook. The resource is now available to other users.

To use the GUI to share resources, follow these steps:

1. Open the Sharing and Connecting notebook and go to the Shares page, as shown in figure 9.15.

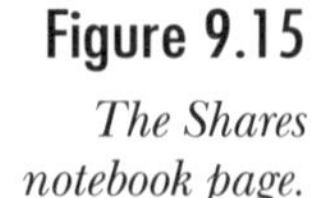

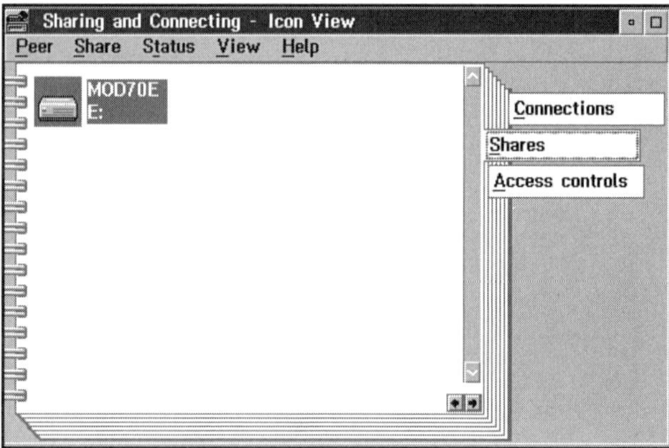

Figure 9.15 *The Shares notebook page.*

2. Select **C**reate from the **S**hare menu. The Select a Resource for Sharing screen appears, as shown in figure 9.16. To share a drive, type the drive letter, or type the name of a directory to share a subdirectory tree.

3. Choose OK. The Configure Sharing screen appears (see fig. 9.17).

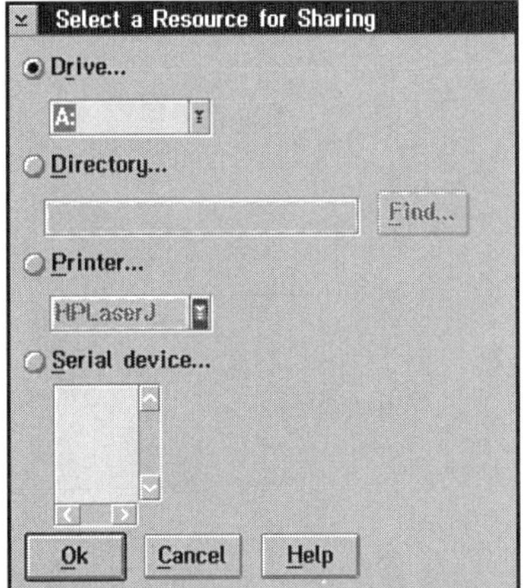

Figure 9.16

The Select a Resource for Sharing page.

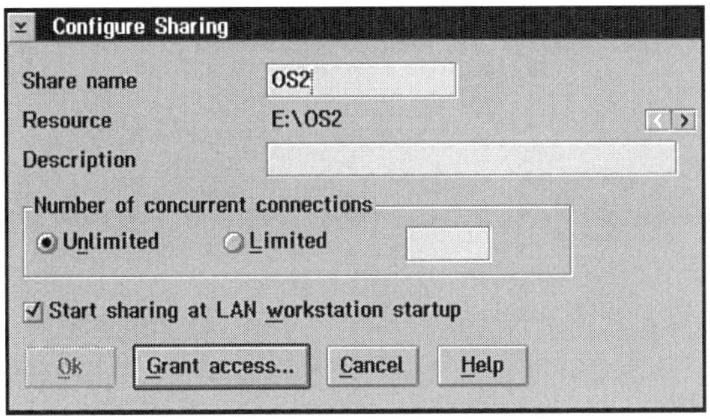

Figure 9.17

The Configure Sharing screen.

Fill in the fields as appropriate. The Share name field is the name that users specify to access this resource. The Resource field is the real name of the resource as determined by the Peer service. The Description field is any meaningful text that you want to describe the resource. You can limit the number of users accessing this resource at one time by setting the Number of concurrent connections parameter to an acceptable value. If you select Limited you must enter a value for the maximum number of systems that can access the resource at one time. The resource can be shared automatically when OS/2 is booted, or only when you take specific action to share it. For automatic sharing, check the Start sharing at LAN **w**orkstation startup box.

4. Next, you must specify who can use the resource. Click on the **G**rant access button to display the screen shown in figure 9.18.

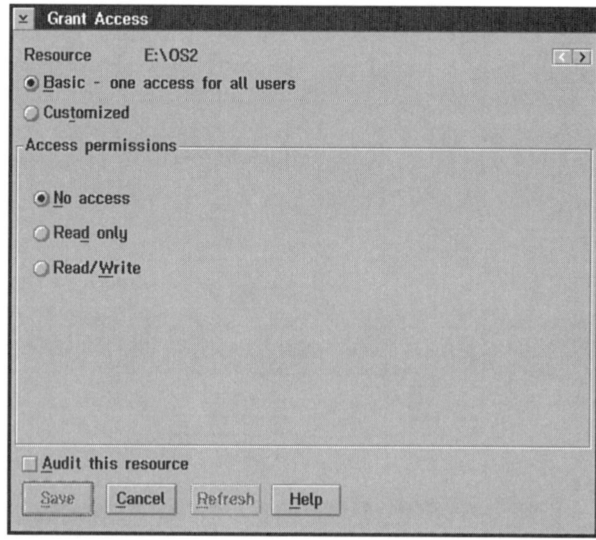

Figure 9.18

The Grant Access panel.

The Grant Access screen lets you chose between **B**asic and Cus**t**omized access control. If you decide to grant **B**asic access to the resource, all users will be treated the same. You can give either no access, read-only access or read-write access.

Selecting Cus**t**omized access displays the screen shown in figure 9.19. Here, you can manage access by individual user or by group. Each individual user or group can be granted specifically tailored access permissions.

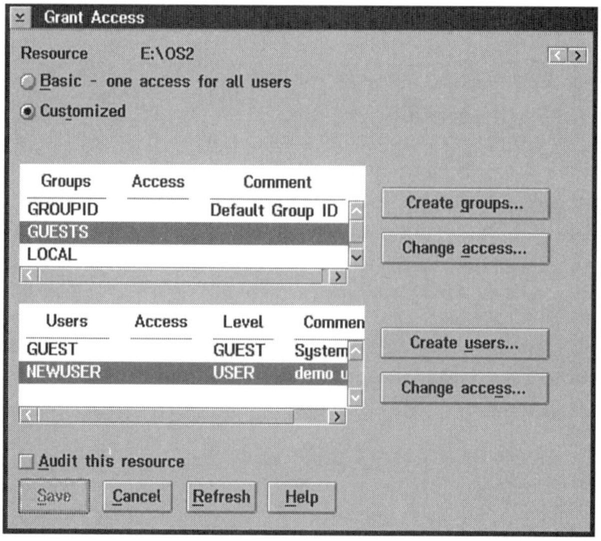

Figure 9.19

The customized access panel.

5. When you have completed specifying the access information, click on OK. The resource will then be available for use by other systems and will be displayed on the Access control page.

The steps you follow to share a printer are similar to those for a drive or directory, with only one slight difference. If you are using Basic access control for the printer, you can give either no access or access. There are no read, read-write or other access types because they are not meaningful to a printer.

You can also use the NET SHARE command to share resources. The following code shows the syntax of the command. Notice that all of the options and parameters that can be set using the GUI are available with the command. Although the GUI is easier to use for sharing a few resources for a few users, you may want to put the NET SHARE command into a batch file if you will be managing many resources with different access permissions for many users.

```
NET SHARE [netname]
            netname=device [password]
                              [/COMM]
                              [/USERS:number ¦ /UNLIMITED]
                              [/REMARK:text]
                              [/PERMISSIONS:XRWCDA]
            netname [PASSWORD]
                              [/PRINT]
                              [/USERS:number ¦ /UNLIMITED]
                              [/REMARK:text]
                              [/PERMISSIONS:XRWCDA]
NET SHARE [netname ¦ device ¦ drive:\path]
          [/USERS:number ¦ /UNLIMITED]
          [/REMARK:text]
          [/DELETE]
          [/PERMISSIONS:XRWCDA]
```

Sharing Resources with Windows 95

Even though Chapter 7 discusses how to use Windows 95 as a server, it is appropriate to include a brief description of how to share resources with Windows 95 here to emphasize the similarities with the OS/2 procedure.

To share a drive on a Windows 95 system, follow these steps:

1. Open the My Computer folder. This brings up the screen in figure 9.20.

2. Select a device to share. In figure 9.20, drive D is selected.

Figure 9.20

The My Computer folder.

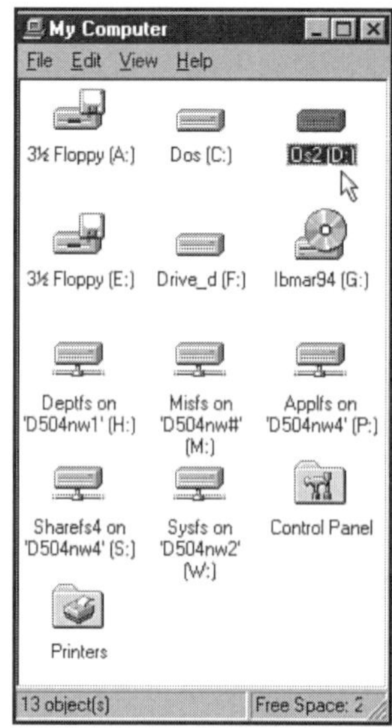

3. Click on the **F**ile menu item to get the drop-down list shown in figure 9.21.

   Open the S**h**aring menu item to get to the sharing page of the properties notebook. As you can see in figure 9.22, this is where you enter the network name of the resource, enter a descriptive comment about the resource, and define the access controls for the resource.

Figure 9.21

The File drop-down menu.

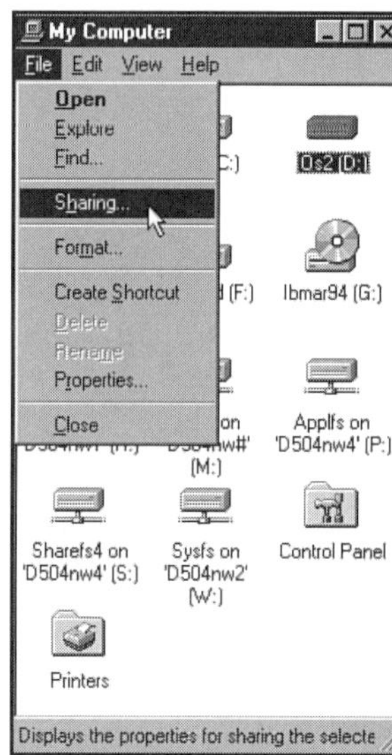

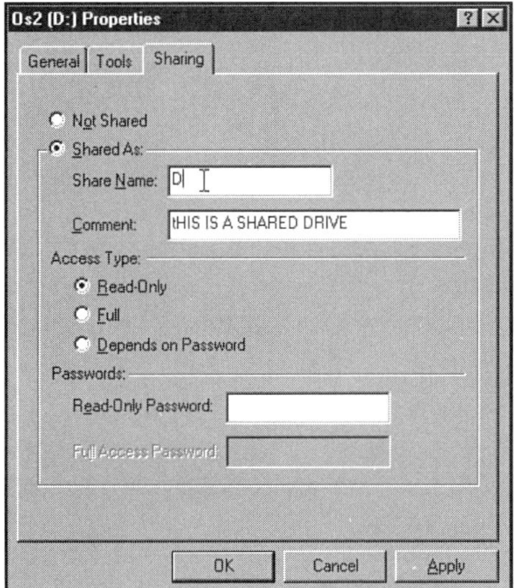

Figure 9.22
The Sharing parameter entry panel.

The technique just described for Windows 95 can also be used with OS/2. As previously mentioned, resources can be shared in multiple ways with OS/2 Warp. In the previous section you dragged the icon for a drive to the sharing folder, and the properties were set. If you right-click on the drive's icon in the drives folder, you see a Share menu item in the pop-up menu, just as you did with Windows 95. You can set the access permissions from there.

Tuning Your System

One reason to use Windows 95 or OS/2 Warp is to get increased 32-bit performance from your system. Some effort will have to be made at system tuning to ensure that you are getting the best performance your system can deliver.

Both Windows 95 and OS/2 Warp are basically self-tuning. During the installation process, both systems pick defaults for certain system functions (such as cache size) based on your hardware. These values are designed to provide the best balance between performance and reliability based on how the development group envisions your use of the system. If your work does not match their ideas, however, you may see improved performance by changing these definitions.

Measuring System Performance

Windows 95 includes a program, called the System Monitor, that is designed to help you tune your system. With OS/2, the only standard tool is the Pulse program that displays total CPU utilization. To do a comprehensive tuning job on an OS/2 system, you need to get a copy of the IBM System Performance Monitor (SPM) program, which provides extremely detailed performance measurements. Without such a tool, you must shoot in the dark, changing a single parameter and then measuring the effect of the change.

You should create batch files that record the time it takes to access files or load programs on your system, whether it is a Windows 95 or OS/2 Warp system. You can then adjust a tuning parameter and run the script again. After comparing results with the original run, you can decide if the change was good or bad. This is the only way to get repeatable real-world data about how the system is running.

You can use the Windows 95 System Monitor to measure the performance of hardware, system software, and application software. To run the System Monitor, click on the Start button on the toolbar, choose Run, and type **SYSMON**. This brings up the last configured display, as shown in figure 9.23.

To add or delete items from the display, click on the Edit menu item, and then choose Add Item. This brings up the screen shown in figure 9.24.

Figure 9.23

The System Monitor display.

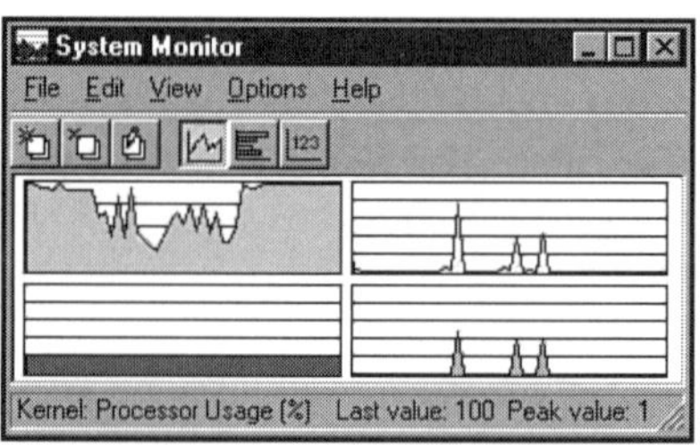

Figure 9.24

The System Monitor Add Item screen.

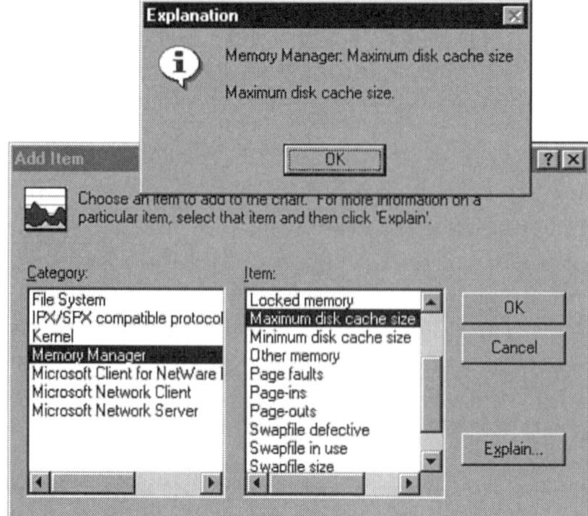

At the left of the panel is the Category list. When you select a category, the Item list in the right window displays the measurable items in that category. If you click on the Explain button (as was done in figure 9.24), an Explanation window appears. It is interesting to go through all of the items reading the explanations. What you are seeing is really a list of the objects used by the Windows 95 system to identify and control its behavior.

After you select the categories to monitor, go back to the System Monitor display shown in figure 9.23. Click on the different graph types on the properties bar to change the appearance of the graphs. Figure 9.25 shows the same data in bar graph format.

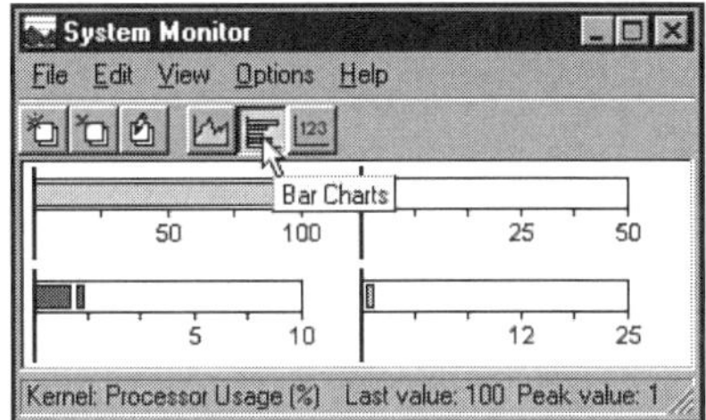

Figure 9.25

The System Monitor with bar graph display.

Notice that the title of the object being measured and the reported data are displayed along the bottom of the window. Clicking on a different graph updates this text accordingly.

You can change the update interval with the Options, Chart menu item. Figure 9.26 shows the control you use to set the graph update speed. Select Options from the menu bar, and then select Chart.

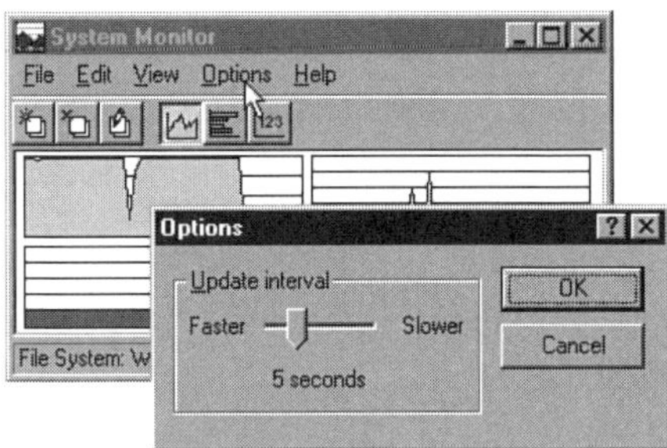

Figure 9.26

The System Monitor Update interval control.

You can also tailor graph colors. From the **E**dit pull-down menu, select the chart for which you want to set the color. Click on Chart Options, and then click the Change button in the color box. This brings up the color selection window shown in figure 9.27.

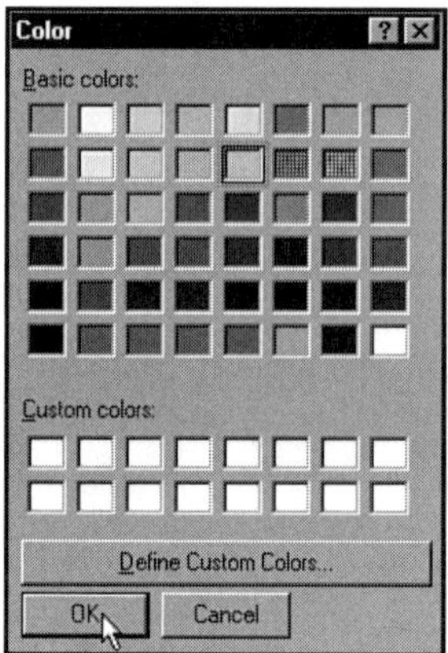

Figure 9.27
The System Monitor color selection screen.

What do you monitor? First, build a reference performance database of several areas. If performance is satisfactory, stop for now. Save another set of charts periodically and look for trends in the changes. If performance is slowing down, you should be able to spot the area of concern. See if you can find the bottleneck. If performance is still adequate but you see a resource's usage increasing, you may be able to predict how soon that resource will become a bottleneck. This is called capacity planning and is used to anticipate the need for system upgrades before there is a performance problem.

Monitoring Use of Your Shared Resources

You can measure how your shared resources are being used with OS/2 Warp Connect. This will help you determine how to set your configuration parameters.

Click on the Sharing and Connecting icon to open its notebook, and then select Status from the menu bar to see a summary of your system's activity (see fig. 9.28).

You can refresh or clear these values by clicking on the appropriate button in the Statistics window. To see a list of files on your system that are being used by other users, select **O**pen Files from the Status drop-down menu. You will see a list of files, some statistical data, and the ID of the person who is using the file (see fig. 9.29).

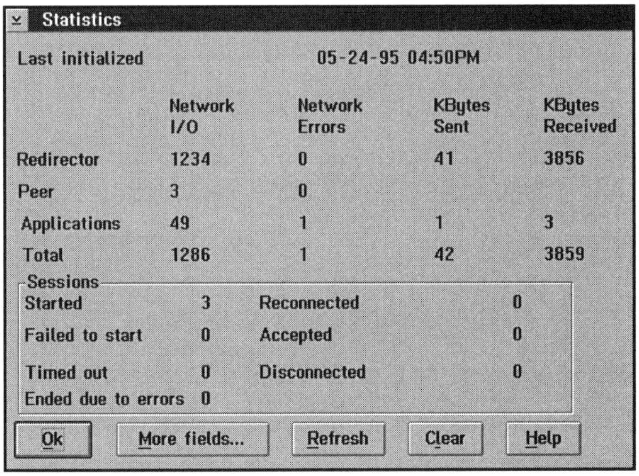

Statistics

Last initialized 05-24-95 04:50PM

	Network I/O	Network Errors	KBytes Sent	KBytes Received
Redirector	1234	0	41	3856
Peer	3	0		
Applications	49	1	1	3
Total	1286	1	42	3859

Sessions

Started	3	Reconnected	0
Failed to start	0	Accepted	0
Timed out	0	Disconnected	0
Ended due to errors	0		

Ok | More fields... | Refresh | Clear | Help

Figure 9.28

System statistics.

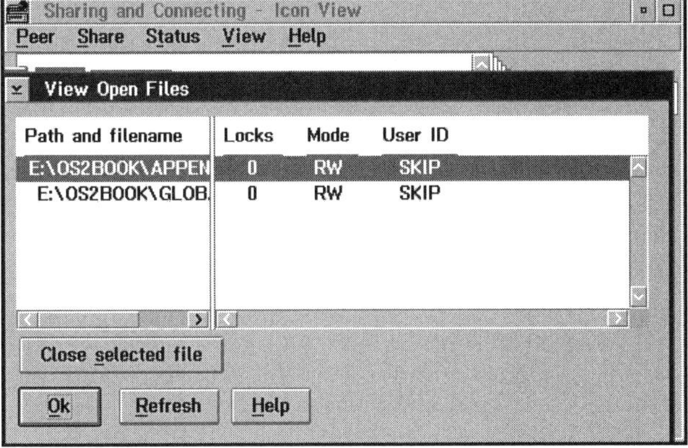

Figure 9.29

The View Open Files screen.

If you click on the Close **s**elected file button, the file that is selected closes immediately. This will probably crash the program that is using the file on the other system, leading to an irate message from that user. Therefore, do this with great care.

If you want to see a list of the people using your resources, select the **A**ctive Sessions menu item from the Status drop-down menu. The View Active Sessions screen appears, as shown in figure 9.30. Notice that like the View Open Files window, you have the ability to delete the selected session. Again, use caution when doing this.

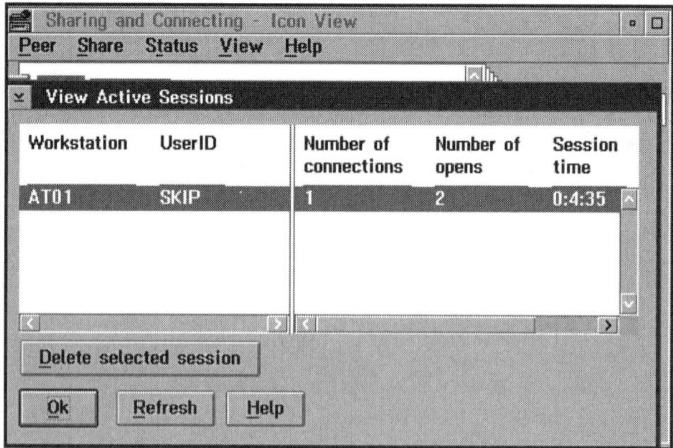

Figure 9.30

The View Active Sessions screen.

Optimizing Swapping and Paging

Some tuning techniques apply equally to both Windows 95 and OS/2 Warp. The swap file, for example, should be located on the most used partition or logical drive on the least used physical drive. This minimizes head movement to satisfy a swap or paging request while minimizing the interference from program loading and data access. Windows 95 supports multiple swap files on multiple disk drives, which can also improve performance. Swap file operations do not go through the disk cache.

Swap file location, minimum size, and starting size, are specified in the CONFIG.SYS file for OS/2 Warp. For Windows 95, you open the Performance tab in the Control Panel and click on the Virtual Memory button. This opens the screen shown in figure 9.31, which enables you to specify the path to the swap file, and the minimum and maximum swap file sizes.

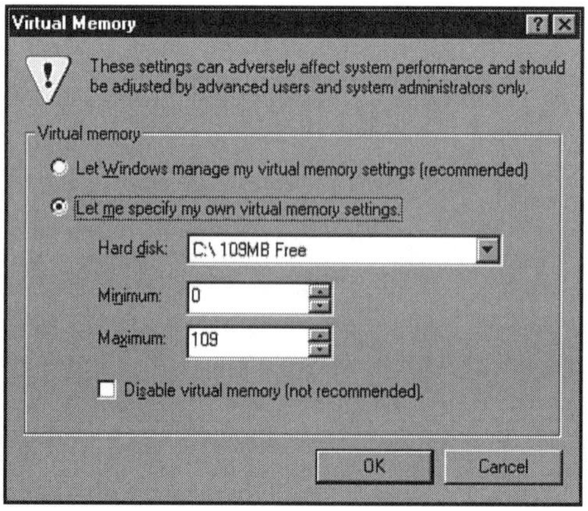

Figure 9.31

Defining Windows 95 swap file parameters.

Virtual Memory

These settings can adversely affect system performance and should be adjusted by advanced users and system administrators only.

Virtual memory

Let Windows manage my virtual memory settings (recommended)

Let me specify my own virtual memory settings.

Hard disk: C:\ 109MB Free

Minimum: 0

Maximum: 109

Disable virtual memory (not recommended).

OK Cancel

Optimizing File System Performance

You may want to adjust the disk cache size (for example, if you are sharing file resources with many other users). Windows 95 automatically adjusts the cache size based on system load. In OS/2, you specify the cache size for FAT and HPFS drives separately in CONFIG.SYS. You have to try several different values and measure their effect on response time. Change the cache size and run your test script again. You should be able to see the effect of the configuration changes.

Another area where you can improve performance is with a disk optimizer. Windows 95 includes a program to do this as part of the system. With OS/2, you will have to buy a package that does this, such as the GammaTech Utilities, which includes a good defragmentation program. It is especially important to keep fragmentation to a minimum on the drive that contains the swap file. HPFS drives are designed to avoid, or at least minimize, this problem.

Windows 95 offers three settings for controlling file system performance based on how the system is used. You can specify that the system is one of the following:

- **Desktop system**—Used primarily as a network client or individual workstation
- **Portable system**—A system that is carried around
- **File Server**—A computer used primarily as a peer server for file and printer sharing

To specify these settings, choose the File System section of the Control Panel. The File System Properties page appears, as shown in figure 9.32. Click on the Typical role of this machine list box and select the profile that most closely matches how the system is being used.

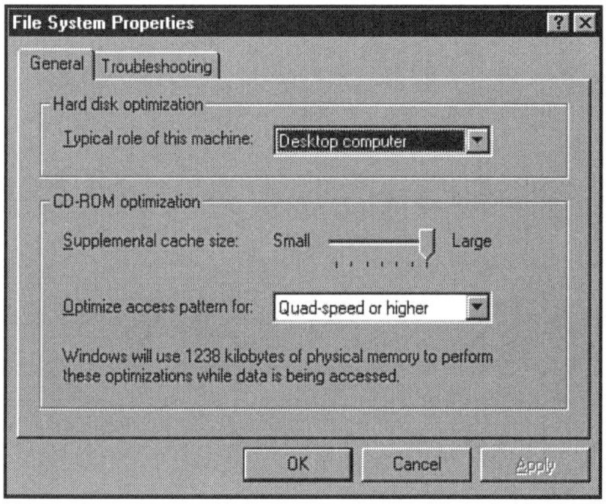

Figure 9.32

Defining Windows 95 file system parameters.

As you can see in figure 9.32, you can also control the size of the CD-ROM cache. The CD-ROM cache is pageable. Even if CD-ROM data has to be paged in, it is still faster than reading from a CD-ROM, and by being pageable, the memory requirement for the system is reduced.

Optimizing Printer Performance

Windows 95 handles printing in the background if there is sufficient system memory. This reduces the time it takes a program to spool its print data. Windows 95 stores the data in a device-independent Enhanced Metafile Format file. A background process then converts this file to the required printer format and sends it to the printer. All you have to do is provide sufficient memory.

If you click on the Printers icon in the Control Panel on your Windows 95 desktop, and then select Details, you see the screen in figure 9.33.

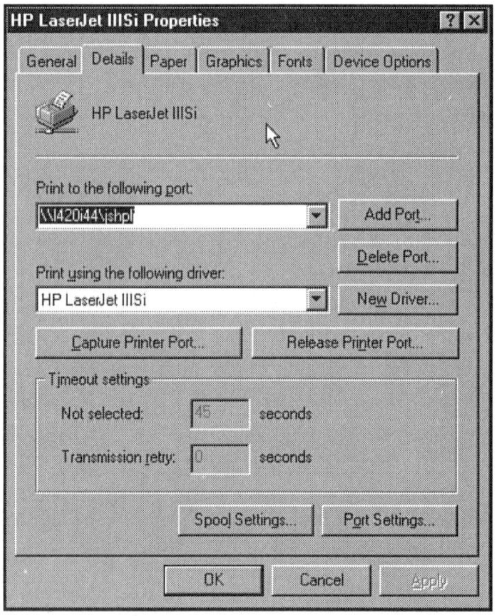

Figure 9.33
Defining Windows 95 printer characteristics.

As you can see, the screen in figure 9.33 enables you to control the hardware settings. To control the spooler settings, click on the Spool Settings button. This brings up the Spool Settings screen, as shown in figure 9.34.

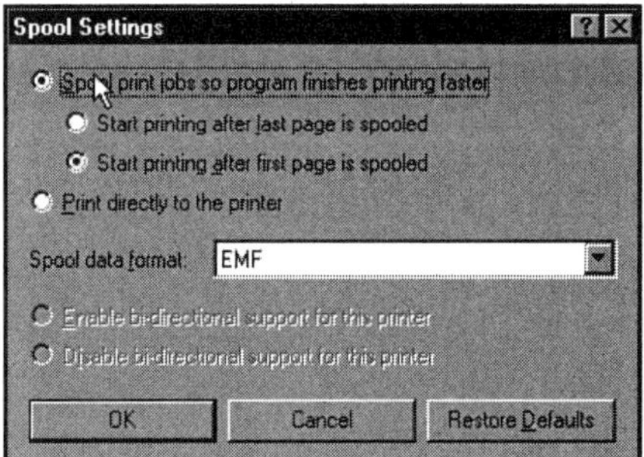

Figure 9.34
Defining Windows 95 spool parameters.

Here, you can turn the spooler on and off and control when the system begins printing.

OS/2 Warp also lets applications spool their print data, which is then sent to the printer by a background process. OS/2 Warp includes an option in Config.sys that lets you control how the printer hardware is controlled, however. This can have a significant performance impact.

Previous versions of OS/2 used an interrupt from the printer to tell the system when to send additional data. Not all printer cables provided connections for the interrupt signals, however, so this caused problems for OS/2 users with the improper cables. IBM changed OS/2 Warp to eliminate this problem. By default, OS/2 Warp polls the printer to see when it is ready to accept data. Depending on relative system and printer speeds, this can cause excessive system load. If this is the case on your system, append /IRQ to the BASEDEV=PRINT0X.SYS line in CONFIG.SYS to tell OS/2 Warp to use interrupt-based control. Just be sure to have a good printer cable.

Using Windows 95 with Windows NT Networks

In today's networking environment, Microsoft's Windows NT system is fast becoming one of the most popular client/server network platforms. If you use Windows NT as your network software, Windows 95 makes an excellent choice for a Windows NT workstation.

Windows NT is Microsoft's entry in the high-end networking arena. It offers 32-bit performance, a new file system, and linear virtual memory. Windows 95 also offers a 32-bit operating system that is a good match for the 32-bit operating system of Windows NT Server. In fact, several Windows 95 features have come from "big brother" NT, such as its Virtual Machine Manager, Linear Model Memory, and object component architecture. A high-performance workstation environment is a welcome change after using Windows 3.*x* on a workstation.

The Windows 3.*x* operating system is dependent on DOS. With DOS, the network drivers load in memory, and then Windows loads on top of them. All this makes for a cumbersome environment that usually teeters on the verge of conventional memory shortage. This is a problem particularly if the workstation has to run DOS programs launched from the Windows environment. At times it is next to impossible to have enough free conventional memory to run certain

DOS programs in this manner. Because Windows 95 does not rely on DOS, however, its performance as a network client is greatly enhanced.

This chapter covers the following issues associated with using Windows 95 as a workstation on a Windows NT network:

- Peer-to-peer services
- Compatibility with future versions of Windows NT
- Flexibility with other network servers
- High performance workstation environment
- Enhancements of Windows 95 over Windows for Workgroups 3.11
- Setting up Windows 95 as a Windows NT workstation
- Security

Exploring the Peer-to-Peer Services of Windows 95

Windows 95 comes with built-in peer-to-peer networking services that can ease the network load on a Windows NT server. Peer-to-peer networking enables users on the network to share the resources on their workstations (such as CD-ROM drives, hard drives, and printers) with other users on the network. The peer-to-peer networking service can be run on top of the client/server network regardless of the type of network topography being used. Even if you are running a Novell network, for example, if your workstations are using Windows 95, you can utilize Windows 95 peer-to-peer services. These Windows 95 peer-to-peer network services include the following:

- Print sharing
- File sharing
- Access control

Print Sharing

With *print sharing,* Windows 95 workstations can offer the use of their printer to the rest of the workgroup. Windows 95 print services run in the background, so the workstation sharing its printer does not suffer a large performance loss when a print job from another station utilizes the computer and printer.

This feature can be useful when a printer attached to a workstation is needed by the network—when the network laser printer runs out of toner, for example. The laser printer attached to a workstation can be shared with the network with just a few steps.

Windows 95 has a 32-bit protected-mode component called the *spooler* that handles the printer sharing. The spooler is comprised of two parts. The first part exists at the application level and accepts print jobs from the applications and passes them to the server (VSERVER). The second part of the spooler is a virtual device driver (VxD) that accepts the print jobs from the server and passes them to a print device, such as a printer connected to the server.

File Sharing

File sharing enables Windows 95 users to share their hard drives, CD-ROM drives, folders, and files with other users on the network. File sharing is performed primarily through the following 32-bit protected-mode components:

- **VSERVER.** VSERVER is a virtual device driver that is multithreaded to handle multiple network requests. This is the main server component of Windows 95. The server (VSERVER) accesses the network via the transport level interface.
- **MSHRUI.** MSHRUI (Microsoft Share Point User Interface) is a Dynamic Link Library (DLL) file that handles the sharing operations initiated by the user of the workstation. This is the component that adds the share point to the local computer when a file or folder is shared on a server.
- **IFS Manager.** IFS (Installable File System) Manager routes file system requests from the server (VSERVER) to either the network File System Driver (FSD) or the local FSD. The IFS Manager in Windows 95 offers multiple redirector support, unified cache (which enables client side redirector caching), and protected mode use (which eliminates real-mode conflicts).

Together these 32-bit protected-mode components handle the brunt of Windows 95's file sharing responsiblities. The user's ability to use these shared resources depends on the access control.

Access Control

Access control is the security component of Windows 95. Access control is also a VxD that controls individual file requests. It uses the *username, password* (if applicable) and *filename* to verify the users rights to use a particular file or resource. Access control offers two levels of security: user-level and share-level.

User-Level Security

User-level security enables you to create a list of users who have access to a particular resource on the server. To gain access to a resource, the user must be on this list of users. When a user logs on to the system, a password can be required to verify the authentication of the logon. User-level security is modeled after NT user-level security. It is not as bullet-proof as NT, however, and does not meet the same level of government approval as NT does.

Share-level Security

With *share-level security*, each shared resource has a particular set of access rights. These access rights apply to the resource regardless of which user is attempting access to the resource.

Future Versions of Windows NT

Many of Windows 95 components are derived from technology put into place in Windows NT. The device drivers, file system access, 32-bit operating environment, and other network components are leveraged from the technology used in NT. This makes for a tight fit between the two operating systems.

Microsoft plans for these two operating systems to go hand-in-hand. Windows NT will be the main network platform handling the client/server, serious desktop, and WAN requirements of business; Windows 95 will be everywhere else, handling smaller systems, workstations, and so forth. Microsoft estimates that twenty percent of desktop PCs will benefit from Windows NT (including future versions) and the other 80 percent will be adequately served by Windows 95 and its future versions.

Using Windows 95 with Multiple Network Servers

One advantage of a Windows 95 client on a Windows NT network is Windows 95's capability to seamlessly act as a client on different types of servers. Windows 95 can simultaneously act as a client on a Novell NetWare server and on a Windows NT server, thus allowing for greater flexibility on the network. You can obtain this flexibility without changing the user's methods of connecting to network resources.

This functionality can be leveraged to your advantage if you are planning to migrate from a NetWare server to a Windows NT server, but you want to ease into the switch.

The first step in migrating from a NetWare server to a Windows NT server is to set up Windows 95 on all the workstations. This gives all users Windows-based desktops that are capable of running older, DOS-based applications. In this first phase, Windows 95 enables you (as the network administrator) to still run older DOS-based applications while you are phasing in new Windows-based applications and training users in the new environment and applications. All this is done with the "old" NetWare server in place.

The next step in this migration process is to bring in the Windows NT server on the network while the NetWare server is still in place. Now, Windows-based applications can operate on the NT server, and new 32-bit applications can be installed on the NT server and accessed by the 32-bit Windows 95 clients.

The final step is to remove the NetWare server after all the network services have been moved onto the Windows NT server.

The network has now successfully migrated to Windows NT, with the users barely aware of NetWare's disappearance. Windows 95 is instrumental in this endeavor because of its capability to act as a client on both of these networks while maintaining a consistent user interface.

Network Provider Interface (NPI)

The network component in Windows 95 that enables this concurrent support for network services is the *Network Provider Interface* (NPI).

The NPI enables you to install multiple network interfaces at the same time. It consists of two parts: the network provider API and the network providers. Windows 95 uses the *network provider API* to request network resources from servers on the network. These requests are then passed to the appropriate *network provider.*

This design of the NPI lends itself well to the open design of Windows 95. The NPI's network provider API communicates well with third-party drivers.

The Windows 95 High-Performance Workstation Environment

Windows 95 offers the highest performance client environment for a Windows NT network (other than a Windows NT workstation). The following are the design concepts that makes Windows 95 the best choice for a Windows NT client:

- Open design
- Multiple network support
- Multiple protocol support
- Plug and Play
- 32-bit VxDs

Open Design

Windows 95's architecture is modular and provides support for third-party products. The three main modular interfaces that are made available to these vendors are IFS (Installable File System) Manager, NPI (Network Provider Interface), and NDIS (Network Driver Interface Specification). Being modular means that the operating system components are fitted together, each performing an exact function. This way there is no redundancy in function among system components.

Open design architecture enables third-party developers to create applications and utilities that can tightly fit into this modular design without duplicating any of the functionality of other system components.

IFS Manager

The IFS Manager routes file system requests from the server (VSERVER) to either the network FSD (File System Driver) or the local FSD. The IFS Manager in Windows 95 offers multiple redirector support, unified cache (which enables client side redirector caching), and protected mode use (which eliminates real-mode conflicts). Client side caching gives Windows 95 a performance boost over other client environments for Windows NT.

NPI

The NPI enables you to install multiple networks simultaneously. The modular design of this interface helps Windows 95 maintain its open design. The interface enables venders to create support for their network server product that "plugs" into the interface. This saves vendors from having to write their own interface, which makes their driver larger and possibly less efficient.

NDIS

NDIS 3.1 for Windows 95 has a smaller driver model that allows for mini-drivers. These drivers are compatible with the mini-drivers used in Windows NT. To provide access to their network operating system protocol, NDIS 3.1 enables third-party vendors to write smaller, more efficient drivers for the Windows 95 environment.

Multiple Network Support

Multiple network support refers to Windows 95's capability to act as different network clients at the same time. This is achieved through multiple network redirectors and drivers written to take advantage of Windows 95's open design. This is achieved through the use of the aforementioned NPI.

This functionality makes Windows 95 a better choice as a Windows NT client. Other client environments don't give the ability to log on to a Windows NT server and NetWare server at the same time.

Multiple Protocol Support

The Protocol Manager enables you to load multiple transport protocols. Windows 95 has built-in support for IPX/SPX, TCP/IP, and NetBEUI. The Protocol Manager enables third-parties, however, to write protocol stacks that can be implemented in addition to the built-in protocols.

Plug and Play

The network components in Windows 95 are designed for dynamic *Plug and Play* operation. Because of the protected-mode NDIS drivers, a PCMCIA Ethernet card can be inserted into a notebook computer that is running Windows 95, and the appropriate NDIS 3.1 driver will automatically be loaded. This means that a user of a notebook computer can insert an Ethernet card and log on to the network without restarting his computer. Another benefit of Plug and Play is that the user doesn't have to be a computer guru with knowledge of IRQs and memory addresses to install a sound card. Plug and Play operation handles all of these issues.

32-Bit VxDs

All the network components in Windows 95 are virtual device drivers (VxDs). These VxDs have no conventional memory footprint and are dynamically loaded as they are needed by the system. These virtual device drivers are significantly faster than their real-mode counterparts.

Because these drivers are dynamically loaded, they do not use any system memory until they are needed. This keeps the system overhead low. Additionally, because these drivers have no conventional memory footprint, they leave more room for older DOS-based applications to run.

Enhancements of Windows 95 over Windows for Workgroups 3.11

Windows 95 offers many improvements over previous versions of Windows that can enhance the performance of a workstation in the role of a Windows NT client. These enhancements include the following:

- High-performance 32-bit network architecture that includes VxDs that run in protected-mode offering protection against memory conflicts that can arise from real-mode drivers
- Multiple redirector and multiple protocol support that allow for simultaneous network interfaces
- Remote access capabilities that even allow Windows 95 to act as a gateway to a Windows NT network
- 32-bit printing services that take advantage of the Windows NT 32-bit environment

Windows 95, in its efforts to replace Windows for Workgroups, provides an excellent client environment for a Windows NT network.

Setting Up Windows 95 as a Windows NT Workstation

You can connect a Windows 95 workstation to a Windows NT server by logging on to a particular domain on the server that you want to access.

To log on to a Windows NT domain, follow these steps:

1. Open the Control Panel folder.
2. Open the Network folder by double-clicking on the Network icon.
3. Click on the Client for Microsoft Networks option, and then click on Properties. Figure 10.1 shows the dialog box that appears.
4. Click on the Log on to Windows NT domain option box, and then enter the domain name in the Windows NT domain field.

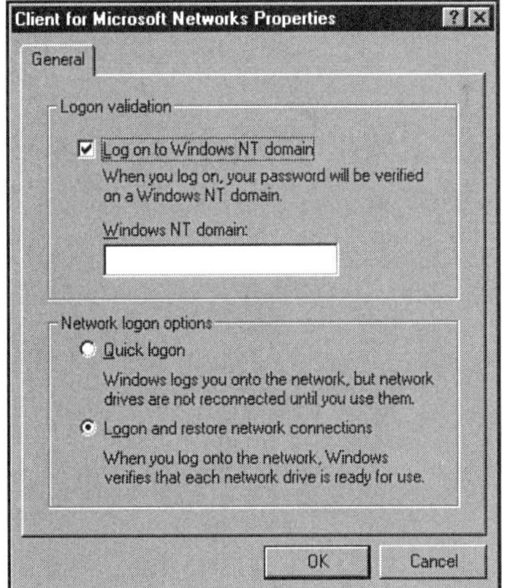

Figure 10.1

The Client for Microsoft Networks Properties property sheet.

5. Select the logon option that you want to use.

   The **Q**uick logon option logs on to the NT domain when you start the computer, but it does not connect the resources until you use them. The drives and printers are connected as they are requested.

   The L**o**gon and restore network connections option logs on to the NT domain and restores all drive connections and Printer connections.

Exploring Security Issues

Windows NT uses user-level security for its primary access control. Windows 95, as a client of Windows NT, fits well into this security scheme. When attached to a Windows NT network, Windows 95 uses the user list that exists for the domain that the client workstation is logged on to.

To enable user-level security in Windows 95, follow these steps:

1. Open the Control Panel folder.
2. Double-click on the Network icon.
3. Select the Access Control panel. The Access Control panel is shown in figure 10.2.

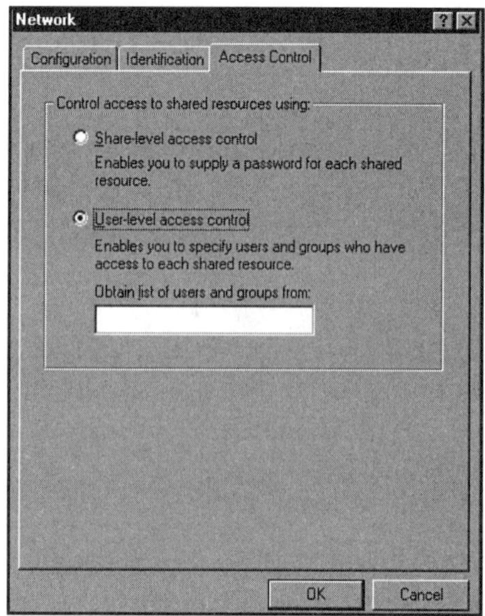

Figure 10. 2

Choose User-level security from the Access Control panel.

4. In the Obtain list of users and groups from option, enter the NT domain that has the user list that you want to use.

The Windows 95 workstation now uses the Windows NT user list at logon when granting access to the user at this Windows 95 workstation.

Remote Access and Management

In today's computing world, the information located on a single personal computer represents but a tiny fraction of the total information available to the computer user. The real power of the desktop personal computer is its ability to communicate with other computers and networks. Windows 95 includes support for remote access that allows users to access other systems and function as a server or gateway to a Windows 95 network.

Remote access refers to the ability to connect one computer to another computer or network via the phone line. This is particularly useful to the mobile workstation such as a notebook computer. Another use of this functionality is remote network access from a home computer. This enables you to log on to the office network from your home Windows 95-based computer to form a mini-network over the phone lines. Your home computer could have full access to all the drives, folders, and printers that your office system has to offer.

This chapter covers the following topics:

- Understanding modems and data communications
- Using Dial-Up Networking
- Using Windows 95 as a gateway to a network
- Understanding other communications programs
- Using the Windows 95 Phone Dialer

Understanding Modems and Data Communications

Before you begin using the remote access features of Windows 95, you should have at least a basic understanding of the key piece of hardware used to connect your local computer to the remote system—the modem. A *modem* is a special piece of computer hardware that converts the data coming from your computer to a signal that can be transmitted through normal telephone lines. This process is called *modulation*. The modem also converts signals from the phone line into data that your computer can understand through a process called *demodulation*. From these two processes (*MO*dulate/*DEM*odulate) comes the term "modem."

Most modems now have the capability to create, send, and receive faxes in addition to sending and receiving data. When purchasing a modem, you should ensure that it has both fax and data capabilities.

Most computers now come with modems already installed. If your computer does not already have a modem, however, you can purchase one separately. There are many brands and varieties of modems available today, though most fall into one of a few main categories: internal, external, PCMCIA format (for notebook computers), and portable.

Modems also have a variety of attributes and features such as error correction, compression, and flow control. Perhaps the most important attribute, however, is the speed with which the modem can transfer data over the telephone line. This speed is measured in bytes per second (Bps). As you might imagine, with transfer rates, faster is generally better. As recently as four years ago, 1,200 Bps was considered standard and 2,400 Bps was fast. Currently, however, 14,400 Bps is common, and many computer systems now have modems that transfer data at 28,800 Bps (also stated as 28.8 Kbps, or kilobytes per second).

Installing and Configuring Modems

Windows 95 makes installing and configuring your modem a simple process. If you have a modem installed in your computer, for example, the Windows 95 Setup program will attempt to detect the modem brand and the modem speed, then install the proper driver files.

If you want to change your modem or install a new modem after you are already running Windows 95, you can install and configure the modem yourself from the Windows 95 Control Panel. You can also reconfigure an existing modem.

Click on the Start button, select Settings, and then click on the Control Panel. From the Control Panel, double-click the Modems icon to reveal a general Modems Properties panel, as shown in figure 11.1.

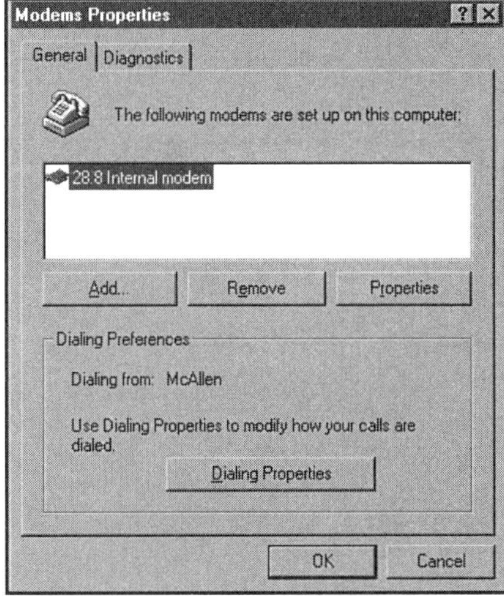

Figure 11.1
The Modems Properties panel.

To reconfigure an existing modem from this panel, click on the Properties button to access these panels (see fig. 11.2).

To change the connection settings, such as stop bits, parity, and data bits, select the Connection panel (see fig. 11.3).

To install a new modem, click on the Add button from the Modems Properties panel (refer to fig. 11.1). A Windows 95 Wizard guides you through the process of installing the new modem. After installing the new modem, you can, if necessary, change its properties using the steps described in the preceding paragraphs.

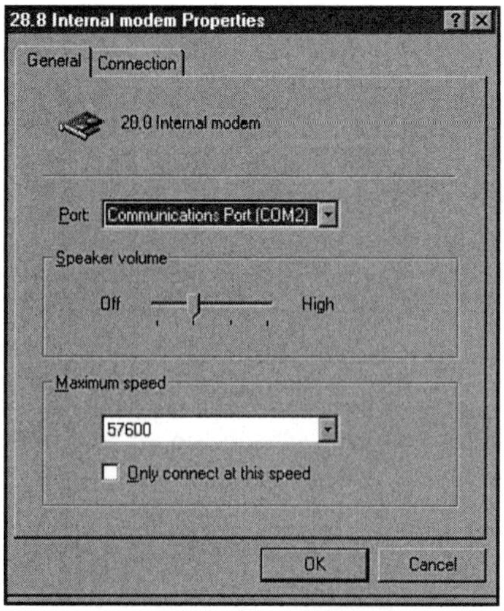

Figure 11.2
The Modems Properties General panel.

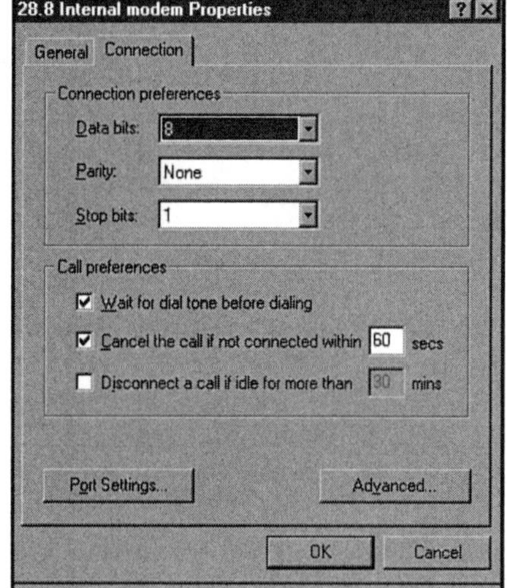

Figure 11.3
The Modems Properties Connection panel.

Examining COM Ports

Modems are configured to transfer data to and from your computer through connections called COM ports. COM ports are connected (either physically or electronically) to your computer's main motherboard and allow communications devices to pass data into and out of the computer (hence the name *COM*munication port).

As mentioned previously, the Windows 95 Setup program automatically detects your COM ports and attempts to configure any devices (such as modems) attached to those ports. Alternatively, you can select a specific COM port for your modem from the Connections panel (refer to fig. 11.3). Windows 95 attempts to communicate with the COM port and creates the computer files and connections necessary to allow data to flow from the computer to the device.

To manually configure a COM port (with or without a modem attached), open the Control Panel and double-click the System icon. Next, select the tab for Device Manager and a list of all of the computer devices in your computer appears.

Double-click on the COM port you want to configure and a Communications Port Properties panel with several tabs appears, as shown in figure 11.4.

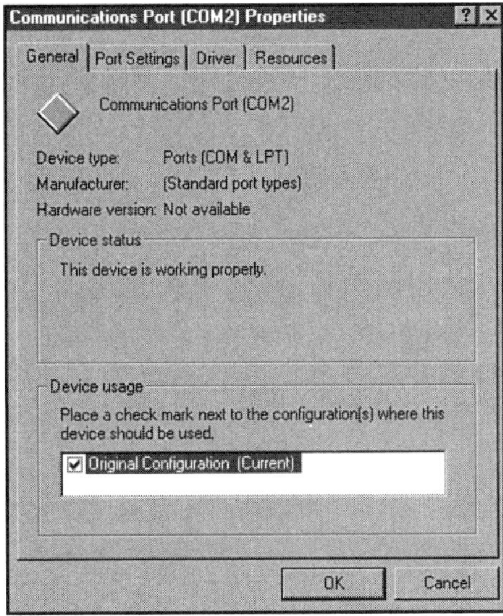

Figure 11.4
The Communications Port Properties panel.

From this panel, you can configure the port to any necessary specifications that you need.

Configuring Other Communications Parameters

After you install and configure a modem, you must specify certain properties. Each modem, for example, has an associated Dialing Properties page. These properties control the manner in which the modem dials the various numbers used to connect to other services.

There are several ways to specify the dialing properties. Most applications, for example, enable you to specify properties from within the application. You can also specify dialing parameters from the Modems icon in the Control Panel, however. To change the dialing properties in this manner, double-click on the icon for the modem you want to change, then select Dialing Properties to reveal this panel (see fig. 11.5).

Figure 11.5

The Dialing Properties panel.

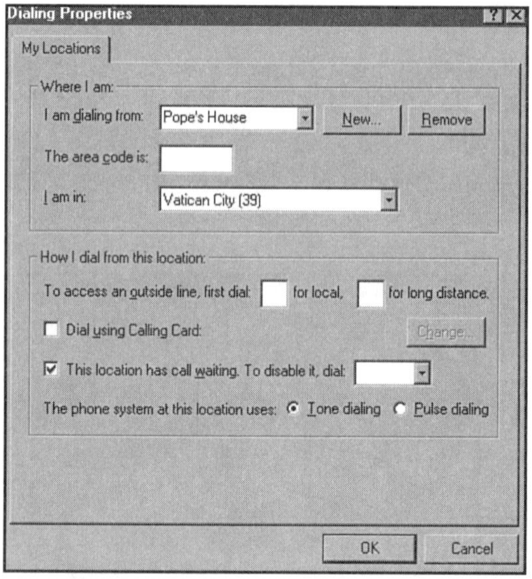

With this panel, you can specify a dialing location, such as Home or Office or you can leave the name as Default Location.

The other settings on this page are largely self-explanatory and include the following:

- **The area code is.** This is the area code from which you are calling.
- **I am in.** Here, select the country of the location from which you are calling. This selection (along with the area code) helps Windows 95 determine when special codes and prefixes are needed to dial long distance.
- **for local.** Here, specify the special accesses number, if any, that you must dial at this location to get an outside, local line. In many telephone systems, for example, you must dial a "9" to get an outside line.
- **for long distance.** This is for any special access number you may need to dial long distance. Note that this number is in addition to the "1" used to dial toll calls. Windows 95 automatically adds the "1" for long distance.
- **Dial using Calling Card.** If you select this option, Windows 95 displays a dialog box in which you can input calling card information.

- **This location has call waiting.** If your telephone system has call waiting, enable this option and provide the code needed to disable call waiting during data communications.
- **Tone dialing** and **Pulse dialing.** Here, select the correct dialing method for your telephone system.

After you have installed and properly configured your modem, you can use Windows 95 (or other communication programs) to remotely access a variety of systems.

Using Dial-Up Networking

One of the most useful features of Windows 95 is Dial-Up Networking. With this feature, you can create custom connections to other computers and then easily use those connections to quickly access other systems.

Setting Up the Remote System

You can access the Dial-Up Networking folder (see fig. 11.6) from the Start button by selecting Programs, then Accessories. On the Accessories list is the selection for Dial-Up Networking.

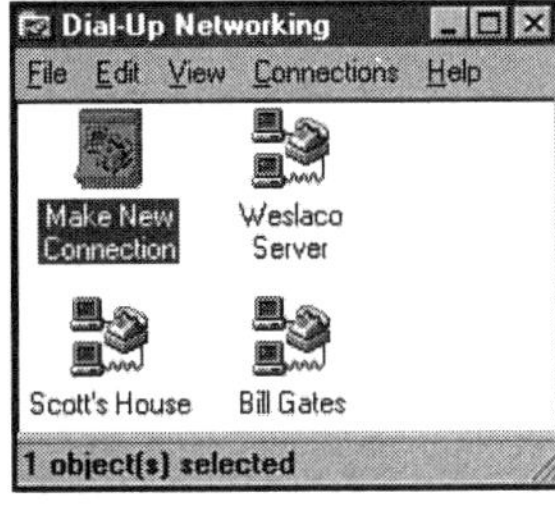

Figure 11.6

The Dial-Up Networking folder.

From this panel, double-click on the Make New Connection icon and a Windows 95 wizard will guide you through the process of creating a new connection. The steps are as follows:

1. Double-click on the Make New Connection icon in the Dial-Up Networking panel.
2. Type in the name for the new connection. (This name will appear with the icon for the connection in the Dial-Up Networking panel.)

3. If you have more than one modem, select the modem you want to use for this connection. (You can also reconfigure the modem from this panel, if necessary.)

4. Click on the Next button near the bottom of the panel. On the new panel that appears, fill in the area code and telephone number of the system to which you will connect, and then click on the Next button.

5. The next panel shows that you have completed creating a new connection. Click on the Finish button to accept the connection, and a new icon will appear on the Dial-Up Networking panel.

The next time you select Dial-Up Networking, the new connection will appear. Now, you can double-click the icon for the connection you want to use. For example, from the previous panel, double-clicking the Weslaco Server button causes the panel shown in figure 11.7 to appear.

Figure 11.7

A sample connection from Dial-Up Networking.

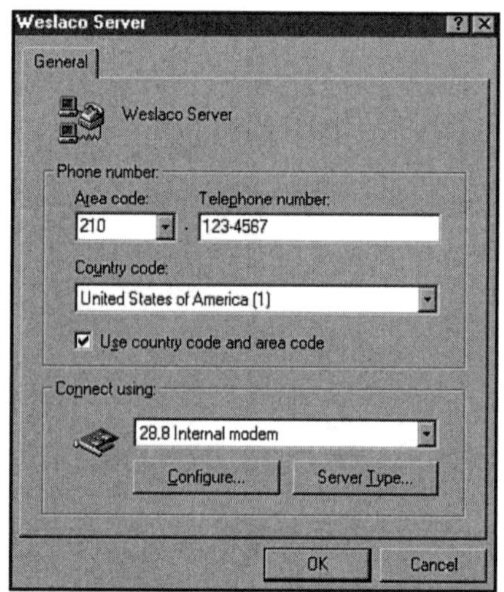

On this panel you confirm that the connection information is correct and enter a password, if necessary. Next, click on the Connect button to dial the remote computer.

Although most of the major online services (CompuServe, Prodigy, America Online, and so forth) have their own communications/interface software, you may want to create a connection to those services yourself, using the Dial-Up Networking options described previously. In addition, many services, such as private bulletin boards and your own local networks, have no such packaged software. Therefore, creating a connection using the Dial-Up Networking may be the best way to connect to those systems.

Setting Up Windows 95 as a Dial-Up Server

In addition to dialing out to other services, you can use Windows 95 to provide remote access and serve as a gateway to a local network, or simply allow other users to access your computer if you set it up as a dial-up server.

To use your PC as a gateway or dial-up server, be sure that you have configured Windows 95 with the following options. First, from the Control Panel, open the Passwords folder and, using the Remote Administration panel, select the Enable Remote Administration check box, and then enter the passwords for remote access to your PC.

Also from the Control Panel, open the Network selection and, from the Configuration panel, select File and Print Sharing and ensure that the appropriate boxes are selected.

Finally, double-click on the My Computer icon and open the Dial-Up Networking item. From here, choose the selection for Dial-Up Server. A panel similar to the one shown in figure 11.8 appears.

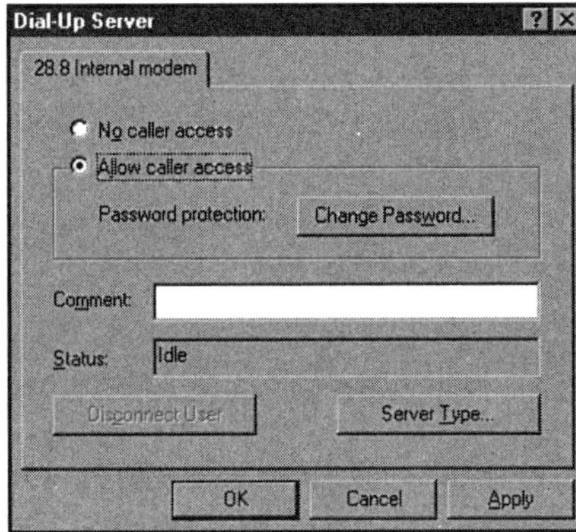

Figure 11.8

The Dial-Up Server property sheet showing that dial-in access to this PC is enabled.

After your Windows 95-based computer is properly configured, you can allow other users to access it just as you would access another system. You can allow file and/or printer sharing and access to any other resources to which your PC has access. If your PC is connected to a Windows 95-based network, another user with dial-up access to your PC can dial up your PC and use it as a gateway to that network.

For more information about using Windows 95 as a network, see Chapter 7, "Windows 95 as a Server."

Using Windows 95 as a Gateway to a Network

The aforementioned process of setting up a computer as a dial-in server enables remote LAN access if the computer is part of a network. Windows 95 enables remote network access not just to Windows 95-based networks, but also to other networks such as Novell NetWare, OS/2, and Windows NT. This gateway functionality is possible through the use of dial-up networking components and Windows 95 flexible network interfaces that are provided by the IFS and NDIS components of Windows 95.

The IFS (Installable File System) and NDIS version 3.1 (Network Driver Interface Specification) are 32-bit protected-mode components of Windows 95 that enable various concurrent network interfaces. The two popular client interfaces that come with Windows 95 are Client for Microsoft networks and Client for NetWare networks. These two client interfaces can both be installed at the same time.

Windows 95's flexibility to function as a NetWare or NT client enables the dial-up server to which the remote computer is dialing to provide network access to the remote computer dialing in. Depending on the level of access, the remote computer can have access to all of the NetWare and Windows NT resources available on the network, including CD-ROM drives and printers.

This remote connection to network resources is done through the normal Windows 95 procedures for connecting to shared resources.

Windows 95 also allows for remote administration of shared resources, depending on access level. This administration includes the ability to set up and remove users, change passwords, and change sharing options on any of the shared resources. Additionally, Windows 95 allows for the remote administration of printing on network printers. You can remotely hold, cancel, resume, and pause print jobs in a network queue.

Registry Editor

In some circumstances, you may need to exercise extensive control over the remote computer, including the remote computer's Registry. To be able to manipulate the registries from your remote location, you must first install the Remote Registry service. To do this, follow these steps.

1. Open the Network icon from the Control Panel.
2. Click on the Add Button in the Configuration tab.
3. In the Select Network Component Type dialog box, click on Service in the list box, and then click on the Add button.
4. In the Select Network Protocol dialog box that appears, click on the Have Disk button and enter the following path in the Install From Disk dialog box: **ADMIN\NETTOLS\REMOTREG**. Click on the OK button.
5. When the Select Network Service dialog box appears, click on the Microsoft Remote Registry in the Models list box.
6. Click on the OK button. Windows 95 copies and installs the appropriate files.
7. Click on the OK button to close the Network dialog box and update the settings. Windows 95 will prompt you to restart the computer.

You must install the Remote Registry service on both the remote and the local computers. These two computers must share at least one network protocol (such as IPX/SPX) in common.

After installing the Remote Registry service, you can connect to a remote registry using the Connect Network Registry item on the Registry Editor's Registry menu. Just enter the name of the computer in the dialog box that appears and click on the OK button.

Understanding Other Communications Programs

In addition to the options outlined above, you can use Windows 95 in conjunction with any of the commercially available communications programs (such as ProComm, ExecCom, and so forth) to access remote services. Each of these programs has unique features and interfaces, but all communications programs share common features and settings.

Windows 95 includes a communications program, called HyperTerminal, that you can also use to dial other services. This section explains some of the features of HyperTerminal and details settings that are useful even if you use another communications program.

Setting HyperTerminal Properties

To launch HyperTerminal, use the Start button to select Programs, then Accessories. Next, double-click on the folder for HyperTerminal. From the items that appear, double-click on the Hypertrm icon. After the startup screen, a Connection Description panel appears. If you choose Cancel, the main HyperTerminal window appears, as shown in figure 11.9. (Clicking OK allows you to create a new connection, as described elsewhere in this chapter.)

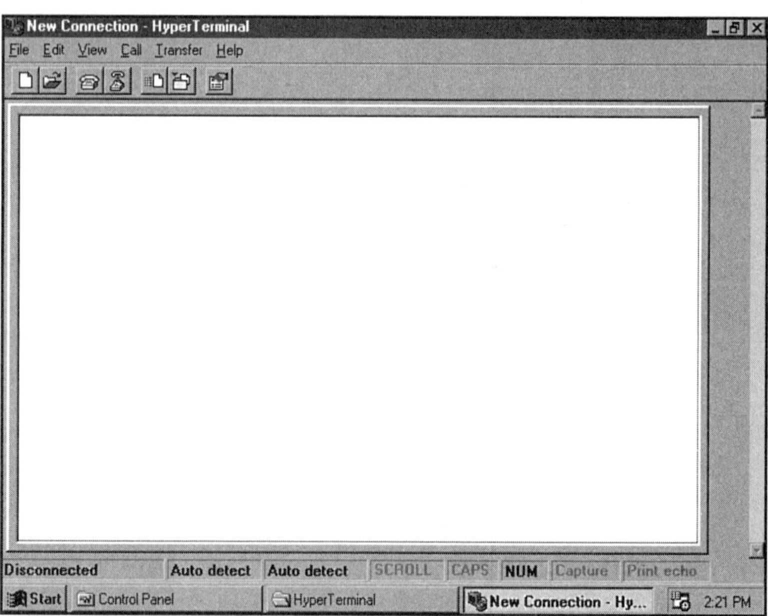

Figure 11.9
The HyperTerminal main window.

Most of the HyperTerminal settings are changed from the Properties page. Click File, then Properties to access the Properties page. From here, you can configure HyperTerminal's two Properties panels: Phone Number and Settings. Figure 11.10 shows the Phone Number panel.

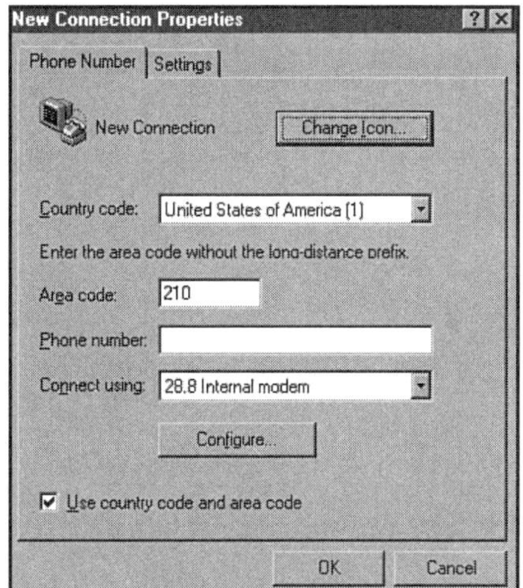

Figure 11.10

The Phone Number panel of the HyperTerminal Properties page.

On this panel, you can enter a telephone number for the connection, select an appropriate icon and, if necessary, configure the modem for this connection. (See the preceding sections for information on how to configure your modem.)

The second panel on the Properties sheet is the Settings panel (see fig. 11.11).

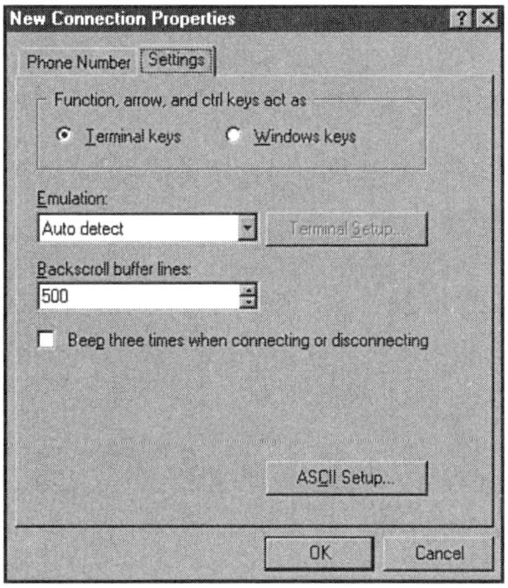

Figure 11.11

The Settings panel from the HyperTerminal Properties page.

The most important setting on this panel is the **E**mulation selection. Each computer or network that you will call expects a certain type of terminal emulation. HyperTerminal includes the most popular emulations as well as a useful feature called Auto detect. If you are unsure of the terminal emulation that the system you are calling uses, you should accept the Auto detect default and allow HyperTerminal to attempt to connect with the correct emulation.

The Settings panel also enables you to set the buffer for the number of lines that you may want to backscroll. This allows you to use the scroll bar to review lines that the terminal program has already received.

Other important settings are accessed from the ASCII Setup screen. To reach this panel, click on the ASCII Setup button; the panel shown in figure 11.12 appears.

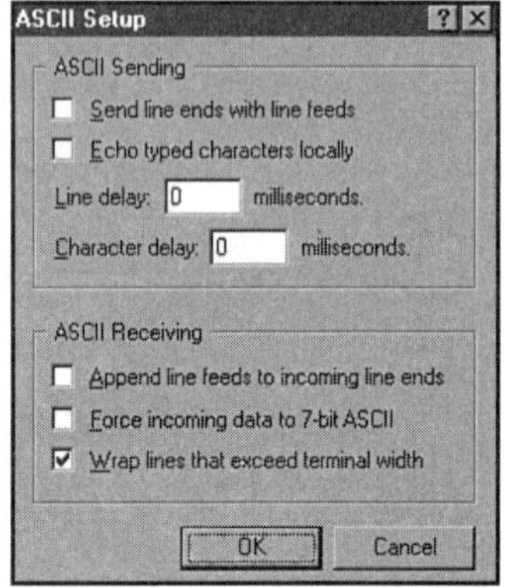

Figure 11.12
The ASCII Setup dialog box.

If you are having difficulties with the service to which you are connected (for example, double typing of characters, improper line wrap, and so forth), try changing these settings.

File Transfer Protocols

When you download (receive) a file from another system, or upload (send) a file to another system, the two computers involved must use the same transfer system, or *file transfer protocol.* There are several protocols in common use and, as with terminal emulation, you should verify the protocols available on the system you are using.

One of the most popular protocols today is called *Zmodem.* Zmodem offers many advantages: for example, it enables you to restart a file transfer that was previously interrupted without having to resend the entire file. This is especially useful if you do transfers of large files. Other popular protocols include Xmodem, Kermit, and Ymodem.

To initiate a file transfer in HyperTerminal, use the Transfer pull-down menu and select the appropriate option. If you want to receive a file from another system, use this menu and select Receive File to access the dialog box shown in figure 11.13.

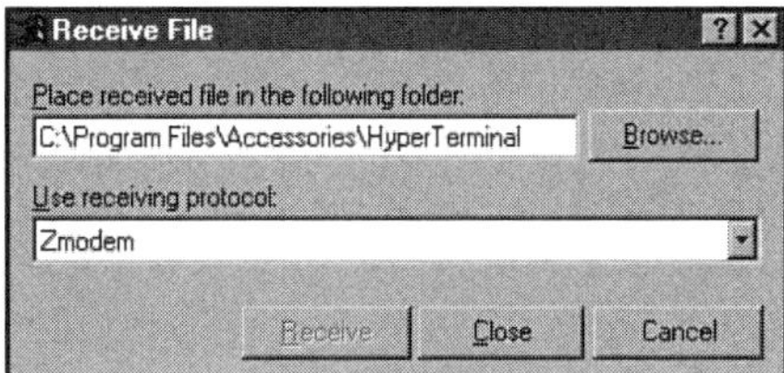

Figure 11.13

The Receive File dialog box.

With the Receive File dialog box, you can select the folder or directory into which you want the downloaded file placed. You can also select the file transfer protocol using the drop-down list box.

The process of sending a file to a computer that you are connected with is practically the same. If you want to send a file to another system, select **S**end File from the **T**ransfer menu. The dialog box that appears has a field for the path and file name that you are uploading and a field for the protocol that you are using.

Using the Windows 95 Phone Dialer

Windows 95 includes a useful accessory program called *Phone Dialer*, which enables you to use your computer to quickly dial phone numbers. You may find it helpful if you have certain numbers that you dial often, especially if you dial those numbers primarily while using your computer.

To access Phone Dialer, select Programs, then Accessories from the Start button. Next, double-click on the Phone Dialer icon and the Phone Dialer screen appears (see fig. 11.14).

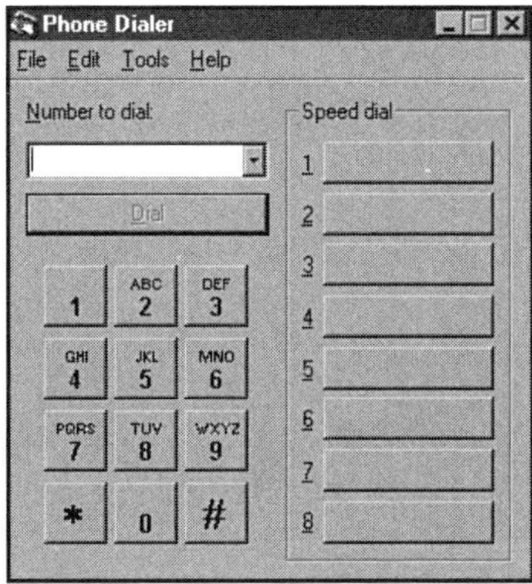

Figure 11.14

The Phone Dialer screen.

To dial a number manually, click on each number and verify that the correct numbers appear in the **N**umber to dial box at the top, and then click on **D**ial. As the computer dials, the dialog box shown in figure 11.15 appears. When the number begins to ring (or someone answers), pick up the receiver of your telephone and click on the **T**alk button. At any time while the dialing is in progress, you can choose **H**ang Up to terminate the call.

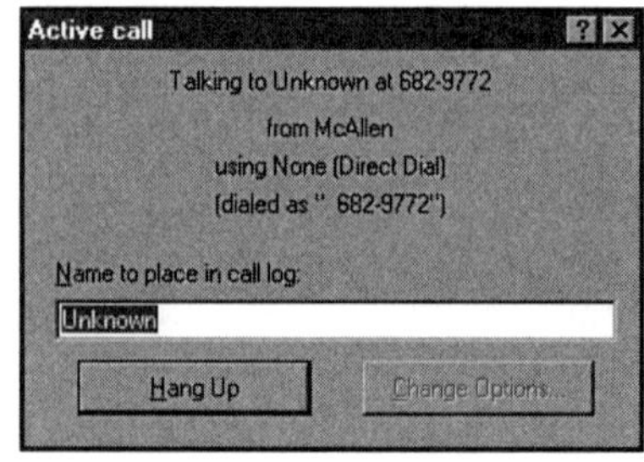

Figure 11.15

The dialog box that appears when you are on the phone.

Phone Dialer saves each number you dial. You can click the drop-down arrow on the **N**umber to dial box and select a number you have previously dialed, even if it does not appear in your speed dial list.

To enter a number in the Speed dial section of Phone Dialer, click on an empty button. Enter the name and number for the speed dial entry and choose **S**ave. The name for the speed dial entry appears on the button you selected. In the future, you can simply click that button to quickly dial the entered number.

Built-In Network Tools

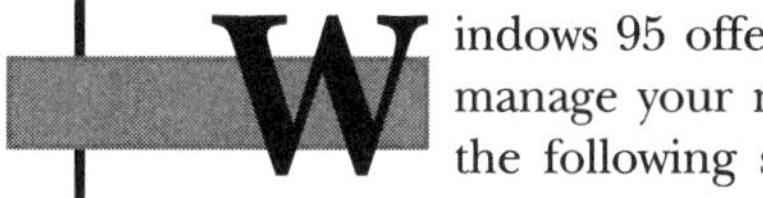

Windows 95 offers several software tools that enable you to manage your network more efficiently. These tools fall into the following seven categories:

- ◆ Control Panel resources
- ◆ Remote administration tools
- ◆ Password List Editor
- ◆ Network print services
- ◆ Network batch and scripting services
- ◆ Macintosh connectivity
- ◆ HOST and LMHOST

These tools are easy to use, but you have to remember that many of them do not install during a standard setup. Many of these tools are optional network services that you install using the Network icon in the Control Panel. Others are applications that you must install independently of the setup program. This chapter describes each of these tools, explains when you would want to use each tool, and shows how to install each one.

Throughout this chapter, you will be instructed to enter paths to various software programs. In every case, you need to be sure to include the appropriate disk drive in the path. In most cases, this will be your CD-ROM drive.

Using Control Panel Resources

After a typical setup of Windows 95, the Control Panel displays several tools that enable you to configure different aspects of a system's interaction with the network (see fig. 12.1). Two of these tools are always present on a system attached to a network: the Network icon and the Passwords icon. Two, the Mail and Fax icon and the Microsoft Mail Postoffice icon, are installed if the Microsoft Exchange and FAX services have been set up on the computer. Another, the Internet icon, is available only if the Microsoft Plus! pack has been installed. The subsequent sections describe how to use these Control Panel applications to configure your network.

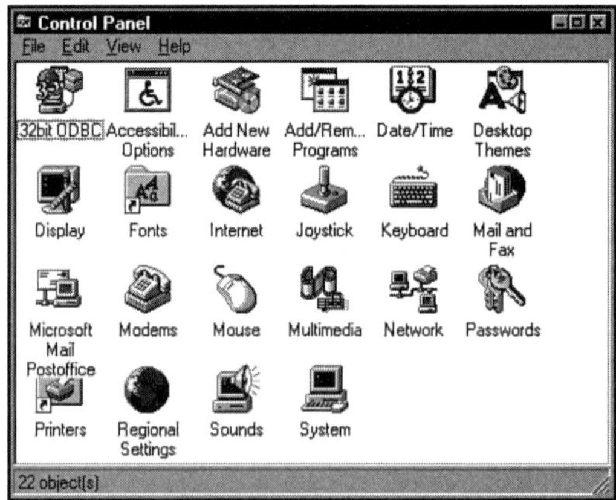

Figure 12.1
The Control Panel icons that configure network functions.

The Microsoft Plus! companion for Windows 95 is sold separately and requires a 486-based computer with 8 MB of RAM and a 256 color display.

The Network Icon

The Network icon, when activated, displays the Network dialog box, as shown in figure 12.2. This dialog box allows you to determine values for the following three types of settings:

- **Configuration** of network clients, adapters, protocols, and services
- **Identification** of the computer to the network
- **Access control** for the computer on the network

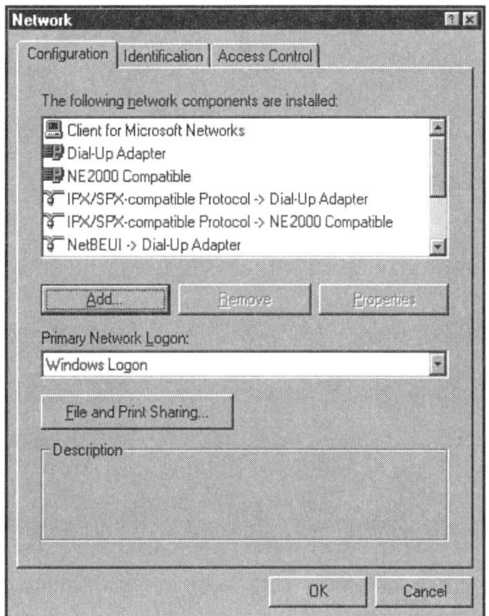

Figure 12.2

The Network dialog box, showing the Configuration tab.

On the Configuration tab, you can perform four activities. First, you can add or remove a network component. Removing a component is the easiest operation. Select the item in the The following network components are installed list box and click on the Remove button. Respond appropriately to the warning dialog boxes that appear, and the component will be removed.

To add a service, click on the Add button. Windows 95 displays the Select Network Component Type dialog box, which enables you to choose among clients, adapters, protocols, or services by selecting one of these items in a list box. Clicking on the Add button after selecting an item from the list displays the Select dialog box for the type of component you chose. (The actual title of the dialog box includes the name of the item you selected—for example, Select Network Client.) These Select dialog boxes present two list boxes, one displaying Manufacturers and the other displaying the items that you can install produced by that manufacturer. Figure 12.3 shows the Select Network Client dialog box, which gives you a sense of how the process works.

After selecting a manufacturer in the Manufacturers list box, you select a client in the Network Clients list box. If your chosen manufacturer or product does not appear on the list and you have a floppy disk or CD containing the Windows 95 (or DOS) drivers for the product, clicking on the **H**ave Disk button displays a standard Browse dialog box that enables you to select the item from the disk. After you have selected the correct item, clicking on the OK button causes Windows 95 to copy the appropriate files to the hard drive and to update the Registry. You might have to restart the computer to complete installation, in which case Windows 95 prompts you to do so.

Figure 12.3
The Select Network Client dialog box.

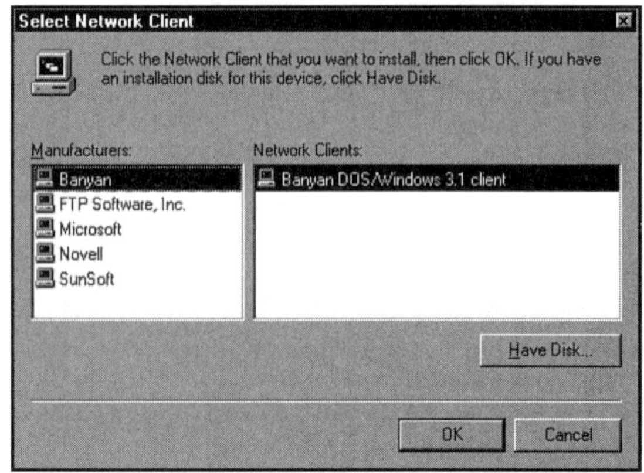

Using DOS device drivers for a network component inevitably degrades system performance. Use them only as a last resort, and call the manufacturer to insist that they provide Windows 95 drivers.

The second task you can perform on the Configuration tab is setting the properties for a network component. To set properties, select a component in the The following **n**etwork components are installed list box and then click on the **P**roperties button. A property sheet unique to the component is displayed, such as the one shown in figure 12.4. Each property sheet includes a Bindings tab and an Advanced tab. Use the Bindings tab to set the network bindings for the component by checking the appropriate check boxes presented on the tab. Use the Advanced tab to determine the settings that the manufacturer considered more advanced than the average user should be concerned about. Use other tabs to determine settings unique to the device. Clicking on the OK button confirms the settings you made in the tabs.

The third task you can perform in the Configuration tab is determining the primary network logon. This is the network the user logs on to by default. A list of available networks is presented in the Primary Network **L**ogon drop-down list box. Select the network to which the user needs to log on when the operating system starts by choosing an item in the list box.

The fourth task you can perform in the Configuration tab is determining whether files and printers attached to the computer can be shared over the network. To make these settings, click on the **F**ile and Print Sharing button. The File and Print Sharing dialog box appears, presenting two check boxes that enable you to share files or printers. Check either or both depending on your needs for this computer.

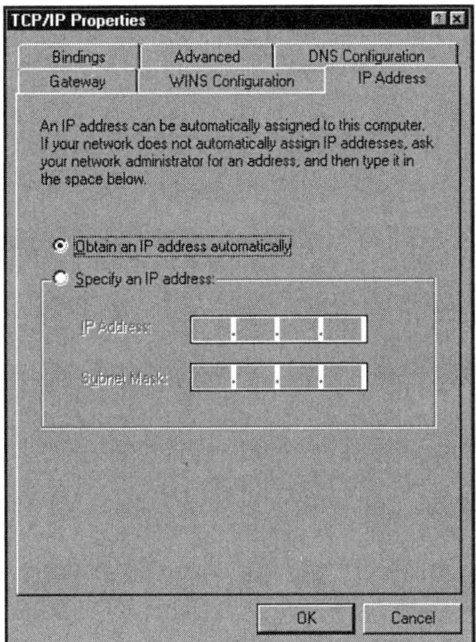

Figure 12.4

The property sheet for the TCP/IP protocol.

Allowing file and print sharing does not mean that files and printers are actually shared. The actual sharing is set in the property sheet associated with the file, folder, or printer to be shared.

The remaining two tabs in the Network dialog box enable you to perform two very straightforward tasks. On the Identification tab, you describe how the computer identifies itself to the network. This tab contains three text boxes that enable you to enter the computer name, the workgroup name, and the computer description that the network uses to identify the computer both internally and to other network users (see fig. 12.5). Fill in these text boxes with the appropriate strings for the computer.

The Access Control tab presents two option buttons that permit you to determine how other computers get access to the resources shared by the computer you are configuring. Figure 12.6 shows the Access Control tab. Set share-level access control by selecting the **S**hare-level access control button. Under this control scheme, you can supply a password for each shared resource. Anyone knowing the password can get access to the resource. Set user-level access control by selecting the **U**ser-level access control button. In this case, Windows 95 seeks the user information in a security provider, which basically is a server running a network operating system like NetWare or Windows NT. The network operating system, rather than Windows 95, enforces user-level security.

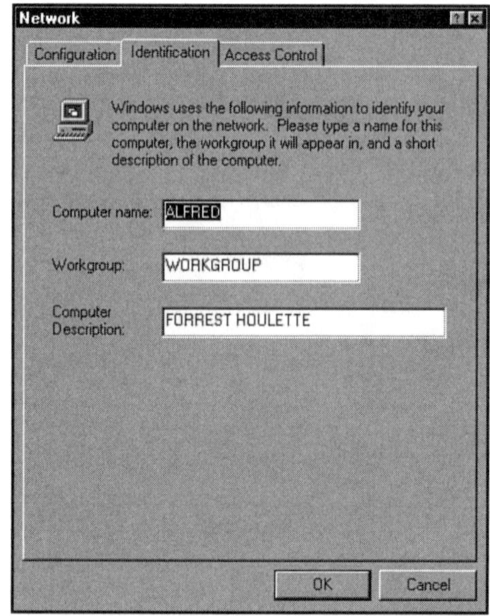

Figure 12.5

The Identification tab in the Network dialog box.

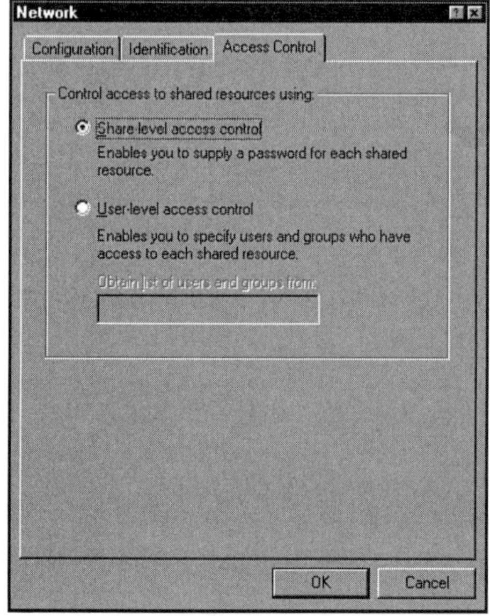

Figure 12.6

The Access Control tab in the Network dialog box.

The Passwords Icon

The Passwords icon in the Control Panel enables you to perform two tasks relevant to networking. First, you can set passwords for a particular user on the computer you are configuring. You set passwords using the Change Passwords tab in the Passwords Properties dialog box that the Passwords icon activates (see fig. 12.7). You can change passwords either for access to the computer itself or for any password-protected service the computer accesses. Clicking on either password-changing button presents a standard password dialog box in which the new password is entered and confirmed.

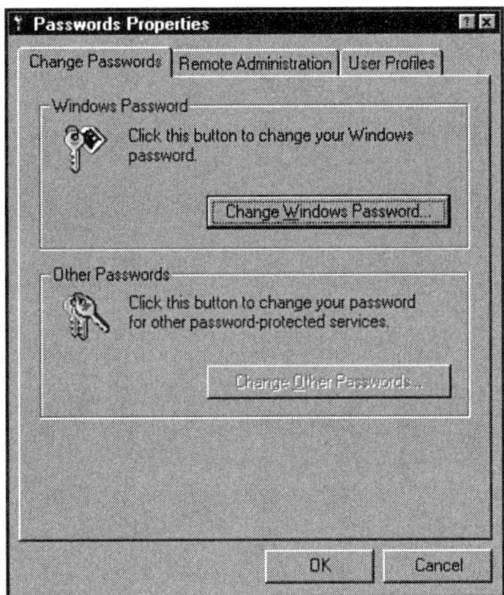

Figure 12.7

The Change Passwords tab in the Passwords Properties dialog box.

The second networking setting available from the Passwords icon allows you to configure the computer for remote administration. To enable or disable remote administration, select the Remote Administration tab, shown in figure 12.8. Check or clear the **E**nable Remote Administration of this server check box to enable or disable this service. If you are enabling this service, enter and confirm the password for remote administration of the server in the text boxes provided.

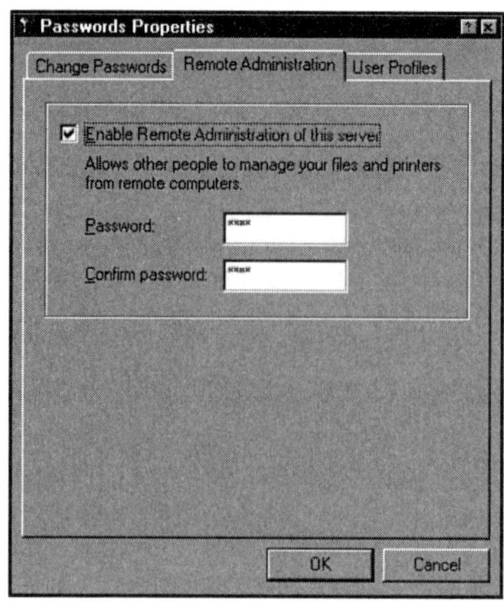

Figure 12.8
The Remote Administration tab in the Passwords Properties dialog box.

The Internet Icon

If you have installed the Microsoft Plus! pack, your Control Panel displays the Internet icon. Activating this icon displays the Internet Properties dialog box, which enables you to configure how your computer accesses the Internet. If access is provided through a local modem dialing out to an Internet service provider, then Internet access is not a networking issue per se, except for arranging security. If Internet access is provided through the LAN to the workstations on the LAN, however, you need to identify the Internet proxy server that provides such access to the local computer. You perform this task using the Advanced tab in the Internet Properties dialog box (see fig. 12.9).

To enable the use of a proxy server from this workstation, check the **U**se Proxy Server check box. Type the address and port number of the proxy server in the **P**roxy Server text box. In the **B**ypass proxy on text box, enter the names of any Internet servers on your LAN (like your Web home page server) that you do not want accessed through the proxy server, but prefer to have accessed directly through the LAN. Use the following syntax for each item, separating items with a comma:

```
writenv.com,:70
```

This line informs this computer and the proxy server to access the server writenv.com on port 70 directly.

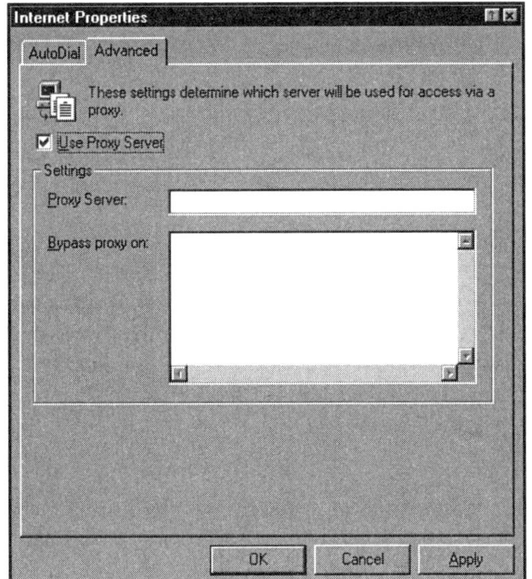

Figure 12.9

The Advanced tab in the Internet Properties dialog box.

The Mail and Fax Icon

The Control Panel's Mail and Fax icon enables you to configure the information services to which the computer can attach. Activating the icon causes Windows 95 to display the configuration dialog box for the currently active user profile. Figure 12.10, for example, shows the dialog box for the user Forrest, displaying the window title Forrest Properties.

Figure 12.10

The properties dialog box for user profile Forrest.

Many of the information services that can be configured using the Mail and Fax icon might have nothing to do with the network; however, several might. The list box in figure 12.10, for example, shows the Microsoft Network Online Service, which users might access through a local modem. Use of this service may not involve the attached LAN at all. Microsoft Mail and the Personal Information Store associated with Microsoft Exchange also show up, however, both of which involve LAN traffic.

The Services tab in the Properties dialog box allows you to add, remove, copy, and display properties for services. To add a service, click on the Add button. The Add Service to Profile dialog box appears, containing a list of available services to choose from. Select the service you desire and click on the OK button. Windows 95 scans its disks or CD for the files and copies them. Alternately, if the service is not listed and you have a manufacturer's disk containing drivers, click on the Have Disk button and use the Browse dialog box to locate the files to copy.

Removing a service is a matter of selecting the service in the list box and clicking on the Remove button. Copying a service is similar. Select the service, click on the Copy button, select the user profile to serve as copy destination in the list box of the Copy Information Service dialog box, and click on the OK button. To display the properties for a service, select it in the list box and click on the Properties button. A service-specific dialog box appears, enabling you to select from the available settings for the service.

If you need to see a list of available user profiles, click on the Show Profiles button in the Services tab.

The Delivery tab (see fig. 12.11) enables you to specify the destination for incoming messages. You can select a primary and a secondary destination using the Deliver new mail to the following location and Secondary location drop-down list boxes. You can determine the order in which the installed services process recipient addresses by using the list box at the bottom of the tab. To change the order of processes, select a service and use the arrow buttons to the right to move it higher or lower in the list. In this way, you can optimize the processing of recipient addresses on messages received by the user on this computer. The most frequently used service should process the address first.

The Addressing tab (see fig. 12.12) enables you to determine where users store addresses and which addresses are displayed by default in the Microsoft Exchange. Select the default address list for display using the Show this address list first drop-down list box. Select the address book for storing personal addresses using the Keep personal addresses in drop-down list box. You can determine the order in which address books are checked for names using the list box at the bottom of the tab. Use the arrow buttons to the right to move the selected service up or down the list. The most frequently used address book should appear first on the list.

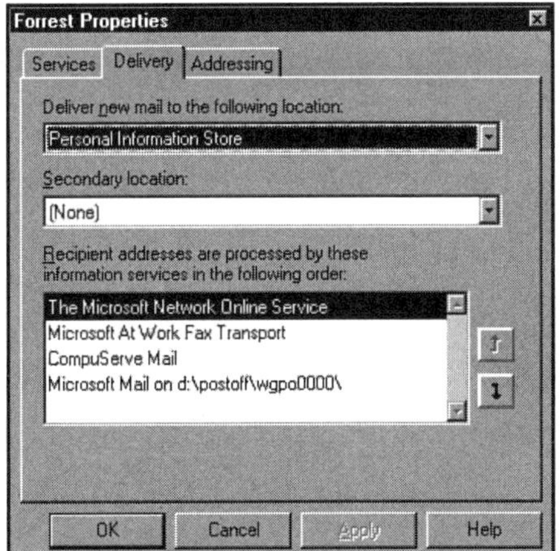

Figure 12.11

The Delivery tab in the properties dialog box for user Forrest.

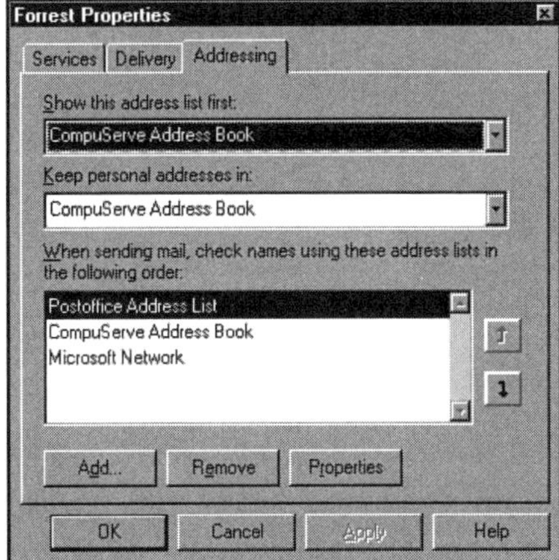

Figure 12.12

The Addressing tab in the properties dialog box for user Forrest.

The Microsoft Mail Postoffice Icon

When you double-click on the Microsoft Mail Postoffice icon, you start the Microsoft Workgroup Postoffice Admin wizard. This wizard guides you through either creating or updating a postoffice on your network. You determine which action you take by selecting between two option buttons in the initial wizard screen (see fig. 12.13). To create a new postoffice, select the Create a new Workgroup Postoffice option and click on the Next button. Specify an existing directory in which to create the postoffice on the next screen of the wizard. Click on Next and review the information the wizard presents about the location of the new postoffice. Click on the Next button to confirm the creation of the new postoffice. In the dialog box that appears, enter the information for the administrator of the postoffice. The most critical matters are the name of the administrator and the administrator's password. Clicking on the OK button causes Windows 95 to create the postoffice in the directory you specified.

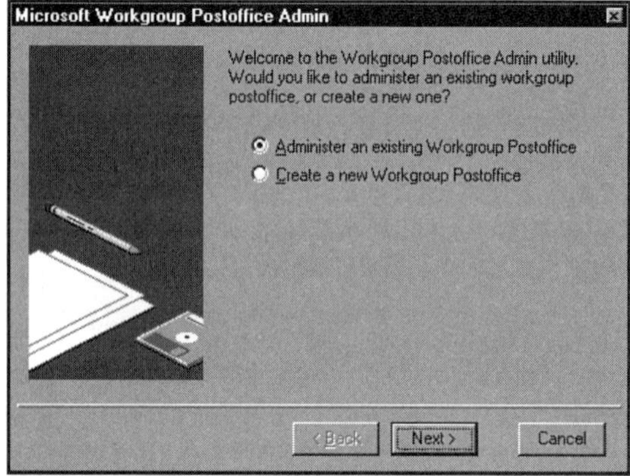

Figure 12.13
The first page of the Microsoft Workgroup Postoffice Admin wizard.

To administer an existing postoffice, select the **A**dminister an existing Workgroup Postoffice button on the first page of the wizard and click on the Next button. Select the location of the postoffice on the next wizard screen, click on the Next button, enter the name of the administrator's mailbox and the administrator's password, and click on the Next button again. You will then see the Postoffice Manager dialog box, shown in figure 12.14. Click on the **D**etails button to reveal the information kept on file for the selected postoffice user. Click on the **A**dd User button to bring up the Add User dialog box, which allows you to fill in the detail information for a new user. Click on the **R**emove User button to remove a user.

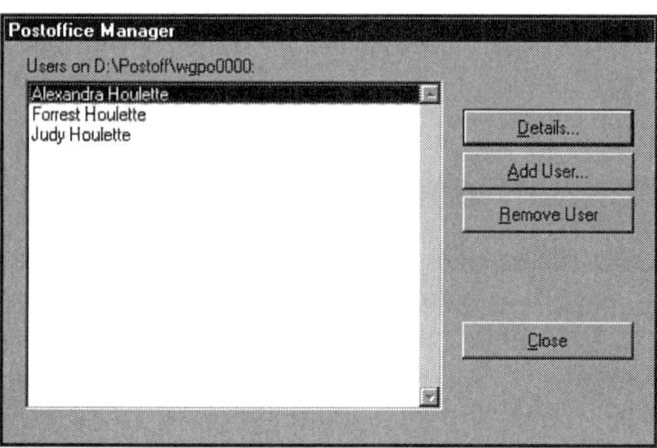

Figure 12.14
The Postoffice Manager dialog box.

In many operations involving the postoffice, you will either view or edit user information. You do so using a dialog box of the type shown in figure 12.15; this dialog box changes titles in its different appearances, but the text boxes remain the same. The information kept on file for any user includes the user's name, mailbox name, and password. In addition, you can keep two phone numbers, the user's office and department, and any informational notes you need.

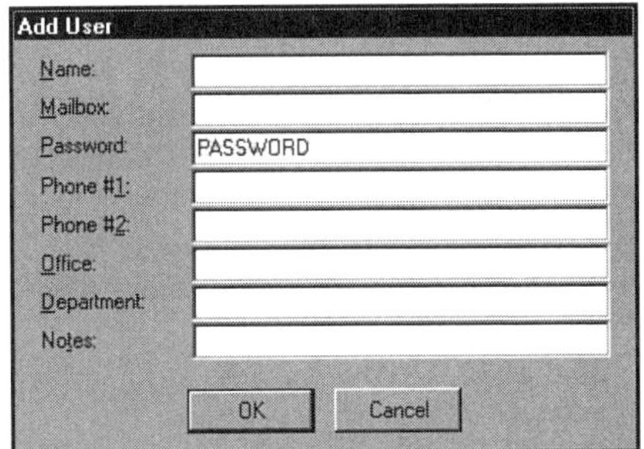

Figure 12.15
The Add User dialog box for administering a postoffice.

Working with Remote Administration Tools

Although understanding how to configure individual machines is important, especially when you are sitting at a computer that must be configured, remote administration is even more critical to managing a network. Network administrators cannot be everywhere at once. Logging on to computers distant from your office to undertake administrative tasks is not just a convenience; on a large network, it is a necessity. Fortunately, Windows 95 provides you with a variety of tools that assist in remote administration. These are described in the next eight sections.

Tip Be sure to enable remote administration when you initially set up each individual machine.

Network Monitor Agent

Windows 95 provides the Network Monitor Agent and protocol driver on the CD. The protocol driver and related executable file enable you to monitor traffic statistics for NDIS 3.1 compliant protected-mode network adapters. You can use this protocol and software to monitor traffic not only on LANs and WANs, but also on the Microsoft Remote Access Server. If you need to troubleshoot network problems, this software is particularly useful.

The Network Monitor Agent is also provided as a component in the Microsoft Systems Management Server, a separate retail network management tool.

You can install the Network Monitor Agent in one of two ways. The first way is to install both the agent and the protocol driver, in which case you plan to use the agent to monitor network traffic and to conduct troubleshooting. To perform this type of installation, follow these steps:

1. Open the Network icon in the Control Panel.
2. Click on the Add button in the Configuration tab.
3. In the Select Network Component Type dialog box, click on Service in the list box, then click on the Add button.
4. In the Select Network Service dialog box that appears, click on the Have Disk button and enter the following path in the Install From Disk dialog box: **ADMIN\NETTOOLS\NETMON**. Click on the OK button.
5. When the Select Network Service dialog box reappears, click on the Microsoft Network Monitor agent.
6. Click on the OK button. Windows 95 copies and installs the appropriate files.
7. Click on OK to close the Network dialog box and update the settings. Windows 95 will prompt you to restart the computer.

The other method is to install only the protocol driver, in which case you use the System Monitor application to monitor network performance. To install only the protocol driver, use the following steps:

1. Open the Network icon in the Control Panel.
2. Click on the Add button in the Configuration tab.
3. In the Select Network Component Type dialog box, click on Protocol in the list box, then click on the Add button.
4. In the Select Network Protocol dialog box that appears, click on the Have Disk button and enter the following path in the Install From Disk dialog box: **ADMIN\NETTOOLS\NETMON**. Click on the OK button.
5. When the Select Network Protocol dialog box reappears, click on the Microsoft Network Monitor agent in the Models list box.

6. Click on the OK button. Windows 95 copies and installs the appropriate files.

7. Click on OK to close the Network dialog box and update the settings. Windows 95 will prompt you to restart the computer.

The Network Monitor Agent can be run either as a service or as an executable file. To run it as a service, follow these steps:

1. Using the Registry Editor, select Hkey_Local_Machine\Software\Microsoft\Windows\CurrentVersion\RunServicesOnce.

2. Open the Edit menu, select New, and then select String Value.

3. Enter a value for the label name. You could use "nm_agent," for example.

4. Select the string value you just created, open the Edit menu, and click on Modify.

5. In the Value Data text box of the Edit String text box, enter **NMAGENT.EXE**.

6. Click on the OK button and exit the Registry Editor.

You can run the Network Monitor Agent as an executable file by clicking on the Start button and selecting the Run option. Enter **NMAGENT.EXE** in the Run dialog box and click on the OK button. The agent starts operation.

If you ever need to stop the Network Monitor Agent, click on the start button and select Run. Enter **NMAGENT-CLOSE** in the dialog box and click on OK. The agent stops operation in response to this command.

Network Backup Agents

If you use network backup software provided by either Arcada (Backup Exec) or Cheyenne (ARCServe), you can use the backup agents provided with Windows 95 to allow backup of individual workstations. To enable such backups, you must first install the agents on each workstation, which you may do during setup or from the Network icon in the Control Panel. To install the agents from the Control Panel, take these steps:

1. Open the Network icon in the Control Panel.

2. Click on the Add button in the Configuration tab.

3. In the Select Network Component Type dialog box, click on Service in the list box, then click on the Add button.

4. In the Select Network Service dialog box that appears, click on the manufacturer in the **M**anufacturers list box (either Arcada or Cheyenne) and the appropriate backup agent in the Network services list box.

5. Click on the OK button.

6. When the Select Network Service dialog box reappears, click on the SNMP agent in the Models list box.

7. Click on the OK button. Windows 95 copies and installs the appropriate files.

8. Click on OK to close the Network dialog box and update the settings. Windows 95 will prompt you to restart the computer.

Each backup agent must be configured to perform the operations you desire. While the Network icon is still open, select the Configuration tab and select the backup agent in the list box. Click on the **P**roperties button to display the property sheet for the agent. For both agents, it is important to set the controls to enable network backup, to determine whether the registry for the computer is backed up, and to set an appropriate password. In addition, these property sheets allow you to select the folders that will be backed up, and some other agent-specific features.

System Policy Editor

You can use the System Policy Editor to control the network settings for an individual workstation and to manage these settings remotely. The System Policy Editor does not install automatically during a standard setup, so you might have to copy it from the \ADMIN\APPTOOLS\POLEDIT directory of the CD to the Windows 95 directory. After you start the System Policy Editor, to configure network policies, make use of the keys under the Network branch of the policy tree for any user, computer, or group. These keys consist of check boxes that can be checked (the policy is in force), unchecked (the policy is not in force), or grayed (the setting is ignored by Windows 95). Figure 12.16 shows sample settings under the network branch for a computer.

To manage a computer's policies remotely, make certain you have the privileges to do so. Then open the **F**ile menu, select Connect, and enter the name of the remote computer in the dialog box that appears. Clicking on the OK button connects you to the Registry on that computer and enables you to set the policies.

The title bar of the System Policy Editor tells you whether you are connected to a local or to a remote Registry.

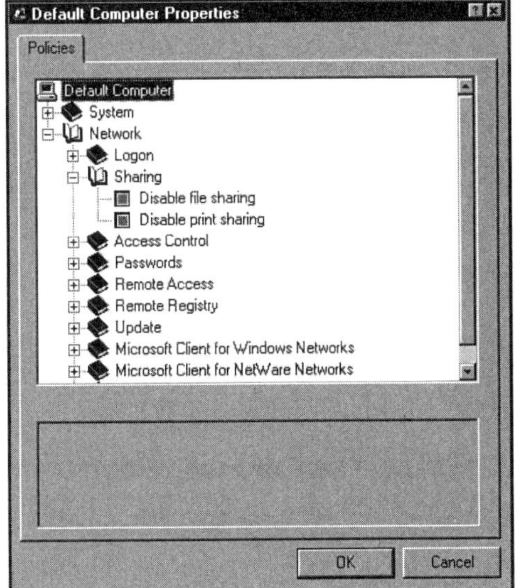

Figure 12.16

The set of network policies for a computer in the System Policy Editor.

Registry Editor

If you need to have complete control over a remote computer's Registry, you should access that computer using the Registry Editor. (You can use the System Policy Editor to manage a Remote Registry, but you get access to only a subset of the keys.) To be able to manage Registries from a remote location, you need to install the Remote Registry Service. To do so, follow these steps:

1. Open the Network icon in the Control Panel.
2. Click on the Add button in the Configuration tab.
3. In the Select Network Component Type dialog box, click on Service in the list box, then click on the Add button.
4. In the Select Network Protocol dialog box that appears, click on the Have Disk button and enter the following path in the Install From Disk dialog box: **ADMIN\NETTOOLS\REMOTREG**. Click on the OK button.
5. When the Select Network Service dialog box reappears, click on the Microsoft Remote Registry in the Models list box.
6. Click on the OK button. Windows 95 copies and installs the appropriate files.
7. Click on OK to close the Network dialog box and update the settings. Windows 95 will prompt you to restart the computer.

You must install the Remote Registry Service on both the administrative and the local computers. These two computers must share at least one network protocol in common. After installing the Remote Registry Service, you can connect to a remote registry using the Connect Network Registry item on the Registry Editor's Registry menu. Just enter the name of the computer in the dialog box that appears and click on the OK button.

For more information on remotely managing the Registry Editor, see Chapter 11, "Remote Access and Management."

System Monitor

Like the Registry Editor and the System Policy Editor, the System Monitor application can be used to monitor several computers operating over a network. Using this technique, you can view performance statistics for multiple LAN nodes to diagnose performance bottlenecks and other problems. To view multiple nodes, you must use multiple instances of the System Monitor. To connect to a remote computer from one instance, use the Connect option on the File menu. Enter the name of the computer to connect to in the Connect dialog box and click on the OK button.

SNMP Agent

If your network uses Simple Network Management Protocol (SNMP) to provide management services, you can use the SNMP agent provided with Windows 95 to facilitate managing Windows 95 computers attached to the LAN. Once installed, this agent makes Windows 95 computers visible to your SNMP console.

1. Open the Network icon in the Control Panel.
2. Click on the Add button in the Configuration tab.
3. In the Select Network Component Type dialog box, click on Service in the list box, then click on the Add button.
4. In the Select Network Service dialog box that appears, click on the Have Disk button and enter the following path in the Install From Disk dialog box: **ADMIN\NETTOOLS\SNMP**. Click on the OK button.

You configure the SNMP agent by editing system policies using one of three methods. You can open the System Policy Editor and edit the policies shown in table 12.1. Double-click the entry for the computer (or create one and then double-click on it). Under the Network branch in the tree, select the SNMP branch. Check each appropriate box and click on the Show button to launch the dialog box that enables you to add entries for each policy.

The System Policy Editor is the easiest and safest way to configure the SNMP agent.

Table 12.1
System Policies to Set for the SNMP Agent

Policy	What to Set
Communities	Add the host or group of hosts that may query this SNMP agent. These are the hosts that may administer the SNMP agent.
Permitted Managers	Add the IPX or IP addresses of the consoles that may display information about this computer.
Traps to Public Community	Add the IPX or IP addresses of hosts in the public community to which traps should be sent.
Internet MIB (RFC 1156)	Add the contact name and location for Internet MIB.

You can also edit the Registry to set these policies. To do so, open the Registry Editor and follow these steps:

1. Select the key Hkey_Local_Machine\System\CurrentControlSet\Services\SNMP\Parameters\TrapConfiguration.
2. Open the Edit menu, select the New item, and then the Key item on the cascading menu.
3. Enter the name for the new community, and then press Enter.
4. Open the Edit menu, select the New item, and then the String Value item on the cascading menu. Enter a Value Name of **1** in the name edit field that appears in the right-hand pane. Press Enter.
5. Select the new name in the right-hand pane, open the Edit menu, and select the Modify item.
6. In the Edit String dialog box that appears, enter the IPX or IP address for the SNMP console to which traps should be sent. Click on the OK button.
7. Repeat steps 4, 5, and 6 for each SNMP console you want traps sent to.
8. Exit the Registry Editor.

You also can configure the SNMP agent by editing the Admin.adm file stored in the \WIN95\INF directory. To do so, follow these steps:

1. Open the Admin.adm file with your favorite text editor.

2. Locate the section titled CATEGORY !!SNMP.

3. Add an entry for the new policy name and new community name, using this template:

```
POLICY "Name Of New Policy"
       KEYNAME
       System\CurrentControlSet\Services\SNMP\Parameters
                             \TrapConfiguration\Name Of New Community
       PART !!Traps_PublicListbox LISTBOX
              VALUEPREFIX ""
       END PART
END POLICY
```

4. Save the file and exit your text editor.

Network Neighborhood

In the Network Neighborhood folder, you can take certain administrative actions for the computers shown. When you right-click on any computer's icon and select Properties from the context menu, you are shown the dialog box in figure 12.17.

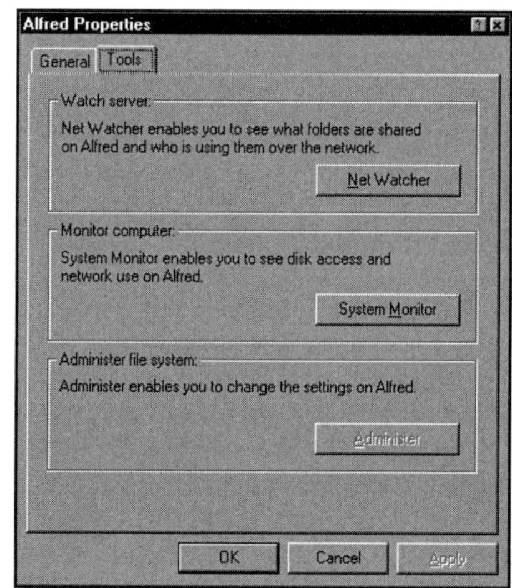

Figure 12.17

The property sheet for a computer in the Network Neighborhood.

The buttons in this dialog box allow you to take the following actions:

- Click the Net Watcher button to access the Net Watcher application. From this application, you can view and manage shared resources on the computer.
- Click on the System Monitor button to start the System Monitor application, which allows you to view performance statistics for the computer.
- Click on the Administer button to access the remote computer's hard disk for administration tasks.

Net Watcher

The Net Watcher application enables you to view shared resources on network computers and to perform certain actions in relation to these resources. The Net Watcher window shows you three types of resources, connections, shared folders, and open files (see fig. 12.18). Which one you view is selectable from the View menu or by clicking buttons on the toolbar. The actions you can take are disconnecting a user, closing a file, adding shared folders, stopping the share of a folder, and setting shared folder properties. All of these actions are selectable from the Administer menu or by clicking buttons on the toolbar.

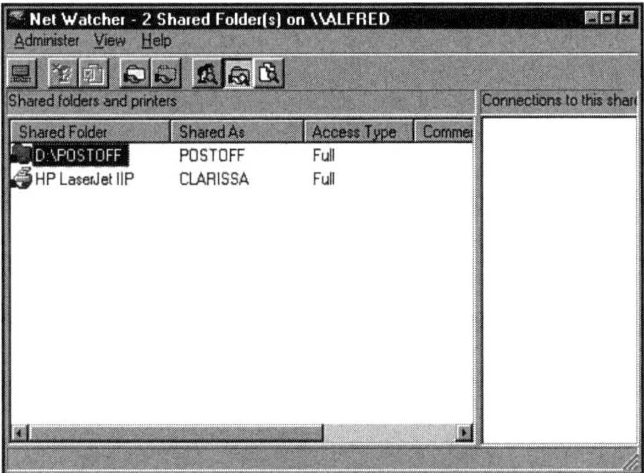

Figure 12.18

The Net Watcher window.

To connect to a remote computer to view shared resources and conduct remote administration, certain conditions must be met. First, the remote computer must have file and printer sharing enabled. Second, your computer must be running at least share-level security. On NetWare networks, two limitations apply. You can connect only to other computers that have enabled file and printer sharing for NetWare networks, and you cannot close files on remote computers.

Using the Password List Editor

Windows 95 uses Pwl files to store lists of resources and their related passwords. So long as a password list file is unlocked, you can edit it using the Password List Editor. You must install the editor first, however, because it is not installed in the normal setup for Windows 95. To install the Password List Editor, follow these steps:

1. Open the Control Panel.
2. Open the Add/Remove Programs icon, select the Windows Setup tab, and then click on the **H**ave Disk button.
3. When the Install From Disk dialog box appears, click on the **B**rowse button. Enter the path to **ADMIN\APPTOOLS\PWLEDIT\PWLEDIT.INF**, and then click OK.
4. In the Have Disk dialog box, click Password List Editor in the list box, and then click **I**nstall. Windows 95 copies the appropriate files to your disk.

After you have installed the Password List Editor, running it presents a window that contains a list of all the password protected services the computer accesses (see fig. 12.19). You cannot add resources or edit the actual passwords. You can, however, remove such services from a particular user's profile. Select the service in the list box and click on the **R**emove button.

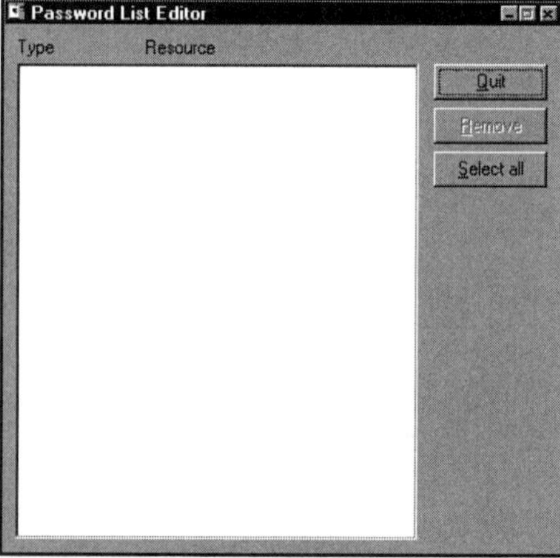

Figure 12.19

The Password List Editor.

Using Network Print Services

Windows 95 makes sharing printers across a network easy. You simply allow sharing using the Sharing tab in the property sheet associated with the printer. Right-clicking on the printer's icon, selecting Properties from the pop-up menu, and selecting the appropriate options in the Sharing tab is all you need to do. On heterogeneous networks, however, special problems can arise. Windows 95 has several tools that provide solutions to these problems. The next three sections describe these printing services.

Print Services for NetWare

Included on the Windows 95 CD is the utility Microsoft Print Services for NetWare, which allows a computer running Windows 95 to despool print jobs from a NetWare print server. The required hardware is a computer running Windows 95 with a local printer installed, a NetWare file server servicing the Windows 95 computer, and a dedicated MS-DOS print server running PSERVER. This configuration is illustrated in the diagram shown in figure 12.20.

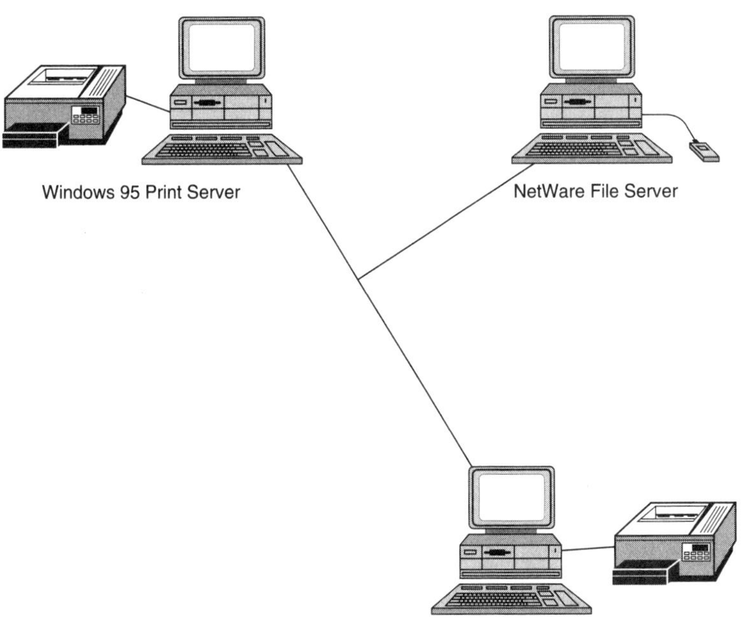

Figure 12.20

The hardware requirements and topology for Microsoft Print Services for NetWare.

Print Services for NetWare is a background utility that requires no resources except the minimal overhead necessary for polling the queue managed by the print server. To minimize the impact on the Windows 95 system, you can determine the polling rate. Print Services uses NetWare's Queue Management Services API to interact with the print server. The utility, when enabled, attaches to the print queue, receiving a handle that identifies it to the operating systems involved. The print server, when polled, returns a header that describes how to carry out the print job, including information such as whether to include a banner and the number of copies to print. After receiving the header, Print Services for NetWare reads the data to be printed from the print server queue and uses the Windows 95 API to print the job. On completion of the print job, the utility informs the print server that the job is finished by returning a function call.

Windows 95 allows the NetWare client to use only three ports.

To install Microsoft Print Services for NetWare, follow these steps:

1. Open the Network icon in the Control Panel.
2. Click on the **A**dd button in the Configuration tab.
3. In the Select Network Component Type dialog box, click on Service in the list box, then click on the **A**dd button.
4. In the Select Network Service dialog box that appears, click on the **H**ave Disk button and enter the following path in the Install From Disk dialog box: **ADMIN\NETTOOLS\PRTAGENT**.
5. Click on the OK button. Windows 95 copies and installs the appropriate files.

To enable Microsoft Print Services for NetWare, follow these steps:

1. Make certain that the MS-DOS computer running PSERVER is running and properly configured as a print server.
2. Open the Printers folder using the **P**rinters option from **S**ettings menu on the Start button.
3. Right-click the printer that will service the queue and select P**r**operties from the pop-up menu. Select the Print Server tab in the property sheet.
4. Select the **E**nable Microsoft Print Server for NetWare option button.
5. Use the **N**etWare Server drop-down list box to select the NetWare server that owns the print queue.

6. Use the Print Server drop-down list box to select the correct print server for the queue.

If you do not see the file server or the print server in the drop-down list boxes, make certain you have access privileges to both.

7. Adjust the time interval for polling the print server using the Polling slider control.
8. Click on either the OK or Apply button.

Hewlett-Packard JetAdmin Utility

If you are using Hewlett-Packard printers, you might also be using HP DirectJet network printer interface cards. If you are, you will want to use the HP JetAdmin utility included with Windows 95. Using this utility, you can perform the following tasks:

- Set up interface cards or printers
- Reconfigure interface cards or printers
- Change printer settings
- Filter and sort printers installed on the network that appear in the utility's list boxes
- Add and remove queues
- Install drivers
- Configure drivers and assign them to printers
- Set printer operating modes
- Set printer descriptions

To install the HP JetAdmin utility, follow these steps:

1. Open the Network icon in the Control Panel.
2. Click on the Configuration tab's Add button.
3. In the Select Network Component Type dialog box, select Service in the list box and click on the Add button.

4. In the Select Network Service dialog box, choose Hewlett-Packard in the **Manu**facturers list box and HP JetAdmin in the Network Services list box.

5. Click on the OK button. Windows 95 copies the appropriate files and installs the HP JetAdmin software.

RPC Print Provider

Windows 95 also includes the Microsoft Remote Procedure Call Print Provider for use with Windows NT servers. This provider supplies Windows APIs for managing printers and queues on the NT Server. Using this provider, the Windows 95 client can get accounting and job status information from the server. This service is a useful addition if you are working with an NT Server on your LAN.

To install the RPC Print Provider, take these steps:

1. Open the Network icon in the Control Panel.

2. Click on the **A**dd button in the Configuration tab.

3. In the Select Network Component Type dialog box, click on Service in the list box, then click on the **A**dd button.

4. In the Select Network Service dialog box that appears, click on the **H**ave Disk button and enter the following path in the Install From Disk dialog box: **ADMIN\NETTOOLS\RPCPP**.

5. Click on the OK button. Windows 95 copies and installs the appropriate files.

Writing Network Batch and Script Files

Many system administrators could not imagine life without DOS batch files, especially those working with command-line interfaces to network services. The good news for these folks is that Windows 95 supports both batch files and special scripting services. Virtually all the DOS commands you are used to are supported in command-line mode, so you can use the batch files you have been using and create new ones using the MS-DOS prompt facility. However, you might want to make use of the scripting facility that Windows 95 supports. The next two sections describe this facility and show how to use it to create setup scripts, perhaps the most useful type of scripts you might need to create.

Creating Setup Scripts

If you worked with setup scripts under Windows 3.1, you will greatly appreciate the tools provided with Windows 95. If you love creating your own scripts, you can read about the file format and all the settings in the *Windows 95 Resource Kit* and continue to write your script files by hand. On the other hand, you can use the Batch.exe utility included with Windows 95. Batch.exe is a Windows 95 utility that enables you to create setup scripts by setting and clearing dialog box controls. You must copy it from the \ADMIN\NETTOOLS\NETSETUP directory on the Windows 95 CD to a directory on your server or local hard disk.

Batch.exe presents the initial window shown in figure 12.21. Using the text boxes in the upper portion, enter the user's name, company name, computer name, workgroup name, and description string. To continue choosing options for the setup script file, click on the buttons displayed in the Setup Options group.

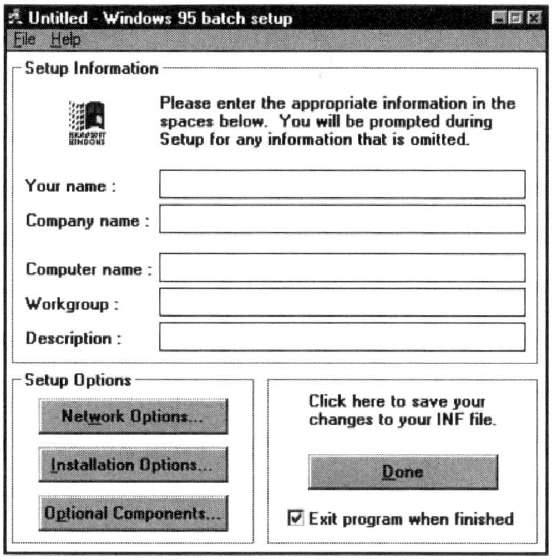

Figure 12.21

The initial window for Batch.exe.

Clicking on the Net<u>w</u>ork Options button displays the dialog box shown in figure 12.22. Using the controls in the Available Protocols group, select which of the three protocols will be installed and with which options. Select the services to be installed from the Available Services group, the security to be installed using the Enable <u>U</u>ser-Level Security check box and related options buttons, and the options for network cards using the Netcard Options group. The controls in the Available Clients group enable you to select which network clients will be installed, and the Ena<u>b</u>le server-based setup check box and related option buttons allow you to determine how setup will take place from the network file server.

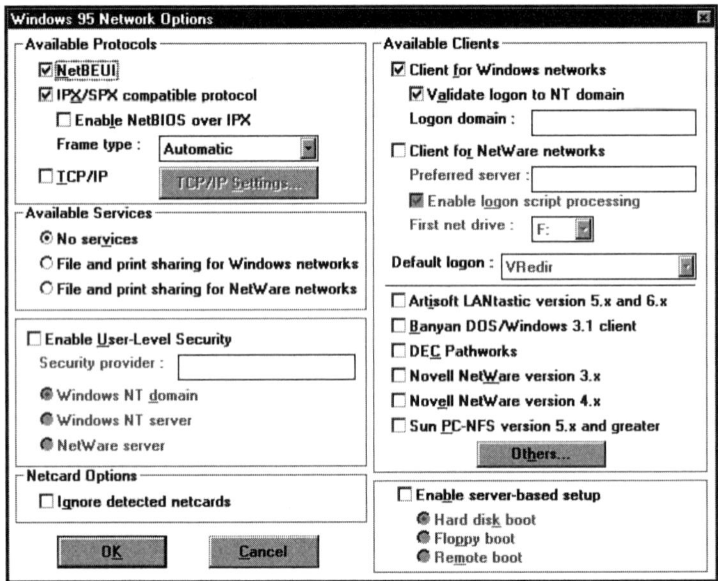

Figure 12.22

The Windows 95 Network Options dialog box in Batch.exe.

Clicking on the Installation Options button in the Windows 95 Batch Setup dialog box displays the Windows 95 Installation Options dialog box, shown in figure 12.23. The Setup Options group of controls allows you to specify the installation directory, type of installation, and specific warnings or promptings that can occur during installation. The Time Zone group enables you to specify the time zone setting, and the Monitor Settings group enables you to select the available display adapter and monitor configuration settings. Clicking on the Set button opens a dialog box that allows you to specify under what circumstances the setup program will stop during execution. Clicking on the Printers button brings up a dialog box that allows you to select a printer to install and lets you determine whether the workstation user will be prompted for information during printer setup.

Clicking on the Optional Components button in the Windows 95 Batch Setup dialog box opens the dialog box shown in figure 12.24. In this dialog box you can select which optional components are installed during setup. Selecting an item in the left-hand list causes the list of components in that group to appear in the right-hand list box. Checking or clearing the check boxes determines whether a component is installed.

You must select an installation type that allows the choice of optional components to enable the appearance of the Windows 95 Optional Components dialog box.

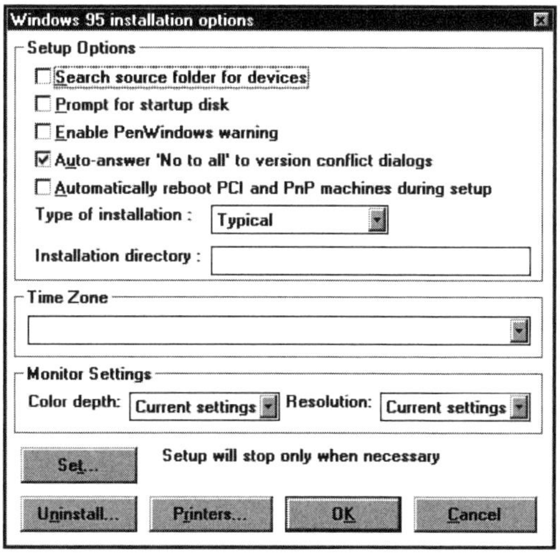

Figure 12.23

The Windows 95 installation options dialog in Batch.exe.

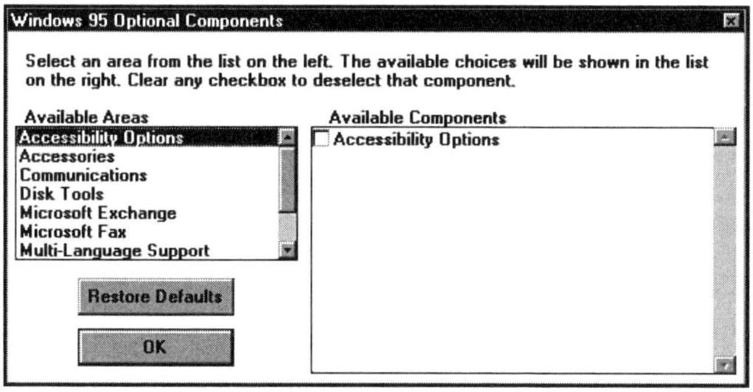

Figure 12.24

The Windows 95 Optional Components dialog box in Batch.exe.

Clicking on the Done button in the main window saves the script file. If the Exit program when finished check box is checked, Batch.exe also terminates.

In addition to Batch.exe, the \ADMIN\NETTOOLS\NETSETUP directory contains another tool named Infinst.exe, which provides a dialog box that prompts you for information about where to install the Inf files for the various optional administrative tools included in the ADMIN directory of the Windows 95 CD. When you run this utility, it provides a button that enables you to select the server directory, a button that launches a Browse dialog box that enables you to select the requisite Inf files, and a button that launches the copying process. Using this utility, you can merge the information on utilities such as Batch.exe into your server installation script, causing the setup program to install them into default directories.

Working with SLIP Scripts

If your user uses dial-up networking (currently available only in the Plus! pack), you might find the scripting feature for this service useful. The Dial-up adapter and software can associate a script with any dial-up service to automate logon and other actions. To create a script, use the following steps:

1. Create the script using the Notepad editor.
2. Open the Dial-Up Scripting Tool by opening the Start menu, selecting **P**rograms, then Accessories, then Dial-Up Scripting Tool (see figure 12.25).

Figure 12.25
The Dial-Up Scripting Tool.

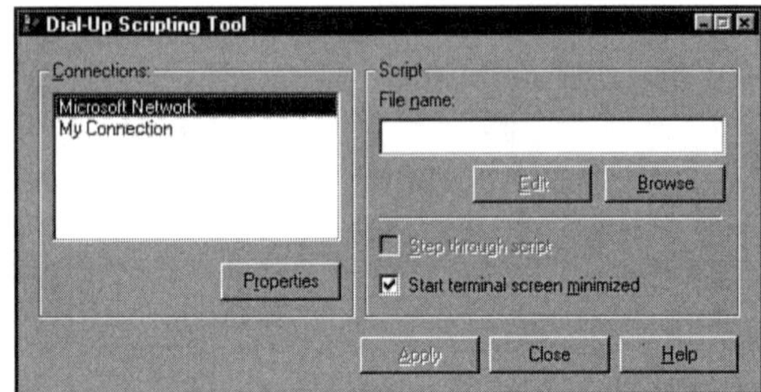

3. Select the service with which the script will be associated in the **C**onnections list box.
4. Enter the text file name containing the script in the File **n**ame text box. (Click on the **B**rowse button to locate the file, or the **E**dit button to start Notepad to examine or edit the file.)
5. Click on the **A**pply button to associate the script with the dial-up service.

When you create a script, you use the commands shown in table 12.2. Windows 95 uses script commands compliant with the SLIP standard. Enter each command on its own line.

Table 12.2
SLIP Scripting Commands for Dial-Up Networking

Command	Meaning
	Commands
proc *name*	Starts the script procedure. You must have a main procedure, named using the command *proc main.*

Command	Meaning
	Commands
endproc	Ends the script procedure.
delay *numseconds*	Pauses the script for *numseconds* seconds.
waitfor "*string*"	Pauses until the cases sensitive *string* is received from the remote computer.
transmit "*string*"|$USERID\|$PASSWORD	Transmits the designated *string*, userid, or password to the remote computer. $USERID and $PASSWORD are automatically set to the values for the selected remote service.
set port databits *number*	Sets the databits for the communications port to a *number* between 5 and 8.
set post stopbits *number*	Sets the stopbits for the communications port to either 1 or 2.
set port parity none|odd|even|mark|space	Sets parity for the communications port to the value selected.
set ipaddr	Sets the IP address.
set screen keyboard on|off	Turns keyboard input to the screen on or off.
getip *optional_index_number*	Returns the IP address from the remote computer. Can be used with set ipaddr to set the local IP address to that of the remote. If more than one address is returned, you can select which one to use by including *optional_index_number*.
halt	Stops the script.
;	Begins a comment.

continues

Table 12.2, Continued
SLIP Scripting Commands for Dial-Up Networking

Character	Meaning
	String Characters
Any character enclosed in double quotes	Indicates a character in a string.
^	Indicates a control character, as in ^M, which indicates a carriage return.
<cr>	Indicates a carriage return.
<lf>	Indicates a line feed.
\"	Indicates a double quote in a string.
\^	Indicates a carat in a string.
\<	Indicates a left angle bracket (or less-than sign) in a string.
\\	Indicates a backslash in a string.

Microsoft recommends using the extension Scp on script files and saving them to the Accessories folder.

Installing Macintosh and OS/2 Connectivity

Windows 95 can exchange files and mail with Macintosh computers. Windows 95 does not, however, provide such services internally. A network file server running a network operating system that supports such connectivity must mediate among the heterogeneous PC operating systems. Windows NT Server includes these services, as does NetWare. All you need to do is to make certain that your server operating system has these features enabled. To allow a Windows 95 Workgroup postoffice on the server to handle mail from several operating systems, you must upgrade it using the Microsoft Mail Post Office Upgrade on the server. After the postoffice is upgraded, it can handle messages from MS-DOS, Windows, Windows for Workgroups, Windows 95, Windows NT, Macintosh, and OS/2 clients.

Using HOSTS and LMHOSTS

HOSTS and LMHOSTS are two files that different networking protocols use to resolve host names and addresses. HOSTS is used as an equivalent for the local Domain Name System (DNS) that resolves host names and IP addresses. LMHOSTS is an equivalent for a Windows Internetwork Name Service (WINS) server, which resolves NetBIOS computer names and IP addresses. Sample files, named HOSTS.SAM and LMHOSTS.SAM, are installed when you install the TCP/IP protocol on your system. The sample files contain comments that explain the syntax of the file lines and the possible command key words that you can include on file lines. To set up your own *host name tables*, as these files are often called, you edit these files as necessary using a text editor.

To use the HOSTS and LMHOSTS host name tables, you must enable DNS using the property sheet for the TCP/IP protocol, which you can reach using the Network icon in the Control Panel.

The HOSTS file uses the same syntax as the /etc/hosts file in Berkeley Standard Distribution Unix, version 4.3. The host IP address is listed followed by the host name, and comments are introduced with a # sign, as in the following line:

```
101.84.44.97    hippo.acme.com     # x client host
```

These entries are read and used when TCP/IP utilities like ping and ftp interact with the computer on which the file is stored, causing a host name to be referenced. Entries are case sensitive, and a HOSTS file must be present on each system in the network. By default, the following entry is included:

```
127.0.0.1    localhost
```

Because HOSTS names are case sensitive, you might want to establish a convention of all upper- or all lowercase entries on your network. Or you can include multiple entries for a given host name, one in all capital letters, the other in lowercase.

The LMHOSTS file is used when you connect computers running Microsoft operating systems through a gateway or router to remote networks. Windows 95, Windows NT, LAN Manager, and Windows for Workgroups automatically map server names to addresses. However, these are NetBIOS names. When accessing remote systems, the LMHOSTS file provides a means of mapping host names to addresses in ways that other computers running TCP/IP protocols other than Microsoft's can understand. The format of the lines in the files is the same as that for the HOSTS file, except the

NetBIOS name replaces the host name. For a computer with a NetBIOS name of alfred and an address of 101.84.44.97, the line appears as follows:

```
101.84.44.97  alfred
```

Table 12.3 shows special keywords you can use in the LMHOSTS file in conjunction with Microsoft TCP/IP to control the loading of entries and association of entries when LMHOSTS is loaded into memory, which normally occurs when the computer starts. Under other protocols, such as LAN Manager, these keywords are treated as comments because they begin with a # sign.

Table 12.3
Keywords for Use with LMHOSTS

Keyword	Meaning
#PRE	Preload this entry into the name cache.
#DOM:*domain*	Associate this entry with the networking domain described by *domain*.
#INCLUDE:*file*	Include the contents of *file* as if it were a part of this LMHOSTS file.
#BEGIN_ALTERNATE	Marks the beginning of a group of #INCLUDE statements. Successfully including one *file* causes all statements to be treated as successes.
#END_ALTERNATE	Marks the end of a group of #INCLUDE statements.
\0xnn	Hexadecimal notation for including nonprinting characters in host names.

The following are example lines from the LMHOSTS.SAM file provided by Microsoft:

```
102.54.94.97     rhino                       #PRE #DOM:networking #net group's DC
102.54.94.102    "appname \0x14"             #special app server
102.54.94.123    popular        #PRE         #source server
102.54.94.117    localsrv       #PRE         #needed for the include

#BEGIN_ALTERNATE
#INCLUDE \\localsrv\public\lmhosts
#INCLUDE \\rhino\public\lmhosts
#END_ALTERNATE
```

The preceding code provides the example from the LMHOSTS.SAM file generated for any computer and demonstrates the use of these conventions. The first line preloads into memory the name for server `rhino` and associates it with the domain named `networking`. The second line demonstrates the use of a nonprinting character using hexadecimal notation in the server name. The third and fourth lines demonstrate preloading two server names, while the last four lines show how to include the LMHOSTS files stored in the PUBLIC directories of the `localsrv` and `rhino` servers in the LMHOSTS file for the local system.

LMHOSTS.SAM contains very complete directions for the use of each of the keywords.

Index

Symbols

A

B

C

D

E

F

K–L

N

Q–R

S

T

U

V

W

X–Y–Z

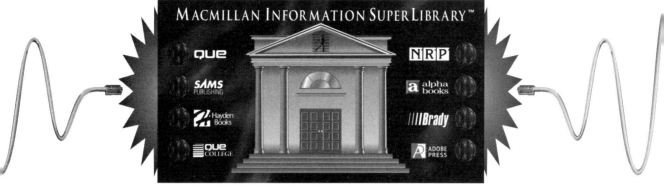